ARDEN EARLY MODERN DRAMA

General Editors: Suzanne Gossett,
John Jowett and Gordon McMullan

PHILASTER,

OR,

LOVE LIES A-BLEEDING

ARDEN EARLY MODERN DRAMA

PHILASTER, OR, LOVE LIES A-BLEEDING

Francis Beaumont and John Fletcher

for the King's Men at the Globe and Blackfriars

Edited by
SUZANNE GOSSETT

Arden Early Modern Drama
1 3 5 7 9 10 8 6 4 2

Arden Shakespeare is an imprint of Methuen Drama

Methuen Drama
A & C Black Publishers Limited
36, Soho Square
London W1D 3QY
www.ardenshakespeare.com
www.methuendrama.com

ISBN 9781408119471 (hardcover) 9781904271734 (paperback)

A CIP catalogue record for this book is available from the British Library

Library of Congress Cataloguing in Publication Data
A catalogue record has been requested

Printed in Croatia by Zrinski

This book is produced using paper made from wood grown in managed, sustainable
forests. It is natural, renewable and recyclable. The logging and manufacturing
processes conform to the environmental regulations of the country of origin.

The Editor

Suzanne Gossett is Professor of English at Loyola University Chicago. She has edited *Pericles* for the Arden Shakespeare (third series), as well as many plays by Shakespeare's contemporaries, including *Bartholomew Fair* for the Revels Student Editions, *A Fair Quarrel* for *Thomas Middleton: The Collected Works* and *Eastward Ho!* for the *Cambridge Edition of the Works of Ben Jonson*. Her recent articles have focused on issues in textual editing such as collaborative authorship and the ideology and ethics of annotation. She is a General Editor of Arden Early Modern Drama.

For Philip, who has been there all along

CONTENTS

PHILASTER, OR, LOVE LIES A-BLEEDING 105

LIST OF
ILLUSTRATIONS

GENERAL EDITORS' PREFACE

Arden Early Modern Drama (AEMD) is an expansion of the acclaimed Arden Shakespeare series to include the plays of other dramatists of the early modern period. The series publishes dramatic texts from the early modern period in the established tradition of the Arden Shakespeare, using a similar style of presentation and offering the same depth of information and high standards of scholarship. We define 'early modern drama' broadly, to encompass plays written and performed at any time from the late fifteenth to the late seventeenth century. The attractive and accessible format and well-informed editorial content are designed with particular regard to the needs of students studying literature and drama in the final years of secondary school and in colleges and universities. Texts are presented in modern spelling and punctuation; stage directions are expanded to clarify theatrical requirements and possibilities; and speech prefixes (the markers of identity at the beginning of each new speech) are regularized. Each volume contains about twenty illustrations both from the period and from later performance history; a full discussion of the current state of criticism of the play; and information about the textual and performance contexts from which the play first emerged. The goal of the series is to make these wonderful but sometimes neglected plays as intelligible as those of Shakespeare to twenty-first-century readers.

AEMD editors bring a high level of critical engagement and textual sophistication to their work. They provide guidance in assessing critical approaches to their play, developing arguments from the best scholarly work to date and generating new perspectives. A particular focus of an AEMD edition is the play as it was first performed in the theatre. The title-page of each volume displays the name of the company for which the play was written and the theatre at which it was first staged: in the Introduction the play is discussed as part of a company repertory as well as of an authorial canon. Finally, each edition presents a full scholarly discussion of the base text and other relevant materials as physical and social documents, and the Introduction describes issues arising in the early history of the publication and reception of the text.

Commentary notes, printed immediately below the playtext, offer compact but detailed exposition of the language, historical context and theatrical significance of the play. They explain textual ambiguities and, when an action may be interpreted in different ways, they summarize the arguments. Where appropriate they point the reader to fuller discussions in the Introduction.

CONVENTIONS

AEMD editions always include illustrations of pages from the early texts on which they are based. Comparison between these illustrations and the edited text immediately enables the reader to see clearly what a critical edition is and does. In summary, the main changes to the base text – that is, the early text, most often a quarto, that serves as the copy from which the editor works – are these: certain and probable errors in the base text are corrected; typography and spelling are brought into line with current usage; and speech prefixes and stage directions are modified to assist the reader in imagining the play in performance.

Significant changes introduced by editors are recorded in the textual notes at the foot of the page. These are an important cache of information, presented in as compact a form as is possible without forfeiting intelligibility. The standard form can be seen in the following example:

31 doing of] *Coxeter;* of doing *Q;* doing *Rawl*

The line reference ('31') and the reading quoted from the present editor's text ('doing of') are printed before the closing square bracket. After the bracket, the source of the reading, often the name of the editor who first made the change to the base text ('*Coxeter*'), appears, and then other readings are given, followed by their source ('of doing *Q;* doing *Rawl*'). Where there is more than one alternative reading, they are listed in chronological order; hence in the example the base text Q (= Quarto) is given first. Abbreviations used to identify early texts and later editions are listed in the Abbreviations and References section towards the end of the volume. Editorial emendations to the text are discussed in the main commentary, where notes on emendations are highlighted with an asterisk.

Emendation necessarily takes account of early texts other than the base text, as well as of the editorial tradition. The amount of attention paid to other texts depends on the editor's assessment of their origin and importance. Emendation aims to correct errors while respecting the integrity of different versions as they might have emerged through revision and adaptation.

Modernization of spelling and punctuation in AEMD texts is thorough, avoiding the kind of partial modernization that produces language from no known period of English. Generally modernization is routine, involving thousands of alterations of letters. As original grammar is preserved in AEMD editions, most modernizations are as trivial as altering 'booke' to 'book', and are unworthy of record. But where the modernization is unexpected or ambiguous the change is noted in the textual notes, using the following format:

102 trolls] *(trowles)*

Speech prefixes are sometimes idiosyncratic and variable in the base texts, and almost always abbreviated. AEMD editions expand contractions, avoiding confusion of names that might be similarly abbreviated, such as Alonzo/Alsemero/Alibius from *The Changeling*. Preference is given to the verbal form that prevails in the base text, even if it identifies the role by type, such as 'Lady' or 'Clown', rather than by personal name. When an effect of standardization is to repress significant variations in the way that a role is conceptualized (in *Philaster*, for example, one text refers to a cross-dressed page as *Boy*, while another uses the character's assumed name), the issue is discussed in the Introduction.

Stage directions in early modern texts are often inconsistent, incomplete or unclear. They are preserved in the edition as far as is possible, but are expanded where necessary to ensure that the dramatic action is coherent and self-consistent. Square brackets are used to indicate editorial additions to stage directions. Directions that lend themselves to multiple staging possibilities, as well as the performance tradition of particular moments, may be discussed in the commentary.

Verse lineation sometimes goes astray in early modern playtexts, as does the distinction between verse and prose, especially where a wide manuscript layout has been transferred to the narrower measure of a printed page. AEMD editions correct such mistakes. Where a verse line is shared between more than one speaker, this series follows the usual modern practice of indenting the second and subsequent part-lines to make it clear that they belong to the same verse line.

The textual notes allow the reader to keep track of all these interventions. The notes use variations on the basic format described above to reflect the changes. In notes, '31 SD' indicates a stage direction in or immediately after line 31. Where there is more than one stage direction, they are identified as, for example, '31 SD1', '31 SD2'. The second line of a stage direction will be identified as, for instance, '31.2'. A forward slash / indicates a line-break in verse.

We hope that these conventions make as clear as possible the editors engagement with and interventions in the text: our aim is to keep the reader fully informed of the editors role without intruding unnecessarily on the flow of reading. Equally, we hope – since one of our aims is to encourage the performance of more plays from the early modern period beyond the Shakespeare canon – to provide texts which materially assist performers, as well as readers, of these plays.

PREFACE

This edition of *Philaster* is the product of a lifetime of interest in the works of Beaumont and Fletcher, and in early modern drama more generally. My debts extend back in time to my late dissertation director, G. E. Bentley, and forward to the other two General Editors of Arden Early Modern Drama, John Jowett and Gordon McMullan. Together we have worked for almost a decade to create the series, and I am delighted that *Philaster*, a play whose absence from the anthologies has led to its undeserved neglect, is among the first published.

Many people have contributed to this volume, some in ways that may not be apparent. The form of these volumes is modelled on the Arden Shakespeare, and Richard Proudfoot was unfailingly helpful and supportive in sharing his General Editorial experience as we began this sister series. John Jowett has lent his scholarly knowledge, and has also become the guru of Guidelines. Gordon McMullan repeatedly assisted me in finding my way through the Fletcher canon, and his careful general editing of my work saved me from many errors. Jonathan Hope helped untangle linguistic matters. Farah Karim-Cooper arranged for me to hear a recording of the reading of *Philaster* in the *Read not Dead* series at Shakespeare's Globe, and Lucy Munro supplied the programme of a recent production. Martin Butler and Valerie Wayne shared their research on *Cymbeline* and David Kathman shared his on the boy actors. Jeffrey L. Forgeng answered a query about the swords in the title-page illustration; Catharine MacLeod of the National Portrait Gallery gave me information about their newly acquired portrait of John Fletcher. Members of the 2007 Shakespeare Association of America seminar on Beaumont and Fletcher were stimulating interlocutors, proof positive that the plays of these authors still merit scholarly attention and performance.

Like many scholars, I could not do my work without the assistance of wonderful, knowledgeable librarians and their staffs. I am especially grateful to everyone at the Folger Shakespeare Library, and particularly to Georgianna Ziegler and Erin Blake, who identified many of the images that illustrate this volume. The Loyola University Chicago library provided regular assistance as well as a rare copy of William Shirley's *Edward the Black Prince*. In the British Library I was permitted to handle their valuable Ashley Collection exemplars of Q1 and Q2, and the Manuscript Room helpfully prepared its copy of Reynolds's adaptation for my arrival. Denise Gallo arranged for me to see the materials from the Federal Theatre Project now in the Library of Congress Music Division. The Houghton Library at Harvard and the University of Chicago library shared rare materials. I am grateful to all of them.

The world of publishing in the twenty-first century is almost as complex as the world of court in the seventeenth. This volume is being published by A&C Black under its Methuen Drama imprint; it started under Thomson Learning and briefly moved with Arden to Cengage Learning. For help in overcoming innumerable obstacles and allowing us to do, as Dion says, all things 'possible and honest', my profound thanks go to everyone who has believed in AEMD from the moment that Jessica Hodge, then the Arden publisher, first commissioned the series. For particular help with *Philaster* I would like to thank Charlotte Loveridge, Alissa Chappell, Kate Reeves and Jane Armstrong, but most of all my thanks go to Margaret Bartley, who has kept us sane and encouraged me at every turn.

INTRODUCTION

Philaster was the first great triumph of the collaborators Beaumont and Fletcher, whose plays continued to be among the most popular and frequently performed on the English stage for almost a century thereafter. Students of early modern drama find *Philaster* intriguing because it is so closely connected to the plays of Shakespeare, some of which it recalls, but others of which it seems to anticipate, perhaps even to stimulate. The tone of the play, as much as its attention to love, honour, politics, and class and sexual tensions, is fundamental to the establishment of tragicomedy, the major formal development in drama in the Jacobean period. And in both its comic prose and its long poetic speeches *Philaster* reveals how the enormous literary talents of its two youthful authors together combined to create a popular masterpiece in a way that neither had quite managed to achieve alone.

The particular success of *Philaster* results from its position at the centre of a number of overlapping networks. The authors were not only collaborators themselves but embedded within a group of early seventeenth-century dramatists with whose work their play is intertextually imbricated. Their transition from the two boys' companies for which they had previously written to the pre-eminent adult company of the period, the King's Men, signalled recognition of their talents; it also responded to situational forces in the theatrical milieu that by 1608 – the year before Beaumont and Fletcher collaborated on *Philaster* – had led to the permanent closure of the children's companies. On one level *Philaster* is a rewriting of Shakespeare's most popular play, with a hero who never lives up to Hamlet but does, however, give great speeches and live happily ever after, complete with the girl and the crown. Yet the collaborators were also rewriting themselves. By

1

recasting elements of their earlier tragedy *Cupid's Revenge* as tragicomedy, as well as by demonstrating that the mixed form could be separated from the pastoral elements that had accompanied it in Fletcher's *Faithful Shepherdess* – a failure on first performance – *Philaster* participated in a generic transition that would affect plays until the closing of the theatres.

Impinging on the dramatists and the play were political and personal forces external to their professional milieu. Although *Philaster* has only a few identifiable topical references, both in its initial production and in revivals throughout the century it repeatedly touched on contested political issues, including some that the playwrights could not have foreseen. Over a sixty-year period of frequent production the play again and again took on new meaning, making it a palimpsest of major political controversies, such as tension over the powers of king and Parliament in 1609; foreign marriage for royal children in 1613; princely ambition and warfare in 1619; and restoration of rightful heirs in 1660. Later adaptations only extended this process, and the history of its interpretation shows how successive critics read the play through the lens of their own political environment.

Finally, *Philaster* was composed when the two young authors were living together on the Bankside, with but one bed and one 'wench' between them, and the sexual tensions in the play seem blown by all the winds of gender ambiguity that a strongly homosocial professional world encouraged. One reason that the play still appeals in the twenty-first century is that its strong heroine, masochistic hero, over-sexualized 'bad girl' and pathetic cross-dressed 'boy'; its midnight assignations, sexual violence and threats of torture; its moments of mutual social incomprehension, are all simultaneously clichéd and yet timelessly familiar.

CONTEXT, CHRONOLOGY, COACTIVITY

Francis Beaumont (born *c.* 1585) and John Fletcher (born 1579) came to London from Oxford and Cambridge respectively, but despite Beaumont's connections to the Inns of Court – he was a member of the Inner Temple and his father was a judge – they moved largely in dramatic circles.[1] By the time they contemplated *Philaster* they had already written, separately and together, at least four and possibly as many as six plays, all for children's companies: certainly *The Woman Hater*, *The Knight of the Burning Pestle*, *Cupid's Revenge* and *The Faithful Shepherdess*, and perhaps also *The Scornful Lady* and *The Coxcomb*. They moved in Ben Jonson's circle: Beaumont had a particular friendship with him, and Fletcher's first undoubted publication was a commendatory poem accompanying *Volpone* (1607). Charles Cathcart suggests that Fletcher may even have been indirectly engaged in the so-called War of the Theatres, taking Jonson's side against John Marston (39–41).

Not surprisingly, both young dramatists show an intense awareness of current theatrical trends. For example, setting out to write *The Faithful Shepherdess*, with its recollections of Guarini's *Il Pastor Fido*, an Italian tragicomedy whose generic innovations were debated in England as well as Italy, Fletcher surely noted the popularity of Marston's 1604 *Malcontent*, which had already borrowed from the translation of *Il Pastor Fido* by Sir Edward Dymock. Marston's play had so attracted the King's Men that, after some now-obscure hanky panky by the boy players, the men had violated the ground rules that usually obtained in the Jacobean theatre and produced Marston's play despite 'another company having interest in it' (*Malcontent*, A4ʳ). Marston's play was entered in the Stationers' Register as a 'tragiecomedia',[2] a

---

1   Precisely when each young man came to London is unknown. Beaumont seems to have left university after the death of his father in 1598; in 1600 he was admitted to the Inner Temple, like his brothers and father before him (Finkelpearl, 18). Fletcher's movements between taking his MA in 1598 and appearing as a playwright in 1607 are 'entirely undocumented' (McMullan, *Fletcher*, 11), but if Cathcart is right in identifying two commendatory poems of 1600 and 1601 as Fletcher's, he is likely to have been in London by then.

2   Hunter suggests that '*Tragicomedia* in the Stationers' Register refers to Marston's programmatic attempt to reconstruct this genre in English' (lxii); McMullan and Hope point out that the first instance of 'tragicomedie' in the Stationers' Register comes in 1598 from Samuel Brandon's 'tragicomedie of the Virtuous Octavia' (19, n. 18).

form that Beaumont and Fletcher would refine and make their own. Beaumont's *The Knight of the Burning Pestle* (1607) is an even more bravura performance, parodying current dramatic styles including citizen comedy, prodigal play and romantic adventure, as well as familiar theatrical tropes such as mock death and unmotivated jealousy.

Most obviously, the young authors knew the works of London's most successful playwright. *Hamlet* had inspired tragedy in Thomas Middleton's *The Revenger's Tragedy* and parody in Jonson, Marston and George Chapman's *Eastward Ho!*; in *The Knight of the Burning Pestle*, *1 Henry IV*'s Hotspur transmogrifies into a romantic apprentice. Thus, when early in the winter months of 1609 the collaborators had what must have been a rather unhappy and worried conversation, it was to Shakespeare and his company that their thoughts turned. The problems the collaborators faced at that moment were both personal and institutional. First, their two most brilliant and individualistic plays, *The Knight of the Burning Pestle* and *The Faithful Shepherdess*, had notoriously failed. Next, they were losing their institutional outlets. Paul's Boys, which had produced *The Woman Hater*, had closed in 1606; the variously titled Blackfriars Boys, who had produced *The Knight of the Burning Pestle*, *Cupid's Revenge* and *The Faithful Shepherdess*, by March 1608 had finally overreached themselves in performing satire, leading King James to swear that 'they should never play more, but should first begg their bred' (Gurr, *Companies*, 354). And, most immediately, after a brief respite that ran from April to June 1608, the plague had returned in full force, closing *all* the theatres, a situation that, although the collaborators could not yet know this, would last until early 1610.

In discussions of *Philaster* the relation of the play to Shakespeare's work has been primarily confined to the question of the priority of *Philaster* and *Cymbeline*, for neither of which is the date more than inferential. In 1901, when Ashley Thorndike radically proposed that from *Philaster* Shakespeare took hints for the writing of *Cymbeline*, his argument was disparaged or dismissed in an atmosphere of bardolatry.[1] But recent scholarship has been more open to this possibility, or at least, this sequence.

The facts are these. *Philaster* must have been written by the middle of 1610, as John Davies of Hereford referred to it by its subtitle in Epigram 206 of his *Scourge of Folly*, which was entered in the Stationers' Register on 8 October 1610:

> *To the well deseruing* M[r] John Fletcher.
>
> *Loue lies ableeding*, if it should not proue
> Her vttmost art to shew why it doth loue.
> Thou being the *Subiect* (now) It raignes vpon:
> Raign'st in *Arte, Iudgement,* and *Inuention*:
>   *For this I loue thee; and can doe no lesse*
>   *For thine as faire, as faithfull* Shepheardesse.
>   (Chambers, 3.223)

Similarly, *Cymbeline* cannot be later than 1611, when it was seen by the astrologer, physician and keen playgoer Simon Forman, who died that September. Although Forman's 'Book of Plays' does not date *Cymbeline*, he summarizes it among a group of plays, including *The Winter's Tale*, which he saw at the Globe in spring 1611. The difficulty is that for neither play is there as clear a *terminus a quo* (that is, a point by which it must have existed) and thus their priority is not established.

For the date of *Philaster* the most important factor is the mention of the 'new platform' that Pharamond has gone to see in 5.3. Andrew Gurr identified this as a reference to the 'great platform' on which Phineas Pett constructed a model of Prince Henry's ship, the *Prince Royal*, and which King James went to visit in May 1609. As Gurr writes,

> the building of the ship was the occasion of a series of charges laid by the Earl of Northampton and others against the Lord Admiral, the Earl of Nottingham, who was responsible for its construction. James himself heard

---

1   See Thorndike, *Influence*, and, for a powerful example of the reaction, Wilson.

the evidence of both sides at the yard where the ship was being built, in Woolwich, on 8 May 1609.

Pett reported that because some of the charges concerned the size of the ship, 'his Majesty referred the trial to be made on the great platform, which was purposely framed of planks to the full scale of the ship' (Gurr, xxvii). The notoriety of all those involved guaranteed the event widespread mention in London. In addition, the confrontation between King James and Sir Edward Coke which is echoed in 4.4 (discussed on pp. 23–5) took place on 13 November 1608; it would have had more resonance in 1609 than a year later.

The dating of *Cymbeline* has traditionally been tied to that of *The Winter's Tale*, and the former has been assumed to precede the latter simply because it is less aesthetically successful. However, Stanley Wells and Gary Taylor, followed by Martin Butler, date *The Winter's Tale* to 1609, and *Cymbeline* to 1610.[1] Their reasons include stylistic and metrical tests, as well as the presence in *The Winter's Tale* of material from Plutarch, also utilized in the immediately preceding *Coriolanus* and *Antony and Cleopatra*. *Cymbeline*, on the other hand, is placed later than *The Winter's Tale* by the absence of verbal echoes from Plutarch and by tests including those of rare vocabulary and colloquialism-in-verse.[2] Furthermore, examined independently, several elements of *Cymbeline* seem tied to the first half of 1610. On 5 June of that year Prince Henry was invested as Prince of Wales and Milford Haven was conspicuously mentioned in the festivities, for example in Samuel Daniel's masque *Tethys' Festival*. Critics since Geoffrey Bullough have connected these events to Shakespeare's sudden preoccupation with 'the iconography and cultural significance of Welshness' (Butler, 5). In addition, on 4 May 1610 Henry IV of France was assassinated and King James ordered that the

---

1 See *TxC* pp. 131–2. Stephen Orgel, in his edition of *The Winter's Tale* (Oxford, 1996), disagrees.

2 For a full discussion, see *TxC*, 'The Canon and Chronology of Shakespeare's Plays'.

Oath of Allegiance be readministered to Catholics. These events may be echoed in Iachimo's mention of 'th'oath of loyalty', and in Innogen's violent reaction to Pisanio, who she believes tried to poison her (Butler, 6).

Despite the counterintuitive implication that the younger authors provided a model for their more experienced colleague, the preponderance of recent investigators assign a date of 1609 to *Philaster* and of 1610 to *Cymbeline*.[1] Theatrical conditions support this sequence. As the Oxford editors point out, 'Beaumont and Fletcher could only have been influenced by Shakespeare's play through performance, and the London theatres were closed because of plague until at least December 1609, and perhaps until January or February 1610' (*TxC*, 132). Yet the topical allusions date *Philaster* to 1609. On the other hand, 'as sharer and primary dramatist for the King's Men Shakespeare would almost certainly have seen the manuscript of *Philaster* before it was performed', possibly months before (*TxC*, 132). It seems likely, then, that *Philaster* was composed in 1609 during the theatre closure and acted for the first time in early 1610, and that *Cymbeline* was being written in May/June 1610, with its first performances in December 1610 (Butler, 6).

The collaborators' play is, nevertheless, enmeshed in the drama of its day. Following no single source, *Philaster* is both highly original, in tone, and deeply derivative, both of the earlier work

---

1   In an attempt to date *Cymbeline* a year earlier, to Christmas 1609, Ros King denies that the mention in *Philaster* of the hero's visit to the 'new platform' refers to the 'great platform'. She argues that the reference is to the lower deck or orlop of the ship, into which a child fell in September of 1610. However, the *OED* finds no use of the term 'platform' for this section of a ship until sixty years later. The 'platform' was clearly new in 1609; a year later a topical reference might have taken a different form. It is also unlikely that Philaster or any prince would make a special visit to the 'new platform' if it were merely a hidden part, a lower deck, of a ship. King makes the assumption that if *Philaster* were written no later than December 1609, 'this in turn would mean that *Cymbeline* could have been written no later than the summer of 1609' (40–1). That is only true if *Cymbeline* came before *Philaster*. In any case, if *Cymbeline* were produced at court in late 1609 while the theatres were closed, it would have been inaccessible to Beaumont and Fletcher, who were not members of the King's Men nor employed by them before *Philaster*.

of the collaborators and of their competitors.[1] *Philaster* is a tragicomedy about a young prince of Sicily whose position has been usurped – the 'late King of Calabria', the current king's father, took Sicily from Philaster's father (see Fig. 1). The first quarto text, discussed below, makes the situation replicate *Hamlet* even more clearly, as there it is the current king who was the usurper. Like Hamlet, the ineffectual but beloved prince continues to live at court, where he resists the encouragement of his gentlemen followers to reclaim his position. The princess Arethusa falls in love with him and he gives her his boy as a go-between. Partly through misunderstanding, partly through an inherent distrust of women, he persuades himself that she is untrue, becomes jealous of her relationship with the boy, and stabs them both. The page, however, as the audience may well suspect, is a cross-dressed woman in love with the prince, which she finally acknowledges. The tragicomic ending comes about because none of the wounds is fatal, the presumed lover is a woman satisfied to live as servant to the princess, and there is a kingdom apiece for the prince and the King. Thus the play is built from plot elements familiar from *Hamlet*, *Othello*, *Twelfth Night*, *Two Gentlemen of Verona* and *Pericles*, as well as reworked from *Cupid's Revenge*, *The Faithful Shepherdess* and even *The Knight of the Burning Pestle*.

Philaster exemplifies what James Bednarz calls 'literary coactivity': the collaborators not only refashioned material each had earlier written alone, but together the two young men seem to have looked at the successful plays of the last decade and played with their hypotheses. What if there had been two kingdoms for Claudius and Hamlet? What if Othello had merely wounded Desdemona, and had finally been persuaded of his error? What if the rebellious citizens in *Cupid's Revenge* had succeeded in

---

1   The claim that the play is based on a section of Alonso Perez's continuation of Montemayor's *Diana*, which was published in Bartholomew Yong's translation in 1598, is unsustainable. For example, Perez's political plot concerns two great houses, the heroine is a widow, and the go-between is an old nurse who is not cross-dressed. The suggestion originated with Weber in 1812, but he did not know that *Twelfth Night* preceded *Philaster*.

1 Map of Sicilia and southern Italy, with Calabria indicated. From George Sandys, *A Relation of a Journey* (1615).

permanently stopping the prince's enemies? Since their goal was performance by the King's Men, they would have been especially conscious of that company's recent productions.[1]

Their most important debts were to themselves. Their attraction to the mixed genre was obvious as early as *The Woman Hater*, whose Prologue announces he 'dare not call it Comedie, or Tragedie; 'tis perfectly neyther'. *The Knight of the Burning Pestle* is even more piecemeal and postmodern, with its send-up of all current modes, and it too foreshadows bits of *Philaster*, as when merely from generalized male suspicion Jasper draws a sword upon Luce to test her love and she responds, 'Strike I am ready, and dying stil I love thee' (3.1.103–4).[2] But the central sources were *The Faithful Shepherdess* and *Cupid's Revenge*, the latter, as Gurr argues, itself a reworking of elements of prose romance, particularly Sidney's *Arcadia*.

Both early plays anticipate actions and characters of *Philaster*. From *The Faithful Shepherdess* comes the focus on female sexual fidelity and male jealousy, the contrast between chaste and unchaste women, the evening assignations and the weak character of the hero. Perigot is easily deceived and discouraged. Like Philaster, he repeatedly threatens suicide, first when the false Amoret (lascivious Amaryllis in disguise) invites him to make love and later in meditation on the 'untrue, unconstant, and unkinde' behaviour of women. He is at the same time dangerous to women, threatening to kill Amaryllis (as Amoret) in the third act and wounding the real Amoret when she enters. In the fourth act, persuaded that 'Men ever were most blessed, till Crosse fate, / Brought love,

---

1 As Lucy Munro notes, 'the institutional dimension of the development of tragicomedy is of central importance. Most of the extant tragicomic plays of the seventeenth century come from the repertories of the Children of the Queen's Revels and the King's Men' (104).

2 Cf. Finkelpearl, 'The interaction between a cowardly, sadistic, weak man with a sword and a "weake, weake" woman with a heroic spirit momentarily derails this hilarious comedy . . . Jasper must be placed among the strange "heroes" of Beaumont and Fletcher's most famous romances, where the pulling out of a sword and sometimes its use against a helpless and usually a loving woman is a frequent gesture. Some version of it occurs in *The Faithful Shepherdess*, *Philaster*, *A King and No King*, and *The Maid's Tragedy*' (87).

and woemen forth unfortunate' '*He hurts her agayne*' (4.4.67–8, 162 SD). Because *The Faithful Shepherdess* is a romance, Amoret is saved first by the God of the River and later by the faithful shepherdess Clorin herself. Notoriously, *The Faithful Shepherdess* was appreciated by the elite but scorned by the public, apparently because, as Chapman says in his commendatory verses, it was 'a Poeme and a play too' and 'holds through all the holy lawes of homely pastorall'. Fletcher, in his irritated preface 'To the Reader' published with the play in 1609, explains pastoral – which however he promptly gave up – and tragicomedy:

> A tragie-comedie is not so called in respect of mirth and killing, but in respect it wants deaths, which is inough to make it no tragedie, yet brings some neere it, which is inough to make it no comedie: which must be a representation of familiar people, with such kinde of trouble as no life be questiond, so that a God is as lawfull in this as in a tragedie, and meane people as in a comedie.

This model, his later works show, he eventually modified, but in its very contradictions the definition exemplifies the difficulty of describing a form more easily labelled than delineated.

Cupid's Revenge, another rehearsal for *Philaster*, foreshadows that play in suffering from tonal dissonance. The premise is that the princess Hidaspes, wishing to purify her kingdom, demands that all the statues of Cupid be plucked down. In response, the god himself descends, promising revenge, and makes Hidaspes fall in love with her father's hideous dwarf. The deluded and ridiculous duke, Leontius, marries his son's mistress Bacha, who nevertheless continues to pursue the prince. The prince is so weak that he lies to his father about his mistress's purity and, when imprisoned, must be saved by a rebellion of citizen-shopkeepers. In a subplot, Bacha's simple, virginal daughter Urania falls in love with the prince, serves him disguised as a 'countrey Lad' and fatally interposes herself when he is attacked. Death comes to all the major characters, but their plights more frequently elicit laughter than pity. *Cupid's Revenge* incidentally demonstrates why the young collaborators did not need *Cymbeline* as a model. Many of the tropes in this play – the cross-dressed girl, the older man deceived by a pretty woman, the weak and dilatory prince, the contrast of pure and lascivious women – are scattered throughout the plays of their contemporaries. Indeed, several moments, such as when Bacha expresses her intention to destroy the rightful prince and 'make *Urania* / My Daughter, the Kings heyre' (3.2.250–1), or when the exiled Leucippus urges the weak, cross-dressed Urania to 'Goe into the Cave and eate' (5.4.26), may be recalled in *Cymbeline*.

Clearly the young authors were almost tactilely conscious of all the plays they perceived as popular. As early as 1750 Seward identified two of their central sources: 'I believe Beaumont aimed at drawing a Hamlet racked with Othello's Love and Jealousy' (Theobald, 1.vii). Philaster's situation and weakness seem modelled on those of the Danish prince, although Lee Bliss points out that the 'isolated figure, cut off from his social and political identity and forced to maintain himself' in a new king's court is a trope found in Marston's *Malcontent* and *Antonio and Mellida*, Edward Sharpham's *Fleer* and John Day's *Humour out of Breath* ('Three Plays', 155). Philaster's jealousy, like Othello's, is aroused by deliberately false insinuations but develops because of his own misogyny and failure to investigate ('I had forgot to ask him where he took them', 3.1.132).

The young authors pillaged freely. In Philaster's threats to his suspected page Bliss sees a debt to Orsino's furious treatment of Viola/Cesario in the final scene of *Twelfth Night*. Lucy Munro demonstrates that once Beaumont and Fletcher were hired by the King's Men their tragicomedies 'reinterpreted many of the preoccupations of the Queen's Revels' version of the form, such as the concern with the relationships between sexuality and political structures' (133). *Pericles*, the first of Shakespeare's tragicomic romances, was also influential. Judging from echoes of that play in *A King and No King* (1611), *The Woman's Prize* (1611) and as late as *A Wife for a Month* (1624), the two dramatists were deeply struck by the play's social commentary, its moments of powerful emotion, and the sexuality of its incest and brothel scenes, all elements suited to adult actors (Gossett). They seem to have particularly remarked the mixture of tones and the radical division of attention between two central figures, father and daughter.

Such a division and a similarly complex, tragicomic tone are notable in *Philaster*. The unheroic protagonist recalls Pericles' weakness, his flight from danger, his almost catatonic withdrawal at Marina's apparent death. More important is the treatment of the female figures. Fletcher's concentration on women is apparent as early as *The Faithful Shepherdess*. But in that play, as in *Cupid's Revenge*, women who choose for themselves and woo are blind, wicked or, like Urania, simple, whereas the women of *Pericles* (and *The Winter's Tale*, if that too preceded *Philaster*) are strong but admirable. Thaisa prefigures Arethusa and Perdita in choosing, wooing and marrying in spite of her father. Another link between *Pericles* and Beaumont and Fletcher's early tragicomedies is its vision of family. Bliss exaggerates in claiming that for Beaumont and Fletcher, 'the interaction between generations holds no interest. *Philaster*'s King exists only as political tyrant and blocking father figure for Arethusa's intended romantic comedy' ('Tragicomic', 152–3). Yet even in *Cupid's Revenge* both plots are based in just such interaction. In *Philaster* the moment when the King demands that the courtiers produce the lost or strayed Arethusa – 'I do command you all, as you are subjects, / To show her me!' – is often noted as an allusion to the contemporary debate over the limits of subjects' obedience, but critics have tended to forget that the King is frantic because 'you've let me lose / The jewel of my life!', that is, his daughter (4.4.30–1, 40–1) (see Fig. 2). The loss and finding of a daughter is reiterated in the second plot, where Dion's recognition of Euphrasia in 5.5 echoes Pericles' step-by-step identification of Marina. Such echoes are a key indicator of the tight-knit, interactive early Jacobean theatrical milieu.

2 'How to flee the Hearon', from George Turberville, *The Boke of Faulconrie* (1575). This image of Queen Elizabeth on horseback suggests what Arethusa looked like as she rode away during the hunting party (cf. 4.4.20).

COLLABORATION

The most important form of coactivity for *Philaster* was the collaboration of its two authors. Somewhat unusually, *Philaster* was published, first in 1620 and again in 1622, with the names of both its authors on the title-page. 'Francis Baymont' (Q1) or 'Francis Beaumont' (Q2) and 'Iohn Fletcher, Gent.' are given credit for the play, and there has never been any doubt that both participated in its creation. The title-page supplies what scholars call 'external evidence', which is confirmed by the reappearance of *Philaster* in the second collection of Beaumont and Fletcher plays, the Folio of 1679. External evidence is useful but not always sufficient, and can even be misleading, as when co-authorship is suppressed (*Cupid's Revenge* was published as 'By Iohn Fletcher' alone) or when title-pages ascribe works to a popular author in hopes of increasing sales (e.g. *The London Prodigal* in 1605, 'By William Shakespeare').

Even when, as in the case of *Philaster*, a title-page does acknowledge collaboration, it does not tell us how the work was divided. Therefore, scholars interested in the authorship of early modern plays search through 'internal evidence' for signs that more than one author is present and for their distinguishing marks. Such evidence is often found in alternative choices of which an author might not even be conscious. These can include a play's vocabulary; its metrics; its 'function words' (*of, and, but*); the forms of its pronouns (*ye/you, thou/you*), verbs (*has/hath*) or grammatical constructions (the auxiliary *do*, as in 'I went home/I did go home'); or the presence or absence of contractions and elisions (*'em/them, i'st/is it*).

More than half of all early modern plays were written by more than one person, either during their original composition or through later revision. 'Beaumont and Fletcher' is shorthand for an extensive canon of plays, a good percentage of which were composed not only after Beaumont ceased to write (*c.* 1613) but after his death in 1616. Fletcher seems to have been the persistent collaborator, and the 'Beaumont and Fletcher' plays are more accurately the canon of 'Fletcher and everyone with whom he collaborated', including Beaumont, Shakespeare, Philip Massinger, Nathan Field, Middleton and several lesser dramatists. As Gordon McMullan observes, Fletcher 'quite clearly *preferred* to collaborate' (*Fletcher*, 133).

Two anecdotes attest to the particular closeness of Fletcher's collaboration with Beaumont. The first is John Aubrey's gossipy comment that Beaumont and Fletcher 'lived together on the

Banke side, not far from the Play-house, both batchelors; lay together; had one Wench in the house between them, which they did so admire; the same cloathes and cloake, &; between them' (Aubrey, 21). Thomas Fuller's report, usually taken to refer to the joint composition of *The Maid's Tragedy*, reveals more about their method of composition:

> Meeting once in a tavern, to contrive the rude draught of a Tragedy, Fletcher undertook *to kill the King* therein; whose words being overheard by a listener . . . he was accused of High Treason, till, the mistake soon appearing, that the plot was onely against a Dramatick and Scenical King, all wound off in merriment.
>
> (cited McMullan, *Fletcher*, 86)

This suggests that their collaborations would begin with meetings at which the plot outline or 'rude draught' would be 'contrived'. Next the sections would be assigned, frequently by parts of the plot; these divisions might later manifest themselves as self-standing scenes or acts. We know that other methods were sometimes employed. For a collaborative play prepared in a hurry, Thomas Dekker testified that he wrote one act and a speech in another act (Bentley, 3.255), while the manuscript of *Sir Thomas More* suggests that Shakespeare, as the King's Men's 'attached dramatist', was called upon to rewrite and add to some scenes in an attempt to make that tragedy playable. Fletcher's own methods may have varied. For example, in *The Two Noble Kinsmen* he wrote primarily the subplot, while Shakespeare handled the main plot. Later, as 'the master', he frequently assigned Massinger, 'the apprentice', the opening and closing sections of a play (Potter; McMullan, *Fletcher*, 143). We know least about the final step, how the individually composed sections were integrated. For a quick potboiler such as *Keep the Widow Waking* this may not have happened at all, but for Chapman, Jonson and Marston's *Eastward Ho!* it seems that Jonson copied out the final draft, smoothing inconsistencies. *Philaster* was probably more like *Eastward Ho!*, as there are indications that the final draft was in Beaumont's hand.

What are these indications? Between 1956 and 1962 Cyrus Hoy published a series of articles in which he attempted to distinguish 'The Shares of Fletcher and his Collaborators in the Beaumont and Fletcher Canon', and Hoy's work has been largely confirmed by subsequent scholars using different methods of analysis. Hoy's evidence was linguistic: he found Fletcher's style characterized by clear preferences such as *ye* over *you*, *has* over *hath*, and contractions such as *'em* over *them* and *i'th'* over *in the*. These differences made for a reasonably easy separation of Fletcher from Massinger, but unfortunately Beaumont's 'linguistic "preferences" – if they can be termed such – are . . . nothing if not eclectic' (Hoy, III, 87), his only invariable choice being *you* over *ye*. Thus if *Philaster* was given its final form by Beaumont (Hoy, III, 86), he probably eliminated many instances of *ye*, Fletcher's most characteristic linguistic trait, somewhat weakening the evidence.

However, the two authors can also be distinguished by their metrics. Fletcher's heavy reliance on the eleven-syllable line with a 'weak' or 'feminine' ending is another of his distinguishing characteristics. Compare, for example, Megra's lines from 2.4, almost all of which end with an unstressed syllable:

> Let 'em enter, prince, let 'em enter;
> I am up and ready. I know their business:
> 'Tis the poor breaking of a lady's honour
> They hunt so hotly after. Let 'em enjoy it.
> (2.4.105–8)

with these lines from the beginning of 4.3, where every line ends with a stress:

> Oh, that I had been nourished in these woods
> With milk of goats and acorns and not known
> The right of crowns nor the dissembling trains
> Of women's looks, but digged myself a cave

Where I, my fire, my cattle and my bed
Might have been shut together in one shed.
(4.3.1–6)

In general Hoy's divisions have been sustained by subsequent scholars. He assigns sections of *Philaster* as follows (III, 95):

Beaumont: I, 2; II, 1, 3, 4a (to Pharamond's entrance); III; IV, 3–6; V, 1–2, 3a (to King's exit), 5.
Fletcher: I, 1; II, 2, 4b (from Pharamond's entrance to end); IV, 1–2; V, 3b (from King's exit to end), 4.

Thus Beaumont is responsible for many of the play's important speeches and striking poetic images, for example, Bellario's comment that if he dies, ''Tis not a life, / 'Tis but a piece of childhood thrown away' (5.2.14–15) and Philaster's description of finding the 'boy' by the fountain (1.2.111–40). Fletcher is assigned almost all the comic prose scenes, for example, those of the citizens, the woodmen (4.1) and the cynical courtiers, as well as all the scenes in which Megra appears except the last. McMullan notes, 'The main Beaumont and Fletcher collaborations . . . provide clear evidence of Fletcher's regular subordination to his younger partner in the writing process' (*Fletcher*, 143), and for *Philaster* Hoy confirms that 'Beaumont's is the controlling hand' (III, 95).

Yet the division here shows that the two collaborators had already identified their individual strengths. Beaumont would give up the stage, but Fletcher would gradually expand his skills, writing comic prose, poetic tragedies and tragicomedies throughout his career. After Shakespeare's retirement he was the most successful dramatist in London; a 1620 portrait of him shows a richly dressed man standing next to the tools of his trade: quills, inkstand and paper (see Fig. 3). His hand rests on a brief poem, which may be modernized as:

Fletcher
The pencil and the pen have strived together
To show thy face and wit, and whether

3   Portrait of John Fletcher, from life, about 1620. Oil on panel, artist unknown.

Have done their best I know not, but confess
None but thy own pen could thy wit express.[1]

READING THE POLITICS OF BEAUMONT AND FLETCHER

Philaster is a play whose framing questions – usurpation and right-ful succession, tyranny and proper rule, foreign and native marriage alliances – are those of the great political dramas of the period, including not only *Hamlet* but also Shakespeare's history plays. Yet the seriousness of these issues is constrained by the tone of romance and by the equal attention given to personal and psychological matters. For some critics this tragicomic balance is a source of weakness. As Bliss puts it, the play shifts from *Hamlet* to romantic intrigue comedy to *Othello* and back, and 'In this blend of genres lies the formal solution to *Philaster* and also, to modern critics, the root of its failure' ('Three Plays', 166). Yet the slipperiness of the play's politics may be intentional: the collaborators knew very well that plays that touched on current matters too closely could land the authors in prison, as had happened to Jonson and Chapman for writing *Eastward Ho!*, or shut down an entire company, as had happened to the Blackfriars Boys. Thus, with the exception of one or two striking topical references, the play hints and suggests rather than directly confronting dangerous topics.

As a result, readings of the play have paralleled more general readings of the politics of the Beaumont and Fletcher canon. Over time these have essentially reversed. Humphrey Moseley's publication of the first Folio collection of Beaumont and Fletcher in 1647 was an implicitly royalist statement in the period when the theatres had been closed by the Puritans; in this 'Tragicall

---

1 In the picture the poem is mislined, with 'Flecher' forced into the third line. John Jowett suggests that in the artist's copy the name was in the margin, and points out that 'The forcing of the name into the poem and the mislineation are signs of reorganisation to fit to a narrow line, but although caps are retained for the original verse-lines, the relineation is disguised by new caps at the beginning of every line but the second' (JJ). In the second line 'with' instead of 'wit' is presumably an error.

Age', James Shirley wrote in his preface 'To the Reader', the Folio would demonstrate the '*Authentick witt that made Blackfriers an Academy . . . and the very Pleasure did edifie*' (A3).[1] Coleridge was more explicit: basing his analysis on lines such as Philaster's assurance to the King, 'I am dead, sir; you're my fate' (1.1.274) and Amintor's submission to tyranny in *A King and No King*, he characterized the collaborators as 'servile jure divino Royalists' (655). This became the dominant view; despite an occasional objection (e.g. Strachey's 1887 Preface), as late as 1952 John Danby was identifying the collaborators as 'brilliantly opportunistic' Jacobean absolutists and Philaster as an 'embryonic Cavalier' (161, 179).

The alternative view was that the plays of Beaumont and Fletcher, rather than royalist, were meaningless. The most negative version was codified by T. S. Eliot, who in his 1922 essay on Ben Jonson described the work of Beaumont and Fletcher as 'superficial in a pejorative sense', based on hollow emotions (115). Eliot influenced even critics who held a higher opinion of the collaborators. Although Lawrence Wallis (1947) was aware that Beaumont and Fletcher were members of a 'ruling class which looked forward to leadership in the affairs of the land rather than to servile compliance with dictatorship or tyranny' (135) and found Coleridge's charge 'baseless' (141), he still believed the plays were merely a 'framework upon which an elaborate emotional tapestry could be woven' (207). Wallis concluded that 'Fletcher, Beaumont and Company had no other significant aim than entertainment' (ix), and Eugene Waith (1952) influentially described their tragicomedies as written to a 'pattern'.

Thus by the middle of the twentieth century there seemed to be general agreement that Beaumont and Fletcher were royalist writers of decorative fairytales, creators of well-structured fables which, like *A King and No King*, had 'no meaning' but were 'an

---

1   *Philaster* did not appear in the 1647 Folio, in which Moseley included only plays never printed before (A4); it was therefore collected for the first time in the second Folio of 1679, *Fifty Comedies and Tragedies*, which added seventeen plays previously published in quarto. Wallis says the 1647 publication has 'a tinge of royalist literary manifesto' (14).

arrangement of dramatic moments in which . . . passions are displayed' (Waith, 41). On such a reading it would be impossible to take the politics of the collaborators seriously.

Nevertheless, a reaction was setting in. Starting with the work of Mary Grace Muse Adkins in 1946 and Clifford Leech in 1962, and continuing in that of Peter Davison (1963), Philip Finkelpearl (1990) and Gordon McMullan (1994), a different picture emerges. Leech, noting that a dramatist who 'directly questioned a sovereign's possession of an inalienable right to obedience . . . was in a particularly dangerous position', found 'the element of open debate which appears in the Beaumont and Fletcher plays . . . remarkable' (15), although he concluded that Fletcher's drama was ultimately 'too sceptical ever to be rebellious' (47). Adkins tried to explain her disagreement with the usual view by distinguishing between the collaborators: while Fletcher was 'uncompromisingly royalist' (209), Beaumont – given credit for most of *Philaster* – was in touch with the changing temper of the people challenging the extent of the king's power. Adkins stressed the power of the citizens, who are 'the means by which the usurping king of Sicily is deposed, the interloper Pharamond shipped back to Spain, and Philaster restored' (203). For Davison, *Philaster* reflected current affairs, especially reaction to claims in King James's writings (such as *The True Law of Free Monarchies*, published in 1603, the year he assumed the English throne) that even a tyrant might not be deposed: only God could punish wicked kings. For example, James asserted that even if he broke his coronation oath the people were still bound to him, and Dion suggestively wishes that 'somebody would draw bonds for the performance of covenants betwixt' king and people (4.4.59–61). In *Philaster*, Davison believes, 'pretensions of absolute power are made to look absurd and contemptible' (10). Furthermore, it is the Country Fellow who saves the princess, and thus despite the crudeness of his behaviour he represents an idealization of the 'country' members of Parliament, that is, those gentry whose attitudes and ethos were anti-court; who held traditional views of religion, hospitality and duty; and who ultimately formed a core of the Parliamentary leaders in the Civil War.

Direct contradiction of Coleridge arrived with Finkelpearl, who categorizes Beaumont and Fletcher's three most famous plays, *Philaster*, *A King and No King* and *The Maid's Tragedy*, as a 'trilogy about the public and private consequences of princely intemperance' (146). For Finkelpearl, too, the Country Fellow is at the heart of the play's politics. Where the court recreations are pernicious, the citizens protect Philaster and the Country Fellow protects Arethusa. Philaster himself is an antihero, a type Beaumont and Fletcher use repeatedly ('A figure of great public esteem, but weak-willed, life-hating, given to extreme, self-defeating, impressively noble gestures', 134) and typical of the manners and morals of the gentry and aristocracy of Jacobean London. Like Gurr, Finkelpearl notes the importance of the play's clearest topical reference, the confrontation in which the King demands that the courtiers produce his missing daughter:

KING

        ... Mark me all, I am your king!
I wish to see my daughter; show her me.
I do command you all, as you are subjects,
To show her me! What, am I not your king?
If ay, then am I not to be obeyed?

DION

Yes, if you command things possible and honest.

KING

'Things possible and honest'? Hear me, thou,
Thou traitor, that dar'st confine thy king to things
Possible and honest:

                    (4.4.28–36)

The dialogue closely parallels King James's clash with Lord Chief Justice Coke on 13 November 1608, which ended with Coke begging pardon on his knees (see Fig. 4). The issue was the

4   Portrait of Sir Edward Coke, by John Payne after unknown artist (1629)

superiority of the king or the common law. Gurr cites Sir Julius Caesar's official report on the incident:

> The comon lawe protecteth the king, quoth the L. Cooke, which the King said was a traiterous speech: for the King protecteth the lawe and not the lawe the King. The King maketh Judges and Bishops. If the Judges interpret the lawes themselves and suffer none else to interpret, then they may easily make of the lawes shipmen's hose.

As Gurr points out, 'It is inconceivable that Beaumont could not have been concerned with the issue; his father was a Common

Law judge, and he himself was a member of Coke's own Inn of Court, the Inner Temple' (lv–lvi); Finkelpearl calls the Beaumonts 'a veritable Inner Temple dynasty' (13).

McMullan elaborates on Fletcher's political and personal alignment with the 'country' party. Like Beaumont, Fletcher was patronized by the Earl and Countess of Huntingdon, and 'symmetries are apparent between the country-based, feminocentric, uncourtly environment cultivated by the Huntingdons at Ashby and the politics of the plays, which are cynical of court and assertions of absolutism' (*Fletcher*, 35). These attitudes become overt in *Philaster* when the hero tells his gentlemen supporters, 'You're all honest. / Go, get you home again and make your country / A virtuous court' (1.1.313–15). Ashby was such a 'center of disagreement with and occasionally of passive resistance to some of the policies emanating from London and the court' (Finkelpearl, 29). McMullan argues that even *The Faithful Shepherdess*, Fletcher's first solo production, far from being merely a pastoral romance, is 'a political play' (*Fletcher*, 65), representing the 'dangerous potential of popular unrest' (55), a particular concern of the Earl of Huntingdon after he was called upon to quell uprisings in Leicestershire in 1607. The scenes of citizen rebellion in *Cupid's Revenge*, like the scenes of Philaster's rescue, are by Fletcher, and McMullan finds that '[a]lready, Fletcher's sense of the possibilities of political unrest can be seen to outweigh Beaumont's aristocratic humor at the expense of the possibility of political collaboration between rulers and common people' (95). It is not surprising, therefore, that even when the collaborators had characters mouth the ideology of divine right or class superiority, their joint plots – *Philaster* included – invited an audience to consider an ironic interpretation.

JACOBEAN POLITICS, PERFORMANCES AND PUBLICATION

Philaster must have been first performed as soon as the theatres reopened in 1610, and its action will inevitably have suggested the central conflicts of the early years of James's reign and the character of the king himself. The play's nameless King has two kingdoms, one from which he comes (Calabria) and one in which he resides and rules (Sicily), just like James, who had been King James VI of Scotland since childhood and King James I of England since Elizabeth's death in 1603. The confrontation over the limits of the King's power takes place in the woods because he is not in court but away hunting, as James, to the annoyance of his Council, so frequently was (see Figs 5 and 6). Philaster's assertion that he is 'no minion' would have resonated as James's predilection for young men became increasingly apparent; the king ceased to cohabit with his wife after the birth and death of the Princess Sophia in 1607, and his special relationship with Robert Carr, his first truly conspicuous 'minion', began in that same year.

Politically the most contested question of James's early reign was the extent of the king's powers and the balance of those powers against those of Parliament. As Davison points out, almost everything contained in King James's 1616 *Works* had been written before 21 March 1610, *The True Law of Free Monarchies* by 1603. Thus the assertions found there – claiming that kings 'exercise a manner or resemblance of Diuine power vpon earth'; asserting the king's right to ignore contracts made with the people; and directing Parliament not to 'meddle with the maine points of Gouernment' – all underlie the confrontations that the usurping King in *Philaster* has with his courtiers, who implicitly represent the aristocrats and gentry that constituted most of Parliament. Informed pragmatically that his attendants cannot find his daughter, the King, like Richard II assuming that angels will fight for him, evokes the ideology of divine right:

KING

                  . . . 'Tis the King
Will have it so, whose breath can still the winds,

5 Three men hawking, with hounds; the title-page image from George Turberville, *The Boke of Faulconrie* (1575); cf. 4.1.1–2.

> Uncloud the sun, charm down the swelling sea
> And stop the clouds of heaven. Speak, can it not?

DION
> No.

KING   No! Cannot the breath of kings do this?

DION
> No, nor smell sweet itself if once the lungs
> Be but corrupted.

(4.4.42–8)

Dion's cynical view that only the gods could enforce 'bonds' between king and people, his attempt to restrict the King's power to 'things possible and honest' (4.4.33), and the echoes of the

The Booke of Hunting. 133

that the Prince or chiefe (if so please them) do alight and take
assaye of the Deare with a sharpe knife, the which is done
A 3   in

6 'The prince or chiefe . . . do alight and take assaye of the Deare', from George Turberville [actually George Gascoigne], *The Noble Art of Venerie* (1611); cf. 4.2.9–14. In this 1611 printing the image of Queen Elizabeth present in the 1575 illustration has been cut out of the woodblock and a picture of King James substituted.

confrontation between James and Coke all suggest that the young authors were titillating their audience with dangerous topicality while revealing their own political allegiances. Nevertheless, their tragicomic plot requires this same Dion to tell Philaster a crucial lie, that Arethusa lives 'dishonestly' with her 'boy' (3.1.28, 96). It is such inconsistencies that allow a critic like Waith to describe the play as 'a world of pseudo-history and romance' (18) and to ignore any immediate political significance.

Philaster's political resonances grew stronger in 1612–13, when it was twice performed at court during the celebrations for the wedding of Princess Elizabeth with Frederick, the Elector Palatine (see Figs 7 and 8). By giving his daughter to Pharamond, 'the Spanish prince that's come to marry our kingdom's heir and be our sovereign', *Philaster*'s King 'labours to bring in the power of a foreign nation to awe his own with' (1.1.7–8, 43–4). As early as 1609 King James had similarly begun to consider marriages for his children as political tools. Unrealistically hoping to ensure future peace through balanced alliances, he proposed a Spanish match for his heir, Prince Henry, although the English hatred of the Catholic Spanish went back at least to Mary Tudor's marriage and had not declined in the years since the 1588 attack by the Spanish Armada. Henry was too young to marry at the time of the first performances of *Philaster*, and to general dismay he died unexpectedly in November 1612. At the time of Elizabeth's marriage – to a staunch Protestant – Charles had become the royal heir, so the drawbacks of Arethusa's proposed marriage to a foreigner were not directly applicable to the English princess.

However, *Philaster* might well have suggested another recent court scandal, the secret marriage of Arbella (or Arabella) Stuart (see Fig. 9). Arbella was King James's first cousin – their fathers were brothers – and she had been born and raised in England, technically giving her a better claim to the throne than his. Contemporaries and modern historians alike frequently describe her behaviour as hysterical or mad, and a recent critic argues that she suffered from porphyria (Norrington). Elizabeth had kept her away from court, but at first James welcomed her, though he would not permit her to marry. Around the time of *Philaster* Arbella, born in 1575, apparently became impatient. She was arrested in December 1609 because of fears that she would marry a foreigner, and

7   Princess Elizabeth, daughter of King James I, at the time of her marriage.
From Crispin van de Passe, *Abbildung dess durchleuchtigen hochgebornen
Fursten und Herrn* (1613), a German edition of *Regiae Anglicae maiestatis
pictura* (1604), with the addition of six plates.

released with a promise that she could marry any loyal subject.
However, her eye had fallen upon William Seymour (b. 1588),
the most threatening match she could have proposed. Seymour
was the grandson of the Earl of Hertford, who had contracted
a secret marriage with Lady Catherine Gray, grandchild of
Henry VIII's younger sister Mary Tudor. In 1608 this match

8   Frederick V, Elector Palatine, at the time of his marriage. From Crispin van de Passe, *Abbildung dess durchleuchtigen hochgebornen Fursten und Herrn* (1613), a German edition of *Regiae Anglicae maiestatis pictura* (1604), with the addition of six plates.

had finally been declared official and its offspring legitimate. Under the will of Henry VIII, who had favoured descendants of his younger sister over those of his older sister Margaret (from whom both James and Arbella descended), the Seymours should have inherited the crown. James, with some difficulty, had this will set aside.

9   Lady Arbella Stuart, by John Whittakers, Sr (1619)

Rumours spread. In February 1610 both Arbella and William were arrested; released in March, they married secretly in June. Both were taken into custody, William to the Tower and Arbella to house arrest. But they managed to remain in contact, and in June 1611 they attempted a co-ordinated escape to France, with Arbella – who had perhaps seen too many plays – dressed as a man. William arrived too late at the rendezvous but made it to Ostend. Arbella, however, was recaptured and brought back to England. She died in September 1615, and only in 1616 did William return. Arbella's actions were intensely theatrical, and it is not surprising that [?Beaumont and] Fletcher's *The Noble Gentleman* (1611), Middleton's *The Lady's Tragedy* (1611) and Webster's *The Duchess of Malfi* (1613) have all been seen as representing aspects of her life and behaviour (see Finkelpearl; Gristwood; Steen). Ironically, considering its cross-dressing plot, Arbella herself apparently had Jonson's *Epicoene* (1609) suppressed for lines she thought reflected badly on her. She seems to be the source of the names of both Are/thusa and Bell/ario, and by 1612 Arethusa's choice of a 'loyal subject' rather than a foreigner as a husband, and the scene in which she and Philaster are shown '*in prison*' (5.2), might have suggested Arbella's history with Seymour.[1]

Understanding the political import of the 1619–20 productions, the next we know about, requires a brief summary of the textual situation (described more fully in the Textual Introduction, pp. 76–102). Not one but two early versions of *Philaster* exist, and the differences between these two versions – one published in 1620 (the First Quarto or, for short, Q1), the other in 1622 (the Second Quarto or Q2) – are both provocative and substantially intertwined with the play's ongoing political impact. In a nutshell, Q2 is the 'cleaner' text – that is, it is apparently complete and has fewer obvious printer's errors – and is the basis for the edition of the play presented here. Q1, though earlier, has features which make it less suitable as a base text for a modern edition but which are significantly revealing about the way in which plays were written, performed, reworked, updated and remembered (see Figs 10 and 11).

Thomas Walkley, publisher of both texts, in an address 'To the Reader' in Q2 describes Q1 as 'maimed and deformed',

1 James Savage, in fact, dates the play to 1610 partly because he thinks the references intentional.

PHYLASTER.

OR,

Loue lyes a Bleeding.

Acted at the Globe by his Maiesties Seruants.

Written by { *Francis Baymont* and *Iohn Fletcher*. } Gent.

The Princes.   *A Cuntrie Gentellman.*   *Phielaster.*

Printed at *London* for *Thomas Walkley*, and are to be sold at his shop at the *Eagle and Child*, in Brittaines Burffe. 1620.

10   Title-page of Q1, 1620

PHILASTER.

OR,

Loue lies a Bleeding.

As it hath beene diuerse times Acted,
at the Globe, and Blacke-Friers, by
his Maiesties Seruants.

Written by { *Francis Beaumont.*
and
Iohn Fletcher. } *Gent.*

The second Impression, corrected, and
amended.

LONDON,

Printed for THOMAS WALKLEY, and are to
be solde at his shoppe, at the signe of the
Eagle and Childe, in *Brittaines Bursse.*
1622.

11   Title-page of Q2, 1622

containing 'dangerous and gaping wounds' (see Quarto paratext for the entire address). Q1 bears the hallmarks of censorship: it eliminates all but two mentions of the 'two kingdoms' and never names Calabria, the King's original realm. The courtiers' discussion of the 'Spanish prince that's come to marry our kingdom's heir and be our sovereign' and the King's intention to 'bring in the power of a foreign nation to awe his own with' are reduced to a reference to 'the intended marriage with the Spanish prince'; satire on the court is softened and the description of lascivious court ladies in the first scene is entirely cancelled; Bellario is married off to a courtier whose interest in her has not previously been mentioned, eliminating any overtone of sexual irregularity. The two texts differ most radically at the beginning and end, but there are also many small changes in wording throughout. Given all the evidence, it seems most likely that Q1 is based on a partially censored, theatrically abridged, performance version, or a reconstruction of one, carelessly written and ultimately badly printed. Q2, on the other hand, is a 'good text'; it may derive from a transcript of the authors' original papers. Significantly, although Q1 was printed first, it is probably a derivative of Q2.

By 1619–20 *Philaster*'s political content had again accreted new political and cultural meaning. James was actively pursuing an unpopular Spanish match for Charles, and Frederick had lost his Bohemian throne and become a dispossessed prince married to the daughter of a rather hostile king. The censored Q1 text was probably created in its published form at this time. Although the passages suggestive of Arbella, by 1613 shut in the Tower, may have been cut at the earlier revival, in 1619–20 the politics of the country were tenser and plays were being used 'for a larger scale of political comment than is evident earlier' (Gurr, *Companies*, 133). For example, in August 1619 the King's Men were ready to stage Fletcher and Massinger's *Sir John van Olden Barnavelt* – a play that dramatized recent political struggles in the Netherlands and that had already

PHILIPPVS III D G, HISPANIARVM
ET INDIARVM REX. *obijt A M DCXXI.*

12   King Philip III of Spain, from Pieter de Jode, *Theatrum Principum* (1651)

been heavily censored by the Master of the Revels – when the Bishop of London attempted, ultimately unsuccessfully, to prohibit the performance. In 1621 there was so much open political anxiety that 'James insisted in Parliament that public discussion of foreign matters be prohibited as an infringement of the prerogative', and a year later he 'was faced with growing demands for a repudiation of the Spanish treaties' (Clare, 208) (see Fig. 12).[1]

Both exclusions and inclusions in Q1 point to 1619. The first is the removal of the satirical description of the court ladies. Attacks on the virtue of aristocratic women and court ladies are endemic in early modern English drama, but after 1615, with the revelation of the part played by Frances Howard in the Overbury affair, they seemed particularly risky. Howard was sexually notorious: she was married at the age of thirteen to the third Earl of Essex, and while he was on the grand tour was rumoured to be the lover of Prince Henry. At Essex's return she claimed he was impotent so that she could marry James's favourite Robert Carr, whom the king had made Earl of Somerset. In September 1613 Howard, probably with Carr, arranged the murder of Carr's former friend Sir Thomas Overbury, who was privy to their affair and may have known about potions Howard had used on the Earl of Essex.[2] The marriage took place in December, but in 1615 Howard and Somerset were found guilty of murder and condemned to death. James, however, had them remitted to the Tower, and there they remained until 1622. Thus, in 1619 a censor may have found descriptions of the court lady who will 'simper when she is courted by her friend, and slight her husband' and of Megra, whose 'name is common through the kingdom and the trophies of her dishonour advanced beyond Hercules' pillars', too suggestive of recent events, and ordered them removed (1.1.50–1, 56–7). Q1 also adds '*in prison*' to the opening direction for 5.2 – '*Enter* Phylaster, *Princesse,* Boy, *in prison*' – which might again suggest Howard and Somerset, although the line 'Come from this prison, all joyful to our deaths' (5.2.25) appears in both versions. *Philaster* kept becoming unexpectedly topical.

1 Savage believed that Q1 was the only version ever performed and that the censorship had been made before the first performance by George Buc, the Master of the Revels.

2 Alastair Bellany, *The Politics of Court Scandal in Early Modern England: News Culture and the Overbury Affair, 1603–1660* (Cambridge, 2002), concludes that Carr's guilt 'cannot be proved' (56).

Even more convincingly tied to 1619–20 are lines found only in Q1 that strikingly suggest Frederick's situation at this time:

> No, he that will
> Bandy for a monarchy must provide
> Brave martial troops with resolution armed
> To stand the shock of bloody, doubtful war,
> Not daunted though disastrous Fate doth frown
> And spit all spiteful fury in their face,
> Defying horror in her ugliest form,
> And grows more valiant the more danger threats.
> Or let lean Famine her affliction send,
> Whose pining plagues a second hell doth bring;
> They'll hold their courage in her height of spleen
> Till valour win plenty to supply them.
>
> (1.1.40–51)

In August 1619 Frederick claimed the monarchy of Bohemia, but in October 1620 he lost the Battle of the White Mountain, and soon thereafter, threatened with famine, he fled with his wife, Elizabeth, later known as the Winter Queen because of the brevity of her reign, to The Hague. King James resisted demands that he go to the defence of his daughter and son-in-law. The adapter of 1619–20 may have allowed himself to add a topical reference knowing that there was much popular support for the prince's attempt to 'bandy for a monarchy'. If so, this is the first time that changes were intentionally made in order to parallel events in the outside world. We do not know who wrote these lines, but a likely candidate is the King's Men's 'attached dramatist', who was none other than John Fletcher. Fletcher's political stance is clear from a verse-letter he wrote at this time to the Countess of Huntingdon: mentioning rumours that 'wee shall haue warrs wth Spaine', he asserts, 'I wolde wee might' (McMullan, *Fletcher*, 18).

Furthermore, McMullan suggests that the woodcut found on the title-page of the 1620 quarto, which seems to misrepresent the events by which Arethusa is saved, may be part of the same attempt to give topical political meaning to the action. The picture shows 'The Princes', with a deep wound on her breast, lying next to a well-dressed, booted and spurred 'Cuntrie Gentellman' holding a very prominent sword, while 'Phielaster', similarly dressed, creeps into the bushes (see Fig. 10). The Gentleman's sword is rather unusual, combining a basket around the knuckles with a long, curved crossguard; its style suggests not only rusticity but 'cultural conservatism' (Forgeng). To elevate the rank of Arethusa's saviour even more, not only does the picture make him a gentleman, but the Q1 stage direction for his entrance calls him a 'Countrey Gallant' rather than a 'countrey fellow'. The readership of the 1620 quarto, McMullan suggests,

> would have seen an overt reference to contemporary politics in the title–page illustration. The equation of the royal body with the state had been a political commonplace for decades, and the immediate context in 1620 provides an obvious parallel to the situation in the illustration. . . . Where a prince is apparently intent on destroying a loyal princess, it is a country gentleman who intervenes, driving away the offender and placing himself between the princess and the sword. It would be difficult to miss the implication that it is only in the country that the excesses and errors of court could be put right.
>
> (*Fletcher*, 112–13)

Taken with Q1's omission of the lines in which Bellario tells Philaster he cannot sell his clothes because 'The silly country people think 'tis treason / To touch such gay things' (4.3.30–1), it certainly seems that the reviser of 1620, while he censored suggestions that came too near the court, felt little compunction about defending the 'country' position.

Finally, in Q1 the speech prefixes for those who capture Pharamond and rescue Philaster are altered from 'Cit[izen]' to 'Soul[dier]'. Citizens served as the militia in London, so to some extent the distinction was blurred. In Fletcher's *The Island Princess*

(1621) the stage direction 'Enter Captaine and Citizens' is immediately followed by the Captain's injunction, 'Up souldiers, up, and deale like men' (2.3.58–9). Nevertheless *Philaster*'s display of the potential power of ordinary citizens – who in Q2 are rougher on the captured prince – may have disturbed the censor. Even in the Q2 text, where the Country Fellow is a 'mean man' who admits he does not know the 'rhetoric' of the courtiers, his instincts upon seeing Philaster with his sword drawn are fundamentally admirable: 'Hold, dastard, strike a woman! Th'art a craven, I warrant thee'. Arethusa's response, 'What ill-bred man art thou, to intrude thyself / Upon our private sports, our recreations?' seems a manifestation of all that is most ridiculous about the court (4.5.81–92).

SEX, GENDER AND DEVIANCE

Philaster is a play concerned with sex, gender and deviance, pushing against physical and psychological norms and boundaries. But gender is also a political issue in this play. As a female heir, Arethusa is inherently disruptive to an orderly succession. Furthermore, while innocent herself, like Prince Hal she is the child of a usurper. The play's King recognizes the danger in a guilty meditation on how the man

> who unrighteously
> Holds wealth or state from others shall be cursed
> In that which meaner men are blessed withal.
> Ages to come shall know no male of him
> Left to inherit, and his name shall be
> Blotted from earth.
>
> (2.4.49–54)

The situation is doubly threatening: in the absence of a male heir a foreign king may be imposed through marriage, blotting out the native line, or the succession may be contested, a widespread fear in Queen Elizabeth's later years. Much of James's behaviour, including his treatment of Arbella, derived from his need to show that he was not only the obvious but also the rightful successor. The play, of course, enables tragicomedy by giving the usurper a daughter and having the 'gods . . . make the passions of a feeble maid / The way unto your justice', that is, leading the princess to reject the foreigner and choose the rightful, native prince (1.2.31–4).

Susanne Collier has argued that during James's reign 'tragicomic romances depict the triumph of a patriarchal royal family whose dynastic succession is secured by the female heir marrying the one suitor whose bloodline can restore patrilinear descent of the throne', while in *Philaster* and *Cymbeline* 'stabbing the woman can be seen as an attempt to eradicate female powers, both physically and politically' (48, 42). This description is truer of *Philaster* than of any of Shakespeare's late romances. Only Arethusa restores *proper* descent by her marriage – the marriages of Miranda and Perdita will unite realms and ensure male rule, and Innogen merely steps aside for her brothers. But just as Arethusa is the only princess actually stabbed, she is also the only one who threatens to *replace* a rightful heir. She epitomizes the nation, and an attack on her is an attack, as Collier says, on 'the future queen's two bodies' (42).

The play also makes the trope of cross-dressing serve its political goals. The eventual submissions of Arethusa and Bellario, the former to a husband/king, the latter to sexual quiescence, ratify the political structure as well as conventional gender hierarchy (see Berek, 369). This is particularly important because Philaster is a weak prince and, as he himself says, frail and edging towards madness.

Philaster is constructed around two love triangles, each centred on a man. The more conventional one comprises Pharamond, Arethusa and Megra, whom he invites to 'love me and lie with me' (2.2.101–2) after the princess refuses him a few 'stolen / Delights' (1.2.195–6). The other comprises Philaster, the princess and Philaster's adoring 'boy', Bellario (see Fig. 13). Not one of these characters entirely adheres to early modern ideals of masculinity

13 Arethusa (Louise Mardenborough) with the cross-dressed Bellario (Ainsley
    Howard); cf. 2.3. Birmingham School of Acting, 2006.

and femininity, and much of the play's interest, as well as the occasional prurience that led Dryden to object that Fletcher did not
understand 'the decorum of the stage' (1.172), comes from their
deviance from gender norms. Both Philaster and his rival are, by
early modern standards, 'effeminate', lacking both power and self-
control. Effeminacy could signify excessive interest in women,
rather than acting as a woman. Pharamond's comment when he is
refused by his betrothed, 'The constitution of my body will never

hold out till the wedding. I must seek elsewhere,' is an example (1.2.199–200). His lust leads him to violate all decorum, refusing the King's guard entry to his lodgings and almost insulting the monarch. His behaviour justifies the King's dismissal: 'Remember 'twas your faults that lost you her / And not my purposed will' (5.5.206–7). Pharamond's terror when captured by the citizens adds to the sense of his insufficiency as prince and man.

The ostensible hero is also less than ideally manly. Philaster manifests his deficiencies politically by refusing to take action to regain his rightful position, despite the encouragement of his followers. When challenged by the King for boldness after a blustering speech, he immediately retreats, recognizing that he is 'too tame, / Too much a turtle, a thing born without passion' (1.1.208–9). He is credulous, accepting the accusations against Arethusa without investigating. Worst of all, he is neither heroic nor altruistic. As Dryden put it, he wounds 'his mistress, and afterward his boy, to save himself', and the Clown 'has the advantage of the combat against the hero' (1.172). More than any other element of the play, even more than his Othello-like stabbing of Arethusa and his inadequacy in fighting a mere churl, it is Philaster's cowardly behaviour when he is pursued that condemns him:

> I'll take this offered means of my escape.
> They have no mark to know me but my wounds
> If she be true; if false, let mischief light
> On all the world at once. Sword, print my wounds
> Upon this sleeping boy. I ha' none, I think,
> Are mortal, nor would I lay greater on thee.
> *Wounds him.*
>
> (4.6.20–5)

He then 'creeps' into the nearby bushes, suggesting that he is more animal than man at this moment.

Despite Philaster's later shame and repeated gestures toward suicide, nothing seems sufficient to excuse stabbing a woman and a boy, even if both welcome the attack (see 4.5.26, 65–6). On one level Philaster's immediate belief in the accusations against his beloved merely reiterates the play's pervasive misogyny. A foundational male concept of the perfect female emerges in the King's opening speech, where he proclaims his daughter 'yet / No woman'. Arethusa, he announces, is a virgin with 'undivided parts' whose 'few years and sex / Yet teach her nothing but her fears and blushes, / Desires without desire' (1.1.99–111). To be or become a 'woman', then, is to be imperfect or divided, presumably through sexual activity, and being sexually active risks making one like Megra. The play's attitude towards such women is embodied in the King's apostrophe as Megra emerges from Pharamond's bedroom (see Fig. 14):

> Thou most ill-shrouded rottenness, thou piece
> Made by a painter and a pothecary,
> Thou troubled sea of lust, thou wilderness
> Inhabited by wild thoughts, thou swollen cloud
> Of infection, thou ripe mine of all diseases,
> Thou all sin, all hell, and last all devils!
>
> (2.4.132–7)

Megra defends the natural sexuality of women – 'I am not the first / That nature taught to seek a fellow forth' – which could be praised as healthy feminism were it not coupled with another false accusation of Arethusa: 'Others took me, and I took her and him / At that all women may be ta'en sometime' (5.5.28–37). Her unusual wickedness emerges when one considers that in none of the other 'slandered woman' plays of the period (*Othello*, *Much Ado About Nothing*, *Cymbeline*, *The Woman Hater*) is the slanderer herself a woman.

Yet, contrary to her father's assumptions, the virginal Arethusa *does* have desires, desires that fortunately will fulfil 'the secret justice of the gods' (1.2.103). Nevertheless, Philaster's reaction when she announces that along with both kingdoms she must have 'Thy love, without which all the land / Discovered yet will serve me for no use', immediately reveals his inherent distrust of women:

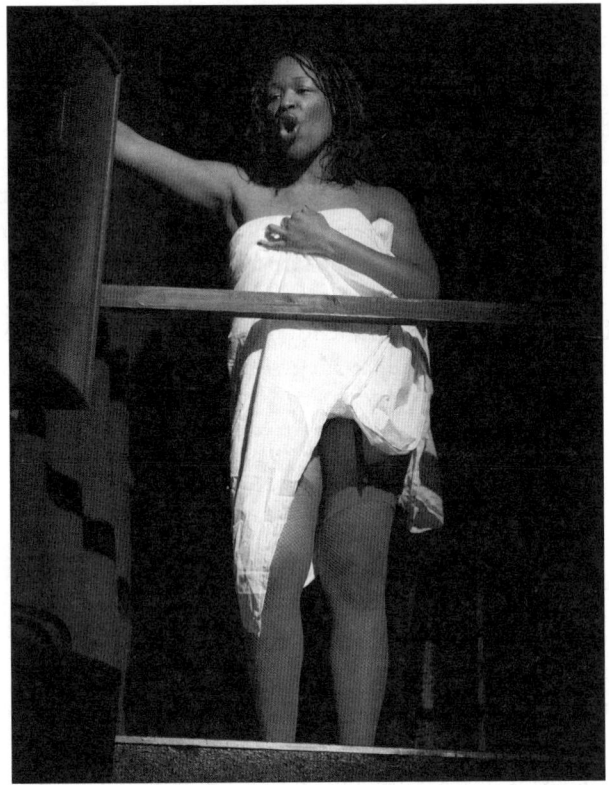

14   Megra (Charlene James) appears on the balcony; cf. 2.4.104 SD. Birmingham
      School of Acting, 2006.

Madam, you are too full of noble thoughts
To lay a train for this contemned life,
Which you may have for asking. To suspect
Were base where I deserve no ill. Love you?
By all my hopes I do, above my life.
But how this passion should proceed from you
So violently would amaze a man
That would be jealous.

(1.2.89–96)

The transition from love to suspicion to hypothetical jealousy is instantaneous, and is as much the cause of the near disasters in the subsequent action as are the treacherous accusations against Arethusa's chastity.

Critics have searched for psychological and ideological explanations for Philaster's actions. For Finkelpearl, '[a]t some unconscious level it would seem that Beaumont suspected heroic, widely admired figures of possessing uncontrollable, perverse impulses' (87). Loughlin reads Philaster's repeated stabbings epistemologically, as a manifestation of his need to uncover hidden truth. The ultimate unknowability of the other frustrates and misleads him just as it frustrates the state, leading to judicial torture. Yet the misogyny seems in some ways simpler and more fundamental. In 3.2 Philaster preaches 'What woman is' on a series of 'sad texts' that climax by calling woman 'A mere confusion and so dead a chaos / That love cannot distinguish' (112–26). He opens 4.3 with another attack on 'the dissembling trains / Of women's looks' based on Juvenal's sixth *Satire*, a core text of western misogyny (1–13). Philaster's attitude thus implicitly parallels the King's: having acknowledged desire, even for him, Arethusa ceases to be 'no woman' and becomes indistinguishable from the unchaste Megra. Her vulnerability comes from the projections of the men around her rather than from her own actions.

The strange, sexually ambiguous, even 'queer' nature of the situation, and of Philaster himself, develops less from the relation of the two lovers, with its echoes of Othello and Desdemona, than from the treatment of the remaining central character, the 'boy' Bellario who is really Euphrasia. In numerous Elizabethan and Jacobean plays a boy, often a page or servant, turns out to be a woman (played, of course, by a boy actor), but *Philaster* is unusual in several ways. First, in contrast to Shakespeare's method in such plays as *Twelfth Night*, the audience is not apprised of the character's 'real' gender until the final scene. Nevertheless, audiences with theatrical experience are likely to be alerted to anticipate

47

further developments by a seemingly unmotivated and irrelevant exchange in the first scene

PHILASTER
    My lord Dion, you had
    A virtuous gentlewoman called you father.
    Is she yet alive?

DION   Most honoured sir, she is,
    And for the penance but of an idle dream
    Has undertook a tedious pilgrimage.
                      (1.1.332–6)

They may then draw a connection to Philaster's long, poetic description in the next scene of the go-between he will send Arethusa, a boy he found weeping by a fountain. The boy had made a garland of flowers and gave 'The prettiest lecture' explaining what each flower 'Did signify'. Philaster 'gladly entertained him, / Who was glad to follow, and have got / The trustiest, lovingest and the gentlest boy / That ever master kept' (1.2.111–40).

The tears, the garland, the gentleness, prettiness and tenderness are all clues that the 'boy' is female. By the time of Field, Fletcher and Massinger's *The Honest Man's Fortune*, which the manuscript identifies as 'Plaide in the yeare 1613' (Hoy, IV, 101), the trope of the boy who is really a girl was available for parody. Veramour, the boy page, explains that he has falsely admitted to being a woman only because he has been persistently harassed to do so: 'I knew it not my selfe, / Untill this Gentleman opend my dull eyes, / And by perswasion made me see it' (5.4.241–3). Where in Middleton's *No Wit, No Help Like a Woman's* (1611) Mistress Low-water reveals her sex with a pun, 'I've my neck-verse perfect here and here' (9.559), presumably exposing her breasts, *The Honest Man's Fortune* ends with a risqué search of Veramour's breeches to know 'the ring from the stone'.

As *The Honest Man's Fortune* indirectly testifies, boys were recognized objects of sexual attraction for men as well as women (Masten; Orgel). For a modern audience the intense scenes between Philaster and Bellario have a homoeroticism that slides towards paedophilia and pederasty. The high point is the masochistic stabbing, with its unmistakable visual and verbal punning on 'die' as death and orgasm:

BELLARIO
> Oh, death I hope is come! Blessed be that hand;
> It meant me well. Again, for pity's sake!
>
> (4.6.26–7)

These homoerotic suggestions do not necessarily conflict with the court's assumption that the boy, 'about eighteen', has also done Arethusa 'service'. The sexuality of the situation is polymorphous. In his furious testing of Bellario Philaster asserts that he charged Arethusa 'to yield thee all delights / Naked, as to her lord; I took her oath / Thou shouldst enjoy her' (3.1.198–200). Bellario indignantly protests against the suggestion. Yet the plan s/he proposes at the end of the play – 'Never, sir, will I / Marry. It is a thing within my vow. / But if I may have leave to serve the princess, / To see the virtues of her lord and her, / I shall have hope to live' (5.5.186–90) – will make the future royal household a *ménage à trois*. Sandra Clark points out that Bellario's sexuality is 'categorically anomalous in that she is female, heterosexual, yet committed to a life of unfulfilled desire' (156). One might more cynically propose that she is committed to a life of desire(s) that may be fulfilled in irregular ways: even while acknowledging that 'complex negotiations' in *Philaster* 'create and then conceal the homoerotic as a discrete category of sexual experience', Nicholas Radel notes that 'marriage in the period does not necessarily stabilize (hetero)sexuality' (63–4).

The extent to which the anomalous ending could seem disturbing may be gauged from its rewriting in Q1. There Bellario acquires a previously unmentioned, pining lover and a marriage is rapidly arranged:

PHYLASTER [*to Bellario*]
> But 'tis you, lady, must make all complete

49

> And give a full period to content.
> Let your love's cordial again revive
> The drooping spirits of noble Trasiline.
> What says Lord Leon to it?

LEON

> Marry, my lord, I say, I know she once loved him –
> At least made show she did.
> But since 'tis my lord Phylaster's desire,
> I'll make a surrender of all the right
> A father has in her. [*to Trasiline*] Here, take her, sir,
> With all my heart, and heaven give you joy.

> > (Q1 5.5.97–107)

This conclusion reintegrates Bellario into heteronormative social roles. Not only will she have a husband, but her father's patriarchal rights are reiterated even as they are transferred to that husband. Q1 also eliminates Bellario/Euphrasia's statement that her desire is 'to serve the Princess', with its disturbing echo of the King's accusation that Arethusa's boy has 'done you / That good service shames me to speak of' (3.2.19–20). Radel believes that the 'potential lesbian desire that we might have expected to materialize once Bellario's true sex is revealed simply does not' (69) – there is hardly time for it to do so – while Masten argues that 'the play both makes impossible and practices a same-sex female eroticism . . . since its impossibility both absolves the Princess from the accusation of having slept with a boy, and remains present in her affection for her page turned woman' (125). No matter which way the Q2 ending is read, apparently the Q1 reviser thought it best to eliminate its remaining whiff of potential homoeroticism.

The play also shows politics impinging on bodies in its persistent mention of torture. In early modern England torture was used particularly against those, including Catholic priests, suspected of treasonous activities. Torture demonstrated the power of the state over the individual, invading the body as a stand-in for the soul in the search for 'truth'. After the discovery of the Gunpowder

Plot in 1605 eight of the conspirators were tortured, then publicly hanged and dismembered; Father Thomas Garnet was executed in 1608, shortly before *Philaster*, in this way.

Nevertheless, torture was regarded as unEnglish. On the continent, where the judicial system followed the Roman canon law, it was employed routinely, but as Sir Thomas Smith wrote in *De Republica Anglorum* (1565), 'torment or question which is used by the order of the civill lawe and custome of other countries . . . is not used in England'. Half a century later Chief Justice Coke – the same Coke who confronted James – reiterated that 'there is no law to warrant tortures in this land' (Hanson, 57). Clues to continuing contemporary objections are found a little later in the sermons John Donne wrote beginning in 1615. No doubt affected by his early experience among Recusant Catholics, Donne argued that torture was of dubious use and, more significantly, morally abhorrent, an offence against the dignity of God's creation.[1]

It is therefore notable that torture and threats of torture occur frequently in the Beaumont and Fletcher canon.[2] The two most striking cases are *The Double Marriage*, where Juliana is racked onstage in an unsuccessful attempt to make her reveal her husband's whereabouts, and *The Island Princess*, where the Princess Quisara announces her readiness to suffer 'fell tortures' to convert to Christianity. Both of these plays have Spanish sources, which may in part explain their acceptance of torture as normal.

In *Philaster*, which has no such source, the scenes in which torture is threatened – particularly 3.1, 4.6 and 5.5 – are all thought to be by Beaumont, who had Catholic relatives and may have been especially sensitive on the issue. Certainly the threat of state torture frightens Bellario. While he claims to be prepared to suffer for his fidelity to Arethusa – 'were she foul as hell / And I did know it, thus: the breath of kings, / The points of swords, tortures

---

1 See John Stubbes, *Donne: The Reforming Soul* (2007), 18, 332–3.
2 LION returns hits for 'torture' in thirty-two of the plays, and while the word is sometimes used metaphorically, actual torture is often threatened and sometimes carried out.

nor bulls of brass / Should draw it from me' (3.1.231–4) – when captured he is terrified: 'For charity let fall at once / The punishment you mean and do not load / This weary flesh with tortures.' English/Spanish differences may be adumbrated at the end of 4.6. Spanish Pharamond replies, 'If tortures can be found / Long as thy natural life, resolve to feel / The utmost rigour,' but when Arethusa requests to 'appoint / Their tortures and their deaths', Dion notes that 'our law will not reach that for this fault' – and the audience knows that Arethusa's real intention is to protect Bellario and Philaster (4.6.66–143).

In the final scene, when the King orders, 'Bear away that boy / To torture,' Philaster is so appalled that he again '*Offers to kill himself*' (5.5.64–79). However, the threat of torture is sufficient justification for Bellario to 'discover all', at which climactic point the play returns to the politics of bodies. 'Discovering all' means revealing the truth of sex. Once again political significance is partly obscured by romantic form. The audience, suspecting all along that the 'boy' is female, is being simultaneously titillated by Dion's insistence that torture will try his/her 'tender flesh' and reminded that political torture is unworthy. Donne, still a layman, could even have been in an early audience.

FORM AND STYLE

The tragicomic form and tone of *Philaster*, as well as its varying styles, are well illustrated in the first few scenes of the final act. In a brief opening, the gentlemen articulate the peril facing the prince as they simultaneously promise to resist it:

> THRASILINE   Has the King sent for him to death?
> DION   Yes, but the King must know 'tis not in his
>   power to war with heaven.
> CLEREMONT   We linger time; the King sent for
>   Philaster and the headsman an hour ago.
> THRASILINE   Are all his wounds well?

DION   All they were but scratches, but the loss of
   blood made him faint.
CLEREMONT   We dally, gentlemen.
THRASILINE   Away!
DION   We'll scuffle hard before he perish.

                                        (5.1.1–11)

These lines neatly fit Fletcher's promise that tragicomedy 'wants
deaths, which is inough to make it no tragedie, yet brings some
neere it, which is inough to make it no comedie', his version of
Guarini's famous criterion that tragicomedy gives us 'the danger,
not the death'. The plot here is close enough to *Cupid's Revenge*
that we cannot be sure that Philaster will escape, but his quick
recovery, the support of the gentlemen and the citizens, and the
love of Arethusa all point toward a happy or comic resolution.

The succeeding scene, 5.2, exemplifies a different aspect of the
tragicomic mixture, the tone of pathos – neither comic nor tragic
– that has characterized particularly Bellario:

PHILASTER

      O Arethusa! O Bellario! Leave to be kind.
      I shall be shot from heaven, as now from earth,
      If you continue so. I am a man
      False to a pair of the most trusty ones
      That ever earth bore. Can it bear us all?
      Forgive and leave me. But the King hath sent
      To call me to my death. Oh, show it me
      And then forget me! And for thee, my boy,
      I shall deliver words will mollify
      The hearts of beasts to spare thy innocence.

BELLARIO

      Alas, my lord, my life is not a thing
      Worthy your noble thoughts. 'Tis not a life,
      'Tis but a piece of childhood thrown away.

Arethusa joins in, promising 'by the honour of a virgin' not
to outlive Philaster, and the scene climaxes with a perfect

tragicomic paradox: 'Come from this prison, all joyful to our deaths' (5.2.3–25).

The next generic move is to introduce echoes of the Jacobean masque. Masques had gradually developed a tragicomic shape, often beginning with a frightening or comic antimasque ultimately banished by idealized or even deified masquers:

> *Enter* PHILASTER, ARETHUSA [*and*] BELLARIO *in a robe and garland* [, *escorted by* THRASILINE].

KING   How now, what masque is this?
BELLARIO
    Right royal sir, I should
    Sing you an epithalamion of these lovers,
    But having lost my best airs with my fortunes,
    And wanting a celestial harp to strike
    This blessed union on, thus in glad story
    I give you all.

Bellario's 'story', with its metaphorical presentation of the lovers as 'two fair cedar branches, / The noblest of the mountain', lasts twenty lines, after which Arethusa attempts an explication:

ARETHUSA   Sir, if you love it in plain truth,
    For now there is no masquing in't: this gentleman,
    The prisoner that you gave me, is become
    My keeper, and through all the bitter throes
    Your jealousies and his ill fate have wrought him,
    Thus nobly hath he struggled and at length
    Arrived here my dear husband.

The furious King continues the masque imagery while inverting its meaning:

KING   Your dear husband! –
    Call in the captain of the citadel. –
    There you shall keep your wedding. I'll provide
    A masque shall make your Hymen

Turn his saffron into a sullen coat
And sing sad requiems to your departing souls!
Blood shall put out your torches, and instead
Of gaudy flowers about your wanton necks
An axe shall hang like a prodigious meteor,
Ready to crop your loves' sweets.

(5.3.19–60)

In early performances these passages would have recalled Ben Jonson's *Hymenaei*, the masque for the marriage of the Earl of Essex and Lady Frances Howard, performed on 5 January 1606 and printed in quarto the same year. *Hymenaei* begins with the entrance of 'fiue Pages, attyr'd in white, bearing fiue tapers of virgin waxe; behind them, one representing a *bridegroome*'. These torchbearers are followed by:

HYMEN (the god of *marriage*) in a saffron-coloured robe, his vnder-vestures white, his socks yellow, a yellow veile of silke on his left arme, his head crowned with *Roses*, and *Marioram*, in his right hand a *torch* of *pine tree*.

After him a *youth*, attyred in white, bearing another light, of *white thorne*; vnder his arme, a little wicker *flasket*, shut: behind him two others, in white, the one bearing a *distaffe*, the other a *spindle*. Betwixt these a personated *Bride*, supported, her hayre flowing, and loose, sprinckled with grey; on her head a *gyrland of Roses*

(see Fig. 15). The masque concluded with a lengthy Epithalamium; only one 'staffe' was sung in performance, but in the quarto Jonson '*set it downe whole*' (Jonson 7.210–11, 225).

The public desire to see these fabulously elaborate court masques, which were usually performed only once, was not easily fulfilled. The audience was restricted to great courtiers: in *The Maid's Tragedy* Beaumont and Fletcher include a scene of officers trying to control potential gate-crashers. Consequently, the public theatres found ways to purvey bits of masques to their paying

15   Hymen, the god of marriage, from Vincenzo Cartari, *Imagini dei Dei degli Antichi* (1581)

customers. Occasionally sections of actual masques could be borrowed, as when part of Beaumont's *Masque of the Inner Temple and Gray's Inn* was inserted into the sheep-shearing scene of *The Winter's Tale*. More frequently a play would incorporate a few masque-like elements or, as in *The Maid's Tragedy*, invent a full masque for the usual occasion, a betrothal or wedding.

In *Philaster* suggestions of a wedding masque at this critical juncture seem intended to create what Brecht called an 'alienation effect': the King is serious about executing Philaster, and audience members might be reminded of Claudius's ultimately successful plot to kill Hamlet. But the action is distanced by its performative elements, which make the threat seem metatheatrically staged. Immediately after Philaster's typically masochistic, tragicomic, 'by the gods, it is a joy to die; / I find a recreation in't', a Messenger bursts in to announce that the citizens have risen in defence of Philaster and, led by 'an old grey ruffian', have taken Pharamond prisoner. The private reaction of the gentlemen moves significantly from high dramatic poetry to carnivalesque prose. Dion apostrophizes his 'dear countrymen what-ye-lacks', promising to have them 'chronicled and chronicled, and cut and chronicled, and all-to-be-praised, and sung in sonnets, and bathed in new brave ballads' (5.3.102–31). By the time the audience encounters the Captain and his 'brave Myrmidons' the action appears to have shifted definitively. The sudden reversal in the very last scene, when Megra renews her charges and Bellario is threatened with torture, is the kind of event that leads those who dislike the play's overt patterning to complain that '*Philaster* is a lively series of incidents contrived with great ingenuity to provide constant excitement and surprise . . . And it is nothing more' (Wilson, 339). In a more sympathetic reading it can be understood as the authors' triumphant demonstration of their control of the form.

The limits of tragicomedy were unclear in the early seventeenth century. Part of the success of Beaumont and Fletcher derived from following Marston's lead in *The Malcontent* and separating the form from pastoral and traditional romance. Despite the see-sawing emotions, the danger and the rescue, the disguise and the revelation, *Philaster* remains tied to a naturalistic world of political intrigue, citizen can-carriers and sexual infidelity, sharp-tongued women unembarrassed to be found *in flagrante* and weak princes dependent on their followers. In *The Faithful Shepherdess* the stabbed heroine is saved by a god; in *Philaster* she is saved by a countryman who is snubbed for his linguistic inadequacy and who, having beaten off Philaster, unheroically harasses the princess, 'I prithee, wench, come and kiss me now' (4.5.108–9). Tragicomic dramaturgy, Berek argues, embodies rather than resolves contradictions; the plays of Beaumont and Fletcher enact their culture's sexual and political ambivalences. The collaborators' generic experiments were ongoing from their time writing for the Children of the Queen's Revels; with *Philaster* they took tragicomedy to the King's Men and together with Shakespeare made it the most popular form of the next few years.

PERFORMANCE HISTORY

'That good old Play Philaster *ne're can fail'* (Settle)

A number of key themes recur as one traces the production history of *Philaster*: the play's popularity, its attractive 'star' roles, its adaptable political significance(s) and its complex representation of gender. The play held the stage for over a century. Yet its history of censorship and adaptation suggests recurrent discomfort, although the elements of the drama that invited intervention varied.

Earliest performances

Philaster was the play that made Beaumont and Fletcher famous. It is somewhat uncertain where the 1610 first performance occurred: the title-page of Q1 asserts that the play was '*Acted at the Globe by his Maiesties Seruants*' but Q2 is less restrictive, stating that the play has been '*diuerse times Acted*, at the Globe, and Blacke-Friers'. Gurr (xlix) suggests that the play's opening line, 'Here's nor lords nor ladies,' would have been more fitting for the Globe, but nothing confirms that the opening was seen as ironic when the play was performed with gentlemen seated on the Blackfriars stage.

Two other elements of the play point in conflicting directions. The exit and immediate re-entrance of the court gentlemen between Acts 2 and 3 and Acts 4 and 5 and of Arethusa between Acts 3 and 4 suggest a private theatre play; the King's Men did not use act intervals until they took over the Blackfriars in 1608, so a play that violates the convention against immediate re-entrance is unlikely to have been written with the Globe solely in mind (Taylor and Jowett). On the other hand, the absence of required stage machinery and music seems odd for the Blackfriars. Perhaps the play was conceived for the Blackfriars, and maintained the pattern of entrances to which the dramatists were accustomed from their experience at the private theatres, but was ultimately modified at least in part for the Globe; or perhaps the collaborators knew that the King's Men were restoring the Blackfriars but, unable to predict when the plague would lift or when the theatre would be ready, they hedged their bets and proposed a play that, with a little tolerance for the re-entrances, could be staged at either venue.[1]

Philaster's popularity was confirmed during the theatrical season of 1612–13, when the King's Men were paid for twenty court performances, of which only two plays were repeated, *Much Ado About Nothing* and *Philaster* (Chambers, 4.127). Apparently somewhat confused, the Revels Office warrant in May calls for payment to 'Hemynges' for 'fowerteene several playes', listing *Philaster* separately under its title and its subtitle (Chambers, 4.180). The other Beaumont and Fletcher plays were *The Maid's Tragedy* and *A King and No King*, but neither was repeated. *Philaster* was produced again at court in

---

1 McMullan argues that *Henry VIII* was also likely to have been written with both theatres in mind, and notes that 'Seventeen editions of ten plays . . . list both the Globe and the Blackfriars on their title-pages' (*H8*, 9–10).

RICHARD BURBADGE.
The first Performer of King Richard III.
From an original Picture in Dulwich College.
London Pub. as the Act Directs March 1.1790 by R.Harding N.º 132 Fleet Street.

16 Richard Burbage, the first Philaster, by Silvester Harding (1790), based on a picture in Dulwich College

1619–20[1] probably in a version approximating that recorded in Q1.

It is possible to infer something of the cast of these three Jacobean productions. Assuming that players acted consistent 'lines', T. W. Baldwin attempted to assign the original performers.

1 Bentley accepts Chambers's suggestion that the list of plays found among recovered waste papers of the Revels Office itemizes those being considered for presentation at court in that season (1.95), but Gurr apparently disagrees, saying there are no records from 1617–21 (*Companies*, 389).

In his view Richard Burbage, the company's leading man, who had played Hamlet, would have played Philaster in both 1610 and 1613, being replaced by Joseph Taylor in 1619, the year of Burbage's death; this same sequence is recorded in the first quarto of *The Duchess of Malfi* for the role of Ferdinand (see Fig. 16). According to Baldwin, John Lowin, another sharer who specialized in bluff counsellor parts, played Dion; John Heminges Cleremont; William Ostler the King; Henry Condell, who specialized in villains or soldiers, the comic Captain; the 'princely villain', Pharamond, 'belonged' to John Underwood. None of these assignments can be demonstrated – the 1679 Beaumont and Fletcher Folio lists names of actors but not their parts – but the castings are superficially reasonable. Yet various roles, for example the Country Fellow, are not accounted for, and there is nothing to make Cleremont 'a comic peppery old man of high rank' except that this suits Baldwin's description of Condell's roles. Baldwin's analysis more persuasively demonstrates that the play reproduces well-established character types (the hero, the citizen/captain, the blunt counsellor, the princely villain), and thus combines the new tragicomic tone and action with material to which the actors could easily adapt.

As usual in the period, there are two boy's parts of considerable size, Arethusa and Bellario, and two smaller ones, Megra and Gallatea. The boys could more accurately be called apprentices, as their ages ranged from twelve to twenty-two, and it seems possible that the ages of the characters, specified as 'About eighteen' in the case of Bellario (3.2.16), may roughly reflect the age of the players. Bellario was the largest boy's part, at 349 lines in Baldwin's count. Baldwin assigned the role to James Sands, but David Kathman's research suggests that it was probably first played by the leading boy John Rice, who was eighteen in 1610, assisted by either Sands or James Jones as Arethusa with 311 lines. Major boy players in 1613 were John Wilson and Richard Robinson, although Robinson, born in 1598, would only have been fifteen, perhaps too young for Bellario (Kathman, 232, and private communication). In 1619 the leading boy was Richard Sharpe, who was just eighteen and would shortly play the Duchess of Malfi; he probably played Bellario but could have played Arethusa.

Philaster *becomes a ladies' play*

In the Caroline period *Philaster* was twice brought to court, on 14 December 1630 and again on 21 February 1636/7 (Bentley, 1.96, 98). Presumably these performances followed or were accompanied by revivals in the theatres. More unusually, the play's popularity continued in the interregnum. Despite the closing of the theatres, other kinds of performance nevertheless took place. Some were private, as emerges in a recollection of the diarist Samuel Pepys. On 30 May 1668, he went

> To the King's playhouse and there saw *Philaster*; where it is pretty to see how I could remember almost all along, ever since I was a boy, Arethusa's part which I was to have acted at Sir Rob[ert] Cooke's; and it was very pleasant to me, but more to think what a ridiculous thing it would have been for me to have acted a beautiful woman.
>
> (9.217–18)

This reminiscence is revealing about both the play's continuing political reverberations and the slipperiness of its gender depictions.

First, the context of the private production. Sir Robert Coke was the eldest son and heir of Chief Justice Edward Coke, whose confrontation with King James over the respective authority of law and monarch is reflected in the clash between Dion and the King in *Philaster*, 4.4. Sir Robert and his wife Lady Theophila lived near Epsom, Surrey: they were 'learned and cultivated; he had added a hall to the house in 1639, in which plays may have been produced' (Pepys, 9.218 n. 1). Pepys would have been introduced into the house when he visited his relative John Pepys, who lived nearby; John Pepys had been secretary (that is, assistant) to Coke's father the Chief Justice.

In his Restoration recollection Pepys uses the hypothetical, remembering what he 'was to have acted' and 'what a ridiculous thing it would have been'. The production at Coke's may ultimately have been cancelled. Earlier, on 18 November 1661 Pepys had gone 'to the Theatre to see *Philaster* (which I never saw before)' (2.216). Yet he seems to have known the part well, suggesting that the private performance had been thoroughly prepared. Of course he may merely mean he had never before seen it on the public stage. Pepys was born in 1633 and Sir Robert died in 1653, so it is likely that Pepys was studying the part in the early 1640s, after the theatres were closed. His biographer Claire Tomalin imagines 'what an adventure' it would have been for a boy who 'can't have been more than nine' to find himself invited 'to show off in a star part in a great house' (10). But the real adventure is likely to have been Sir Robert's: the choice to stage this particular play, with its unmistakable echo of Coke's father articulating anti-Divine Right theory, in the presence of his former secretary and no doubt others who shared similar views, seems rather risky as war raged between King Charles and his opponents. One can only speculate about the events that may have led to cancellation of the performance, but both the undertaking and the hypothetical suppression are likely to have been political.

Unquestionably political was the choice of *Philaster* 5.4, in which the citizens capture and bait the foreign prince Pharamond, as the basis of the commonwealth droll *The Clubmen*. The 1662 publication of these short entertainments, *The Wits*, makes the error of identifying *The Clubmen* as a scene from *Cupid's Revenge*. Contrarily, it misidentifies a different droll, *The Loyal Citizens*, in which citizens rescue their condemned prince, as derived from *Philaster* when it is in fact from *Cupid's Revenge*, 4.3. Nevertheless, it is significant that in both scenes the citizens take matters into their own hands, defying state power. The preface to *The Wits* asserts that these 'rump drolls' are just meant for amusement, but the repeated confrontation between citizens and aristocracy was certainly pointed in the Commonwealth context. It may also be relevant that the three times authorities halted performance of an identifiable play during the Civil War, the play in question came from the Beaumont and Fletcher canon: *A King and No King*, *The Bloody Brother* and *Wit Without Money* (Wallis, 10). The collaborators' plays had always been popular, but these wartime choices confirm that they supplied more than 'entertainment for the gentry'.

Philaster was one of the 'great favorites' in the Restoration vogue for Beaumont and Fletcher plays (*London Stage*, 1.cxxviii). The play was revived immediately upon the reopening of the theatres, first at the Red Bull in 1659–60 and then in November 1660 by the King's Company under Thomas Killigrew at Gibbons' Tennis Court. It played frequently throughout the 1660s and 1670s; Charles II saw it repeatedly, in 1667 possibly with Hart playing Philaster and Nell Gwyn playing Bellario (*London Stage*, 1.124).[1] Performances were not restricted to London theatres; in 1662 or 1663 Sir Thomas Brown's son Edward, a medical student, saw *Philaster* at an inn called 'the Cardinal's Cap' in Cambridge. It was given in the Temple Hall in November 1671 (Sprague, 41), and apparently George Farquhar appeared as Dion in a production at Ashbury's Smock Alley playhouse in Dublin around 1696 (Sprague, 89 n. 5).

Pepys, dismissing as ridiculous the idea of a boy playing 'a beautiful woman', was writing after actresses began to appear on the English stage. What seemed absurd to him in 1668 would not have been so to adults of the 1640s, for whom clever boys like Pepys had been accepted performers of female roles. But the arrival of actresses may have been one cause for *Philaster*'s continued popularity. Although recently *Philaster* has been discussed as a 'boy's play' (Masten; Radel), in the Restoration it was fast becoming a 'ladies' play'. In June 1672 *Philaster* was one of the plays 'represented at the old Theatre in Lincoln's-Inns-Fields,

---

1 Sprague (40) notes that Genest, in his *Account of the English Stage from the Restoration in 1660 to 1830* (1832), seemed to assume this cast was for the performance of May 1668, but by then Nell Gwyn had quit the King's Company.

when the Women acted alone. The Prologue and Epilogue were spoken by Mrs Marshall, and printed in *Covent-garden Drollery'* (Langbaine, cited *London Stage*, 1.194). Without making specific reference to the action of the play, in her epilogue Mrs Marshall makes a plea for the actresses that suggests the androgynous nature of the parts:

> Gallants; your Fathers with one sex made shift,
> Sure our's of pleasing has the better gift.
> A bearded Princess their concern could move,
> Why may not now, a beardless Prince make Love.
> Nor should soft lines; for youth, and beauty meant,
> Be on Men's blew, and wither'd faces spent.
>
> > (Covent Garden, 19–20)

As late as 1695 the epilogue to Settle's revision (see pp. 67–9) recalled this all-female performance: it begins '*Once our* Philaster *was a Lady's Play*'. The term could be applied both to performers and to audience. In October 1711, after a hiatus of fifteen years, *Philaster* was twice revived 'At the Desire of several Ladies of Quality'; and this happened again in January 1712 and January 1716 (*London Stage*, 2.261, 268).[1]

Improving the decorum of the stage: Philaster *adapted*

The Restoration saw the first two revisions of *Philaster*. Mrs Marshall's Prologue had insisted that the actresses:

> much mistook the age,
> If we thought virtue, must support the Stage;
> Our Bawdery will lose you here 'tis true,
> Some civel women; and of them but few.
> The most discreet amongst 'em will come still,
> Good soules,
> They neither hear nor understand, what's ill:

---

1 In May of 1715 'Tickets for *Philaster* [were] taken this day'; possibly the performance did not take place, as in December of 1715 it was revived 'Not Acted these Three Years' (*London Stage*, 2.356, 382).

65

Nevertheless, the discernible intention of these adaptations was to reduce the shocking nature of the play's actions, especially the hero's phallic stabbing of two defenceless women. As mentioned earlier, in his 'Defence of the Epilogue', published the same year as the all-female performance of the play, Dryden asserts that 'our admired Fletcher . . . neither understood correct plotting, nor that which they call *the decorum of the stage*'. In particular Dryden objects to 'Philaster wounding his mistress, and afterwards his boy, to save himself, not to mention the Clown, who . . . not only has the advantage of the combat against the hero, but diverts you from your serious concernment with his ridiculous and absurd raillery' (1.172). Consequently, Restoration adaptations tried to improve both plotting and decorum, either by modifying the offending actions or by changing their motivation and circumstances.

The first revision, *The Restauration: or, Right will take Place*, was printed in 1715 as by George Villiers, late Duke of Buckingham. The Prologue and Epilogue had been previously published in Buckingham's *Miscellaneous Works* of 1704. Both the authorship of this adaptation and its staging are uncertain: Robert Hume and Harold Love conclude that the 'attribution problems surrounding Buckingham' are 'insoluble' (Buckingham, 1.vii). Langbaine claimed that

> His Grace . . . bestow'd some time in altering . . . *Philaster* . . . He made very considerable Alterations in it, and took it with him, intending to finish it the last Journey he made to *Yorkshire* in the Year 1686

but in 1719 the play was said to be 'Injuriously father'd' upon Buckingham (1.454–5). Topical references in the Epilogue to Buckingham's enemy Shaftesbury, who died in exile in January 1683, suggest that the play appeared shortly thereafter; Hume and Love, like *The London Stage*, are inclined to believe it was performed and point out that in 1683, their first season, the United Company mounted productions of several favourites by Beaumont and Fletcher (1.458–9).

The goals of the asynchronous collaborator are evident. First, the play's new title recalls the greatest success of Buckingham's life, the 1660 restoration of the monarchy in the person of Charles II, with whom Buckingham had been raised. Aside from a slighting reference to a standing army, deeply hated in the Restoration, topical references are restricted to the Prologue and Epilogue. The former regretfully suggests Buckingham's exclusion from government: the author promises to try '*to mend a Play*' although '*Perhaps he wish'd it might have been his Fate / To lend a helping Hand to mend the State.*' The Epilogue more specifically attacks Shaftesbury, who '*since he could not living act with Reason, 'Twas shrewdly done of him to die in Season*'.[1]

The major revisions of 1683 concern the conduct of the central figure. Rather than stabbing Araminta (Arethusa), losing his battle with the Country Fellow and wounding Endymion (Bellario) to lead his pursuers astray, Philander (*sic*) '*Runs* at Endymion, and *hurts* Araminta' by accident. He defeats the 'Clown' in their battle, and wounds Endymion because 'I'm sure I saw him take her in his Arms; / And he deserves to lose his Life for that.' Sprague thought that Arethusa's part had been restrained for reasons of decorum (192–3), but Hume and Love, noting the 'careful reworking' of the parts for boys and their accommodation 'to a more passionate, less poetic style of performance', propose that 'Women actors did not need to mediate female sexuality through the use of ornate language, since they could do it directly with their voices and their bodies' (Buckingham, 1.458).

Elkanah Settle's adaptation dates from 1695. Settle was a man who could tack with the winds: first a supporter of Shaftesbury, then a supporter of James II, after the accession of William and Mary he ceased political activity and returned to the stage (Brown, 27). His Philaster has won the crown of Calabria for the King but has been refused forces to recover his own kingdom, Aragon, 'Torn from him in his weak and sleeping Infancy / By *Spain's*

---

1   Hume and Love largely dismiss more specific political applications.

encroaching Monarch'. The trope of the 'loyal subject' not properly rewarded recurs throughout the Beaumont and Fletcher canon, and in 1695, with William simultaneously Stadtholder of the Dutch United Provinces and King of England after his father-in-law's flight, it was clearly better to avoid depicting a usurping foreign king. In fact, the opening description of Philaster, 'this most generous Stranger, / The *Atlas* of our Kingdom' may be meant as a compliment to William himself. Eventually this Philaster does regain his lost Aragon, as well as Calabria and Sicily by marriage, another echo of William's situation.

Settle outdoes Buckingham in 'improving' the behaviour of his central characters: he effectively rewrites the last two acts, starting when Philaster comes upon Bellario and Arethusa in the woods. Arethusa has fainted, Bellario kneels to help her, but misunderstanding their intimacy Philaster becomes enraged. He orders Bellario to fly, which Bellario does, praying for his prince's 'benighted Reason'; the despairing Arethusa begs for death, but Philaster orders her to kill him. Instead Arethusa '*Falls on his Sword*' and '*Faints away as if she dyed*'. As Philaster, in turn, '*Goes to fall on his Sword*, Bellario *beats it away*'.

Thus there is no need for the 'low' Country Fellow: Arethusa wounds herself out of altruistic love; Philaster wounds no one and does not accuse Bellario. Dion, too, is saved from lying consciously. Instead he and the other courtiers infer that Philaster accuses himself for love of Arethusa, but killed her when he found her with the boy. All is resolved when, just as Philaster and Bellario each take responsibility for Arethusa's death, a Messenger informs the King 'Your Beauteous Daughter Lives.' Love and Honour are vindicated in the best Restoration manner, and the political implications are also defanged. Although the confrontation between Dion and the King is unchanged, the insurrection of the Citizens is reduced to the entrance of the 'Rabble' with Pharamond, and when the Captain promises to protect Philaster from the King, the prince orders, 'forbear this impious profanation! / The King's all God-like good.' Politically as well as sexually the play avoids offending.

Settle's *Philaster* was produced by Rich's company in its first season of competition with Betterton and his associates at Lincoln's Inn Fields. Few of their new plays had 'more than minimal success' (*London Stage*, 1.449); Settle's *Philaster* was no exception. When *Philaster* reappeared at Drury Lane in 1711, the Beaumont and Fletcher version was restored (Sprague, 89).

The third adaptation, in 1763, was by George Colman the Elder (1732–94). Colman considered that his 'Age', while applauding Shakespeare, 'too grossly neglected the other great Masters in the same School of Writing', particularly Beaumont and Fletcher (Colman, 'Adaptation', A2r). He would produce a ten-volume edition of their plays in 1778. He was a professional playwright and theatre manager, and by 1763 was acting as director of the Drury Lane theatre. *Philaster* had not been staged since 1722 and Colman's revision was a hit, assisted by a strong cast (*London Stage*, 4.1011). There were seventeen performances in the first season, with repeats and revivals throughout 1774. By 1780 the play may have ceased to please, as it was played on 3 October and on 4 October *The Suspicious Husband* was the 'Mainpiece in place of *Philaster*' (*London Stage*, 5.376–7). Nevertheless, Colman's version of *Philaster* was again staged in the seasons of 1785–6 and 1796–7, by which time the *Monthly Mirror* objected that 'the beauties and absurdities of this play are equally striking!' (Rulfs, 1252–3).

In the 'Advertisement' to the revision, Colman specifies that his 'sole Ambition' is 'To remove the Objections to the Performance of this excellent Play on the Modern Stage'. As usual these objections are to 'Ribaldry and Obscenity, and . . . a gross Indecency in the original Constitution of the Fable', that is, the scenes in which Philaster wounds Arethusa and Bellario. Colman also omits Dion's 'Falsification of Facts' as 'inconsistent with the rest of his Character' (A2ᵛ).

Once again the focus of the revision is primarily sexual. Colman does his best to avoid staging immoral conduct. Megra becomes Pharamond's Spanish mistress, sent with him to wait upon Arethusa, and her objections to being neglected lead to scenes of jealousy rather than flirtation. Pharamond's illicit proposal to Arethusa is corrected to an invitation to 'solemnize a private Nuptial', and Arethusa's response is less to his sexual demands than to the proposed violation of filial duty: she cannot 'give my Fancy or my Will / More Scope than [my father] shall warrant'. Presumably for the same reason she does not secretly marry Philaster, and the scene where the newlyweds are presented to the King by Bellario is eliminated.

Colman prided himself on the 'simple Means' he used to alter the plot (A3r). He has the Country Fellow 'prevent' Philaster from wounding Arethusa, and Bellario is wounded while interposing in the fight. Thus the Fellow can report that a Knave 'would' have hurt her, and many lines require only a similar change of verb to the hypothetical. Yet, despite the lack of blood, Colman classified the play as a tragedy, comparing it to *Lear*, *Hamlet* and *Othello*, which similarly introduce 'comick Circumstances in the natural Course of the Action', and distinguishing it from the tragicomedies of his period 'in which two distinct Actions, one serious and the other comick, are unnaturally woven together' (A3v).

The Harvard Theatre Collection contains Colman's marked promptbook for the performance of 8 October 1763. The cuts marked reveal Colman's aesthetic – his desire to make the play more delicate, less bawdy, less open about social and political conflict – and a practical theatre manager's eye for reducing lines and scenes not focused on the major characters. The promptbook also shows that despite his dedication to the 'other' playwrights, Colman still read them through Shakespeare. Alongside what is now 3.2.89–94:

> O you gods,
> Give me a worthy patience! Have I stood
> Naked, alone, the shock of many fortunes?
> Have I seen mischiefs numberless and mighty

> Grow like a sea upon me? Have I taken
> Danger as stern as death into my bosom . . .

he notes, 'Fine imitation of Othello'.

After Colman's adaptation *Philaster* almost disappeared from the stage. Rulfs attributes the decline in the fame of Beaumont and Fletcher to the 'greatly increased size of the new Drury Lane and Covent Garden theaters built during the early 1790's', which required spectacular productions, as well as to increased concentration on Shakespeare (1252). The only nineteenth-century revival of *Philaster* known was at the Theatre Royal, Bath, on 12 December 1817 (Gurr, lxxiii).

Yet even so, the disappearance was not quite complete: in 1828 the well-known playwright Frederick Reynolds cannibalized large sections of *Philaster* in adapting William Shirley's *Edward the Black Prince* (1750) as *Edward the Black Prince, or, She Never Told her Love*.[1] Here Reynolds adds romance to Shirley's 'historical tragedy', which Mrs Inchbald's prefatory 'Remarks' had criticized for lacking an attractive woman's part. Helena, daughter to Rousillon, Marshal of France, is prisoner of the English. Ribemont, who loves her, sends his page Julio, whom he found while hunting, to serve as a go-between; the relationship of Helena and Julio is suspected, Ribemont goes mad with jealousy and wounds both of them by accident; Julio begs him to creep into the bushes and save himself; finally Julio's female sex is revealed. In a modification of *Philaster* she marries Ribemont because Helena has fallen in love with an Englishman. In addition to taking key emotional moments from *Philaster*, Reynolds plagiarizes freely from its lyrical speeches, including the finding of the page (1.2.111ff.), Philaster's desire to live in a cave and preach against women (3.2.89ff.), and the page's account of how he first saw the hero (5.5.150ff.). In classical fashion the bloodletting is reported

---

1 *Edward the Black Prince Licensed 14 January 1828 . . . An Historical Play in three acts Interspersed with Music Founded on Shirley and Beaumont and Fletcher. Plays from the Lord Chamberlain's Office*, Vol. XXV, January–February 1828. BM Additional MS 42889, Fols 1–329.

rather than staged. For good measure, Reynolds also adapted the scenes of Caratach and his nephew from *Bonduca* and had Julio and Helena sing 'Tell, Oh tell me, what is love' based on 'Tell me dearest what is Love?' from *The Knight of the Burning Pestle* and *The Captain*. The greater importance of the romantic plot was reflected in a shift in casting: in Shirley's version the company stars, David Garrick and John Philip Kemble, had successively played Prince Edward, while in Reynolds' version the lead tragedian William Charles Macready played Ribemont.

Philaster *in the twentieth and twenty-first centuries*

A bit more than a century later, on 22 November 1938, *Philaster* was revived as a radio broadcast on New York City's WQXR. Condensed to one hour, the play lost much of its sex and poetry, but the surrounding circumstances are, yet again, political. The broadcast was sponsored by the Federal Theatre Project (FTP) of the Works Progress Administration, created by President Roosevelt in 1935 to employ theatre professionals put out of work by the depression. The FTP's general director was Hallie Flanagan; in New York the FTP's first director was the playwright Elmer Rice. The FTP was responsible for hundreds of stage productions as well as the so-called 'Living Newspapers'.[1] In their third year Flanagan reported that 'to date 445 plays have been submitted to the Bureau, and read and reviewed by a staff of experienced play readers and playwrights'. Most of the plays they produced were classics; 'Beaumont and Fletcher' were first represented by *The Knight of the Burning Pestle*.

By 1937 the FTP was under pressure for its politics, considered by some to be too socialistic. In 1938 Flanagan was called before the notorious UnAmerican Activities Committee of the House of Representatives. All funding was stopped and the

---

1   The papers of the FTP are in the Music Section of the Library of Congress; many of Flanagan's papers are at the New York Public Library. Quotations are from the Library of Congress. Boxes 872 and 942 have files on Elizabethan Theatre; Box 282 has a Playscripts file that includes the readers' reports on *Philaster*.

FTP came to an end on 30 June 1939. The broadcast of *Philaster* thus occurred late in the FTP's history, and was no doubt affected by the increasing tension. One possible reason why *Philaster* and seven other Elizabethan and Jacobean plays were still broadcast was that the 'musical supervisor' was WQXR's director Eddy Brown, a pioneer of American radio as a source of cultural education. Another is suggested by a 'Brief' Flanagan delivered to the Committee on Patents of the House of Representatives in February 1938. She listed radio as one of eight lines of work for the FTP and described how the new 'Federal Theatre of the Air', which had produced cycles of Shakespeare, Ibsen and Gilbert and Sullivan, was doing an 'Epic of America'. With accusations of socialism flying and understandings of what was 'American' ideologically charged, Elizabethan plays must have seemed non-controversial.

The choice of *Philaster* was probably made by the National Play Policy Board.[1] Readers seem to have examined the play uncut, and as they carefully detail the number of sets and actors required it is probable that a radio production was not the original intention. The readers' reactions reveal contrasting responses to tragicomic romance – one complains:

> One simply can't take the graver side of Beaumont and Fletcher seriously, unless it be with a nice grain of salt. When they take to moralizing they end up like a couple of sly old shams; when they go out tear-splashing on the sorrows of humankind, they come wallowing home like a pair of blinking crocodiles. As bawdy biting farceurs though, they're inevitably both glorious and grand. Strip this play of its solemnities . . . and you'll be rewarded with high handsome comedy.

Another objects that the 'whole play is based on a misunderstanding that is prolonged at least four acts beyond its natural course'

---

1 These readers passed on newly written plays; it is not entirely clear whether it was they who issued the reports on *Philaster* found in the Library of Congress.

and despite 'fine, flowing rhetoric' the play 'would sound fowl [*sic*] and phony to a modern audience'. A more sympathetic reader compares Bellario to Viola and Innogen, and the most knowledge-able commentator astutely notes the 'effective scenes and beautiful lyrics' but lack of consistent characterization. The recommenda-tion concludes that 'Prudent abridgement would greatly help a modern staging.'

The abridgement was made, the title-page of the script announces, by 'Philip Ansell Roll'. This name is most familiar as a pseudonym of Hugo Butler, a Hollywood screenwriter. In the early 1950s Butler was blacklisted as a subversive. Along with members of the 'Hollywood ten' he moved to Mexico, where he wrote screenplays for the directors Carlos Velo and Luis Buñuel. However, according to Butler's wife, Roll was real, a 'generous New York radio producer we had never met' who lent Butler his name because studios were aware that pseudonyms were used to shield blacklistees (Rouverol, 61). Nothing else is known of the actual Philip Roll, but whichever 'Roll' made the *Philaster* adaptation was fully conscious of what it meant to remove political content from a drama.

Philaster was third in the series of Elizabethan Plays, following *Volpone* and *The Duchess of Malfi*. Each had ten minutes of inter-mission music, shortening them even further. One effect of the intense condensation in *Philaster* is that there is very little character development. For example, all of 2.1, which displays Bellario and Philaster's affection but does not advance the action, disappears, as does the King's guilty soliloquy in 2.4. The confrontation between Dion and the King is eliminated and much of the sexuality is removed, but, oddly, the very action that most disturbed earlier adapters – Philaster's wounding of both Arethusa and Bellario – remains. A peculiar change occurs in the final line, where the King asserts not that what heaven wills 'can never be withstood' but, instead, that what heaven wills 'can never be understood'. The adaptation retains much of the play's language and diction but is typed entirely as prose, suggesting that it was performed in a conversational style, de-emphasizing the 'fine, flowing rhetoric'.

The Federal Theatre Project *Philaster* seems to have been the last, possibly the only, performance in North America. Most subsequent performances have been by students: at Worcester College Oxford in 1947 (Gurr); at the Guildhall School of Music and Drama in 1953; in 2005 at RADA, with Heather Davies directing; and in 2006 at the Birmingham School of Acting in the Birmingham Crescent Theatre, with Stephen Simms directing. That production used the subtitle 'Love Lies a Bleeding' and was updated to the present: for instance, an early scene showed Pharamond speaking into a microphone, as if at a news conference, behind a dais bearing the text, 'Sicily & Calabria Unite'; one actor played an FBI agent. Lascivious Megra was played by a black actress (Charlene James), which could be understood either as a reference to such Jacobean characters as the promiscuous Moor Zanche in Webster's *White Devil* or as modern 'colour-blind casting'. Large modern paintings of nudes hung above the stage. Philaster was Frank Doody, Arethusa, Louise Mardenborough; Drew Webb played Pharamond and Ainsley Howard, Bellario (see Figs 17, 18 and 14).

There was a staged reading of *Philaster* at Shakespeare's Globe Theatre, directed by Alan Cox, on 2 November 1997, and a professional performance at the London Courtyard Theatre in March and April 2004. At the Globe, *Philaster* was part of the *Read Not Dead* series, a project to read all extant plays from the early modern stage. A number of TV and film actors took part: Alisdair Simpson played Philaster; Lucy Whybrow, Euphrasia; Frances Barber, Megra. Judging from the live recording, the audience laughed frequently, and the part of Dion (Christopher Cazenove) came through strongly. Once again *Philaster* was made more of a 'ladies' play': the presence of women among the Citizens who capture Pharamond in the final act strengthened the sexual byplay in lines like 'Shall's geld him, Captain?' (5.4.61).

The Courtyard Theatre production, directed by Anthony Cornish, was not as well received. *Time Out London* thought that Philaster was 'not a native English speaker', and the actors seemed

SICILY & CALABRIA UNITE

17   Pharamond (Drew Webb) gives a political speech while Arethusa (Louise
      Mardenborough) observes; cf. 1.1.131–62. Birmingham School of Acting,
      2006.

baffled by the tone (GM). Apparently tragicomedy can be as problematic in the early twenty-first century as it sometimes was in the
early seventeenth, but the successes at Birmingham and the Globe
suggest that with a little inventiveness *Philaster* can still please.

TEXTUAL INTRODUCTION

As summarized above, there are two textual sources for *Philaster,
or Love Lies a-Bleeding*, Q1 (1620) and Q2 (1622). Because the
play was apparently as popular with readers as with audiences,
it was frequently reprinted, for a total of nine quartos in the
seventeenth century. It was not included in the first Beaumont and
Fletcher Folio of 1647, which omitted plays previously printed.
In the comprehensive 1679 second Folio, *Fifty Comedies and
Tragedies*, *Philaster* was conspicuously placed second, after *The
Maid's Tragedy*. Nevertheless, from a textual point of view only
Q1 and Q2 are of significance; all of the other texts, including that

18   Philaster (Frank Doody) threatens Bellario (Ainsley Howard); cf. 4.5.23–5.
Birmingham School of Acting, 2006.

in the Folio, derive directly or indirectly from Q2 (see Turner, 370, for details of later quartos).

Q1 (1620) is a quarto of sixty-six numbered pages of text, plus a title-page and a list of *The Actors Names*. The title-page includes authorship, 'Francis Baymont [*sic*] and Iohn Fletcher Gent.'; performance history, '*Acted at the Globe by his Maiesties Seruants*'; and publication information, 'Printed at *London* for *Thomas Walkley*, and are to be sold at his shop at the *Eagle and Child*, in Brittaines Bursse. 1620'. It features a large woodcut based on 4.5 and showing 'The Princes', the 'Cuntrie Gentellman' and 'Phielaster' (see Fig. 10).

Q2 lacks the illustration but lives up to its claim to be 'The second Impression, corrected, and amended'. Again printed 'for Thomas Walkley', and by the same printer, whom W. W. Greg identified through type ornaments as Nicholas Okes (2.510), this 1622 quarto begins its corrections on the title-page, where it changes the spelling of Beaumont's name and revises the performance information to 'at the Globe, and Blacke-Friers' (see Fig. 11). This version has seventy-eight pages of text, adding about 200 lines to the play as found in Q1. Walkley's preface 'To the Reader' metaphorizes the relationship:

> Courteous Reader. *Philaster*, and *Arethusa* his loue, haue laine so long a bleeding, by reason of some dangerous and gaping wounds, which they receiued in the first Impression, that it is wondered how they could goe abroad so long, or trauaile so farre as they haue done. Although they were hurt neither by me, nor the Printer; yet I knowing and finding by experience, how many well-wishers they haue abroad, haue aduentured to bind vp their wounds, & to enable them to visite vpon better termes, such friends of theirs, as were pleased to take knowledge of them, so mained [*sic*] and deformed, as they at the first were; and if they were then gracious in your sight, assuredly they will now finde double fauour,

being reformed, and set forth suteable, to their birth, and
breeding.

Inspection confirms Walkley's description of the first impression.
The text is poorly printed, with much verse mislined or set as prose,
and passages of prose printed with capitals at the beginning of each
line, as if verse. Most notably, the two versions contain different
texts at the beginning and the end of the play. Yet these texts are
sufficiently similar that both must be based on at least a recollection
of a common original. In the first scene the texts diverge until 'A
sweeter mistress than the offered language / Of any dame' (112–13
in this edition), when they come together. At the end divergence is
more gradual, but the two last scenes show only a rough similarity
in their language. Furthermore, the final scene is notably shorter
in Q1, with two brief passages condensing nearly 150 lines of Q2.
Those lines contain both the climax of the disguised–page plot and
Bellario's narration of 'his' history. There are in addition 'approximately 775 substantive variations' scattered throughout the body
of the play, without counting 'Stage-directions, punctuation variants, obvious misprints, and speech–prefixes' (Turner, 386). Q1 is,
then, a very bad text, as its own publisher acknowledged within two
years of offering it for sale.

Unfortunately Walkley, while exonerating himself and his
printer, did not offer any explanation of how Q1 came by its 'gaping wounds'. Subsequently a variety of theories have been offered
for the condition of Q1 and for the relationship between the two
quartos: that Q1 was based on a manuscript whose outer gatherings had been destroyed, and a hack writer was called in to supply
the missing material (Dyce); that Q1 was a censored text (Savage);
that Q1 was a pirated version of Q2 (Thorndike); that the two
texts derive from 'different states' of the authors' copy (Gurr).
Robert K. Turner, editing the play for the Cambridge *Beaumont
and Fletcher*, concludes that 'The middle part of Q1 copy was a
poorly written manuscript which came into being through some
kind of reporting; perhaps it descended from the foul papers of a

bad quarto, or . . . a slovenly transcript of a reported text', while 'the origin of the Q1 beginning and end is obscure' (393, 386).

Since the 1960s there has been a revolution in thinking about the nature and provenance of early modern texts, good and 'bad'. Turner's work exemplified the text-critical method known as the New Bibliography, whose main goal, in the words of Fredson Bowers, General Editor of the Cambridge edition, was to 'lift the veil of print' in order to identify the characteristics of the manuscript which underlay any text. The New Bibliographers attempted to find economical explanations for textual conditions; to reduce possibilities to binary divisions (e.g., prints were based either on 'foul papers', that is, an author's rough draft, or on 'fair copy'); and to seek uncomplicated lines of transmission, preferably direct descent. Such thinking underlies Turner's table of the *Philaster* editions, which shows Q1 set from manuscript, Q2 set from Q1, Q3 from Q2 and so on (370). This obscures two matters: the relation between the two significant texts, where, as I will argue, despite the chronological priority of Q1's printing the earlier version derives from the later one; and, as a result, the source of Q2.[1]

Current textual theory proposes that the condition of a text is likely to result from multiple, not-mutually-exclusive causes. It may reflect the condition of the underlying manuscript containing corrections, insertions or cancellations. A dramatic text may show the effect of passage through production, including cuts for particular performances. Some texts may reflect dictation by actors, once assumed to imply illicit activity but increasingly seen as a method that could be used by a company when a text was missing, or to prepare parts while the fair copy was awaiting

---

1 In an article which preceded his edition, Turner, 'Printing', maintained that close examination of Q2 and Q1 reveals none of the bibliographical links one would expect to find between reprint and original and argued more credibly that Q2 was set from a manuscript with a copy of Q1 available 'for occasional consultation'. Such consultation would explain the misnumbering of pages after 50 in Q2, where the compositor may have unwittingly carried over Q1's page numbers into the Q2 forme he was working on. Apparently Fredson Bowers persuaded Turner to change his opinion: see the edition, 378 n.1.

approval by the Master of the Revels (McMillin, 43). A text may reflect interference by the Master, that is, censorship, or show the consequences of interference in the printing house, whether that means correction, in-house censorship or compositorial error.

Textual theorists have also undermined the premise that printers always proceeded in logical ways that can be inferred by working inductively from their products (see McKenzie), and much the same can be said of the scribes who produced 'fair copies' for companies and patrons. Ernst Honigmann's research shows that Ralph Crane, a regular scribe for the King's Men, changed words, omitted passages and followed his own taste, or that of the patron for whom he was copying, in expurgating profanity. Honigmann thus weakened the assumption that texts purged of profanity were necessarily created after the 1606 Act to Restrain Abuses of Players, which forbade oaths, or, correspondingly, that those texts which contain profanity must date from before 1606.[1]

Lukas Erne has further argued that in the case of early modern plays, different versions may derive from a dramatist's divergent goals as literary creator and as purveyor of popular entertainment. He proposes that the longer texts of some of Shakespeare's plays may be 'literary versions' intended for publication, while the shorter texts reproduce versions used in performance. Erne's analysis of the way in which such texts were cut is suggestive for *Philaster*, but the 'badness' of Q1, as with many Shakespeare plays, cannot be comprehensively explained in this way, because many of the variants in the body of the play do not constitute cuts.

The more complex view of textual history is exemplified by Scott McMillin's comments on Q1 *Othello*, printed by Walkley in the same group as *Philaster*. Arguing that this quarto records theatrical cuts and yet seems to have been made for a reader, McMillin concludes that it was probably taken from dictation by a scribe from the actors, who, making changes each time a play was

---

1 See Honigmann, 77–81; Taylor and Jowett; and Werstine, 'Othello'.

revived, would occasionally need a new 'book'. McMillin's comment that 'a transcript made for a private patron who was himself interested in the third or fourth revival of the play might be a copy of a copy of a copy' (7), may help us avoid premature closure as we consider the two texts of *Philaster*.

These texts raise several questions: the source and nature of Q1 and Q2; whether the texts have a genealogical connection; and finally, how much each quarto should be followed in a modern edition. We will need to consider how Walkley came to publish these texts, as well as the implications of his addresses to readers not only in *Philaster* but also in *A King and No King* and *Othello*. Aligning Walkley's statements with others by Heminges and Condell to readers of the Shakespeare First Folio (1616) and by Humphrey Moseley, the publisher of the 1647 Beaumont and Fletcher Folio, illuminates the situation of stationers or publishers as they gathered texts for conversion from the stage to the page and is suggestive about the particulars of *Philaster*'s double publication.

Q2

Q2 proclaims itself to be a good text. Despite typical printing errors such as occasional mislineation of verse and a few mistaken or omitted speech prefixes, the text appears dependable. The plots are complete and there are no significant loose ends. At roughly 2,783 lines the play here is as long as the longest of Shakespeare's comedies, *All's Well* (2,760 lines), and a bit shorter than *The Winter's Tale* (2,946 lines). Such a length may suggest a version close to the collaborators' original text before theatrical cutting: Erne notes that at 3,049 lines Walkley's 1619 quarto of *A King and No King* is considerably longer than the longest of the thirty-four plays in the 1647 Beaumont and Fletcher Folio, and therefore is unlikely to have been set from a theatrically abridged transcript (183). A full text of this kind might be based on a fair copy, authorial or scribal, of the authors' final draft; it might come from the theatre or from an intermediate transcript made for a patron, itself based on an (uncut) promptbook or a fair copy.

The text of the *Philaster* Second Quarto does not immediately reveal much about its origins. For example, it does not contain directions that point directly to a promptbook origin, such as are found elsewhere (e.g., '*A bed thrust out upon the stage*', *Chaste Maid*, 3.2, Middleton, 932) or stage directions as detailed as those in Q1. Even Turner, who argued in his edition that the middle section of Q2 was set up from Q1, concedes that in that case the section must have been 'very heavily annotated' and concludes uncertainly that 'the annotator (so to call the man who prepared the Q2 copy for the press) had at his disposal either the prompt-book or authorial fair copy or a transcript of one of them' (379–80).

It has long been noticed that between 1619 and 1622 there was a flurry of publication of plays owned by the King's Men. Four of the five were published by Walkley, and four of the five appeared shortly thereafter in different, usually better, texts. These plays were first identified by Kenneth Cameron, who referred to them as the 'Burse quartos' after Walkley's shop (672); McMillin calls them the 'Cameron Group'. The group included *Othello* and four by Beaumont and Fletcher: *Philaster*, *A King and No King*, *The Maid's Tragedy* and *Thierry and Theodoret*. All but one had been performed in the 1612–13 season of celebrations for the wedding of Princess Elizabeth and Frederick the Elector Palatine (*Thierry and Theodoret* was probably written later). And all were printed with act divisions, which suggests that these texts, including that of *Othello*, date from the period after the King's Men took control of the Blackfriars.[1]

For his 1619 publication of *A King and No King* Walkley helpfully explains where he got his copy. The quarto preface is addressed to '*the right worshipfvll*, and worthie *Knight*, *Sir* Henrie Nevill' and begins:

> Worthy Sir, *I present, or rather returne vnto your view, that which formerly hath beene receiued from you, hereby effecting*

---

1 *The Maid's Tragedy* was published by Francis Constable and Richard Higgenbotham, not Walkley, although like *Philaster* it was printed by Nicholas Okes; *Thierry and Theodoret* was not republished until 1648.

> *what you did desire. To commend the worke in my vnlearned*
> *method, were rather to detract from it, then to giue it any*
> *luster. It sufficeth it hath your Worships approbation and*
> *patronage, to the commendation of the Authors, and incour-*
> *agement of their further labours.*

The most straightforward interpretation of these sentences is that
Walkley was approached by a Sir Henry Neville with a private transcript – or several – to set into print. This was probably the second
Sir Henry, who died in 1629; he may have inherited the material
from his father, the better known Sir Henry Neville (1561/2–
1615), a diplomat, courtier and MP from Berkshire who served
as ambassador to France, played a minor role in Essex's plot and
in 1612 made a bid to become Secretary of State 'by guaranteeing
James that . . . he could manage the Commons into voting supplies' (Lesser, 170). Despite his presence at court the elder Neville
remained identified with the country; he moved in circles connected
to Beaumont through the Inns of Court (Gayley; Lesser).[1]

Thus one possibility is that *Philaster* Q2, like *A King and
No King*, is a transcript of a version of the authors' original
papers copied for a private patron, Neville or another. Humphrey
Moseley, the publisher of the expensive 1647 Folio, reassured
potential purchasers about his sources: 'here is not any thing
Spurious or *impos'd*; I had the Originalls from such as received
them from the *Authours* themselves; by Those, and none other, I
publish this Edition.'

It is, however, possible that the text for Q2 came to Walkley
directly from the surviving author rather than from an inter-
vening source. P. A. Daniel pointed out in 1904 that while we
cannot know who supplied Walkley with a better text, 'it is to
be remembered that Fletcher was then still living' (118). Too
little attention has been paid to this fact. Fletcher, present in
London as the chief dramatist of the King's Men (between

---

1   Lesser (169ff.) reads *A King and No King* 'through Neville's eyes' as a play about the
mutual dependence of king and Parliament.

1620 and 1622 he wrote ten new plays, alone or with collaborators [McMullan, *Fletcher*, 268]), might have objected to his play
'going abroad' with gaping wounds. Richard Proudfoot suggests
that the original publication may even have been intended to
pry out a better version, presumably from someone – Fletcher?
the company? – who was known to possess it (RP). In Walkley's
preface to *A King and No King*, he speaks of printing 'to the
commendation of the authors, and encouragement of their further labours'. Taking 'authors' literally would mean that in 1619
Walkley did not know that Beaumont was dead – although surely
Neville did. Walkley paid attention to such matters, as he shows
in his epistle to the reader of Q1 *Othello* (1622), written because
'*the Author being dead, I thought good to take that piece of worke
vpon mee*'. One may suspect that by 1622, after publishing *A
King and No King*, *Philaster* and *Thierry and Theodoret*, Walkley
had made the surviving author's acquaintance.

Q1

Turning to Q1, it is well to remember the kinds of copy that
Moseley rejected in 1647:

> When these *Comedies* and *Tragedies* were presented on
> the Stage, the *Actours* omitted some *Scenes* and Passages
> (with the *Authour's* consent) as occasion led them; and
> when private friends desir'd a Copy, they then (and justly
> too) transcribed what they *Acted*. But now you have both
> All that was *Acted*, and all that was not; even the perfect
> full Originalls without the least mutilation.
>
> (The Stationer to the Readers)

Moseley's comment is evidence that multiple copies of popular
plays were in circulation.[1] Taking a negative view, Heminges and
Condell warn readers against 'diuerse stolne, and surreptitious

---

1 Further evidence that multiple copies circulated is provided by the sixty substantive corrections in a seventeenth-century hand found in the copy of Q1 *A King and
No King* now in the Dyce Collection. These annotations are based on an otherwise
unknown early manuscript (Williams, *King*, 176–80).

copies, maimed, and deformed by the frauds and stealthes of iniurious impostors'.[1] Such a copy, maimed but not necessarily stolen, could have come to Walkley among a group of transcripts that he obtained from the younger Neville, or from the King's Men during the difficult year 1619 (see pp. 95–6). Lesser hints that Walkley may have sought out the play, as it sustained his political position, and then used the title-page image 'to elucidate its political application to its readers'. For Lesser, like McMullan, the 'gap between the rustic boor in the text' and the illustration of the 'Cuntrie Gentellman' saving the princess reflects the view that only in the country can 'the excesses and errors of the court' be corrected (194–5; McMullan, *Fletcher*, 113). If this was the only copy that Walkley could get, then, he might have accepted it even knowing it was imperfect.

However Walkley obtained it, the First Quarto of *Philaster* is, I believe, based on one of the 'diverse' copies in circulation, in this case a copy of a partially censored, theatrically abridged, performance version, or a recollection of one, carelessly written and then badly printed.[2] Hypothetically, it could have come from the papers of Richard Burbage, who died in March 1619. One sign that this quarto reflects performance is its tendency to put entrance stage directions a few lines earlier than needed, typical of promptbook texts. For example, in 2.3, in Q1 the direction '*Enter* GALLATEA' appears during Arethusa's conversation with her Gentlewoman; in Q2 it appears two lines later, immediately before Arethusa welcomes Gallatea. Q1 also has two music directions; neither is present in Q2 (Cameron, 681 n. 51).

At some point – either in the playhouse or in the copying – this text was damaged. Dyce thought that the manuscript had lost

---

1 Heminges and Condell are usually taken to be referring to inferior printed copies. In the view of the New Bibliographers these were 'bad' quartos, such as *Hamlet* Q1, but Erne argues that the reference is to the Pavier quartos (255–8).

2 Turner concludes that Q1 is a 'slovenly transcript of a reported text', although he notes that 'many of the classical stigmata are lacking . . . there are no passages interpolated from other plays, and there is no gag or added comedy' (393). However, he does not attempt to account for the extra scene between the gentlemen that begins the Q1 version of 5.5.

its outer gatherings, but while that might explain the completely different opening passage (1–88), it does not account for the gradual divergence from Q2 at the end or the smaller differences in the parallel sections.[1] Just who wrote the substitute opening and closing lines it is impossible to tell. Comparison of characteristic phrases from these passages with the database of early modern drama available through *Literature Online* does not yield meaningful parallels. If a play was repaired in the playhouse in this period the most likely repairer ought, in fact, to have been Fletcher himself as the 'attached dramatist', and as that seems not to be the case, we are left with the often-abused and nameless 'hack' writer.[2]

All of the elements of this explanation have been proposed and rejected by one or another previous editor searching for a single line of causation. Once we admit the possibility of multiple factors and multiple agents of change, the situation clarifies.

Censorship of the text was proposed by J. E. Savage in an analysis that remains persuasive. Savage's general argument is that 'Quarto One represents that version of *Philaster* that the King's company was presenting on the stage about 1619; and that Quarto Two presents, not a theatrical, but a literary,

---

1 Gurr suggests that 'the beginning and end were missing from the transcript originally, possibly from the same cause as led the Pied Bull *King Lear*'s first and last scenes to be transcribed largely from memory' (lxxvii–viii).
2 Using the method pioneered by McDonald P. Jackson, a comparison of characteristic phrases from the first 109 lines and the last two scenes of Q1 with the database in LION of drama performed between 1605 and 1625 was made, giving the following results for authors in descending order of frequency: Fletcher 17; anon 10; Heywood 9; Middleton 8; Chapman 7; Field 6; Massinger 6; Ford 4; Goff(e) 4; Beaumont 3; Carlell 3; Rowley 2; Shakespeare 1; Armin 1. Many collocations appear nowhere else. The frequency with which the phrases of Fletcher's plays appear suggests a familiarity unsurprising in the period, yet Jackson points out that the links to Beaumont and Fletcher are not high when taken in relation to the number of Beaumont and Fletcher plays (personal communication). The results of testing for three phrases in the conversation in 5.5 that has no basis in Q2 are inconclusive. The results for 'beat* near brain*' in plays performed in 1605–25 gives fourteen plays of the Beaumont and Fletcher canon, as well as many Dekker citations; the results for mudd*brain* are only two, one in Chapman and one in Ford; the results for the expletive 'uds death' yields parallels only in Dekker's *Match me in London* and Webster's *White Devil*. Whoever wrote these lines was very familiar with the current theatrical language, but did not leave an identifiable fingerprint.

version of the play as originally written' (448). As evidence of intervention by the Master of the Revels, George Buc, Savage cites the removal 'of all references to the second kingdom, Calabria', including in the list of 'The Actors Names'; he observes that 'all references to the double kingdom are removed in the revised scenes; and on all but two occasions in the central part of the play . . . the word "kingdoms" is changed to "kingdome"'. Satire on the king and the court is removed or replaced by satire on the subject; lines that might reflect on 'James's love of hunting, his taste for fine clothes, and his addiction to favorites' disappear. To explain the introduction of a conventional marriage for Bellario, Savage proposes a desire to avoid directing 'the minds of the audience towards the unhappy Lady Arabella Stuart' (449–51).

The case for censorship of *Philaster* is dismissed by Turner on the grounds that it 'does not explain Q1's omission of the discussion between the three ladies in 1.1 nor its trumpery ending, nor does it account for the retention in Q1 of passages like . . . the confrontation between the King and Dion' (385). Gurr objects more particularly that while Calabria, the second kingdom, is not named in Q2, and some of the references to the dual kingdoms are removed, two remain, as Savage acknowledged.

Yet that the censorship of *Philaster* was inadequate does not prove it was absent, as a glance at other contemporary cases will show (see Clare; Dutton; Finkelpearl). An example is *Eastward Ho!* (1605), a subversive play whose original text seems to have been hurriedly cleaned up first by the printer and again by the removal and substitution of two leaves. Nevertheless, the second issue, which eliminates two satirical passages on the Scots at court, still contains a scene inviting parody of King James.[1] In censoring *Philaster* it would be easier to miss mentions of 'kingdoms' than of Calabria; more to the point, the two kingdoms

---

1   For full discussion see the edition by Suzanne Gossett and W. David Kay in *The Cambridge Edition of the Works of Ben Jonson*, forthcoming.

are necessary for the tragicomic conclusion. McMullan further suggests that the difference between Q2's 'Country Fellow' and Q1's 'Country Gallant' or 'Country Gentleman' (in the woodcut) came about not through a reduction in rank, as Turner thought (389), but the reverse: a promotion by the censor, so that the character's interaction with the princess would be more acceptable (*Fletcher*, 110–15).

It seems most likely that the censorship in Q1 dates from the revival of 1619. At this time description of promiscuous court ladies and, especially, emphasis on a Spanish prince 'come to marry our Kingdom's heir' might be dangerously suggestive, as negotiations for a Spanish match for Prince Charles intensified following the signing of a draft treaty of marriage in 1617 (Redworth, 15–18). On the other hand, the provocative confrontation between Dion and the King that remains recalls an incident a decade in the past. After the prolonged controversy of 1607–11 between king and Commons, James had dismissed Parliament while apparently conceding the primacy of law over prerogative. Dutton and Finkelpearl demonstrate that censorship was erratic and uneven; and even in 1634, a time of 'major examples of dramatic censorship', the changes in *Philaster* Q4 are 'concerned exclusively with oaths; passages that have been regarded as politically subversive, such as the dialogue between Dion and the King in Act 4, scene 4, were completely untouched' (Bawcutt, 76).[1]

On the assumption that Q1 is a text censored for performance, an apparent problem is posed by those places where Q1 contains oaths in which the speaker swears by God and Q2 has weaker imprecations. Yet, while the Act to Restrain Abuses of

---

1 Davison suggests that the differences between the 'brutal baiting' of Pharamond in Q2 and the less extreme version in Q1 may reflect censorship. The most significant difference is the elimination of explicitly political comment; the Captain's lines in Q2, 'Nay, my beyond sea sir, we will proclaim you. / You would be king! / Thou tender heir apparent to a church-ale, / Thou slight prince' (5.4.53–6), are roughly replaced in Q1 by 'You see, my scurvy don, how precious you are in esteem amongst us. Had you not been better kept at home' (5.4.50–2).

Players was not to be taken lightly – printed profanities were not in violation of the Act, but profanity in public performance could, in theory, call for a fine of ten pounds – 'all of the plays in the Cameron Group . . . have some oaths . . . yet all but *Othello* were written after 1606'. Thus the Act may not have been strictly applied (McMillin, 45). Cameron's table of the appearance of oaths in Q1–4 of *Philaster* (676–7) shows them as most notably absent in the first two scenes of Q1, with little change thereafter; either the censor tired of marking them or the oaths appeared in the Q1 manuscript and were unchanged in printing. It is the two Hawkins Quartos, Q3 of 1628 and Q4 of 1634, that eliminate the oaths with increasing rigour.

McMillin's theatrical analysis of the cutting of *Othello* suggests a different explanation for the condition of Q1 *Philaster*. Studying the distribution of the 160 lines present in F *Othello* but absent from Q1, he finds that

> Act 4 has the largest number of omitted lines, nearly 50 per cent of the total. Acts 4 and 5 together have 67 per cent. Moreover, the Act 4 omissions centre on Desdemona and Emilia . . . Forty-five of the omitted lines are from Desdemona's part, 36 from Emilia's – again, about 50 per cent of the total.

He proposes 'that the play was cut towards the end because it was running too long. Perhaps the performance sagged because the boy-actors were not at their best here' (9). Similarly, in the transcript of *Sir John van Olden Barnavelt* made for the King's Men in 1619 by a scribe thought to be Ralph Crane, 'If the cuts required by the censor are disregarded, the bulk of the theatre abridgement, 59 of 73 lines, or about 80 per cent, falls in Acts 4 and 5. Two small parts for boy-actors are removed by the final cut' (28). McMillin concludes:

> The final scenes of the 1620 *Philaster* are about 200 lines shorter than the corresponding scenes in the 1622

Philaster Quarto . . . owing to the different endings of the two versions. The roles for boy-actors are noticeably shorter in the final scenes of the 1620 edition. Where the 1622 edition has 25 speeches for women characters, totalling 106 lines, the 1620 edition has only 9 speeches for women, totalling 28 lines. The lead boy's role (Bellario) is 75 lines in the final scenes of the 1622 edition, but only 17 lines in the 1620 edition. The roles for boy-actors appear to have been reduced in the later scenes of the 1620 *Philaster* . . . All of the texts in the group show signs of theatrical abridgement, and they are more or less the same signs. (28)

(See Figs 19 and 20 for an example of Bellario's reduced role in Q1.)

It seems likely, then, that Q1 *Philaster* reflects a performance text that, like *Barnavelt*, had been cut *both* by the censor to avoid offence to powerful people *and* by the company to fit the allotted time and/or to reduce the length of the roles for boy-actors. Yet that does not explain the weakening and distortion of its lines. Even more agents – dictating actors, an overworked or inadequate scribe, a penny-pinching printer and his compositors – may bear some responsibility for its condition.

Moseley mentioned the role of actors in creating texts, and they may be partly responsible for Q1. Turner notes '775 substantive variations between the two corresponding versions' of which 'about 250 readings in Q1 . . . can only be corruptions of Q2 readings'; disagreements in speech assignments; and finally Q1's 'tendency in stage-directions and speech-prefixes towards generic designation' (that is, *Princess* instead of *Arethusa*, *Boy* instead of *Bellario*). From these signs he concludes that 'Q1 readings are what might be produced by a man with a trained mind who had a close familiarity with the Q2 text but not an absolutely precise memory of it or by one who was reading from a manuscript of the Q2 text so illegible that occasionally he had to call on his memory

Philaster. 75

Ki. Walke aside with him.

Di. Why speak't thou not?

Bel. Know you this face my Lord?

Di. No.

Bel. Haue you not seene it, nor the like?

Di. Yes I haue seene the like, but readily
I know not where.

Bel. I haue bin often told
In Court, of one *Euphrasia,* a Lady
And daughter to you, betwixt whom and me
(They that would flatter my bad face would sweare)
There was such strange resemblance, that we two
Could not be knowne asunder, drest alike.

Di. By heauen and so there is.

Bel. For her faire sake
Who now doth spend the spring time of her life
In holy Pilgrimage, mone to the King
That I may scape this torture.

Di. But thou speak'st
As like *Euphrasia* as thou dost looke,
How came it to thy knowledge that she liues
In Pilgrimage?

Bel. I know it not my Lord,
But I haue heard it and doe scarse beleeue it.

Di. Oh my shame, ist possible? draw neere
That I may gaze vpon thee, art thou she,
Or else her murderer? where wert thou borne?

Bel. In Siracusa.

Di. What's thy name?

Bel. Euphrasia.

Di. O tis iust, tis she,
Now I doe know thee, oh that thou hadst dyed
And I had neuer seene thee, nor my shame,
How shall I owne thee, shall this tongue of mine,
Ere call thee Daughter more?

Bel. Would I had died indeed, I wish it too,
And so must haue done by vow, ere publish'd
                         L 2   What

19   Q2, page L2ʳ, the conversation between Bellario and Dion; cf. 5.5.91–119.

64   *Phylaſter.*

KIN. But heauen hath made aſignement vnto him,
And brought your contract to anullity:
Sir, your entertainment hath beene moſt faire,
Had not your hell-bred luſt dride vp the ſpring,
From whence flow'd forth thoſe fauours that you found:
I am glad to ſee you ſafe, let this ſuffice,
Your ſelfe hath croſt your ſelfe.
LEON. They are married ſir.
PHAR. How married? I hope your highneſſe will not vſe me ſo,
I came not to be diſgraced, and returne alone.
KING. I cannot helpe it ſir.
LEON. To returne alone, you neede not ſir,
Here is one will beare you company,
You know this Ladies proofe, if you
Fail'd not in the ſay-taging.
ME. I hold your ſcoffes in vildeſt baſe contempt,
Or is there ſaid or done, ought I repent,
But can retort euen to your grinning teeths,
Your worſt of ſpights, tho Princeſſe lofty ſteps
May not be tract, yet may they tread awry,
That boy there ----
BEL. If to me ye ſpeake Lady,
I muſt tell you, you haue loſt your ſelfe
In your too much forwardneſſe, and hath forgot
Both modeſty and truth, with what impudence
You haue throwne moſt damnable aſpertions
On that noble Princeſſe and my ſelfe : witneſſe the world ;
Behold me ſir.   *Kneeles to* LEON, *and diſcouers her haire.*
LEON. I ſhould know this face ; my daughter.
BEL. The ſame ſir.
PRIN. How, our ſometime Page, *Bellario*, turn'd woman ?
BEL. Madame, the cauſe induct me to transforme my ſelfe,
Proceeded from a reſpectiue modeſt
Affection I bare to my my Lord,
The Prince *Phylaſter*, to do him ſeruice,
As farre from any laciuious thought,
As that Lady is farre from go odneſſe,
                                                    And

20 Q1, page I4ᵛ, the abridged conversation between Bellario and Leon, with the
     additional stage direction; cf. Appendix 1, Q1, 5.5.35–69.

for words that could not be made out . . . somewhere in the Q1 line of transmission there was a memorial link – that is, that Q1 is a bad quarto' (386–91).[1]

In general the 'bad quarto' or 'memorial reconstruction' explanation, a favourite of the New Bibliographers, has been overused. After full investigation Laurie Maguire, while conceding that such reconstructions did exist, concludes that *Philaster* is not one (296–7). But memory always plays an important part in the theatre, where actors must memorize and repeat lines. Consequently Turner's idea that 'The middle part of Q1 copy was a poorly written manuscript which came into being through some kind of reporting' may still have merit, particularly the argument that the 'theory of communal reconstruction might be applicable to Q1, and, if only the company's principals were involved, might help to explain the misassignment of the speeches of the three gentlemen, who even in Q2 are not strongly individualized' (394). From the point of view of company practice, McMillin explains, 'a scribal copy taken from the dictation of actors who had memorized their parts would have been an economical way of putting together a new prompt book' (38). The examples of mishearing in 1620 *Philaster* – McMillin cites 'miracles' for Q2's 'Miraculous' and 'choller' for 'Call our', and Turner provides a list (393) – suggest dictation. If the original of the beginning and ending of the play were lost or unavailable, this might have stimulated an effort to recreate first those scenes and then the entire play.[2]

As one sign that a scribe was listening to, rather than copying, the *Othello* text, McMillin notes errors in transition from prose to verse corrected after a few lines. Such errors also occur in *Philaster* Q1: many speeches begin with a line of verse before reverting to

1 Gurr (lxxviii) proposes that the use of 'generic' designations in Q1 indicates a text that comes from an earlier stage of the authors' papers, rather than from dictating actors.

2 The lines of the old Captain at the beginning of 5.4 sound enough like Q2 to suggest someone trying to remember speeches. However, the lines then differ more completely. Also, the presence in Q1 of a discussion between the three gentlemen at the beginning of what is 5.5 in Q2, where the discussion does not appear, cannot be explained by memory alone, unless this is a memory of a different performance text.

prose. Scribes also intervened in their texts (see McMillin, 26–8). The extensive stage directions in Q1 may be based on a theatrical manuscript but could instead have been inserted by a scribe trying to assist a reader. Either way they do seem to reflect Jacobean performance, and are largely adopted here.

Not only censorship suggests that the Q1 version of *Philaster* was prepared for the 1619 revival. In 1612–13 both authors were still present in London: Beaumont wrote a masque for the royal wedding and married and withdrew to the country only later that year. Thus there should have been no need for anyone else to supply substitute lines. The year 1619, on the other hand, was critical for the King's Men. In January, after a complaint to the Lord Mayor, the company was ordered to cease playing at Blackfriars, although they managed to have their patron rescue them from this misfortune; on 2 March Queen Anne died and all playing was stopped for eleven weeks; on 13 March Burbage died. Playing was only permitted again after Anne's funeral, not held until 13 May (Gurr, *Companies*). Meanwhile the company seems to have begun thinking about producing a folio collection of Shakespeare's plays, but found that Pavier had had a similar idea and had hired Jaggard to print individual volumes for eventual collection. The players intervened and 'In May, 1619, the Lord Chamberlain instructed the Stationers' Company that no plays belonging to the King's Men should be printed without their consent,' which led to the Pavier quartos with false dates (Blayney, 4).[1] In August the King's Men were ready to stage *Sir John van Olden Barnavelt* when the Bishop of London attempted to prohibit the performance. Given this much disruption, a text of *Philaster* may have been cobbled together in Fletcher's absence. Or, in a reversed sequence, the 1619 revival of the play may have led to a request for copies, at least one of which was deeply inadequate.

It was this kind of copy that first came into Walkley's hands, but his ability to print requires explanation. Before 1619 only

---

1   This is the usual explanation (see Erne, 256ff.), but cf. Sonia Massai, *Shakespeare and the Rise of the Editor* (Cambridge, 2007), for a revisionist theory.

those plays of Beaumont and Fletcher that had originally been acted by the defunct children's companies had come into print. *Philaster*, the play that made their reputation, had been kept off the market for a decade. Yet starting in 1619 four Beaumont and Fletcher plays for the King's Men emerge: *The Maid's Tragedy* and *A King and No King* in 1619, *Philaster* in 1620, *Thierry and Theodoret* in 1621. Similarly, for the first time since 1609 a previously unpublished Shakespeare play, *Othello*, appeared.

If at this time Walkley (and Higgenbotham and Constable) came upon, or were offered, a small group of play manuscripts, the order of the Lord Chamberlain would have driven them to ask permission of the King's Men and presumably to offer some compensation. Given the difficult year that the company had had, the sharers may have welcomed both publicity and income. Cameron proposes that 'the absence of any clamor over the Burse printings subsequent to the Lord Chamberlain's letter seems a clear indication that the quartos were published with the consent of the company' (673); he assumes the company also furnished the copy. There was nothing illicit about Walkley's publication of Q1. He entered it in the Stationers' Register on 10 January 1620; *The Maid's Tragedy*, *A King and No King* and *Othello* were all similarly registered before publication.

The printing of Q1 and Q2

Walkley had only been in business since 1618, and 'at the beginning of his career . . . seems to have been in almost constant financial trouble' (Lesser, 160). Perhaps for this reason, it appears that in Q1 Walkley and Okes were attempting to save on paper, the greatest of a printer's expenses.[1] Q1 collates A^2 B–I^4 K^2, requiring nine sheets. (Turner shows that K was printed as a half-sheet and A may have been as well, possibly with K; the blanks A^1 and K^2 are preserved in the British Library copy

---

1 R. A. Foakes concludes that Okes's desire 'to economize on paper, and not use more than ten sheets' is the best explanation for 'why so much verse was interpreted by the compositors as prose' in the 1608 first quarto of *King Lear* (122).

(373–4)).[1] Q2 collates A^2 B–L^4, requiring ten and a half sheets (on the supposition that A was double printed by half-sheet imposition (JJ)).[2] The text of Q2 is longer, but in Q1 devices of compression, not present in Q2, are nonetheless apparent. The most striking is the printing of passages of verse – especially long speeches – as prose. This occurs both in the variant beginning and end and in the middle sections; examples include Pharamond's speech, 'Kissing your white hand' (1.1.131–62), Philaster's 'I have a boy' (1.2.111–40), and Bellario's 'If it be love' (2.3.48–60) and 'Right royal sir' (5.3.20–44). Stage directions are crowded to the right: 'He offers to draw his sword, & is held' (3.1.64) is broken onto the ends of four lines. Turner assumes that the mislineation was due to the nature of the manuscript, which he calls 'truly miserable' (375). As there are places where prose is printed in lines as if verse, and the space around entrances varies from none ($G3^r$) to considerable ($I2^r$ and $I4^r$), this explanation is also possible.[3] Q1 was apparently written in the same hand throughout (Turner, 384), which, together with its hundreds of small variations from Q2, supports the idea that it was based on a scribal copy.

Less persuasive are Turner's claims regarding the origins of Q2; his Textual Introduction argues that the middle sections of Q2 were set from Q1 'very heavily annotated'. While printers normally did prefer to work from print rather than manuscript – and Okes himself had printed Q1 – the many small changes in the parallel parts of the play work against this supposition. Turner cites some parallels in capitalization and italicization, but his examples of parallel mislineation are weaker. He includes as 'mislineation' passages which a modern editor rearranges to clarify the

---

1 Turner uses the reappearance of running-titles to show that K was printed as a half-sheet, but A has no running-titles to confirm its place in the order of printing. There is no 'J' signature.

2 See Turner's Textual Introduction for technical details of the printing of Q1 and Q2, including the sequence of setting by formes.

3 Turner has shown that Q1 was set by two compositors, A setting signatures B to E and F outer, and B setting signatures F inner and G to K (373).

pentameter but whose lineation may have recurred in separate sources of Q1 and Q2. For example, an exchange from 4.4 is thus printed in both Q1 and Q2:

K. Where is she?
Cle. Sir, I cannot tell.
K. How's that? Answer me so againe.
Cle. Sir, shall I lie?

Turner edits to:

King. Where is she?
Cleremont.   Sir, I cannot tell.
King.   How's that?
Answer me so againe.
Cleremont.   Sir, shall I lie?

While there is much to be said for Turner's rearrangement, the printer, probably following the manuscript, simply begins each new speech on a new line, and since neither of Walkley's texts indents to indicate split verse lines, not too much weight can be put on these similar 'mislineations'.

Turner's other evidence is equally inconclusive: where he sees 'reproduced prose lineation' with 'minor changes due to textual change', the present writer sees different lineation. Of the two transpositions Turner finds significant, the reversed lines at 1.1.178-9 are easily confused. Jowett suggests that the error may have originated as an ambiguously located marginal addition, misinserted when transcribed and never corrected. Furthermore, if the transposed lines were mistaken in the source of Q2 and transmitted to the actors in that way, the error would naturally appear in both Q2 and Q1. The other transposition, 'thou didst' for 'didst thou', persisted through all eight quartos and the folio, apparently troubling no early printer. Most important is Turner's concession that there is 'general uniformity of Q2 accidentals' (that is, spelling and punctuation). This drives him to imagine his 'annotator' to have 'scrupulously brought the

Q1 readings and lineation into conformity with the [proposed] manuscript . . . and to have imposed his own or the manuscript's accidentals on to the Q1 copy' (380). But would Walkley really have depended upon a text to which he himself raised such strong objections? Surely it is a simpler premise that the whole of Q2, which is uniform throughout, was based on a manuscript fairly close to the authors' full text, and that the compositors occasionally consulted Q1, printed in the same house, as a reference.[1]

This edition

The two texts of *Philaster* raise problems for the modern editor. Q2 is probably closer to the authors' original words; Q1's directions are enlightening about contemporary staging. Variations between the two texts include not only the lengthy opening and closing passages but single words, character names, and prose and verse throughout. A particular challenge is posed by the question of (re)lineation. Further, the play has an extensive editorial history.

The body of this edition is based on Q2, with the introduction of a number of directions from Q1 and some emendations from the editorial tradition. In addition, the two passages of Q1 that are significantly different, the first 88 lines and the last two scenes, 5.4 and 5.5, are fully modernized and edited and appear in an appendix facing the similarly modernized and edited versions in Q2. In this way the reader can encounter the play in the full text of Q2 without distraction, but has the opportunity to evaluate the extent of the textual divergences. Q1 is fully collated in the textual notes except for these two passages.

Modernization and regularization have been extended to the names. The hero is thus Philaster, the Spanish prince

---

1   Turner had earlier concluded that 'The number of changes between Q1 and Q2 is so great that annotation of a Q1 exemplar to produce the Q2 text would have resulted in a very cumbersome affair, and composition from such copy would have been such a difficult task that one is inclined to favour manuscript copy on practical grounds alone' ('Printing', 29).

Pharamond. (Q1 names these characters Phylaster/Philaster and Pharamont.) The princess is Arethusa, the modern spelling for the nymph who turned into the Sicilian fountain; this is the spelling Walkley uses in his address 'To the Reader' of Q2, although she is Arathusa in the text and stage directions. The names of the courtiers are more problematic. In Q2 they are Dion, Cleremont and Trasiline; in Q1 they are Lyon/Leon, Clerimon/Clerimont, and Trasiline/Trasilin. Not only are they spelled differently, but about fifty of the sixty-five instances in which Q1 and Q2 assign lines to different speakers involve the three gentlemen (Turner, 387). Ashe may be right that in the manuscript behind Q1 the men were 'designated "1, 2, 3, Gent." and that confusion arose when specific names were assigned by the printing-house or by the composer of the beginning and end' (cited Turner, 387 n. 2).

In this edition the gentlemen are consistently Dion, Cleremont and Thrasiline. The latter change, which restores the Greek root (from *thrasos*, braggart, like the thrasonical *Miles Gloriosus*) appears as early as the list of '*persons presented*' in Q3, 1628. That Trasiline is merely a spelling variation is evident from Q3's use of this form in stage directions despite the change in the list of persons. The alteration of Dion to Leon or Lyon in Q1 is harder to explain. Savage suggested that it might be part of the censorship and then proposed that it could have been made 'because Shakespeare was at about the same time using the name 'Dion' in *The Winter's Tale*' (449, n. 21). Shakespeare's Dion is one of the two lords sent to the oracle at Delphi by Leontes; his role consists of three speeches in 3.1 and a line shared with Cleomenes in 3.2. He is named in the dialogue only once and does not seem sufficiently significant to justify renaming the more important courtier in *Philaster*. In any case early modern playgoers did not see the plays of Beaumont and Fletcher as necessarily having to stand aside for those of Shakespeare. It is more likely that the error was made because Leon was a favourite name in Fletcher's plays, some form appearing in *The Lovers' Progress*, *Rule a Wife and Have a Wife*, *The Humorous Lieutenant*, *Cupid's Revenge* and *Love's Pilgrimage*.[1]

Determining the lineation of the text can be difficult. Q1 is entirely undependable, converting large amounts of verse to prose and sometimes treating prose as verse, as in Pharamond's opening speech in 2.2, which in Q1 begins:

> Why should these Ladies stay so long, they must
> Come this way, I know the Queene imployes vm not,
> For the reuerend mother sent me word,
> They would all be for the garden: if they should all
> Proue honest now, I were in a faire taking:

Consequently, some of the indications in the textual collation that 'Q1 lines' in a particular way actually record instances of prose laid out as verse. On the other hand, usually Q2 properly distinguishes verse and prose. The question for an editor remains when and how much to relineate. The prose of the collaborators, like Shakespeare's, is 'often hard to distinguish from verse; it is highly patterned and often falls into iambic rhythms' (Wright, 110–11). Also debatable is when and whether to indicate pentameter lines shared between speakers. Indicating shared lines by printing them on the same type-line, which had precedents in classical drama and in the printing of Jonson's works, begins as early as Q5 (1639) and is frequent in Q6 (1652). Q2's intentions are often unclear because it deeply indents the beginning of each new speech, as in

> But miserable man!
> *Phi.* See, see, you gods,

Often such speeches form perfect pentameters, and no matter how they are presented on the page they reflect the consistency with which Beaumont and Fletcher wrote pentameter verse.

---

1 In 'Printing' Turner shows that the Leon/Lyon variation is a 'compositorial aberration' and suggests that 'Dion/Dyon' may have stood in the manuscript, being altered in two stages (23).

George T. Wright has shown that in Shakespeare's late plays speeches characteristically end midline, with the next speaker's utterance completing the pentameter. Occasionally 'short lines at the hinges will be completed in the next half-line, even as that half-line is itself completed by its own second half' (103). Such short or half lines had a double motive: dramatically they created a sense of continuous conversation, and practically they may have made cue lines visible to actors and scribes (see McMillin, 39–40). Beaumont and Fletcher seem to have been following the same practice.

Editors of *Philaster*, beginning with the quarto correctors, have arranged short lines to display the linking of speeches. By Q6 there were even linkages of three short lines; see 2.4.87 and Werstine, 'Division'. This method was expanded by Theobald, but a general reversion to the quarto lineation followed until Boas (1904). Gurr objects (lxxxi), but because Beaumont and Fletcher wrote in pentameters that the audience would have perceived aurally, it seems best to assist the reader by indicating the verse even though the breaks between lines are sometimes uncertain. The sharing of lines is a fundamental indication of engagement between characters; it is well exemplified in the tragicomic moment when the protagonists are reconciled (5.2.37–45).

In the end, all editors of *Philaster* follow Walkley, binding up such 'wounds' as they find in the text, and attempting to set the play forth 'suitable'. The goal of this edition is to allow the play to visit its 'well-wishers', make new friends and once again find the 'double favour' that made it famous in its own time and for centuries to follow.

QUARTO PARATEXT

PRELIMINARIES FROM QUARTO 1, 1620

The Actors Names

King of Sicily
Arathusa, *the princess*
Phylaster
Pharamont, *a Spanish prince*   5
Leon, *a lord*
Clerimon ⎫
Trasiline ⎭ *two noble gentlemen*
Bellario, *a page, Leon's daughter*
Gallatea, *a lady of honour*   10
Megra, *another lady*
A Waiting-Gentlewoman
Two Woodmen
A Country Gallant
An old Captain   15
And Soldiers
A Messenger

PRELIMINARIES FROM QUARTO 2, 1622

To the Reader

Courteous Reader.

Philaster and Arethusa, his love, have lain so long
a-bleeding, by reason of some dangerous and gaping
wounds which they received in the first impression,   5
that it is wondered how they could go abroad so long,
or travel so far, as they have done. Although they were
hurt neither by me nor the printer, yet I, knowing and
finding by experience how many well-wishers they have
abroad, have adventured to bind up their wounds and   10
to enable them to visit upon better terms such friends
of theirs as were pleased to take knowledge of them, so
maimed and deformed as they at the first were. And if
they were then gracious in your sight, assuredly they
will now find double favour, being reformed and set   15
forth suitable to their birth and breeding.

By your serviceable friend,
Thomas Walkley

3–4 **love . . . a-bleeding** Walkley adopts the play's subtitle, *Love Lies a-Bleeding*, to describe the textual imperfections of Q1.
4–5 **dangerous . . . wounds** For analysis of the *wounds* or defects that *maimed and deformed* Q1, see the Introduction (pp. 78–81).
5 **impression** printing
7 **travel so far** a reference to the success of the play, which had several revivals before publication, including performances at court in 1612–13
8 **hurt . . . printer** Walkley does not explain who did damage the text.
 printer Nicholas Oakes, who printed both Q1 and Q2, as well as the 1608 quarto of *KL*
10 **adventured** undertaken
18 **Thomas Walkley** For discussion of Walkley's role, see pp. 83–5.

PHILASTER,
OR,
LOVE LIES
A-BLEEDING

LIST OF ROLES

KING	*of Sicily and Calabria*	
ARETHUSA	*his daughter*	
PHILASTER	*rightful heir to Sicily*	
PHARAMOND	*prince of Spain*	
DION		5
CLEREMONT	*courtiers*	
THRASILINE		
BELLARIO	*servant to Philaster, later revealed as*	
	Euphrasia, daughter to Dion	
GALLATEA	*a court lady attending on Arethusa*	
MEGRA		10
LADY	*court ladies*	
GENTLEWOMAN	*to Arethusa*	
2 WOODMEN		
COUNTRY FELLOW		
CAPTAIN	*of the Citizens*	15
5 CITIZENS		
2 MESSENGERS		

Attendants and Guards

LIST OF ROLES There is a list of *The Actors Names* in Q1 (see Paratext) but none in Q2.

1 KING The nameless King has apparently inherited his position in Sicily from his father, the *late* King of Calabria, who *unrighteously deposed* Philaster's father (see 1.1.25–7). The cast list of Q1 calls him King of Sicily, part of that text's usual reduction of his realm to one rather than two kingdoms.

2 ARETHUSA Arethusa was a nymph and daughter of Nereus. Fleeing the unwanted attentions of the river god Alpheus, she was transformed by Artemis into a fountain on the island of Ortygia in Syracuse, Sicily. The story is told in Ovid's *Metamorphoses*, Book 5. In Q1 her speech prefixes are regularly Princess and the spelling varies between Arethusa and Arathusa.

3 PHILASTER in Q1 regularly Phylaster. Ashe (xvii) suggests that the name is an adaptation of Astrophil, the star-lover of Sidney's sonnet sequence *Astrophil and Stella*.

4 PHARAMOND in Q1 regularly Pharamont

5 DION in Q1 regularly Leon. No convincing explanation has been offered for the alteration.

6 CLEREMONT usually spelled Clerimon in Q1

7 THRASILINE usually spelled Trasiline in both early quartos, but *thrasos* or θρασος is Greek for boldness or courage and Θρασων (Thrason) is the name of a braggart soldier in Roman New Comedy. The correction in the list of characters appears first in Q4, when someone in the print shop may have known Greek, but the speech prefixes remain 'Tra' until F2 in 1679.

8 BELLARIO usually Boy in Q1 stage directions and speech prefixes. The audience is not informed that this character is disguised and cross-dressed until the final scene. The Q1 cast list identifies Bellario as Leon's daughter, but the name Euphrasia never occurs in that text.

9 GALLATEA Gallatea was a nymph who mocked the love of Polyphemus, the Cyclops, 'much as Galatea in *Philaster* scorns Pharamond's overtures to her' (Ashe, xvi). She recounts her own story in *Metamorphoses*, Book 13. John Lyly's *Gallathea* (Paul's Boys *c.* 1585), about two girls each disguised as a boy to avoid being sacrificed to a sea monster, instead develops elements of the myth of Iphis and Ianthe from *Metamorphoses*, Book 9. 'Callatea', the form that appears in Q1's listing of *The Actors Names*, is presumably a compositorial error, as she is otherwise Gallatea in that text.

10 MEGRA Gurr suggests that the name may 'have been intended to suggest Megaera, one of the Erinyes, a Fury or goddess of vengeance' (7); she threatens to enact 'a woman's madness, / The glory of a fury' at 2.4.157–8.

11 LADY The nameless Lady who appears in 1.1 is of unsavoury reputation; presumably this is the same Lady who calls Arethusa to hunt at 3.2.167–8. She is not described in Q1 and is absent from Q1's list of characters. That text may be attempting to conflate her with the 'Waiting Gentlewoman': see Notes to Appendix 2: Casting *Philaster*, for details.

12 GENTLEWOMAN Arethusa's personal attendant

14 COUNTRY FELLOW Q1 calls him a 'Countrey Gallant' and depicts him dressed as elaborately as Philaster in its title-page woodcut (see Fig. 10). Nevertheless he refers to himself as a *mean man* (4.5.81) and his language, like that of the Clown in *WT*, emphasizes his social distance from the courtiers he stumbles upon.

15 CAPTAIN According to the Messenger, 'an old grey ruffian' (5.3.113). His leading of the Citizens suggests he is one of the Captains of London's trained bands.

16 CITIZENS in Q1 called 'Souldiers' in *The Actors Names* and in speech prefixes, although the Q1 entry direction is for '*a crew of Citizens*'. The distinction was not absolute when England did not maintain a standing army. These citizens are London

shopkeepers (*what-do-you-lacks*) who
in time of danger clap their 'musty
morions on / And trace the streets in
terror' (5.4.94–5). The London militia trained at Mile End, as described
by Rafe in Beaumont's *Knight of the
Burning Pestle*.

18 **Guards** There must be at least two;
see 2.4.34 SDn.

PHILASTER,
OR,
LOVE LIES A-BLEEDING

1.1   *Enter* DION, CLEREMONT *and* THRASILINE.

CLEREMONT   Here's nor lords nor ladies.

DION   Credit me, gentlemen, I wonder at it. They received
strict charge from the King to attend here. Besides, it
was boldly published that no officer should forbid any
gentlemen that desired to attend and hear.   5

CLEREMONT   Can you guess the cause?

DION   Sir, it is plain about the Spanish prince that's come
to marry our kingdom's heir and be our sovereign.

1.1 Location: a public reception room in
the court; see 2.3.25n. on 'the presence'.
As the action contains a formal meeting
between the King and the visiting prince
Pharamond, the original staging may
have included a 'state', a raised chair
with a canopy or throne (*OED n.* 20).

1 Gurr (xlix) suggests that this line refers
implicitly to the real audience and
indicates anticipated performance at
the Globe rather than the Blackfriars.
However, the Globe audience, although
not as exclusive as that at the indoor
theatres, nevertheless included some
persons of high status. There were
so-called lords' rooms, 'partitioned off
from the galleries closest to the stage,
at the Theatre, Rose and Globe' (Gurr,
Stage, 122). On the other hand, an
actor at the front of the Globe stage
looking sneeringly at the groundlings
might have raised an instant laugh with
this line (GM).

2–5 Dion's response prepares the audience
for a full court scene.

3   **attend** be present
4   **boldly published** widely announced
7   **plain** plainly, obviously
7–8 **Spanish . . . sovereign** The prenuptial visit would have had special
resonance in 1612–13, when *Philaster*
was twice performed at court during
the period when Frederick, the Elector
Palatine, had *come to marry* Princess
Elizabeth. Elizabeth, however, was
not the *kingdom's heir*, distinguishing
the dramatic situation from reality. At
the revival of 1619, a time of public
resistance to King James's attempt
to secure a Spanish match for Prince
Charles, by then the *kingdom's heir*,
Pharamond's nationality would have
instantly condemned him. English
hostility to the marriage of one of their
rulers to a Spanish prince went back
at least as far as the marriage of Mary
Tudor to Philip II (1554).

8   **sovereign** supreme ruler, used
interchangeably with 'king' but also
sometimes applied to the Deity.

1.1] *(Actus* I. *Scaena* I.*)*   0 SD] *Enter at seuerall doores Lord* LYON, TRASILINE *followes him,* CLERIMON
meetes them. Q1   THRASILINE] *Q4; Trasiline Q2 throughout*   2+ SP] LYON *Q1*

THRASILINE   Many that will seem to know much say she
looks not on him like a maid in love.   10

DION   Faith, sir, the multitude, that seldom know anything
but their own opinions, speak that they would have. But
the prince, before his own approach, received so many
confident messages from the state that I think she's
resolved to be ruled.   15

CLEREMONT   Sir, it is thought with her he shall enjoy
both these kingdoms of Sicily and Calabria.

DION   Sir, it is, without controversy, so meant. But 'twill
be a troublesome labour for him to enjoy both these
kingdoms with safety, the right heir to one of them   20
living, and living so virtuously – especially the people
admiring the bravery of his mind and lamenting his
injuries.

CLEREMONT   Who, Philaster?

DION   Yes, whose father, we all know, was by our late King   25
of Calabria unrighteously deposed from his fruitful

12 **speak . . . have** make statements that
reflect their desires

12–15 **But . . . ruled** The King apparently
pre-empted Arethusa's resistance to
the marriage by assuring Pharamond
before his visit that the princess would
definitely be his.

17, 19–20 **both these kingdoms** The
parallel to James VI and I's rule of *both*
the *kingdoms* of Scotland and England
may have made these lines dangerous;
the phrase, and its variations at 30–1 and
35, is not present in Q1. See pp. 87–9.

17 **Sicily and Calabria** like England
and Scotland, two territories in close
proximity, although in this case separated
by the Straits of Messina. (See Fig. 1 for
a seventeenth-century map.) By the time
of *Philaster* the Spanish controlled both.
Sicily was under Aragonese and Spanish
rule from the thirteenth century until
the eighteenth, usually through a viceroy.

Calabria, the south-western extremity of
the Italian peninsula, the toe of the 'boot',
was in the early seventeenth century
part of the Spanish-ruled Kingdom of
Naples. By the eighteenth century under
the Bourbons this became the Kingdom
of the Two Sicilies, ruled from Naples
until the Italian *Risorgimento*. The
play evokes simultaneously a world of
realpolitik and national conflict and the
pastoral Sicily of Theocritus (see Bliss,
Beaumont, 77–8).

25-6 **whose father . . . deposed** Like
Hamlet, Philaster is a *right heir* (20),
whose father lost his kingdom, but
here the son excluded from the throne
faces not the *late King* who carried
out the deposition but that king's
son. In Q1 the situation is simplified
and replicates the plot of *Ham*: 'the
King usurped the kingdom during
the nonage of the prince Phylaster'.

11 Faith] O *Q4*

Sicily. Myself drew some blood in those wars which I
would give my hand to be washed from.

CLEREMONT   Sir, my ignorance in state policy will not
let me know why, Philaster being heir to one of these   30
kingdoms, the King should suffer him to walk abroad
with such free liberty.

DION   Sir, it seems your nature is more constant than to
inquire after state news. But the King, of late, made a
hazard of both the kingdoms – of Sicily and his own   35
– with offering but to imprison Philaster. At which
the city was in arms, not to be charmed down by any

The existence of two kingdoms foreshadows a non-tragic solution to
the conflict. Adaptations of the play
change its politics: in Buckingham's
Restauration the Spanish prince's
father 'usurp'd the Kingdom where
he reigns'; and in Settle Philaster is
the (foreign) Prince of Aragon, which
was born from him in his infancy but
'Spain's encroaching monarchy'. For
discussion see pp. 65–9.

27–8 **Myself . . . from** Similar regret is
expressed in *R3*, 1.4, by Clarence,
who considers himself perjured for
swearing to fight on the side of Henry
VI but then supporting his brother
Edward and killing Henry's son.
Ordinary soldiers were exempt from
such responsibility: as Bates tells the
disguised Henry V, 'we know enough
if we know we are the King's subjects.
If his cause be wrong, our obedience to
the King wipes the crime of it out of
us' (*H5*, 4.1.130–3).

31 **suffer . . . abroad** permit him to
circulate freely

33–4 **it . . . news** In 1609 courtiers' fear
of inquiring after *state news* might
reflect King James's insistence on his
right to protect *arcana imperii* or royal
secrets. In *Basilikon Doron* James had
defended the king's right to secrecy,
and in his *Speech to the Lords and*

Commons 21 March 1609 he warned
members of Parliament not to 'meddle
with the maine points of Gouernment;
that is my craft: *tractent fabrilia fabri*;
to meddle with that, were to lesson
me . . . I must not be taught my Office'
(E1ʳ). James again insisted on *arcana
imperii* in his 1616 speech to the Star
Chamber, where he ordained for the
judges the 'limits wherein you are to
bound your selues . . . Incroach not
vpon the Prerogatiue of the Crowne: If
there fall out a question that concernes
my Prerogatiue or mysterie of State,
deale not with it, till you consult with
the King or his Councell, or both:
for they are transcendent matters,
and must not be sliberely carried with
ouer-rash wilfulnesse . . . That which
concernes the mysterie of the Kings
power, is not lawfull to be disputed; for
that is to wade into the weaknesse of
Princes, and to take away the mysticall
reuerence, that belongs vnto them that
sit in the Throne of God' (D1ᵛ–D2ʳ).

33 **constant** steadfast, resolute

34–5 **made a hazard of** risked

36 **offering** attempting

37 **the city** the citizens. Q2's capital (see
t.n.) may imply that for the Jacobean
audience the phrase suggested the City
of London.
charmed conjured; calmed

37 city] *(City)*

state order or proclamation till they saw Philaster
ride through the streets pleased and without a guard.
At which they threw their hats and their arms from   40
them, some to make bonfires, some to drink, all for his
deliverance. Which, wise men say, is the cause the King
labours to bring in the power of a foreign nation to awe
his own with.

[*Enter* GALLATEA, *a* LADY *and* MEGRA.]

THRASILINE   See, the ladies. What's the first?   45
DION   A wise and modest gentlewoman that attends the
    princess.
CLEREMONT   The second?
DION   She is one that may stand still discreetly enough
    and ill-favouredly dance her measure, simper when she   50
    is courted by her friend, and slight her husband.
CLEREMONT   The last?
DION   Faith, I think she is one whom the state keeps for
    the agents of our confederate princes. She'll cog and lie
    with a whole army before the league shall break. Her   55

---

39 **pleased** contented
42–3 **King . . . nation** At the time of
Philaster's double publication (1620/22)
this line might suggest King James's
hope that a large dowry accompanying
a Spanish alliance would keep him from
having to call on Parliament for supply
(Lesser, 195–8).
44 SD *The order of characters in Q2's
stage direction (see t.n.) follows the
convention of listing named characters
first. However, Dion's descriptions of
the women (46–61) fit Gallatea, then
the nameless Lady and finally Megra,
whose attraction to foreigners and
promiscuity is demonstrated by the
subsequent action.
50 **measure** a stately court dance

51 **friend** lover
53–5 **state . . . break** Dion is ironic not
only about Megra's special fondness for
foreigners but also about the political
relationship, the *league*, between the
state and *confederate princes*, presumably
including Pharamond.
54 **confederate** united by treaty
54–5 **cog . . . army** To *cog* is to employ
fraud or deceit, to cheat (*OED v.* 3),
frequently coupled with lie; cf. *MA*,
5.1.94–5, 'boys, / That lie, and cog, and
flout, deprave, and slander'. *OED* cites
Martin Marprelate's *Hay any Work*
(1589) 'thou canst cog, face, & lye,
as fast as a dog can trot'. However,
Dion's turn of phrase, *lie with*, suggests
Megra's sexual activity.

44 SD] *Theobald (Seward); Enter* Gallatea, Megra, *and a Lady. opp. 44–5 Q2*

name is common through the kingdom and the trophies
of her dishonour advanced beyond Hercules' pillars.
She loves to try the several constitutions of men's
bodies and indeed has destroyed the worth of her own
body by making experiment upon it for the good of the   60
commonwealth.

CLEREMONT   She's a profitable member!

MEGRA [*to Gallatea and Lady*]   Peace, if you love me.
You shall see these gentlemen stand their ground and
not court us.   65

GALLATEA   What if they should?

LADY   'What if they should'!

MEGRA [*to Lady*]   Nay, let her alone. [*to Gallatea*] What if
they should? Why, if they should, I say, they were never
abroad; what foreigner would do so? It writes them   70
directly untravelled.

GALLATEA   Why, what if they be?

LADY   'What if they be'!

---

57 **advanced . . . pillars**   metaphorically, beyond the end of the known
world. Traditionally Hercules' pillars
were the promontories that flanked
the eastern entrance to the Strait of
Gibraltar. According to Greek mythology, Hercules broke through the
mountain barrier that had locked the
Mediterranean, creating an outlet to
the Atlantic.

58–9 **constitutions . . . bodies**   sexual
natures or abilities; cf. 1.2.199 where
Pharamond blames 'the constitution of
my body' for his lack of chastity.

62 **member** citizen of the commonwealth;
sexual organ

63–87 *The speech prefixes for Megra and
the Lady are reversed in the original of
this passage; see t.n. Although Q2's
assignment of lines is playable, Seward
argued persuasively that its prefixes are

mistaken: 'all the Speeches which the
anonymous Lady speaks, her excessive
Fondness for the Courtship of Men,
and of Foreigners in particular' exactly
suit Megra. Furthermore, the 'long and
distinguishing Character' that Dion
gives in 53–61 is unlikely to describe
'a mere Cypher' (Theobald, n.2).
Gurr suggests that the problem arose
because the order of the descriptions
did not match the order of the entrance
direction, and confusion in the speech
prefixes followed.

71 **untravelled** The value of travel as
part of a young English gentleman's
training had been debated at least since
Roger Ascham's *Schoolmaster* (1570);
see *TGV*, 1.1.3, as well as Jonson's
satire on Puntarvolo in *Every Man Out*
and on Sir Politic and Lady Would-be
in *Volpone*.

63+ SP] *Theobald (Seward); La. Q2*   63 SD] *this edn*   67+ SP] *Theobald (Seward); Meg. Q2*
68 SD1] *this edn*   SD2] *this edn*

MEGRA [*to Lady*] Good madam, let her go on. [*to
      Gallatea*] What if they be? Why, if they be, I will   75
      justify they cannot maintain discourse with a judicious
      lady, nor make a leg, nor say 'excuse me'.

GALLATEA Ha, ha, ha!

MEGRA Do you laugh, madam?

DION Your desires upon you, ladies.   80

MEGRA Then you must sit beside us.

DION I shall sit near you, then, lady.

MEGRA Near me, perhaps. [*Indicates Gallatea.*] But there's
      a lady endures no stranger, and to me you appear a very
      strange fellow.   85

LADY Methinks he's not so strange; he would quickly be
      acquainted.

THRASILINE Peace, the King!

Enter KING, PHARAMOND, ARETHUSA *and train.*

KING

To give a stronger testimony of love
Than sickly promises, which commonly   90

75–7 **I . . . 'excuse me'** Megra's list of what
a gentleman learns from foreign travel
ignores all its usual justifications, such
as the acquisition of languages, cultural
knowledge and political information.

77 **make a leg** Bow formally; make an
obeisance by drawing back one leg and
bending the other (*OED* leg *n.* 4)

80 Dion's greeting, ostensibly a polite
formula, carries a sexual suggestion
immediately picked up by Megra.

82 Having earlier deplored Megra's
behaviour, Dion proceeds to flirt with
her.

84–5 **stranger . . . strange** The scene
puns repeatedly on *stranger* (foreigner)
and *strange* (odd, peculiar).

88 SD *train* The *train* that follows the
King is presumably the same as the
Attendants who accompany him at the
beginning of Act 4, though it may be
filled out with other actors if available.
Two is probably the minimum required
in both cases. Depending on the
company's resources, these actors may
also double as the *Guard* who appear
with the King in 2.4.

89–121 The King's speech is modelled on
Claudius's opening speech in *Ham*, 1.2.
It is officially addressed to Pharamond,
worthy sir (92), but like Claudius's it is
public (116), establishes the *succession*
(120) and attempts to reassure *nobles
and gentry* (119).

74 SD] *this edn*   74–5 SD] *this edn*   83 SD] *this edn*   86 be] *Q3;* to bee *Q2*

In princes find both birth and burial
In one breath, we have drawn you, worthy sir,
To make your fair endearments to our daughter
And worthy services known to our subjects
Now loved and wondered at. Next, our intent   95
To plant you deeply, our immediate heir,
Both to our blood and kingdoms. For this lady,
The best part of your life, as you confirm me
And I believe: though her few years and sex
Yet teach her nothing but her fears and blushes,   100
Desires without desire, discourse and knowledge
Only of what herself is to herself
Make her feel moderate health, and when she sleeps,
In making no ill day, knows no ill dreams.
Think not, dear sir, these undivided parts   105
That must mould up a virgin are put on
To show her so, as borrowed ornaments,
To talk of her perfect love to you or add
An artificial shadow to her nature.
No, sir, I boldly dare proclaim her yet   110
No woman. But woo her still, and think her modesty

92–5 The syntax is unclear. Is Pharamond
to make known to the King's *subjects*
both his unidentified *worthy services*
and his *endearments* to Arethusa, and
therefore to be 'loved and wondered at'?
Or is he *drawn* to make his endearments
to Arethusa and to make known his
service to subjects that are now loved?
Q3's emendation (see t.n.) does not
clarify.
93 **fair endearments** actions or utter-
ances 'expressive of love or fondness'
(*OED* endearment 2; the first example
is 1702)
95 **intent** intent is
99–104 **though . . . dreams** The King
stresses Arethusa's female innocence

and sexual inexperience. The meaning
of 'discourse and knowledge / Only
of what herself is to herself' remains
vague but emphasizes that no one else
has (sexual) knowledge of Arethusa.
Cf. *Son* 4, 'having traffic with thyself
alone, / Thou of thyself thy sweet self
dost deceive'.
105–6 **undivided . . . virgin** Again
stressing Arethusa's untouched per-
fection, the King unwittingly suggests
her intact hymen.
111 **No woman** a virgin; at the feast in
Honest Man's Fortune, when Lamira is
to choose a husband, Orleans says, 'My
Lady now shall see you made a Woman'
(5.4.6).

91 burial] *(buriall.)*   94 our] your *Q3*   95 Now] Both *(conj. this edn)*   108 talk of] speake *Q3*

A sweeter mistress than the offered language
Of any dame – were she a queen – whose eye
Speaks common loves and comforts to her servants.
Last, noble son, for so I now must call you,   115
What I have done thus public is not only
To add a comfort in particular
To you or me, but all, and to confirm
The nobles and the gentry of these kingdoms
By oath to your succession, which shall be   120
Within this month at most.

THRASILINE [*aside to Cleremont and Dion*]   This will be
hardly done.

CLEREMONT   It must be ill done, if it be done.

DION   When 'tis at best, 'twill be but half done whilst so   125
brave a gentleman is wronged and flung off.

THRASILINE   I fear –

CLEREMONT   Who does not?

DION   I fear not for my self, and yet I fear, too. Well, we
shall see, we shall see. No more.   130

PHARAMOND

Kissing your white hand, mistress, I take leave
To thank your royal father and thus far

---

112 At this point the first and second
quartos begin to correspond.

114 **comforts** Q2's plural is probably
correct, as the King contrasts Arethusa's
singular reserve or *modesty* to the *dame*
with *common* [i.e. shared, multiple] *loves*
and *servants* or lovers.

116 **public** publicly

121 **Within this month** The King
anticipates only a brief prenuptial visit.
See 1.2.191–2n.

122 SD From this point until the King's
exit at 294 the three gentlemen keep
up a separate conversation, marked

by prose and by its hostile commentary on the King's speeches. The
formal distinction emphasizes the
political distance between the King's
intentions and the desires of the
courtiers.

123 **hardly** with difficulty; barely, perhaps
not at all

131–62 As Cleremont will note (164–6),
Pharamond's speech, full of rodomontade and exaggerated self-praise,
expresses what the English considered typically Spanish egotism and
ostentation.

112] *Comprehensive collation of Q1 begins here; see p. 99.*   114 comforts] comfort *Q1*   116 only]
om. Q1   117 a] *Q1; not in Q2*   119 these kingdoms] our Kingdome *Q1*   122 SD] *Spencer subst.*
125 'tis] it is *Q1*   125–6] *Gurr; Q2 lines* done, / off. /; *Theobald lines* whilst / off /   129–30] *Gurr;
Q2 lines* too: / more. /

To be my own free trumpet. Understand,
Great King, and these your subjects, mine that must
  be –
For so deserving you have spoke me, sir,   135
And so deserving I dare speak myself –
To what a person, of what eminence,
Ripe expectation, of what faculties,
Manners and virtues, you would wed your kingdoms.
You in me have your wishes. Oh, this country,   140
By more than all the gods I hold it happy! –
Happy in their dear memories that have been
Kings great and good; happy in yours that is;
And from you, as a chronicle to keep
Your noble name from eating age, do I   145
Opine myself most happy. Gentlemen,
Believe me: in a word, a prince's word,
There shall be nothing to make up a kingdom
Mighty and flourishing, defenced, feared,
Equal to be commanded and obeyed,   150
But through the travails of my life I'll find it
And tie it to this country. By all the gods,
My reign shall be so easy to the subject
That every man shall be his prince himself
And his own law, yet I his prince and law. —   155

---

145 **eating age** time that will consume the present King's memory; cf. *Son* 1, where the poet tells his lover to 'Pity the world, or else this glutton be / To eat the world's due, by the grave and thee'. The phrase *eating age*, which appears repeatedly in seventeenth-century poetry, seems to originate in *Philaster* in imitation of Ovid's *Metamorphoses*, Book 15, translated by George Sandys as 'nor Sword shall raze, nor eating Age' (1632).

146 **Opine** consider
149 **defenced** defended
151 **travails** Q2's 'trauells' includes both the primary meaning here, the efforts Pharamond promises for the kingdom, and the sense of 'travels', re-emphasizing Pharamond's foreignness.
156–62 As Pharamond concludes, his hyperboles (*man of men*) and superlatives (*dearest, blessed'st*) increase; presumably the *Great queens* will die of heartbreak when he marries Arethusa.

140 You] and *Q1* your] *Q1; you Q2* 141 the gods] my hopes *Q4* 145 eating] rotting *Q1* 146 Opine] *F2;* Open *Q2* 151 travails] *(*trauells*)* it] it out *Q1* 152 By all the gods] And I vow *Q4* 153 so] as *Q1* subject] subiects *Q1*

And, dearest lady, to your dearest self,
Dear in the choice of him whose name and lustre
Must make you more and mightier, let me say,
You are the blessed'st living. For, sweet princess,
You shall enjoy a man of men to be   160
Your servant: you shall make him yours for whom
Great queens must die.

THRASILINE [*aside to Cleremont and Dion*]   Miraculous!

CLEREMONT   This speech calls him Spaniard, being
nothing but a large inventory of his own commen-   165
dations.

DION   I wonder what's his price? For certainly he'll sell
himself, he has so praised his shape.

Enter PHILASTER.

But here comes one more worthy those large speeches
than the large speaker of them. Let me be swallowed   170
quick if I can find, in all the anatomy of yon man's
virtues, one sinew sound enough to promise for him he
shall be constable. By this sun, he'll ne'er make king,
unless it be of trifles, in my poor judgement.

PHILASTER [*to the King*]
Right noble sir, as low as my obedience   175
And with a heart as loyal as my knee,
I beg your favour.

KING   Rise: you have it, sir.

---

159 **blessed'st** elided to two syllables
171 **yon man's** Pharamond's
173 **constable**   Constables were
notoriously unintelligent; cf. Dent,
C616, 'you might be a constable for
your wit', and *MA*, 3.3.22–3, 'You

are thought here to be the most
senseless and fit man for the constable
of the watch.' Slow-witted constables
frequently appear in Fletcher's plays:
see *Coxcomb* (1.6) and *Maid in the
Mill* (5.2).

163 SD] *Spencer subst.* Miraculous] Miracles *Q1* 167–74] *Langbaine lines* certainly / shape: /
Speeches, / them. / find, / Virtues, / him, / Constable. / King / Judgment. / 168 himself] him
Q1 so] so be *Q1* SD] *Q1; opp. 166 Q2* 169 speeches] praises *Q1* 171 in] *om. Q1* 172 one sinew]
vnseene to *Q1* 175 SD] *this edn; Kneeling | Gurr* 176 And] *om. Q1* 177 your] for *Q1*

118

DION

Mark but the King. How pale he looks! He fears.

Oh, this same whoreson conscience, how it jades us!

KING

Speak your intents, sir.

PHILASTER   Shall I speak 'em freely?   180

Be still my royal sovereign.

KING   As a subject

We give you freedom.

DION   Now it heats.

PHILASTER   Then thus:

I turn my language to you, prince, you foreign man.

Ne'er stare nor put on wonder, for you must

Endure me and you shall. This earth you tread upon,   185

A dowry as you hope with this fair princess,

By my dead father – oh, I had a father,

Whose memory I bow to – was not left

To your inheritance and I up and living,

Having my self about me and my sword,   190

178–9 Shakespeare's usurpers typically suffer pangs of *conscience*; see Claudius, 'How smart a lash that speech doth give my conscience' (*Ham*, 3.1.49), and Henry IV, 'How I came by the crown, O God forgive' (*2H4*, 5.1.218), and cf. Fletcher, *Valentinian*, 4.1.87–8, 'What an afflicted conscience doe I live with, / And what a beast I am growne?'

179 **jades** 'Wearies, exhausts by driving hard' (*OED v.* 1)

183 **prince . . . man** Philaster emphasizes the contrast between himself, the *right heir* (20), and the outsider, Spanish Pharamond. Cf. *thy nation*, 200. The competition between the two men is emphasized by the use of *prince* in reference to both.

184 **stare** Q1's 'start' is the kind of plausible error that may arise either through mishearing or in an actor or compositor's memory. At this point Pharamond is merely looking with *wonder* at Philaster, who has not yet said anything to make him 'start'.

put on pretend to

187–8 *These lines are reversed in Q2; as several phrases ('left / By my dead father' and even 'princess, / Whose memory I bow to') make superficial sense, a scribe or compositor may have reversed them in copying.

189 **up** alert; adult

178 He fears] with feare *Q4*   179 Oh] and *Q1*   how] ah how *Q1*   180 intents] *Q1;* intent *Q2*   'em] *(vm);* on *Q1*   182–3] *this edn; Q2 lines* freedome. / heates. / turne / man: / *; Theobald lines* Subject, / heats. / turn / Man. /   184 stare] start *Q1*   for] *om. Q1*   186 fair] sweet *Q1*   187–8] *Theobald;* Whose . . . left / By . . . father) *Q2*

The souls of all my name and memories,
These arms and some few friends, besides the gods,
To part so calmly with it and sit still
And say 'I might have been'. I tell thee, Pharamond,
When thou art king look I be dead and rotten   195
And my name ashes, as I. For hear me, Pharamond,
This very ground thou goest on, this fat earth
My father's friends made fertile with their faiths,
Before that day of shame shall gape and swallow
Thee and thy nation like a hungry grave   200
Into her hidden bowels. Prince, it shall:
By the just gods it shall.

PHARAMOND

He's mad, beyond cure mad.

DION [*aside*]   Here's a fellow has some fire in's veins; the
outlandish prince looks like a tooth-drawer.   205

PHILASTER

Sir prince of popinjays, I'll make it well

---

191 **all my name** my kin
194 **might have been** might have been king
196 **as I** Although omitted by Q4 and by many editors to regularize the metre, the phrase adds emphasis: Philaster warns Pharamond that he will not be safe unless not only Philaster but all knowledge of him is reduced to dust.
197–9 *****this . . . shame** Q2's comma (see t.n.) is misleading: with it the phrase *this fat earth* appears complete, with *friends made fertile* an independent clause. Q1's punctuation clarifies that *made fertile* is a participial phrase controlling the description of the earth that will *gape* for Pharamond.
203–12 ¹**mad . . . tainted** Philaster's behaviour is frequently excessive and eccentric, characterized by the mood swings and lack of control exemplified

here. The play's parallels to *Ham* keep the question of Philaster's sanity constantly before the audience, but he is never unquestionably *mad*. Cf. 3.1.123, *I am distracted*, and note.
205 **outlandish** foreign; bizarre, odd
tooth-drawer barber surgeon, regarded as practising a purely mechanical, low trade. In Cornwallis's *Essays*, cited *OED*, he expresses contempt for 'tooth-drawers' by comparing them to rat-catchers.
206 **popinjays** literally, parrots, but metaphorically the popinjay was taken as a type of vanity or empty conceit, in 'allusion to the bird's gaudy plumage, or to its mechanical repetition of words and phrases', and thus applied contemptuously to a person (*OED* 2b); cf. Hotspur's complaint about being 'so pestered with a popinjay' (*1H4*, 1.3.50).

---

192 besides] *Q1;* beside *Q2*   196 as I] *om. Q4*   197 earth] *Q1;* earth, *Q2*   201 her] his *Q1*   202–3] *one line Q6*   202 the just gods] *Nemesis Q4*   204 SD] *Spencer*   in's] in his *Q1*   206–7] *Boas; Q2 lines* appeare / mad. / vs, /; *Weber lines* well / mad. / us: /   206 popinjays] popines *Q1*   I'll] I will *Q1*

Appear to you I am not mad.

KING   You displease us.
You are too bold.

PHILASTER   No, sir, I am too tame,
Too much a turtle, a thing born without passion,
A faint shadow that every drunken cloud   210
Sails over and makes nothing.

KING   I do not fancy this.
Call our physicians. Sure he's somewhat tainted.

THRASILINE [*aside to Cleremont and Dion*]   I do not think
'twill prove so.

DION   He's given him a general purge already, for all the   215
right he has, and now he means to let him blood. Be
constant, gentlemen. By heaven, I'll run his hazard,
although I run my name out of the kingdom.

CLEREMONT   Peace, we are all one soul.

PHARAMOND

What you have seen in me to stir offence   220
I cannot find, unless it be this lady,
Offered into my arms with the succession,
Which I must keep though it hath pleased your fury
To mutiny within you, without disputing
Your genealogies or taking knowledge   225
Whose branch you are. The King will leave it me,
And I dare make it mine. You have your answer.

---

209 **turtle** turtle dove, traditionally viewed as particularly pacific

215 **general purge** Early modern medicine, based on galenic theory, believed that health required a balance of humours or fluids; physicians thus forced the body to expel excess or corruption through purges or enemas.

216 **let him blood** Bleeding was also used to purge the body of poisons and illness.

217 **run his hazard** take a chance for him (Philaster)

225–6 **Your . . . are** Pharamond treats Philaster as if he were a pretender to the throne from a remote branch of the royal family.

207 displease] do displease *Theobald*   209 turtle] Turcle *Q1*   211–12 this . . . physicians] this choller *Q1*   213 SD] *Spencer subst.*   215–18] *Weber lines* already, / means / gentlemen: / hazard, / kingdom. /   215 He's] *(Has)*   217 gentlemen. By heaven] gentle heauens *Q1*   heaven] these hilts *Q4*   223 it] is *Q1*   226 me] to me *Q1*

PHILASTER

If thou wert sole inheritor to him
That made the world his and couldst see no sun
Shine upon anything but thine – were Pharamond   230
As truly valiant as I feel him cold,
And ringed amongst the choicest of his friends,
Such as would blush to talk such serious follies
Or back such belied commendations,
And from this presence – spite of these bugs, you should   235
Hear further from me.

KING   Sir, you wrong the prince.

I gave you not this freedom to brave our best friends.
You deserve our frown. Go to, be better tempered.

PHILASTER

It must be, sir, when I am nobler used.

GALLATEA [*aside to Megra and Lady*]

Ladies,   240
This would have been a pattern of succession
Had he ne'er met this mischief. By my life,
He is the worthiest the true name of man
This day, within my knowledge.

MEGRA

I cannot tell what you may call your knowledge,   245
But th'other is the man set in my eye.
Oh, 'tis a prince of wax!

228–30 **If . . . thine** if you were to inherit
   the whole world from God (rather than
   one country from its king)
234 **belied commendations** false self-
   praises
235 **from . . . presence** not in the court
   bugs threats; Q1's 'brags' is also
   possible.

240–7 The comments of the ladies, like
   those of the gentlemen, continue apart
   from the main conversation around
   the King.
246 **set in my eye** that I admire
247 **prince of wax** perfect, as if modelled
   in wax. Cf. *RJ*, 1.3.76, 'why, he's a man
   of wax.'

235 this] his *Q1*   spite of these bugs] Spit all those bragges *Q1*   235–6] *this edn; Q2 lines* bugs, /
me. / Prince: /   237–8 to . . . frown] *om. Q1*   238 deserve] do deserve *Theobald*   239 nobler] noblier
Q1   240 SP] LEON *Q1*   SD] *Spencer subst.*   242 ne'er] neuer *Q1*   243 He] this *Q1*   245 your] *om.
Q1*   246 th'other is] i'm sure tothers *Q1*

GALLATEA   A dog it is.

KING

Philaster, tell me

The injuries you aim at in your riddles.

PHILASTER

If you had my eyes, sir, and sufferance,   250

My griefs upon you and my broken fortunes,

My wants great, and now nothing – hopes and fears –

My wrongs would make ill riddles to be laughed at.

Dare you be still my king and right me?

KING

Give me your wrongs in private.

PHILASTER   Take them,   255

And ease me of a load would bow strong Atlas.

　　They whisper.

CLEREMONT [*aside to Dion and Thrasiline*]   He dares not

stand the shock.

DION [*aside to Cleremont and Thrasiline*]   I cannot blame

him; there's danger in't. Every man in this age has   260

not a soul of crystal for all men to read their actions

through. Men's hearts and faces are so far asunder that

they hold no intelligence. Do but view yon stranger

---

252 **nothing . . . fears** – Q4's emendation
(see t.n.) creates clearer syntax but
assumes that Philaster is entirely
coherent as he spells out his *griefs* and
wants. There is no difference in the
meaning.

253 **ill riddles** unfit mysteries

254 Philaster asks the King if he can
do the apparently impossible, retain
his own position and yet compensate
Philaster for his loss of the throne.
Q3's addition of 'not' (see t.n.) may be
correct: it regularizes the metrics of

the line and alters the question so that
Philaster asks whether the King dares
to keep his throne, which inevitably
requires *not* compensating Philaster.
The implicit threat recalls the opening
conversation about the *hazard* the King
ran by threatening 'but to imprison
Philaster' (1.1.35–44).

256 **Atlas** In Greek mythology, Atlas
carried the world on his shoulders.

263 **hold no intelligence** do not
communicate; do not correspond to
each other

---

251 griefs] griefe *Q1*　252 wants] *Q1;* want's *Q2*　nothing – hopes and fears –] *(*nothing hopes
and feares*)*; nought but hopes, and feares, *Q4*　254 me] me not *Q3*　255–6 Take . . . Atlas] *om.*
Q1　256 SD] *opp. priuate 255 Q2; Phy. whisper the King Q1; They walk apart | Weber*　257 SD] *this edn*
259 SD] *this edn*　261 not] *om. Q1*　261–2 for . . . faces] to read their actions, though mens faces
Q1　263 Do] *om. Q1*　yon] the *Q1*

well, and you shall see a fever through all his bravery
and feel him shake like a true tenant. If he give not   265
back his crown again upon the report of an elder-gun,
I have no augury.

KING

Go to!
Be more yourself, as you respect our favour;
You'll stir us else. Sir, I must have you know   270
That y'are – and shall be – at our pleasure, what fashion
We will put upon you. Smooth your brow,
Or by the gods –

PHILASTER

I am dead, sir; you're my fate. It was not I
Said I was wronged. I carry all about me;   275
My weak stars lead me, too – all my weak fortunes.
Who dares in all this presence speak that is

---

264 **bravery** boasting; swaggering; fine
clothes
265 **tenant** A dependent who shakes from
fright in the face of his lord and master,
in contrast to Pharamond's assertion
of royal sovereignty. Q1's 'truant',
one who recognizes his own failure or
criminality, is possible, but the repetition
in 'true truant' suggests confusion by
the compositor. Theobald's conjecture,
'recreant', would clarify.
266 **elder-gun** a pop gun made from a
shoot of elder wood; metaphorically, a
useless or toy weapon. Cf. *H5*, 4.1.195–
6, 'That's a perilous shot out of an
elder-gun'.
271 **y'are** This form, rather than the usual
modernization *you're*, emphasizes the
contrast between the present *are* and
shall be.
271–2 **what . . . you** whatever status I
choose to accord you

274 **I am . . . fate** Philaster's acqui-
escence sounds servile, but the rest
of his speech is so excessive that it
makes the King suspicious (*Sure he's
possessed*, 280), raising the possibility
that the hyperbole is parodic or ironic.
See pp. 20–5 for discussion of the
play's politics.
275–6 **I carry . . . fortunes** The repetition of *weak*, present in both early
quartos, may suggest an error of
transmission. Theobald's emendation
(see t.n.) would change the meaning
to 'Everything that I am, all the
poverty and lack of power which I
am accorded by my poor fortunes, you
may see in me.' In Q2 the speech is less
coherent, with *all my weak fortunes* only
connected by parallel to *weak stars*; the
loose construction contributes to the
King's sense that the speech indicates
madness.

---

264 through] throw *Q1*   bravery] braueries *Q1*   265 shake] shacke *Q1*   tenant] truant *Q1;* Recreant
Theobald   267 have] am *Q1*   271–3] *this edn; Q2 lines* we / gods. /.; *Dyce lines* what / brow, / gods – /
271 y'are] you are *Q1*   272–3 brow, / Or] selfe, ore or *Q1*   273 gods –] *Q1* (gods); gods. *Q2*
274 you're] you are *Q1*   275 me;] (me,); me *Theobald*   276 me, too –] *this edn;* me too; *Q2*
277 dares] dare *Q1*   speak that] *Q1;* (speak, that *Q2*

But man of flesh and may be mortal, tell me
I do not most entirely love this prince
And honour his full virtues.

KING   Sure he's possessed.   280

PHILASTER

Yes, with my father's spirit. It's here, O King:
A dangerous spirit. Now he tells me, King,
I was a king's heir, bids me be a king,
And whispers to me these are all my subjects.
'Tis strange. He will not let me sleep, but dives   285
Into my fancy and there gives me shapes
That kneel and do me service, cry me king.
But I'll suppress him; he's a factious spirit
And will undo me. [*to Pharamond*] Noble sir, your hand;
I am your servant.

KING   Away! I do not like this.   290
I'll make you tamer or I'll dispossess you
Both of life and spirit. For this time
I pardon your wild speech without so much
As your imprisonment.

               Exeunt King, Pharamond [*and*] *Arethusa.*

DION [*aside*]

I thank you, sir. You dare not for the people.   295

---

280 **possessed** mad, taken over by demonic powers

281–4 **father's spirit . . . subjects** A recollection of the scenes (*Ham*, 1.4–5) in which Hamlet actually sees his *father's spirit*, who bids him kill the usurper.

284 **these . . . subjects** Cf. *R2*, 4.1.168–70, 'Yet I well remember / The favours of these men. Were they not mine? / Did they not sometime cry "All hail" to me?'

287 **cry** call; proclaim

288 **factious** seditious; inclined to form a party, in this case against the King

289 SD The offer to shake hands is made to Pharamond, as Philaster kneels to show respect to the King. See 175–7.

290–2 **I do . . . spirit** Some part of the King's comment may be spoken aside, though it is more threatening if addressed directly to Philaster.

295 SD Although his words take the form of direct address to the King, Dion waits until the monarch has left to comment.

295 **for** because of, for fear of

---

278 man] *Q1;* men *Q2*   280 Sure] *om. Q1*   281 It's] is *Q1*   282 Now] and now *Q1*   288 he's] heas *Q1*   289 SD] *Daniel*   292 life] your life *Q1*   294 your] *om. Q1*   SD] *om. Q1*   and] *F*   295 SD] *Spencer*

GALLATEA

Ladies, what think you now of this brave fellow?

MEGRA   A pretty talking fellow, hot at hand. But eye yon
stranger: is he not a fine, complete gentleman? Oh,
these strangers, I do affect them strangely. They do the
rarest home things and please the fullest. As I live, I   300
could love all the nation over and over for his sake.

GALLATEA   Gods comfort your poor head-piece, lady: 'tis
a weak one and had need of a nightcap!   *Exeunt Ladies.*

DION [*to Cleremont and Thrasiline*]

See how his fancy labours! Has he not spoke
Home, and bravely? What a dangerous train   305
Did he give fire to! How he shook the King,
Made his soul melt within him and his blood
Run into whey. It stood upon his brow
Like a cold winter dew.

---

297 **hot at hand** easily aroused

299–300 **do . . . things** perform the most
wonderful, implicitly sexual, actions
in private

303 **nightcap** literally, head clothing
worn in bed for warmth (cf. *Knight
of Malta*, 3.4.12–14, 'had but I a kind
wench / To pull my Boot-hose off,
and warm my night-cap, / There's no
charme like it'), but in early modern
drama frequently associated with
cuckoldry: cf. *Oth*, 2.1.305, 'I fear
Cassio with my night-cap too', and
Westward Ho, 1.1, 'why should a man
bee such an asse to play the antick for
his wiues appetite? Immagine that I, or
any other great man haue on a veluet
Night-cap, and put case that this
night-cap be to little for my eares or
forehead, can any man tell mee where
my Night-cap wringes me, except I be
such an asse to proclaime it.' There are
no examples in the drama of women
wearing nightcaps.

304–5 **spoke / Home** spoken directly, to
the point

305–6 **dangerous . . . fire to** a *train* is 'a
line of gunpowder or other combustible
substance laid so as to convey fire to
a mine or charge for the purpose of
exploding it' (*OED n.*[1] II 13a); it is
used figuratively here, as in 'a train of
thought'.

307–8 **blood . . . whey** Blood, one of the
four humours, was believed to carry the
'vital spirits'; for it to turn to 'whey',
the watery portion of milk, was a sign
of weakness. As Paster explains, 'The
materialism so dominant in Renaissance
thinking about behavior and the faculties
of the soul allows blood's physical
attributes to receive a high praise
suffused with ethical implication . . . In
one's blood were carried the decisive
attributes of one's cultural identity'
(*Body Embarrassed*, 65–72). Cf. Goneril's
attack on her husband: 'Milk-livered
man' (*KL*, 4.2.51).

---

296 SP] TRA. *Q1*   301 the] their *Q1*   302 SP] LAD. *Q1*   Gods] Pride *Q4*   lady] om. *Q1*   303 had] has
Q1   a] an *Q1*   SD *Exeunt*] *(Exit)*   304 SD] *this edn*   304–5] *Theobald lines* not / Train /

PHILASTER   Gentlemen,
You have no suit to me? I am no minion.   310
You stand, methinks, like men that would be courtiers,
If you could well be flattered, at a price
Not to undo your children. You're all honest.
Go, get you home again and make your country
A virtuous court, to which your great ones may   315
In their diseased age retire and live recluse.

CLEREMONT
How do you, worthy sir?

PHILASTER   Well, very well.
And so well, that if the King please, I find
I may live many years.

DION   The King must please
Whilst we know what you are and who you are,   320

---

310 **minion** a young male courtier/
flatterer, often with suggestion of a
homoerotic relationship. Philaster
implicitly denigrates Pharamond by
contrast to himself.

311–13 **like men . . . children** a crux,
sometimes emended so that the person
well flattered is Philaster (see t.n.), but
the lines make sense as they stand.
The primary sense of *would be* is
'would like to be': the men aspire to be
courtiers, but as they are *all honest* (313)
they set two conditions: that they be
complimented and not endanger their
children's future. Alternatively they
would be courtiers already if it had been
possible to be flattered without harming
their children. If emended so that it is
Philaster who requires flattering, the
meaning is that the men would like to
serve him but set limits to what they
will do.

314–15 **get . . . court** Throughout
his reign King James attempted to

convince the gentry to return to
their country estates; he reiterated in
a speech to Star Chamber in 1616
his earlier proclamation 'That all
Gentlemen of qualitie should depart
to their owne countreys and houses,
to maintaine hospitalitie amongst their
neighbours; which was equiuocally
taken by some, as that it was meant
onely for that Christmas: But my wil
and meaning was . . . that it should
alwaies continue' (H1ᵛ). In the plays
of Beaumont and Fletcher virtuous
characters like Archas in *Loyal
Subject* retreat to the country when
abused. See p. 24 on the alignment
of Beaumont and Fletcher with the
'country' faction.

316 **live recluse** conduct private lives

317–19 **How . . . years** Cf. the exchange
between Ophelia and Hamlet in the
Folio text, 'How does your honour for
this many a day?' 'I humbly thank you,
well, well, well' (3.1.91–2).

---

312 you] I *Weber (Mason)*   313 You're] you are *Q1*   316 and live recluse] liue recluses *Q1*
317 you, worthy] your worth *Q1*   318 I find] *om. Q1*   319 The] Sir, the *Q1*   320 what . . . who] who . . .
what *Q1*

Your wrongs and injuries. Shrink not, worthy sir,
But add your father to you, in whose name
We'll waken all the gods and conjure up
The rods of vengeance, the abused people,
Who like to raging torrents shall swell high   325
And so begirt the dens of these male-dragons
That through the strongest safety they shall beg
For mercy at your sword's point.

PHILASTER   Friends, no more;
Our ears may be corrupted. 'Tis an age
We dare not trust our wills to. Do you love me?   330

THRASILINE

Do we love heaven and honour?

PHILASTER

My lord Dion, you had
A virtuous gentlewoman called you father.
Is she yet alive?

DION   Most honoured sir, she is,
And for the penance but of an idle dream   330
Has undertook a tedious pilgrimage.

---

326 **male-dragons** men who threaten or, metaphorically, breathe fire like Pharamond. Women, presumably, threaten in a different way. Cf. *Cor*, 5.4.28–9, 'There is no more mercy in him than there is milk in a male tiger.' There may also be a suggestion of 'dragoon', 'A species of cavalry soldier' (*OED* 2). F. Markham's 1622 *Decades of Epistles of War*, the earliest *OED* citation, comments that the Low Countries 'haue produced another sort of Horse-men . . . and they call them *Dragoons*, which I know not whether I may tearme them Foot-Horse-men, or Horse-Footmen' (Decade 3, Epistle 1).

327 **safety** protection, safeguard (*OED* n. 3)

332–6 These lines might alert an audience familiar with such plays as *TGV* and *AW* to anticipate the eventual appearance of Dion's daughter, possibly cross-dressed. In *AW* Helena dresses as a pilgrim to 'Saint Jaques le Grand' in her pursuit of Bertram; in *TGV* Julia, desiring to see Proteus, denies that the way is 'wearisome' to a 'true-devoted pilgrim' and, dressed as a 'well-reputed page', is employed by Proteus as a go-between to his new beloved.

336 SD *GENTLEWOMAN Q1's '*Gentlewoman*' identifies this character as the same person who enters with Arethusa in 1.2 ('*her Gentlewoman*') rather than, as in Q2, '*a Lady*'. The nameless lady of easy virtue who appeared earlier in Q2 1.1, with Gallatea and Megra is

---

321 injuries] vertues *Q1*   322 add] call *Q1*   325 to] *om. Q1*   328 Friends] Friend *Q1*   332–3] *Theobald lines Dion, / Father; /*   332 Dion] *Lyon Q1*   335 the] a *Q1*   336 SD] *after* aliue. *334 Q1; Enter a Lady Q2*

Enter a [GENTLEWOMAN].

PHILASTER

Is it to me or any of these gentlemen you come?

GENTLEWOMAN

To you, brave lord. The princess would entreat
Your present company.

PHILASTER

The princess send for me? You're mistaken.   340

GENTLEWOMAN

If you be called Philaster, 'tis to you.

PHILASTER

Kiss her fair hand, and say I will attend her.

[Exit Gentlewoman.]

DION

Do you know what you do?

PHILASTER

Yes, go to see a woman.

CLEREMONT

But do you weigh the danger you are in?   345

PHILASTER

Danger in a sweet face?
By Jupiter, I must not fear a woman.

THRASILINE

But are you sure it was the princess sent?
It may be some foul train to catch your life.

omitted entirely from Q1, as are the lines describing her. Q3, 1628, enumerating '*The persons presented*', attempts to clarify the matter by including both 'An old Wanton Lady, or Croane' and 'Another Lady attending the Princesse'.

343–9 The nervousness of the gentlemen and their attempts to keep Philaster from going to Arethusa parallel the attempts of Horatio and Marcellus to keep Hamlet from following the ghost in *Ham*, 1.4.

346–52 **sweet . . . out** Philaster's comments prepare for the Gentlewoman's comment to Arethusa that Philaster's 'looks hid more / Of love than fear' (1.2.16–17).

349 **train** a lure or bait to entice an animal or person into a trap or snare (*OED n.*²)

337 Is it] I'st *Q1*   any] to any *Q1*   338, 341 SP] *Q1* (GENT. Woo); La. *Q2*   340 You're] you are *Q1*   341 to] *om. Q1*   342 SD] *Q1 (Exit. Gent.woo.) opp. 343; not in Q2*

PHILASTER

    I do not think it, gentlemen. She's noble;   350
    Her eye may shoot me dead, or those true red
    And white friends in her face may steal my soul out;
    There's all the danger in't. But be what may,
    Her single name hath armed me.   *Exit.*

DION   Go on,

    And be as truly happy as thou art fearless.   355
    Come, gentlemen, let's make our friends acquainted
    Lest the King prove false.   *Exeunt.*

[1.2]   *Enter* ARETHUSA *and* [*her* GENTLEWOMAN].

ARETHUSA

    Comes he not?

GENTLEWOMAN   Madam?

ARETHUSA   Will Philaster come?

GENTLEWOMAN

    Dear madam, you were wont to credit me
    At first.

ARETHUSA   But didst thou tell me so?

    I am forgetful, and my woman's strength

351–4 Philaster's use of the conventional images of love poetry further reveals his feelings for Arethusa. Cf. *Astrophil and Stella*, 9, describing '*Stella's* face . . . / Whose porches rich (which name of cheekes endure) / Marble mixt red and white do enterlace', and 20, where the speaker complains he has his 'death wound' because he looked in his mistress's 'heav'nly eye' in which Cupid had hidden, and, having 'descried the glistring of his dart . . . ere I could flie thence, it pierc'd my heart'.

354 **single name** name alone

1.2 Location: Arethusa's chamber. This need not have included a bed and on the early modern stage was probably suggested only by the private conversation.

1 Arethusa's anxiety is revealed by her negative construction and the unidentified 'he'; her rephrasing shows an attempt to recover her dignity.

2 **wont** accustomed
  credit believe

350 do] dare *Q1*   352 friends] fiend frends *Q1*   face] cheekes *Q1*   354 SD] *(Exit.* Phil.*)*   355 thou art] *Q1;* th'art *Q2*   357 SD] *(Exit Gentlemen.)*   **1.2**] *Weber*   0 SD *her* GENTLEWOMAN] *Q1;* a Lady *Q2*   1–3] *Boas; Q2 lines* not? / Madam? / come? / wont / first. / so? /; *Q1 lines* not. / Madam? / come? / first. / so. /; *Q6 lines* Madam? / wont / first. / so? /   1+ SP GENTLEWOMAN] *Q1* (Woo.*); La. Q2*   3 first] the first *Q1*   4–34 I . . . your] *prose Q1*

Is so o'ercharged with dangers like to grow   5
About my marriage that these under things
Dare not abide in such a troubled sea.
How looked he when he told thee he would come?

GENTLEWOMAN
Why, well.

ARETHUSA   And not a little fearful?

GENTLEWOMAN
Fear, madam? Sure he knows not what it is.   10

ARETHUSA
You all are of his faction. The whole court
Is bold in praise of him, whilst I
May live neglected and do noble things
As fools in strife throw gold into the sea:
Drowned in the doing. But I know he fears.   15

GENTLEWOMAN
Fear? Madam, methought his looks hid more
Of love than fear.

ARETHUSA   Of love? To whom? To you?
Did you deliver those plain words I sent
With such a winning gesture and quick look
That you have caught him?

5–6 **dangers . . . marriage** Neither the *dangers* nor the *marriage* is specified; the phrase at first seems to refer to the courtiers' objections to Pharamond, but implicitly it anticipates the more risky marriage Arethusa is contemplating.

6 **under things** minor details, lesser considerations

13–15 **do . . . doing** My noble actions gain no attention and destroy themselves, even as fools, by fighting, unwittingly lose whatever of value they have. The final phrase may mean either that the gold or the fools are drowned. Turner points out that 'In Q1, where this entire speech is printed as prose, a suspicious amount of white space is left before and after *and doe noble things*'. Turner, who assumes that Q1 was the basis of Q2, suggests that 'some words were omitted by Q1 and that the annotator failed to correct the passage when he prepared copy for Q2' (487). As Q1 instead probably derives from Q2, the spaces may reflect the printer's uncertainty about whether the text was complete.

7 Dare] dares *Q1*   13–15] things: . . . sea, . . . doing: *Turner*   16 Fear?] *om. Q1*   methought] mee thoughts *Q1*   19 winning] woing *Q1*

GENTLEWOMAN   Madam, I mean to you.   20

ARETHUSA

Of love to me? Alas, thy ignorance
Lets thee not see the crosses of our births.
Nature, that loves not to be questioned
Why she did this or that, but has her ends
And knows she does well, never gave the world   25
Two things so opposite, so contrary,
As he and I am. If a bowl of blood
Drawn from this arm of mine would poison thee,
A draught of his would cure thee. Of love to me?

GENTLEWOMAN

Madam, I think I hear him.

ARETHUSA   Bring him in.   [*Exit Gentlewoman.*]

You gods that would not have your dooms withstood,   31
Whose holy wisdoms at this time it is
To make the passions of a feeble maid
The way unto your justice, I obey.

Enter [GENTLEWOMAN *with*] PHILASTER.

GENTLEWOMAN

Here is my lord Philaster.

22 **crosses . . . births** the ways in which
our inherited positions keep us apart
27–9 **bowl . . . thee** Arethusa's image
depends on two early modern medical
practices: bleeding and 'drinking
animal or human blood . . . widely
recommended as a curative for states
like sorrow, which cooled and dried the
body' (Paster, *Humoring*, 57). In Galenic
physiology all of the body's constituent
fluids were 'reducible to blood' and
'the relationship between blood and
the individual body containing it was

no less ideological than physiological.
In one's blood were carried the decisive
attributes of one's cultural identity'
(Paster, *Body Embarrassed*, 9, 66).
31 **gods** These justice-seeking gods are
presumably the same as those Dion
promised to *waken* on Philaster's behalf
at 1.1.323; cf. 100–3, 112, 144.
dooms judgements; irrevocable destiny
33–4 **passions . . . justice** Unlike women
who choose husbands in opposition to
the desire of their fathers only to satisfy
their *passions*, Arethusa sees her desires

20 him] *om. Q1*   24 her] his *Q1*   26 contrary] bound to put *Q1*   28 of mine] *om. Q1*   29 Of] *om. Q1*
30 SD] *Dyce subst.*   31 would] will *Q1*   dooms] dens *Q1*   33 passions] passion *Q4*   34 unto] into
Q1   SD] *Q1; opp. Philaster 35 Q2; om. Q1u;* GENTLEWOMAN *with* | *Dyce subst.*

ARETHUSA   Oh, it is well.   35
Withdraw yourself.   [*Exit Gentlewoman.*]
PHILASTER   Madam, your messenger
Made me believe you wished to speak with me.
ARETHUSA
'Tis true, Philaster, but the words are such
I have to say and do so ill beseem
The mouth of woman that I wish them said   40
And yet am loath to speak them. Have you known
That I have aught detracted from your worth?
Have I in person wronged you? Or have set
My baser instruments to throw disgrace
Upon your virtues?
PHILASTER   Never, madam, you.   45
ARETHUSA
Why, then, should you, in such a public place,
Injure a princess and a scandal lay
Upon my fortunes, famed to be so great,
Calling a great part of my dowry in question?
PHILASTER
Madam, this truth which I shall speak will be   50
Foolish. But for your fair and virtuous self,
I could afford myself to have no right
To anything you wished.
ARETHUSA   Philaster, know

as bringing about the political *justice*
called for earlier by the courtiers.
39–40 **ill . . . woman** Arethusa is concerned with the gender-appropriateness
of her behaviour even in objecting to
actions that *Injure a princess*, 47.
42 **aught . . . worth** spoken ill of you
44 **baser instruments** servants
51–3 **But . . . wished** Philaster's *foolish*

truth is that he could be indifferent
to the kingdoms and allow her to
have them, if it were not for (*but
for*) his appreciation of the princess's
qualities; implicitly he wants them for
and together with her. Paradoxically,
'it is because he loves her that he
cannot afford to give up his right to her
inheritance' (Gurr, 23).

36 SD] *Weber subst.*   38–45 'Tis . . . virtues] *prose Q1*   39 do] dos *Q1*   beseem] become *Q1*   47–9]
prose Q1   47 Injure] Iniury *Q1*   48 famed] found *Q1*   51–3] *prose Q1*   51 and] *om. Q1*   53–4
Philaster . . . kingdoms] *one line Q1*

I must enjoy these kingdoms.

PHILASTER   Madam, both?

ARETHUSA

Both, or I die. By heaven I die, Philaster,   55

If I not calmly may enjoy them both.

PHILASTER

I would do much to save that noble life,

Yet would be loath to have posterity

Find in our stories that Philaster gave

His right unto a sceptre and a crown   60

To save a lady's longing!

ARETHUSA   Nay, then, hear.

I must and will have them, and more –

PHILASTER   What more?

ARETHUSA

– or lose that little life the gods prepared

To trouble this poor piece of earth withal.

PHILASTER

Madam, what more?

ARETHUSA   Turn, then, away thy face.   65

PHILASTER

No.

ARETHUSA

Do.

54–6 **kingdoms . . . both? . . . both**
See pp. 26, 87–9 for discussion of
the political significance of the two
kingdoms and Q1's failure to censor
these two references.

61 **lady's longing** a phrase usually
describing the irrational desires
associated with pregnancy but frequently carrying sexual implications:
in *Eastward Ho!* (1605) Quicksilver
warns Petronel that his new wife
Gertrude will 'tie you to your tackling
till she be with child' and always insist
on fulfilment of her desires: 'She would
long for everything when she was a
maid, and now she will run mad for
'em.' Gertrude asserts her indifference
to other people's inconvenience 'rather
than I lose my longing' (2.3.53–6,
125).

55 ¹die] do *Q1*   56 may] die *Q1*   58–61 Yet . . . longing] *prose Q1*   61–2 Nay . . . and more.] *one
line Q1*

PHILASTER

I can endure it. Turn away my face?
I never yet saw enemy that looked
So dreadfully but that I thought myself 70
As great a basilisk as he, or spake
So horrible but that I thought my tongue
Bore thunder underneath as much as his,
Nor beast that I could turn from. Shall I then
Begin to fear sweet sounds – a lady's voice 75
Whom I do love? Say you would have my life:
Why, I will give it you, for it is of me
A thing so loathed, and unto you that ask
Of so poor use, that I shall make no price.
If you entreat, I will unmovedly hear. 80

ARETHUSA

Yet for my sake a little bend thy looks.

PHILASTER

I do.

ARETHUSA   Then know I must have them and thee.

PHILASTER

And me?

ARETHUSA   Thy love, without which all the land

---

71 **basilisk** 'A fabulous reptile, also called a *cockatrice*, alleged to be hatched by a serpent from a cock's egg; ancient authors stated that its hissing drove away all other serpents, and that its breath, and even its look, was fatal' (*OED* 1); cf. *Four Plays in One*, 'Art thou there, Basilisk? remove thine eyes, / For I am sick to death with thy infection' (*Triumph of Honour*, 2.167–8) and *WT*, 1.2.388–90, 'Make me not sighted like the basilisk. / I have look'd on thousands, who have sped the better

/ By my regard, but kill'd none so.'
75–6 **lady's . . . love** The previous relationship between Arethusa and Philaster is never clarified.
76–9 **Say . . . price** the first of Philaster's statements of self-loathing and willingness to die
79 **make no price** ask nothing for it
80 **unmovedly** unmoved; *OED*'s earliest citation of this usage
83–4 **land . . . yet** The European kingdoms Arethusa demands are well established, but in 1609 this phrase would remind

---

68–80] *Q1 lines* face, / dreadfully, / he, / tongue / his: / begin, / loue, / it you, / beg, / price, / heare. /   68 can] cannot *Q3*   69 yet saw] saw yet *Q1*   71 spake] speake *Q1*   75 lady's voice] womans tongue *Q1*   77 me] *Q1;* me, *Q2*   78 ask] beg *Q1*   81–2 Yet . . . do] *one line Q1*   82–3 Then . . . me?] *one line Q1*   83–5 Thy . . . possible?] *Q1 lines* yet, / possible. /

Discovered yet will serve me for no use
But to be buried in.

PHILASTER   Is't possible?   85

ARETHUSA

With it, it were too little to bestow
On thee. Now, though thy breath do strike me dead –
Which know it may – I have unripped my breast.

PHILASTER

Madam, you are too full of noble thoughts
To lay a train for this contemned life,   90
Which you may have for asking. To suspect
Were base where I deserve no ill. Love you?
By all my hopes I do, above my life.
But how this passion should proceed from you
So violently would amaze a man   95
That would be jealous.

ARETHUSA

Another soul into my body shot
Could not have filled me with more strength and spirit
Than this thy breath. But spend not hasty time
In seeking how I came thus: 'tis the gods,   100
The gods, that make me so, and sure our love
Will be the nobler and the better blessed
In that the secret justice of the gods
Is mingled with it. Let us leave and kiss,

---

audiences of ongoing voyages of discovery to North America; Jamestown, the first permanent settlement, was established just as *Philaster* was written.

87 **breath . . . dead** recalling the basilisk of 71

88 **unripped my breast** revealed my feelings; the phrase foreshadows the wound that Arethusa later receives: 'he's hurt her in the breast', 4.5.116–17.

90 **contemned** contemnèd

94–6 Philaster's immediate suspicion of Arethusa's violent *passion* and his hypothetical jealousy are apparently based on misogynistic distrust of women rather than political suspicion.

103 **secret justice** because their love will restore Philaster's political rights

104–6 **leave . . . without it** Whether Philaster follows Arethusa's invitation at this point is uncertain and may vary in production. The lovers may kiss,

86–8] *prose Q1*   87 do] *om. Q1*   91–6] *prose Q1*   91 may] might *Q1*   100–6 In . . . it] *Q1 lines* so, / better / gods / some / vs, / it. /   101 The gods] *om. Q1*   102 nobler] worthier *Q1*

Lest some unwelcome guest should fall betwixt us   105
And we should part without it.

PHILASTER   'Twill be ill
I should abide here long.

ARETHUSA   'Tis true, and worse
You should come often. How shall we devise
To hold intelligence, that our true loves
On any new occasion may agree   110
What path is best to tread?

PHILASTER   I have a boy
Sent by the gods, I hope, to this intent,
Not yet seen in the court. Hunting the buck,
I found him sitting by a fountain's side,
Of which he borrowed some to quench his thirst   115
And paid the nymph again as much in tears.
A garland lay him by, made by himself,

---

but it is also possible that Philaster's
discomfort about Arethusa's forwardness (see 94–6n.) inhibits
him.

104 **leave** cease to talk
109 **hold intelligence** communicate
110 **any new occasion** when a new
  situation arises
111–39 **I have . . . kept** This speech, with
  its pastoral imagery and its roots in
  tales of abandoned children nourished
  by nature, is central to the play's tone
  of romance and its tragicomic structure
  of loss and recovery. The fountain with
  surrounding flowers is a *locus amoenus* of
  classical tradition, recalling the garden
  of Adonis in *FQ* and the fountain or
  holy well in *Faithful Shepherdess*: 'And
  but that matchlesse spring which Poets
  know, / Was nere the like to this: by it
  doth growe / About the sides, all hearbs
  which witches use, / All simples good
  for medicine or abuse, / All sweetes

that crowne the happy nuptiall day, /
With all their colours: there the month
of May / Is ever dwelling, all is young
and greene, / There's not a grasse on
which was ever seene, / The falling
Autume or cold winters hand, / So full
of heate and virtue is the land / About
this fountaine' (2.3.69–79).
113 **Hunting the buck** Most
  contemporary images of hunting show
  men in groups (see Figs 5 and 6) but
  Philaster seems to have been alone.
116 **the nymph** Fountains of romance are
  presided over by nymphs. Usually these
  are harmless, but in Book 2 of *FQ* Guyon
  finds in the Bower of Bliss a fountain 'of
  richest substaunce, that on earth might
  bee' in which 'Two naked Damzelles he
  therein espyde', almost distracting him
  from his righteous quest.
117 **garland . . . himself** Crowning with
  flowers is typical of pastoral. In *Faithful
  Shepherdess* Clorin recalls 'How often

---

105 unwelcome] Vnwelcom'd *Q1*   106–11 'Twill . . . tread] *Q1 lines* long. / often. / intelligence?
/ agree, / tread. /   110 any] an *Q1*   111–40 I . . . love] *prose Q1*   114 fountain's] fountaine *Q1*
116 again as much] as much againe *Q1*

Of many several flowers bred in the vale,
Stuck in that mystic order that the rareness
Delighted me. But ever when he turned   120
His tender eyes upon 'em he would weep
As if he meant to make 'em grow again.
Seeing such pretty helpless innocence
Dwell in his face, I asked him all his story.
He told me that his parents gentle died,   125
Leaving him to the mercy of the fields,
Which gave him roots, and of the crystal springs,
Which did not stop their courses, and the sun,
Which still, he thanked him, yielded him his light.
Then took he up his garland and did show   130
What every flower, as country people hold,
Did signify, and how all, ordered thus,

have I sat crownd with fresh flowers / For Summers queene' (1.1.18–19). Such garlands are usually woven by female characters: Perigot tells Amoret 'by this / Fresh Fountaine many a blushing maide / Hath crownd the head of her long loved shepheard, / With gaudy flowers' (1.2.110–13) and Cloe promises Daphnis that she will 'pull / Fresh blossomes from the bowes, or quickly cull / The choisest delicates from yonder meade, / To make thee chaines or chaplets' (1.3.105–8). Lear, crowned with 'all the idle weeds that grow', has presumably woven the crown of flowers himself; the gender reversal is one indication that he is 'mad as the vexed sea' (4.3.2–5). The boy's activity here signals gender ambiguity to an alert audience.

118 *bred . . . vale* Q1's *vale* reiterates the secluded location of the fountain. Q2's 'bred in the bay' is usually taken as referring to the construction of the garland; Gurr emends to *breded* and glosses 'entwined (braided) in the

garland (laurel)' with *bred* as a past participle of 'brede', to intertwine or braid. However, the only form of this participle that *OED* finds is 'breaded', in *FQ*, 3.2.50, 'Taking thrise three heares from off her head, / Them trebly breaded in a threefold lace', and Gurr is driven to assuming the 'past participle, being unmetrical, was written in an elided form in the manuscript'. More probably *bred* is the past participle of the verb 'breed' (*OED* 12c); cf. Baron's *Gripus and Hegio*: 'When gaudy *Flora* in her prime / Observing it was Summer-time / . . . Olympick *Iove* / Commanded *Aprels* balmy shoures, / To refresh the *March* bred flowers'.

119 **that mystic** such an esoteric or mysterious (*OED* B 2)

125 **gentle** of gentry or aristocratic status

128 **did . . . courses** continued to run and supply him with water

131–2 **flower . . . signify** The most familiar of the *country people* explaining the meaning of flowers is Perdita, in *WT*, 4.4, but cf. Ophelia, 'There's rosemary,

118 bred] breded *Gurr*   vale] *Q1 (*vayle*);* bay *Q2*   121 eyes] eye *Q1*   122 'em] *(vm);* them *Q1*
128 their courses] the course *Q1*   129 still, he thanked him,] still he thankt, it *Q1*   light] life *Q1*

Expressed his grief, and to my thoughts did read
The prettiest lecture of his country art
That could be wished, so that, methought, I could   135
Have studied it. I gladly entertained him,
Who was glad to follow, and have got
The trustiest, lovingest and the gentlest boy
That ever master kept. Him will I send
To wait on you and bear our hidden love.   140

ARETHUSA

    'Tis well. No more.

Enter [GENTLEWOMAN].

GENTLEWOMAN

    Madam, the prince is come to do his service.

ARETHUSA

    What will you do, Philaster, with yourself?

PHILASTER

    Why, that which all the gods have appointed out for me.

ARETHUSA

    Dear, hide thyself. –   145

    Bring in the prince.   [*Exit Gentlewoman.*]

PHILASTER   Hide me from Pharamond?

When thunder speaks, which is the voice of God,
Though I do reverence yet I hide me not.
And shall a stranger prince have leave to brag

---

that's for remembrance . . . And there is pansies; that's for thoughts' (*Ham*, 4.5.169–71).

136 entertained him took him into my service

142 do his service to salute you

143–4 do . . . with yourself Arethusa means because of the arrival of Pharamond; Philaster's reply more

generally affirms his intention to follow what he perceives as divine will, that is, to pursue his throne.

147 thunder . . . God a commonplace; cf. *Woman Killed*, 'Thou God of thunder' (vi.21) and *2H6*, 4.1.104–5, 'O, that I were a god, to shoot forth thunder / Upon these paltry, servile, abject drudges!'

135 methought] me thoughts *Q1*   137 Who] whom *Q1*   141 SD GENTLEWOMAN] *Q1 (woman); Lady Q2; after 140 Q3*   142 SP] *Q1 (*Woo.*); La. Q2*   143 do, Philaster] *Phylaster* doe *Q1*   145–6 Dear . . . prince] *one line Q1*   146 SD] *Dyce subst.*   148 hide me not] doe not hide my selfe *Q1*

Unto a foreign nation that he made   150
Philaster hide himself?

ARETHUSA   He cannot know it.

PHILASTER

Though it should sleep forever to the world,
It is a simple sin to hide myself,
Which will forever on my conscience lie.

ARETHUSA

Then, good Philaster, give him scope and way   155
In what he says, for he is apt to speak
What you are loath to hear. For my sake, do.

PHILASTER
I will.

Enter PHARAMOND.

PHARAMOND

My princely mistress, as true lovers ought,
I come to kiss these fair hands and to show   160
In outward ceremonies the dear love
Writ in my heart.

PHILASTER [*to Arethusa*]

If I shall have an answer no directlier,
I am gone.

PHARAMOND   To what would he have answer?

---

153 **simple sin** an ignorant or foolish
error (by transference from simple,
OED n. 9, 'Deficient in knowledge
or learning; characterized by a
certain lack of acuteness or quick
apprehension')
155 **scope** 'Room or freedom to act' (*OED*
7a)

158 SD In Q1 Pharamond is escorted in
by the Gentlewoman, but this in turn
requires a subsequent exit for her (see
160 t.n.). Pharamond can enter alone
or the direction to *Bring in the prince*
(146) can be satisfied if the attendant is
glimpsed gesturing him forward.
163 **directlier** more directly

150–1 Unto . . . himself] *Q1 lines* Phylaster / himselfe. /   153–4] *Q1 lines* euer / lie /   153 sin]
*(*sinae*)*   157 for my sake, do] *om. Q1*   158 SD] *Enter* PHARAMONT *and a woman. Q1*   160–2] *prose
Q1*   160 show] shew, [*Exit* Lady *Dyce*   162 Writ in] *Q3;* Writ it *Q2;* within *Q1*   162–3] *one line
Q5*   163–4 If . . . gone] *one line Q1*   163 SD] *this edn*   163 no directlier,] or no, derectly *Q1*   164
what] what? what *Q1*

ARETHUSA

    To his claim unto the kingdom. 165

PHARAMOND

    Sirrah, I forbare you before the King.

PHILASTER

    Good sir, do so still. I would not talk with you.

PHARAMOND

    But now the time is fitter. Do but offer

    To make mention of right to any kingdom,

    Though it lie scarce habitable –   *[Seizes Philaster.]*

PHILASTER *[Pushes Pharamond off.]*   Good sir, let me go. 170

PHARAMOND

    And by the gods –

PHILASTER   Peace, Pharamond. If thou –

ARETHUSA

    Leave us, Philaster.

PHILASTER   I have done.   *[Starts to leave.]*

PHARAMOND

    You are gone? By heaven, I'll fetch you back.

PHILASTER *[Returns.]*

    You shall not need.

PHARAMOND   What now?

PHILASTER   Know, Pharamond,

    I loathe to brawl with such a blast as thou, 175

    Who are naught but a valiant voice. But if

---

166 **Sirrah** Pharamond's attitude toward Philaster is embodied in this term, which expresses 'contempt, reprimand, or assumption of authority on the part of the speaker' (*OED*).
forbare endured, tolerated. Both forbare and forbore were available past tenses at the time of *Philaster*; 'bare' was the original past tense form, but 'bore'/'forbore' appeared around 1400 and became general after 1600 (JH). See *OED forbear* and *bear v.*1.

175 **blast** both a loud empty noise (*OED n.*1 3a) and a pernicious influence or curse (*OED n.*1 6c)

168–70 But . . . habitable –] *prose Q1* 170 lie] be *Q3* SD1] *this edn* SD2] *this edn* 171 the gods] my sword *Q4* thou –] then *Q1* 172 SD] *Dyce subst.* 173] *om. Q1* PHA. You] *catchword* C3ʳ *Q1* 174–5] *Boas; Q2 lines* need. / now? / *Pharamond,* / thou, / ; *Q6 lines* now? / *Pharamond,* / thou, /   174–8 Know . . . it] *prose Q1* 174 SD] *Dyce subst.* 176 naught] nothing *Q1*

Thou shalt provoke me further, men shall say
Thou wert and not lament it.

PHARAMOND   Do you slight
My greatness so, and in the chamber of the princess?

PHILASTER

It is a place to which, I must confess,   180
I owe a reverence, but were't the church –
Ay, at the altar – there's no place so safe
Where thou dar'st injure me but I dare kill thee.
And for your greatness, know, sir, I can grasp
You and your greatness thus, thus, into nothing.   185
Give not a word, not a word back. Farewell.   *Exit.*

PHARAMOND

'Tis an odd fellow, madam. We must stop
His mouth with some office when we are married.

ARETHUSA

You were best make him your controller.

PHARAMOND

I think he would discharge it well. But madam,   190
I hope our hearts are knit, but yet so slow
The ceremonies of state are that 'twill be long

---

178 **Thou wert** i.e. you have died
185 **thus, thus** an invitation to the actor
    to make a gesture, such as pinching his
    fingers together and then blowing the
    imaginary Pharamond away
187–8 **stop . . . office** Presumably if
    given an official court position Philaster
    would be compelled to swear allegiance
    and obedience to the ruler.
189 **controller** Pharamond misses
    Arethusa's pun. He understands the
    term as reference to the 'household
    officer whose duty was primarily to
    check expenditure, and so to manage in
    general; a steward. Now chiefly used in

the household of the sovereign, and in
those of members of the royal family'
and usually spelled comptroller (*OED*
2); cf. *H8*, 1.3.67. Arethusa, however,
implies 'One who controls or keeps
under control; one who restrains,
directs, or manages' (*OED* 4a).
191–2 **slow . . . state** Although the
    King promises that the oath to the
    succession will take place *Within this
    month* (1.1.121), preliminaries to a
    state marriage could stretch over
    considerable time. Frederick, the
    Elector Palatine, arrived in England in
    October 1612 for his marriage to the

178–9 Do . . . Princess] *Q1 lines* much, / Princesse? /   179 so] so much *Q1*   180–8] *prose Q1*   181
were't] (wer't); wert *Q1*   182 Ay, at the altar] (I at the Altar); at the high Altar *Q1*   183 injure] iniurie
Q1   184 sir] *om. Q1*   190–8] *Q1 lines* well. / *followed by prose*   190 SP] *Q1*; Phi. Q2*   But] *om. Q1*

142

Before our hands be so. If then you please,
Being agreed in heart, let us not wait
For dreaming form but take a little stolen   195
Delights and so prevent our joys to come.

ARETHUSA

If you dare speak such thoughts
I must withdraw in honour.   *Exit.*

PHARAMOND   The constitution of my body will never   199
hold out till the wedding. I must seek elsewhere.   *Exit.*

2.1   *Enter* PHILASTER *and* BELLARIO.

PHILASTER

And thou shalt find her honourable, boy,

Princess Elizabeth, which did not take place until St Valentine's Day, 1613. The delay was partly caused by the death of Elizabeth's brother, Prince Henry, heir to the throne.

195–6 **stolen / Delights** Although it seems unlikely that a princess would have sufficient privacy even if she wished to violate the rules of sexual propriety, Prospero's repeated admonitions to Ferdinand not to break Miranda's 'virgin-knot before / All sanctimonious ceremonies may / With full and holy rite be ministered' (*Tem*, 4.1.15–17; cf. 4.1.51–3) suggest how much anxiety the topic could arouse.

196 **prevent** anticipate

199–200 Pharamond's lack of sexual control indicates his inability to rule himself more generally; the consequences are implied in Ferdinand's reply to Prospero's fears (see 195–6n.): 'As I hope / For quiet days, fair issue

and long life / . . . the strong'st suggestion / Our worser genius can, shall never melt / Mine honour into lust' (*Tem*, 4.1.23–8). Fletcher's young gallants are often sexually freer than Shakespeare's (see *Night Walker* and *Chances*) but intemperance among royalty is treated seriously, as in *Maid's Tragedy*.

199 **constitution . . . body** The echo of 1.1.58 emphasizes the similarity of Pharamond and Megra.

2.1 Location: Philaster's lodging

1 **boy** The repeated use of this term in the audience's first view of Bellario gives a homoerotic tone to the encounter. The emphasis on honour, tenderness and modesty may instead suggest femininity. Masten describes 'the boy or youth or young man as a "universal object of desire" – a figure of erotic and affective attraction and availability for men and women alike'

193 hands] hearts *Q1*   If then] then if *Q1*   197 such] your *Q1*   198 SD] *(Exit* Ar:*)*   200 SD] *(Exit* Ph.*)*   **2.1**] *(Actus. 2. Scaena* I.*)*   0 SD] *Enter* PHYLASTER, *and his boy, called* BELLARIO. *Q1*
1–5 And . . . deserve] *Q1 lines* regard / modesty, / aske, / deserue /

Full of regard unto thy tender youth,
For thine own modesty and for my sake
Apter to give than thou wilt be to ask –
Ay, or deserve.

BELLARIO   Sir, you did take me up   5
When I was nothing, and only yet am something
By being yours. You trusted me unknown,
And that which you were apt to construe
A simple innocence in me perhaps
Might have been craft, the cunning of a boy   10
Hardened in lies and theft. Yet ventured you
To part my miseries and me, for which
I never can expect to serve a lady
That bears more honour in her breast than you.

PHILASTER
But boy, it will prefer thee. Thou art young   15
And bearest a childish overflowing love
To them that clap thy cheeks and speak thee fair yet,
But when thy judgement comes to rule those passions,
Thou wilt remember best those careful friends
That placed thee in the noblest way of life.   20
She is a princess I prefer thee to.

BELLARIO

In that small time that I have seen the world
I never knew a man hasty to part

---

(117). He refers to Q1, which uses *Boy* as the speech prefix for Bellario throughout, as 'the boy quarto'.

6–7 **something . . . yours** my only identity is as your servant

8 **construe** interpret

15 **prefer** advance

19–20 **careful . . . thee** Friends, in this sense, included all of an individual's supporters, whether relatives or associates, who could assist in finding a satisfactory life situation. For men this might mean placement at court or, on a lower social level, employment; for women *friends* might arrange marriages.

3 thine] thy *Q1*   5–10 Sir . . . boy] *Turner; Q2 lines* nothing: / yours; / apt, / me, / boy /; *Q1 lines* nothing, / yours, / *followed by prose*   5+ SP] BOY *Q1*   6 only yet am] I am onely yet *Q1*   8 were] are *F2*   construe] *Langbaine;* conster *Q2*   10 craft] crafty *Q1*   16–21] *prose Q1*   17 clap] claps *Q1*   yet] om. *Q1*   18 thy] *om. Q1*   to] no *Q1*   23–7] *prose Q1*

With a servant he thought trusty. I remember
My father would prefer the boys he kept   25
To greater men than he, but did it not
Till they were grown too saucy for himself.

PHILASTER

Why, gentle boy, I find no fault at all
In thy behaviour.

BELLARIO   Sir, if I have made
A fault of ignorance, instruct my youth: 30
I shall be willing, if not apt, to learn.
Age and experience will adorn my mind
With larger knowledge, and if I have done
A wilful fault, think me not past all hope
For once. What master holds so strict a hand   35
Over his boy that he will part with him
Without one warning? Let me be corrected
To break my stubbornness – if it be so –
Rather than turn me off, and I shall mend.

PHILASTER

Thy love doth plead so prettily to stay   40

24–7 **I . . . himself** This description of *boys* being preferred to *greater men* (*prefer* appears three times from 15 to 25) suggests King James's well known penchant for beautiful male favourites and in particular for Robert Carr, who came to James's attention in 1607 and was given increasingly important titles, culminating in Earl of Somerset in 1613. Carr married Frances Howard in 1609 and fell at the revelation of the Overbury murder in 1615.

27 **too saucy** Carr's arrogance was notorious.

28 **I . . . all** In early modern drama *fault* is 'perhaps allusive of vagina, certainly fornication' (Williams, *Glossary*, 121); if the audience suspects Bellario's gender, Philaster's finding *no fault* may suggest poor judgement.

37 **corrected** punished, probably physically, as suggested by the *hand* of the *master . . . Over his boy* (35–6) and *break my stubbornness* (38). Studies of pedagogic beating in the period have suggested that 'this imagined scene of correction is itself not necessarily separate from or devoid of eroticism' (Masten, 119).

27 grown] *om. Q1*   29–39 Sir . . . mend] *Q1 lines* ignorance, / learne, / larger / fault / once / boy, / warning, / stubbornnesse, / off, / mend. /   40–50 Thy . . . princess] *Q1 lines* stay, / thee: / businesse / her, / full / trust, / ioy, / weepe / Princesse. /   40 doth] dos *Q1*

That, trust me, I could weep to part with thee.
Alas, I do not turn thee off. Thou knowest
It is my business that doth call thee hence,
And when thou art with her thou dwellest with me.
Think so, and 'tis so. And when time is full   45
That thou hast well discharged this heavy trust,
Laid on so weak a one, I will again
With joy receive thee; as I live, I will.
Nay, weep not, gentle boy! 'Tis more than time
Thou didst attend the princess.
BELLARIO   I am gone.   50
But since I am to part with you, my lord,
And none knows whether I shall live to do
More service for you, take this little prayer.
Heaven bless your loves, your fights, all your designs.
May sick men, if they have your wish, be well,   55
And heaven hate those you curse, though I be one.   *Exit.*
PHILASTER
The love of boys unto their lords is strange.
I have read wonders of it, yet this boy
For my sake – if a man may judge by looks
And speech – would outdo story. I may see   60
A day to pay him for his loyalty.   *Exit.*

---

42 **turn thee off** dismiss you
44 **when . . . me** a typical lover's paradox; cf. *Son* 36 and 43.
46 **heavy** serious, burdensome
57 The 'love of boys unto their lords' is shown as unreliable, if not *strange*, in *Cym*: in 4.2 the disguised Innogen's tale of affection for her 'master / A very valiant Briton' moves Lucius to take 'Fidele' as a page because 'Thy

name well fits thy faith', yet Innogen has invented this master and is actually lying on the body of Cloten. Later, when Lucius assumes that 'Fidele' will use the boon offered by Cymbeline to beg his life, the page informs him, 'Your life, good master, / Must shuffle for itself' and Lucius concludes that 'Briefly die their joys / That place them on the truth of girls and boys' (5.5.104–7).

---

43 doth] dos *Q1*   44 dwellest] dwest *Q1*   50–61 I . . . loyalty] *prose Q1*   54 fights] sighes *Q1*
56 heaven] heauens *Q1*   60 may] must *Q1*   61 SD] *(Exit Phi.)*

[2.2]   *Enter* PHARAMOND.

PHARAMOND   Why should these ladies stay so long? They
must come this way; I know the Queen employs 'em
not, for the reverend mother sent me word they would
all be for the garden. If they should all prove honest
now, I were in a fair taking! I was never so long without   5
sport in my life, and in my conscience, 'tis not my
fault. Oh, for our country ladies! Here's one bolted; I'll
hound at her.

Enter GALLATEA.

Madam.
GALLATEA   Your grace.   10
PHARAMOND [*Approaches her.*]   Shall I not be a trouble?

2.2 Location: the court

2 **the Queen** A queen never appears
and is not otherwise mentioned in the
play. Arethusa, like many early modern
dramatic heroines, does not seem to
have a mother. All arrangements for her
future are made by her father.

3 **reverend mother** This may be a false
start; no such person appears in the play.
In *Woman Hater* the Count describes
one waiting woman as if she were older
and in charge: 'the Lady *Honoria* cares
for you as she doth for all other young
Ladies, shee's glad to see you, and will
shew you the privie Garden, and tel you
how many gownes the Duchesse had'
(1.3.4–7). The phrase may have bawdy
overtones: in *Humorous Lieutenant*
Leucippe, the Bawd, tells the Woman
who brings in her daughter, 'I am full
of Maids' (2.3.63). Cf. 4.2.21n.

4 **honest** chaste

5 **a fair taking** an unfavourable plight
or condition (*OED* taking *vbl. n.* 4a);
colloquially, 'a pretty mess'

6 **sport** sexual activity

7 **our country ladies** ladies from our
country (a slur on Spain); rural women,
perceived as sexually free. The phrase
includes a pun on *cunt*, as in Hamlet's
'country matters' (3.2.110).
   bolted suddenly escaped from its
burrow, like a rabbit. *OED v.²* 3 cites
this line and *Humorous Lieutenant*,
4.8.28, 'He will bolt now for certaine.'

8 **hound at** pursue harassingly (*OED*
v. 2)

9 *Madam Turner points out that this
word is omitted in Q2 but appears
mistakenly in Q1 at 114 following *maid*.
He proposes that it was 'added as a
proof correction, but the compositor,
instead of putting the word into D2,
put it into approximately the same
position in D3ᵛ, which lay adjacent to
D2 in the forme' (487). Something
more may have gone wrong to confuse
the compositor: Turner does not note
that in Q2 leaf D2 is mistakenly signed
D3.

2.2] *Weber* 1–9] *Q1 lines* must / not, / word, / should all / taking: / life, / fault / boulted, /
Madame. / 6 sport] sport before *Q1* 8 SD] *after 7* fault. *Q1* 9 Madam] *Q1; not in Q2* 11–12]
one line Daniel 11 SD] *this edn*

147

GALLATEA [*Moves away.*] Not to me, sir.

PHARAMOND   Nay, nay, you are too quick. By this sweet
hand –

GALLATEA   You'll be forsworn, sir, 'tis but an old glove. If   15
you will talk at distance, I am for you, but good prince,
be not bawdy nor do not brag. These two I bar, and
then I think I shall have sense enough to answer all the
weighty apothegms your royal blood shall manage.

PHARAMOND   Dear lady, can you love?   20

GALLATEA   Dear, prince? How dear? I ne'er cost you
a coach yet nor put you to the dear repentance of a
banquet. Here's no scarlet, sir, to blush the sin out it
was given for. This wire mine own hair covers, and
this face has been so far from being dear to any that it   25
ne'er cost a penny painting. And for the rest of my poor
wardrobe, such as you see, it leaves no hand behind it to

13–15 **By . . . glove** Pharamond apparently grabs Gallatea's gloved hand.

16 **at distance** from a proper distance

19 **weighty apothegms** An apothegm is
a 'terse, pointed saying . . . a pithy or
sententious maxim' (*OED*). Gallatea is
mocking the prince.

21 ***Dear, prince?** Q2 has no comma, and
Gallatea's response is ambiguous, either
imitating Pharamond's address to *Dear
lady* or challenging the suggestion that
she is expensive (and by implication,
kept).

21–2 **cost . . . coach** Coaches, symbols of
wealth and status, were notorious as
places for assignations: the 'physic' that
will impregnate Lady Kix in *Chaste
Maid* must be 'taken lying . . . A-bed,
or where you will for your own ease, /
Your coach will serve' (3.3.150–2). Q1
strengthens the sexual implication by
reading 'Couch'.

23 **scarlet** 'In early use, some rich cloth,
often of a bright red colour, but . . . also
sometimes of other colours' (*OED n.*
1a, citing Hickok, *Frederick's Voyage*,
'Ships bring cloth of Wooll, Scarlets,
Veluets, Opium' (1588))

24 **wire** a frame to support an elaborate
hairdo (*OED n.* 9b, citing Stubbes, *The
Anatomy of Abuses* (1595), 'least it [the
hair] should fall down it is vnder propped
with forks, wyers, and I cannot tel what',
and Zanthia's attack on other women in
Knight of Malta, 1.1.183–5, 'unfledge
'em of their tyres, / Their wyres, their
partlets, pins, and perriwigs, / And they
appeare like bald cootes, in the nest')

26 **cost . . . painting** required expenses
for make-up

27–8 **leaves . . . doings** Daniel suggests
that 'no hand behind it' means 'no
acknowledgment of indebtedness'
because the debt is paid. More generally

12 SD] *this edn; going | Spencer*   13 you are] y'are *Q1*   15–19] *Theobald lines* Glove. / for you; / brag; /
bar; / enough / Apothegmes / manage. /   15 but] *om. Q1*   17 These] those *Q1*   bar] onely barre *Q1*
21 Dear,] *F2;* Deare *Q2*   22 coach] Couch *Q1*   22–3 a banquet] a play and a banquet *Q1*   23–4 to . . . for]
to make you blush *Q1*   24 This . . . covers] this is my owne hayre *Q1*   26 a penny] *Q1;* penny *Q2*

make the jealous mercer's wife curse our good doings.

PHARAMOND   You mistake me, lady.

GALLATEA   Lord, I do so. Would you or I could help it.   30

PHARAMOND   Do ladies of this country use to give no more respect to men of my full being?

GALLATEA   Full being? I understand you not, unless your grace means growing to fatness, and then your only remedy, upon my knowledge, prince, is, in a morning, a   35 cup of neat white wine brewed with carduus, then fast till supper. About eight you may eat. Use exercise and keep a sparrowhawk. You can shoot in a tiller. But of all

Gallatea suggests that, unlike other women, she has not had cloth from the mercer in exchange for *good doings* of a sort to make the mercer's wife *jealous*.

30 The extra lines added by Q1 at this point (see t.n.) may be 'gag' ad-libbed in performance. They carry through the imagery of medicine and time wasting, so it is also possible they were accidentally omitted from Q2.

32, 33 **full being** Pharamond means 'complete masculine physique and status'; Gallatea intentionally misunderstands him to be worried about his figure.

33–40 Gallatea's directions follow recommendations in early modern 'dietaries', including Thomas Elyot, *The Castle of Health* (1539, 1595) and William Vaughan, *Naturall and Artificial Directions for Health* (1600). Vaughan states that 'White wine, drunk in the morning fasting, cleanseth the lunges' (10). However, he also permits 'Sower whay' as 'a temperate drink, which mundifieth the lunges, purgeth bloud, and alayeth the heat of the liuer' (13). Pork 'hurteth them that bee subiect to the gout and *Sciatica*, and annoyeth old men and idle persons'

(16). Vaughan recommends exercise 'when the body is fasting and emptie' (35) but counsels 'them, that vse any moderat exercise, not in any case to be let bloud' (37–8); cf. *fly phlebotomy*. Elyot, typically, ties the correct diet to the 'vniuersal complexions' (62) or dominant humours prevalent in a body. For example, Timothy Bright, *A Treatise of Melancholy* (1586), urges the melancholy person to eschew pork 'except it be yong' and milk and 'whatsoeuer is made thereof' (28–9).

36 **carduus** *cardus benedictus* or holy thistle; cf. *MA*, 3.4.68–70, 'Get you some of this distilled *carduus benedictus*, and lay it to your heart; it is the only thing for a qualm.'

36–7 **fast till supper** The dietaries give differing directions for the right number of meals; Vaughan writes that 'Moderate fasting, as, to omit a dinner or a supper once a weeke, is wonderfull commodious for them, that are not cholerick or melancholick, but full of raw humours' (45).

38 **sparrowhawk** 'A species of hawk (*Accipiter nisus*) which preys on small birds, common in the British Islands' (*OED* 1, citing this line). *OED* records

28 mercer's] silke-mans *Q1* good doings] doing *Q1* 29 mistake] much mistake *Q1* 30 it] it. / PHA. Y'are very dangerous bitter, like a potion. / GAL. No sir, I do not mean to purge you, though I meane to purge a little time on you. *Q1* 33–40] *Q1 lines* grace / remedy / morning, / Cardus, / exercise, / Tiller, / Flebotamie, / whay: / anymales. / 37 eight] fiue *Q1*

149

your grace must fly phlebotomy, fresh pork, conger and
clarified whey: they are all dullers of the vital spirits.   40
PHARAMOND   Lady, you talk of nothing all this while.
GALLATEA   'Tis very true, sir. I talk of you.
PHARAMOND [*aside*]   This is a crafty wench. I like her wit
well; 'twill be rare to stir up a leaden appetite. She's
a Danae and must be courted in a shower of gold. –   45
Madam, look here. [*Offers gold.*] All these, and more
than –
GALLATEA   What have you there, my lord? Gold? [*Takes
gold.*] Now, as I live, 'tis fair gold; you would have silver
for it to play with the pages. You could not have taken   50

a description from 1752, '*The Sparrow
hawk*. The yellow-legged Falco, with
a white, undulated breast, and a
fasciated brown tail'. Going hawking
involves physical exercise, but the
nobility used falcons. Sparrowhawks
were more likely to be kept by citizens,
and Gallatea may be subtly insulting
Pharamond. See Fig. 5.

shoot in a tiller exercise yourself at
archery: a *tiller* is a 'stock or shaft fixed
to a long-bow to admit of its being used
as a cross-bow, for greater convenience
or precision of aim' (*OED n.*[2] 1b, citing
this line).

39 **phlebotomy** therapeutic bleeding
conger eel, but Gurr (34) notes
that conger was 'a common term for
cucumber in the Midlands'. According
to Vaughan, 'Cucumbers are of a cold
temperature, and fit to be eaten only of
cholerick persons' (27).

40 **whey** the watery liquid left after the
coagulation of milk to make cheese. See
33–40n.
vital spirits those forces which sustain
life, usually in the plural. *OED* vital,

a. and *n.* 2b, cites Lodowick Bryskett's
Civil Life (1606, 'The heart, wherein all
the vitall spirits are forged, and receiue
their strength', and Bacon's *Sylva*
(1626) §30, 'As for liuing creatures it
is certaine, their Vital Spiritts are a
Substaunce Compounded of an Airy
and Flamy Matter.'

45 **Danae** In Greek mythology Danae was
the daughter of King Acrisius of Argos.
Learning from an oracle that her child
would kill him, Acrisius shut her in a
tower, but Zeus came to her in a golden
shower and she became the mother
of Perseus. In Heywood's *Golden Age*
(1611) Homer recounts: 'of *Danae* that
bright lasse, / How amorous *Ioue* first
wrought her to his power, / How shee
was closed in a fort of brasse, / And how
he skal'd it in a golden showre' (G3ᵛ).

49 **silver** small change

50 **play . . . pages** gamble with the boys,
with pederastic overtones

50–1 **You . . . time** I'm sorry that just
at this moment I have no change; also
implying Pharamond's unsuccessful
'taking' of her.

39 conger] and Conger *Q1*   40 all] *om. Q1*   spirits] anymales *Q1*   41 while] time *Q1*   43 SP] *Q1;*
Phi. Q2   SD] *Dyce, after 45* gold   43–7] *Q1 lines* well, / appetite. / gold, / then – /   45 a Danae]
daintie *Q1*   in] with *Q1*   46 SD] *Dyce, after 47* than –   48–9 SD] *Dyce, after 53* you.   49 you would]
you'd *Q1*   50 for it] fort *Q1*

me in a worse time, but if you have present use, my
lord, I'll send my man with silver, and keep your gold
for you.

PHARAMOND   Lady, lady!

GALLATEA   She's coming, sir, behind, will take white   55
money. [*aside*] Yet for all this I'll match ye.

Exit Gallatea behind the hangings.

PHARAMOND   If there be but two such more in this
kingdom and near the court, we may even hang up our
harps! Ten such camphor constitutions as this would
call the golden age again in question and teach the old   60
way for every ill-faced husband to get his own children.
And what a mischief that will breed, let all consider.

Enter MEGRA.

51 **have present use** need it now
55–6 **take . . . money** accept silver; can
be bought
56 SD *behind the hangings* Hangings, or
'arras' in Q1, are tapestries hung on
castle walls, often at a sufficient distance
'to allow of people being concealed in
the space between' (*OED*). Cf. *MW*,
3.3.82–3, 'She shall not see me; I will
ensconce me behind the arras', and
Woman Hater, 1.3. 50–1, where the
count admonishes his sister, 'if you
stay in the presence till candlelight,
keep on the foreside oth' Curtaine'. On
stage the *hangings* covered the central
opening in the tiring-house wall.
58–9 **hang . . . harps** To *hang up* may
mean 'to put aside in disuse; to give up
using' (*OED* hang *v*. 29b); apparently
by *our harps* Pharamond means,
metaphorically, his songs of wooing.
59 **camphor** 'A whitish translucent
crystalline volatile substance, belonging

chemically to the vegetable oils, and
having a bitter aromatic taste and a
strong characteristic smell' (*OED n.*1).
Camphor is traditionally cold: *OED*
cites Dryden, *Spanish Friar*, 'Prescribe
her an Ounce of Camphire every
Morning . . . to abate Incontinency.'
60 **golden age** The traditional *golden
age* is described by Fulke Greville
in *Caelica*, Sonnet 43: 'The *Golden-
Age* was when the world was yong,
/ Nature so rich, as Earth did need
no sowing, / Malice not knowne, the
Serpents had not stung, / Wit was
but sweet Affections ouerflowing. /
Desire was free, and Beauties first-
begotten; / Beauty then neither
net, nor made by art, / Words out
of thoughts brought forth, and not
forgotten, / The Lawes were inward
that did rule the heart.' Pharamond,
however, considers it primarily a time
of sexual licence.

51 time] time sir *Q1*   52 gold] gold safe *Q1*   55–6] *Q1 lines* behind, / this / will . . . ye] Will ye
take white money yet for all this. *Q1*   56 SD1] *Dyce after* ye.   match] watch *Settle*   SD2] *She slips
behind the Orras. after 53 Q1*   57–8 more in this kingdom] in this Kingdome more *Q1*   58 even]
ene *Q1*   59 camphor] *Q1 (*Campher*); Champhier Q2*   61 ill-faced] *(*ill fac't*); ill fast Q1*   62 will]
would *Q1*

Here's another; if she be of the same last, the devil shall
pluck her on. – Many fair mornings, lady.

MEGRA

As many mornings bring as many days   65
Fair, sweet and hopeful to your grace.

PHARAMOND [*aside*]

She gives good words yet. Sure this wench is free. –
If your more serious business do not call you,
Let me hold quarter with you. We'll talk an hour
Out quickly.

MEGRA   What would your grace talk of?   70

PHARAMOND

Of some such pretty subject as yourself.
I'll go no further than your eye or lip;
There's theme enough for one man for an age.

MEGRA

Sir, they stand right, and my lips are yet even,
Smooth, young enough, ripe enough and red enough,   75
Or my glass wrongs me.

PHARAMOND

Oh, they are two twinned cherries dyed in blushes,
Which those fair suns above, with their bright beams,
Reflect upon and ripen. Sweetest beauty,
Bow down those branches, that the longing taste   80
Of the faint looker-on may meet those blessings
And taste and live.   [*They kiss.*]

---

63 **of . . . last** made in the same mould
67 **free** sexually available
69 **hold quarter with** 'To remain beside'
    (*OED n.* 16, citing this line)
77 **twinned cherries** a standard image
    in a conventional poetic catalogue or

blazon of a woman's beauty and virtues;
cf. *TNK*, 1.1.177–9, 'Oh, when / Her
twinning cherries shall their sweetness
fall / Upon thy taste-full lips'.
80 **those branches** again Megra's lips, the
    cherries now being full trees

67 SD] *Dyce after* free   68 you] you Lady *Q1*   69 talk] take *Q2u*   70 Out] Ont *Q1*   71–3] *Q1 lines*
selfe, / enough / Age. /   72 or] your *Q1*   73 theme] time *Q1*   74–5] *Q1 lines* smooth, / red enough,
/ even, /   Smooth] euen smooth *Q1*   75 and] *om. F2*   77 blushes] blush *Q1*   78 bright] deepe
Q1   81 faint] sweete *Q1*   those] these *Q1*   82 SD] *Q1; not in Q2*

MEGRA   O delicate sweet prince,
She that hath snow enough about her heart
To take the wanton spring of ten such lines off
May be a nun without probation. Sir,   85
You have in such neat poetry gathered a kiss
That if I had but five lines of that number,
Such pretty begging blanks, I should commend
Your forehead or your cheeks and kiss you too.

PHARAMOND
Do it in prose; you cannot miss it, madam.   90

MEGRA   I shall, I shall.

PHARAMOND   By my life, you shall not. I'll prompt you
first. [*Kisses her.*] Can you do it now?

MEGRA   Methinks 'tis easy now I ha' done't before. But
yet I should stick at it.   95

PHARAMOND   Stick till tomorrow. I'll ne'er part you,
sweetest. But we lose time. Can you love me?

MEGRA   Love you, my lord? How would you have me love
you?

PHARAMOND   I'll teach you in a short sentence, cause I   100

85 **May . . . probation** requires no further test of her chastity. Q1's 'bee a number without Probatum' suggests both mishearing and misunderstanding. 'Probatum', from the Latin phrase '*probatum est*', it has been proved or tested, means a demonstrated conclusion, a proof.

88 **begging blanks** lines of blank verse requesting a kiss; for this usage *OED* 8 cites Greene, *Menaphon*, 'Lest . . . they bewaile in weeping blankes the wane of their Monarchie'.

90 **Do . . . prose** The scene becomes less

formal and more intimate as the sexual tension rises.

94 **Methinks . . . before** Now that I have done it once, the second time is easy. Q2's comma after 'easie' may belong after 'now', in which case Megra actually admits her sexual experience. Q1's 'you ha' don't before me' avoids this possibility.

95–6 **stick at . . . Stick** scruple at (*OED* v.¹ IV.24); remain fast

96 **part you** part with you; separate you from your intention

82–9 O . . . too] *prose Q1*   84 off] *om. Q1*   85–6] *Colman; Q2 lines* probation. / kisse, /; *prose Q1*   85 May . . . probation] it may bee a number without Probatum *Q1*   86 in] by *Q1*   90 you] *Q1;* yon *Q2*   92 life] life but *Q1*   93–7] *Gurr; Q2 lines* not: / now? / before: / it. / morrow, / time; / me? / 93 SD] *Weber*   94 easy] *(*easie,*)*   I] you *Q1*   before] before me *Q1*   But] and *Q1*   95 I should] should I *Daniel*   99 you] ye *Q1*   100–2] *Q1 lines* sentence, / memory, / me. /

will not load your memory. This is all: love me and lie
with me.

MEGRA   Was it lie with you that you said? 'Tis
impossible.

PHARAMOND   Not to a willing mind that will endeavour.   105
If I do not teach you to do it as easily in one night as
you'll go to bed, I'll lose my royal blood for't.

MEGRA   Why, prince, you have a lady of your own that yet
wants teaching.

PHARAMOND   I'll sooner teach a mare the old measures   110
than teach her anything belonging to the function.
She's afraid to lie with herself if she have but any
masculine imaginations about her. I know when we are
married I must ravish her.

MEGRA   By mine honour, that's a foul fault indeed, but   115
time and your good help will wear it out, sir.

PHARAMOND   And for any other I see, excepting your
dear self, dearest lady, I had rather be Sir Tim the
schoolmaster and leap a dairy maid.

MEGRA   Has your grace seen the court star, Gallatea?   120

PHARAMOND   Out upon her! She's as cold of her favour as
an apoplex. She sailed by but now.

MEGRA   And how do you hold her wit, sir?

110] **the old measures** a stately dance,
here treated as old-fashioned

112–14 **She's . . . her** This description
of Arethusa as afraid even to think
about sex echoes the King's view at
1.1.97–111. It is contradicted by her
behaviour with Philaster, for example
her invitation, 'Let us leave and kiss'
(1.2.104), which stimulates his fear of
her sexual forwardness.

114 **ravish** rape, force

118 **Sir Tim** apparently a conventional
name for a country schoolmaster. In
Chaste Maid the foolish city heir Tim
returns from Cambridge with his
equally foolish Tutor.

119 **leap** attack sexually

122 **apoplex** apoplexy, stroke

123–4 **hold** Megra means 'esteem';
Pharamond takes the verb literally.

105–7] *Q1 lines* endeauour, / night, / for't. /   108–9] *Dyce lines* own / teaching. /   110–14] *Q1
lines* measures, / function, / selfe, / about her, / rauish her. /   112 any] my *Q1*   113 imaginations]
imagination *Q1*   115–16] *Q1 lines* indeed, / sir. /   115 mine] my *Q1*   117 any] my *Q1*   118 Tim the]
Timen a *Q1*   119 leap] keepe *Q1*   maid.] *Q1;* maid. Madam *Q2*   123 And] om. *Q1*   sir] om. *Q1*

PHARAMOND I hold her wit? The strength of all the
guard cannot hold it. If they were tied to it she would   125
blow 'em out of the kingdom. They talk of Jupiter!
He's but a squib cracker to her. Look well about you
and you may find a tongue bolt. But speak, sweet lady,
shall I be freely welcome?

MEGRA Whither?   130

PHARAMOND To your bed. If you mistrust my faith you
do me the unnoblest wrong.

MEGRA I dare not, prince, I dare not.

PHARAMOND Make your own conditions: my purse shall
seal 'em, and what you dare imagine you can want I'll   135
furnish you withal. Give two hours to your thoughts
every morning about it. Come, I know you are bashful:
speak in my ear. Will you be mine? [*Gives money*.]
Keep this and with it, me. Soon I will visit you.

MEGRA My lord, my chamber's most unsafe, but when   140
'tis night I'll find some means to slip into your lodging.
Till when –

PHARAMOND Till when, this [*kissing her*] and my heart
go with thee.   *Exeunt.*

---

126 **Jupiter** king of the Greek gods
127 **squib cracker** a setter-off of firecrackers
128 **tongue bolt** a fastener to silence her; the sentence is obscure, and is omitted in Q1.
138 SD Weber has Pharamond give Megra a ring, but Pharamond has earlier offered Gallatea gold (43–51) and promises to meet Megra's conditions with his *purse* (134). When, as in *AW*, a ring is used to seal a sexual arrangement, it is mentioned explicitly.

140 **my . . . unsafe** In a royal lodging there would be very little privacy for anyone other than the King and perhaps the princess. 'The great houses of the fifteenth and sixteenth centuries had been constructed of interlocking suites of rooms without corridors, so that the only way of moving about was by passing through other people's chambers' (Stone, 169). Waiting women and courtiers slept in corridors and rooms adjoining those of their superiors.

124–9] *Q1 lines* guard / toot: / *Iubiter,* / Lady, / welcome? /   125 to it] toot *Q1*   127–8 Look . . . bolt] *om. Q1*   132 unnoblest] most vnnoblest *Q1*   133 ²I dare not] *om. Q1*   136 two . . . your] worship to you *Q1*   137 you are] y'are *Q1*   138 SD] *Thorndike; Gives her a ring.* | *Weber*   139 will] shall *Q1*   140 unsafe] vncertaine *Q1*   143 this] *Dyce;* this, *Q2*   SD] *this edn*   144 SD1] *Exit ambo. Q1; Ex. seueral waies Q4*

Enter GALLATEA *from behind the hangings.*

GALLATEA   Oh, thou pernicious petticoat prince, are   145
these your virtues? Well, if I do not lay a train to blow
your sport up, I am no woman. And, Lady Towsabell,
I'll fit you for't.   *Exit.*

[2.3]   *Enter* ARETHUSA *and* [*her* GENTLEWOMAN].

ARETHUSA   Where's the boy?
GENTLEWOMAN   Within, madam.
ARETHUSA   Gave you him gold to buy him clothes?
GENTLEWOMAN   I did.
ARETHUSA   And has he done't?   5
GENTLEWOMAN   Yes, madam.
ARETHUSA   'Tis a pretty, sad-talking boy, is it not?
Asked you his name?
GENTLEWOMAN   No, madam.

Enter GALLATEA.

ARETHUSA
Oh, you are welcome. What good news?   10

---

145 **petticoat prince** regal woman-
chaser
146 **lay a train** set a trap
147 **Towsabell** Q1 alters to Dowsabell, a
more conventional name for a forward
woman, but Turner points out that
'Gallatea is punning on "Dowsabell"
and "tousle"' (488). Cf. Dromio in *CE*,
4.1.111, 'Where Dowsabel did claim me
for her husband'.
2.3 Location: Arethusa's chamber
0 SD *her* GENTLEWOMAN In Q2 both

here and in 1.2 Arethusa enters with
an unidentified 'Lady' rather than 'her
gentlewoman'. The more consistent
identity in Q1 probably reflects stage
practice limiting the number of small
parts for boys.
1–9, 13–15 These lines, especially 3 and
4, could be combined into verse, but
as they are 'squints' permitting various
arrangements they are here presented
as in Q2.
7 **sad-talking** melancholy

144 SD2 *hangings*] *Orras Q1*   147 Towsabell] *Dowsabell Q1*   148 for't] *for it Q1*   SD] *(Exit
Gall.)*   2.3] *Weber*   0 SD *her* GENTLEWOMAN] *Q1; a Lady Q2*   1–9] *Langbaine lines* Madam, /
Cloaths? / don't? / Madam. / not? / Madam. /   2+ SP] *La. Q2*   2 madam] *om. Q1*   7–8] *one line
Q1*   7 is it] *i'st Q1*   9 SD] *opp.* 6 Madam *Q1*

GALLATEA

As good as any one can tell your grace
That says she has done that you would have wished.

ARETHUSA Hast thou discovered?

GALLATEA I have strained a point of modesty for you.

ARETHUSA I prithee, how? 15

GALLATEA In listening after bawdry. I see, let a lady live
never so modestly, she shall be sure to find a lawful time
to hearken after bawdry. Your prince, brave Pharamond,
was so hot on't.

ARETHUSA With whom? 20

GALLATEA Why, with the lady I suspected; I can tell the
time and place.

ARETHUSA Oh, when and where?

GALLATEA Tonight, his lodging.

ARETHUSA

Run thyself into the presence; mingle there again 25
With other ladies. Leave the rest to me. *[Exit Gallatea.]*
If destiny, to whom we dare not say
Why thou didst this, have not decreed it so
In lasting leaves – whose smallest characters
Was never altered – yet this match shall break. 30

13 **discovered** discovered anything, found the information I sent you for
16 **listening after** eavesdropping on, searching for
25 **the presence** the presence chamber, the reception room at court in which the sovereign gave audience. Unlike the privy chambers, those who might *mingle* there were of varying kinds. The Count in *Woman Hater* warns his sister, 'if you stay in the presence till candlelight . . . take heed of the old Bawd, in the cloth of Tissue-sleeves, and the knit Mittins' (1.3.50–2).
28 **thou didst** Langbaine's inversion (see t.n.) is attractive but unnecessary.
29 **lasting leaves . . . characters** Arethusa imagines Destiny's decree written in *characters* or letters on durable *leaves* or pages, as if engraved on metal.
30 **altered – yet** Dyce's reading, 'alter'd yet', suggests that Destiny's decrees could be altered in the future. In Q2's punctuation Arethusa emphasizes that despite Pharamond's arrival and the King's promise of his daughter, the match will be broken off unless it has been decreed by Destiny.

14–22] *Dyce lines* point / you. / how? / lady / find / bawdry. / on't! / whom? / suspected: / place. / 17 she] they *Q1* 25–31] *prose Q1* 26 SD] *Dyce* 28 thou didst] didst thou *Langbaine* 30 Was] Were *F2* altered – yet] ((atlterd:) yet,); altred, yet *Q1;* alter'd yet), *Dyce*

Where's the boy?

Enter BELLARIO.

GENTLEWOMAN   Here, madam.

ARETHUSA

Sir, you are sad to change your service. Is't not so?

BELLARIO

Madam, I have not changed: I wait on you

To do him service.

ARETHUSA   Thou disclaim'st in me.

Tell me thy name.

BELLARIO   Bellario.

ARETHUSA   Thou canst sing and play?   35

BELLARIO

If grief will give me leave, madam, I can.

ARETHUSA

Alas, what kind of grief can thy years know?

Hadst thou a curst master when thou went'st to school?

Thou art not capable of other grief;

Thy brows and cheeks are smooth as waters be   40

When no breath troubles them. Believe me, boy,

Care seeks out wrinkled brows and hollow eyes

---

32 **change your service** have a new master or mistress

34 **disclaim'st in me** Dyce thought this meant simply 'disclaimest me', but Daniel comments, 'the Princess, however, does not here intimate that Bellario disclaims or renounces her, but only that he disclaims or repudiates any inherent right in her to his service; he waits on her not as her servant but as servant to his lord'.

38 **curst** disagreeable, irritable

40–1 **Thy . . . them** Cf. *TN*, 1.4.30–4, 'For they shall yet belie thy happy years / That say thou art a man. Diana's lip / Is not more smooth and rubious. Thy small pipe / Is as the maiden's organ, shrill and sound, / And all is semblative a woman's part.'

42–3 'The caue where horride care doth dwell' (Lodge, *A Marguerite for America*, 1596, f4[r]) reappears in Greene's *Mamillia* and Marlowe's *Edward II*, 5.1. In *FQ*, 4.5, Care is

31 SD BELLARIO] *Boy Q1*; Bellario, *richly dressed* | *Dyce*   32 you are] your *Q1*   33–4 Madam . . . service] *one line Q1*   34 Thou disclaim'st] Then trust *Q1*   35] *Boas; Q2 lines* name. / Bellario. / play. /   38 curst master] crosse schoole-maister *Q1*   40 waters] water *Q1*   42 out] *om. Q1*

And builds himself caves to abide in them.
Come, sir, tell me truly: doth your lord love me?

BELLARIO
Love, madam? I know not what it is.   45

ARETHUSA
Canst thou know grief and never yet knewest love?
Thou art deceived, boy. Does he speak of me
As if he wished me well?

BELLARIO   If it be love
To forget all respect to his own friends
With thinking of your face; if it be love   50
To sit cross-armed and think away the day,
Mingled with starts, crying your name as loud
And hastily as men i'the streets do 'Fire!';
If it be love to weep himself away
When he but hears of any lady dead   55
Or killed, because it might have been your chance;
If when he goes to rest, which will not be,
'Twixt every prayer he says to name you once
As others drop a bead, be to be in love:
Then, madam, I dare swear he loves you.   60

ARETHUSA
Oh, you're a cunning boy and taught to lie

---

a blacksmith with 'hollow eyes and
rawbone cheekes'; his cottage 'placed
was, / There where the mouldred earth
had cav'd the banke'.

48–60 The rhythm and structure of
Bellario's speech parallels Innogen's
response to Pisanio: 'False to his bed?
What is it to be false? / To lie in
watch there, and to think on him? / To
weep 'twixt clock and clock? If sleep

charge Nature, / To break it with a
fearful dream of him, / And cry myself
awake? That's false to's bed, is it?'
(*Cym*, 3.4.40–4).

51 **cross-armed** the conventional
position of the lover; *OED* cites
Lady Mary Wroth, *Urania*, 'Then
I . . . walked cross armed, sighed, cast
vp mine eyes.'

59 **drop a bead** as in saying a rosary

---

43 himself] it selfe *Q1*   45 Love . . . not] I know not Madame *Q1*   48–60 If . . . you] *prose Q1*
52 Mingled with] with mingling *Q1*   crying] and crying *Q1*   53 And hastily] om. *Q1*   i'the] in
Q1   55 lady] woman *Q1*   59 a bead] *Q2c;* a beard *Q2u;* beades *Q1*   60 you] yee *Q1*   61–6] *Q1 lines*
credit, / sound, / sayes / too, / away. /   61–2 lie / For] *om. Q1*

159

For your lord's credit; but thou knowest a lie
That bears this sound is welcomer to me
Than any truth that says he loves me not.
Lead the way, boy. [*to Gentlewoman*] Do you attend me,
   too. –   65
'Tis thy lord's business hastes me thus. Away!   *Exeunt.*

[**2.4**]   *Enter* DION, CLEREMONT, THRASILINE, MEGRA
                   [*and*] GALLATEA.

DION

Come, ladies, shall we talk a round? As men
Do walk a mile, women should talk an hour
After supper. 'Tis their exercise.

GALLATEA

'Tis late.

MEGRA

'Tis all   5
My eyes will do to lead me to my bed.

GALLATEA [*aside*]

I fear they are so heavy you'll scarce find
The way to your own lodging with 'em tonight.

2.4 Location: This scene begins in a
presence room of the palace, but by
78 has moved in front of Pharamond's
lodging, which is imagined as being on
the upper storey and accessible by a
front and *back door*. The front door
where the courtiers *press to come in*
(93 SD) would have been represented
by one of the stage entrances. The
above where first Pharamond and then
Megra appear may have been the stage
balcony or a window.
0 SD Q1 brings on '*another Lady*',
probably in recollection of the entrance
of the three ladies in 1.1. She has no
lines and is superfluous here.
1 **talk a round** Dion puns on the
more usual use of 'round', 'A turn,
a walk or drive, round a place or to
a series of places, for the purpose of
recreation, sight-seeing, purchasing,
etc.; esp. in phr. *to make, go, take a
round*' (*OED* round *n*.[1] 16a, citing
this line).
3 **'Tis their exercise** Attacks on women
for excessive talking are pervasive in
the literature of the early modern
period.

65 SD] *Spencer subst.* 66 thus. Away!] *(*thus: Away.*);* thus away. *Q1* **2.4**] *Weber* 0 SD] *Enter the
three Gentlewomen,* MEGRA, GALLATEA, *and another Lady. Q1* 0.2 *and*] *F* 1 SP] TRA. *Q1* 1–3] *prose
Q1* 5–6] *one line Q1* 7 SD] *Spencer* 7 they are] theyre *Q1* you'll] *Q1;* theile *Q2*

Enter PHARAMOND.

THRASILINE

The prince.

PHARAMOND

Not abed, ladies? You're good sitters-up!   10
What think you of a pleasant dream to last
Till morning?

MEGRA

I should choose, my lord, a pleasing wake before it.

Enter ARETHUSA *and* BELLARIO.

ARETHUSA

'Tis well, my lord: you're courting of these ladies.
Is't not late, gentlemen?

CLEREMONT   Yes, madam.

ARETHUSA [*to Bellario*]   Wait you there.   *Exit.*

MEGRA

She's jealous, as I live! Look you, my lord,   16
The princess has a Hylas, an Adonis.

---

8 SD Q1 has Pharamont enter with '*the Princesse boy, and a woman*'. As Q1 has no later direction for the entrance of Arethusa, possibly '*the Princesse boy*' means the Princess *and* the boy, though it may mean 'the Princess's boy', with a later entrance for Arethusa intended but omitted. The direction suggests that in performance Arethusa was regularly accompanied by her 'gentlewoman'. But even if Q1 reflects performance it has passed through a memorial stage and is untrustworthy, as seen in the inadequate entrances.

17 **Hylas . . . Adonis** types of youthful male beauty. Hylas, beloved of Hercules, was said to have been ravished away by nymphs during the expedition of the Argonauts because of his beauty. Venus' description of Adonis (*VA*, Stanza 2) is appropriately androgynous: '"Thrice fairer than myself," thus she began, / "The field's chief flower, sweet above compare, / Stain to all nymphs, more lovely than a man, / More white and red than doves or roses are; / Nature that made thee, with herself at strife, / Saith that the world hath ending with thy life."'

8 SD] *Enter* PHARAMONT, *the Princesse boy, and a woman. Q1*   11 pleasant] pleaing *Q1*   13 SP] GAL. *Q1*   should] shall *Q1*   SD] *om. Q1*   14+ SP] PRIN. *Q1*   14 my lord] *om. Q1*   15] *Boas; Q2 lines* Gentlemen? / Madam. / there. /; *Q6 lines* Madam. / there. /   SP1] GAL. *Q1*   SD1] *Gurr* SD2] *(Exit* Arethusa.*); Exit Princesse. Q1*   16 you] *om. Q1* 17 has] *om. Q1*

PHARAMOND

His form is angel-like.

MEGRA

Why, this is he that must, when you are wed,

Sit by your pillow like young Apollo, with   20

His hand and voice binding your thoughts in sleep.

The princess does provide him for you and for herself.

PHARAMOND

I find no music in these boys.

MEGRA   Nor I.

They can do little, and that small they do

They have not wit to hide.

DION   Serves he the princess?   25

THRASILINE

Yes.

DION   'Tis a sweet boy. How brave she keeps him!

PHARAMOND

Ladies, all good rest. I mean to kill a buck

Tomorrow morning ere you've done your dreams.

MEGRA

All happiness attend your grace.   [*Exit Pharamond.*]

Gentlemen, good rest.

Come, shall we to bed?

GALLATEA   Yes, all good night.   30

---

19 *The line in Q2 is short a syllable that
  can be made up in the pauses, but
  Dyce's emendation (see t.n.), which
  combines Q1 and Q2, is convincing.
20–1 **Apollo . . . voice** Apollo, son of Leto
  and Zeus, was the Greek god of healing
  and music.
22 **provide . . . herself** Megra implies
  the boy will serve both sexually; see
  Masten on the androgynous attraction

of boys.
23 **music** charm
24 **can do little** are not very useful; are
  not sexually proficient
26 **brave** richly dressed
27 **Ladies, all good rest** Editors often
  follow Colman and have Pharamond
  address the assembly as 'Ladies all',
  but Q2's 'all good rest' is echoed at 30,
  'all good night'.

19–22] *Q1 lines* by / hand / Princesse / selfe. /   19 he that] *Dyce;* he *Q2;* that *Q1*   are] once are
Theobald   25 hide] hide it *Q1*   27 Ladies, all] *(*Ladyes all*);* Ladies all, *Colman*   28 you've] you haue
Q1   29 SD] *Dyce; after* dreams *28 Theobald; not in Q2*   30 Come] *om. Q1*

162

DION

    May your dreams be true to you.

                    Exeunt Gallatea [and] Megra.

    What shall we do, gallants? 'Tis late. The King

    Is up still: see, he comes, a guard along

    With him.

            Enter KING, ARETHUSA *and Guard.*

KING   Look your intelligence be true.

ARETHUSA

    Upon my life it is, and I do hope   35

    Your highness will not tie me to a man

    That in the heat of wooing throws me off

    And takes another.

DION   What should this mean?

KING   If it be true,

    That lady had been better have embraced

    Cureless diseases. Get you to your rest;   40

---

31 SD Presumably the ladies exit only after Dion salutes them, and hence the stage direction must be moved from the Q2 placement. See t.n.

34 SD *Guard* The term may be singular (*OED n.* 7) or plural (*OED n.* 9). The number of guards is never specified, and the blocking will vary accordingly. The number was probably determined by the resources the company could spare. Two was usual (see Bradley), and the King's threat that the guard 'see that none pass, upon your lives' (77) suggests this was the minimum. At least one must go to Pharamond's *back door* (76) and one must escort him out at 123.

34 **intelligence** information

39 **had ... have** To support a claim that this verb form was 'common', Daniel cites *Oth*, 3.3.365, 'Thou hadst been better have been born a dog.'

40 **Cureless diseases** presumably the pox, a risk Arethusa would run if she *embraced* (39) the promiscuous Pharamond. The situation resembles that in *Per*, 'The potential polluter of a beautiful young woman is a luxurious gentleman who abuses the privileges his nobility favours him with. Through marriage, an innocent young woman will be placed at his disposal by the very person who should most seek to protect her – her father' (Healy, 100–1). A diseased son-in-law would endanger not only Arethusa but also the King's future heirs and thus the country.

---

31 SD] *Dyce; opp. 30 Q2; om. Q1 and*] F   34 SD] *after* late *32 Q1 Guard*] *a guard Q1;* Guards *Dyce*   38] *Boas; Q2 lines* another. / meane? / true, /; *Q5 lines* meane? / true, /   39 have] *om. Q1*

You shall be righted.   *Exeunt Arethusa and Bellario.*
                              Gentlemen, draw near;
We shall employ you. Is young Pharamond
Come to his lodging?
DION   I saw him enter there.
KING
    Haste some of you and cunningly discover
    If Megra be in her lodging.   [*Exit Dion.*]
CLEREMONT   Sir,   45
    She parted hence but now with other ladies.
KING
    If she be there, we shall not need to make
    A vain discovery of our suspicion.
    [*aside*] You gods, I see that who unrighteously
    Holds wealth or state from others shall be cursed   50
    In that which meaner men are blessed withal.
    Ages to come shall know no male of him
    Left to inherit, and his name shall be
    Blotted from earth. If he have any child
    It shall be crossly matched: the gods themselves   55
    Shall sow wild strife betwixt her lord and her.
    Yet, if it be your wills, forgive the sin
    I have committed: let it not fall
    Upon this undeserving child of mine;

47–62 This speech is modelled on Claudius's in *Ham*, 3.3.36–72, in particular: 'But O, what form of prayer / Can serve my turn: "Forgive me my foul murder"? / That cannot be, since I am still possessed / Of those effects for which I did the murder, / My crown, mine own ambition, and my Queen.' There are also echoes of Lear's curse on Goneril, 1.4.267–81.

47–8 It is possible that these lines, like the rest of the speech, are spoken aside.

52–3 **Ages . . . inherit** The problem of the female heir is one cause of the political discomfort with Arethusa's foreign marriage; the issue is implicit in *Cym* and *KL* and had its background in the debates over the marriage of Mary Tudor to Philip of Spain and the marriages proposed for Elizabeth I.

59 *****undeserving** This word's opposing meanings lead to confusion. The King

---

41 SD] *Dyce; opp.* rest *40 Q2; om. Q1; Exeunt* Arethusa, Bellario *and* Lady. *Turner*   42 you] ye *Q1*   45 SD] *Q1 (Exit.* LEON.*); not in Q2*   SP] LEON *Q1*   49 SD] *Weber, after* unrighteously; *after* wrong *62 Dyce*   54 earth] the earth *Q1*   59 undeserving] *Q1;* vnderstanding *Q2*   of mine] *om. Q1*

She has not broke your laws. But how can I   60
Look to be heard of gods that must be just,
Praying upon the ground I hold by wrong?

Enter DION.

DION   Sir, I have asked, and her women swear she is
within, but they, I think, are bawds. I told 'em I must
speak with her; they laughed and said their lady lay   65
speechless. I said my business was important; they
said their lady was about it. I grew hot and cried my
business was a matter that concerned life and death;
they answered so was sleeping, at which their lady was.
I urged again, she had scarce time to be so since last I   70
saw her; they smiled again and seemed to instruct me
that sleeping was nothing but lying down and winking.
Answers more direct I could not get. In short, sir, I
think she is not there.

KING

'Tis then no time to dally. You o'the guard,   75
Wait at the back door of the prince's lodging
And see that none pass thence, upon your lives.
                                    [*Exeunt some of the Guard.*]

considers Arethusa, as in *OED ppl.a.*
2, 'Not deserving (harsh treatment,
etc.); guiltless, innocent'. But the
word's first meaning is 'Not deserving
(something good); lacking desert or
merit; unworthy', which may explain
why Q2 has the more complimentary
'understanding'. However, the King is
focused here on Arethusa's innocence
rather than her intelligence, so
'undeserving' was probably the original,
with the change made at a later point.
Turner argues that 'understanding' 'in
the sense of standing under (*OED v.* 9)
is justified by the idea of the King's sin

falling upon the next generation' and
by 'the principle of the harder reading'
(488), but Gurr rightly objects that this
sense was rarely used except punningly,
as in the Prologue to *Pestle*.
63–74 Dion's speech is full of sexual
suggestion and double entendres
(*bawds, lay speechless, business, about it,
nothing but lying down*).
63 **her women** Megra is an important
court lady; see 130, *lady of honour*. Like
the princess she has waiting women or
servants.
75, 77 SD **You o'the guard** . . . *some of
the Guard* See 34 SDn.

60 She] if she *Q1*   can] could *Q1*   62 by] in *Q1*   73 get] get from them *Q1*   73–4 I think she is] shee's
Q1   77 SD] *Dyce subst.* (*Exeunt* Guards.*)*

Knock, gentlemen, knock loud. Louder yet.
What, has their pleasure taken off their hearing?
I'll break your meditations! Knock again.   80
Not yet? I do not think he sleeps, having his
Larum by him. Once more.   [*Calls.*]
                                   Pharamond! Prince!   [*They knock.*]

[*Enter*] PHARAMOND *above.*

PHARAMOND

What saucy groom knocks at this dead of night?
Where be our waiters? By my vexed soul,
He meets his death that meets me, for this boldness.   85
KING

Prince, you wrong your thoughts; we are your friends.
Come down.
PHARAMOND   The King?
KING   The same, sir. Come down:
We have cause of present counsel with you.

[*Enter*] PHARAMOND *below.*

PHARAMOND

If your grace please to use me, I'll attend you

---

78 **Knock . . . loud** At this point the
scene has moved to directly outside the
prince's lodging.
80 **your meditations** Turner emends to
'their' meditations to parallel 79, *their
hearing*, but the King is agitated and
alternately addresses the gentlemen with
him and Pharamond and Megra within.
82 **Larum** 'An apparatus attached to a
clock or watch' (*OED n.* 2) for purposes

of being awoken, here metaphorical
84 **waiters** members 'of the retinue or
household of a royal or noble person-
age', often of high rank (*OED* 6a)
vexed vexèd
85 **He . . . me** I will kill whomever I
encounter.
88 SD Pharamond exits above, or
withdraws his head from a window, and
then emerges onto the main stage.

---

78 Louder yet] *om. Q1*   79 their . . . their] your . . . your *Q1*   80 your] their *Turner*   meditations] meditation *Q1*   again.] againe, and lowder, *Q1*   81 his] such *Q1*; this *Q3*   82 Larum] larumes *Q1*   Prince]
om. Q1   SD1] *this edn*   SD2] *Q1; not in Q2*   SD3 Enter] *Q1; not in Q2*; Pharamond *appears at a window.*
| *Dyce*   86 Prince] Prince, Prince, *Q1*   87 The same, sir. Come down:] The same sir. Come downe sir *Q1;*
The same. Come down, sir *Daniel*   88 SD] *Dyce*; Pha. *below. opp.* chamber *90 Q2; om. Q1*

To your chamber.   90

KING

No, 'tis too late, prince: I'll make bold with yours.

PHARAMOND

I have some private reasons to myself

Makes me unmannerly and say you cannot.

[*They press to come in.*]

Nay, press not forward, gentlemen. He must come

Through my life that comes here.   95

KING

Sir, be resolved. I must and will come. Enter!

PHARAMOND

I will not be dishonoured thus.

He that enters, enters upon his death.

Sir, 'tis a sign you make no stranger of me,

To bring these renegadoes to my chamber   100

At these unseasoned hours.

KING   Why do you

Chafe yourself so? You are not wronged, nor shall be.

Only I'll search your lodging for some cause

To ourself known. Enter, I say.

PHARAMOND   I say no.

---

96 **Enter** Q4 makes this a stage direction (see t.n.). It is not entirely clear who does attempt to enter; at 94 Pharamond urges the *gentlemen* not to press forward, but the King may be directing either gentlemen or guards.

100 **renegadoes** The word is an insult whether it refers to the gentlemen of the court or to the King's guard. *OED* cites only this line for *renegado* as 'a vague term of abuse'; usually the word indicated one who had changed sides or religions. *OED* also cites Hakluyt,

'he was a Renegado, which is one that first was a Christian, and afterwards becommeth a Turke' (*Voyages*, 2.1.186). In Massinger's *Renegado* (*c.* 1624) the title character, Grimaldi, is a Venetian who is serving the Turk.

101 **unseasoned** unseasonable; late

104 SD–129 SD Like Pharamond, Megra is first seen above, then exits within and re-enters on the main stage. It is unclear who, if anyone, enters the chamber. Q2's direction, '*Enter with* Megra' (129 SD), suggests she appears accompanied

92 some] certaine *Q1*   myself] my selfe sir *Q1*   93 SD] *Q1 opp. 92–3; not in Q2*   94 gentlemen] *om. Q1*   96 must] must come *Q1*   come. Enter!] *(come: Enter);* come Enter *Q1;* come: *with* Enter *as SD opp. 95 Q4*   97 thus] *Q1; not in Q2*   100 renegadoes] runagates *Q1*   102 so] *om. Q1*   103 I'll] *om. Q1*   104 known] *om. Q1*   ²say] so *Q1*   SD] *om. Q1; Enter*] Dyce subst. (MEGRA *appears at a window.*)

[Enter] MEGRA *above.*

MEGRA

Let 'em enter, prince, let 'em enter;   105
I am up and ready. I know their business:
'Tis the poor breaking of a lady's honour
They hunt so hotly after. Let 'em enjoy it.
You have your business, gentlemen: I lay here.
O my lord the King, this is not noble in you,   110
To make public the weakness of a woman.

KING

Come down.

MEGRA

I dare, my lord. Your hootings and your clamours,
Your private whispers and your broad fleerings
Can no more vex my soul than this base carriage.   115
But I have vengeance yet in store for some
Shall in the most contempt you can have of me
Be joy and nourishment.

KING   Will you come down?

MEGRA

Yes, to laugh at your worst, but I shall wring you

---

by gentlemen or a guard. Cleremont and Dion speak while she is within, so the only named gentleman available is Thrasiline. Thus the reference is probably to one or more guards. If so, the guard, possibly accompanied by Thrasiline, may enter the chamber either at the King's order at 104 or when Megra says *let 'em enter* at 105, and reappear with her at 129. In Q1 there is no separate entrance for Pharamond and the direction '*they come down to the* King', even though illogical following the King's dismissal of Pharamond at 123, may suggest that in some performances the staging was simplified and Megra and Pharamond entered together.

114 **broad fleerings** open mocking, grimaces
115 **base carriage** unworthy behaviour
116–18 **But . . . nourishment** Megra may speak these lines aside; she is unlikely to threaten the King openly. Similarly, her promise to *wring you* (119) is probably spoken out of his hearing.
119 **wring** distress, injure

105–6] *Theobald; Q2 lines* Prince, / businesse, /; *Q1 lines* vp, / *followed by prose*   106 and ready] *om.*
Q1   107 the] a *Q1*   113 hootings] *(*whootings*)*; whoting *Q1*   116 yet] still *Q1*

If my skill fail me not. [*Exit above.*]

KING [*to Pharamond*]

Sir, I must dearly chide you for this looseness; 121
You have wronged a worthy lady. But no more.
[*to a Guard*] Conduct him to my lodging and to bed.
[*Exeunt Pharamond and Guard.*]

CLEREMONT [*aside to Gentlemen*]

Get him another wench and you bring him to bed
indeed.

DION [*aside to Gentlemen*]

'Tis strange a man cannot ride a stage 125
Or two to breathe himself without a warrant.
If this gear hold, that lodgings be searched thus,
Pray God we may lie with our own wives in safety,
That they be not by some trick of state mistaken.

Enter [Guard] *with* MEGRA.

KING

Now, lady of honour, where's your honour now? 130
No man can fit your palate but the prince?
Thou most ill-shrouded rottenness, thou piece

---

123 Pharamond is taken to the King's lodging, a kind of polite house arrest. As Megra is still in his own lodging he cannot be taken there.
125–6 **ride . . . two** have a sexual encounter
127 **gear** nonsense, foolish goings on (*OED* 11)
130–7 **Now . . . devils** In a classic manifestation of the double standard, the King's speech, with its accusations of sexual *rottenness* and metaphors of sin and physical infection, is addressed exclusively to the woman involved;

Pharamond is merely chided for *looseness* (121).
130 **lady of honour** a title, like lady-in-waiting
131 **but the prince** One of Megra's sins is social climbing.
132 **ill-shrouded** badly concealed (*OED* shroud *v.*[1] 4), with suggestion of a death shroud
piece a derogatory reference to a woman considered as sexual object (*OED n.* II 9b, citing Burton, *Anatomy of Melancholy*, 'A waspish cholerick slut, a crased peece')

---

120 SD] *Dyce* 121 SD] *this edn* dearly chide you] chide you deerely *Q1* 122 worthy] *om. Q1* 123 SD1] *this edn* my] his *Q1* SD2] *Dyce subst.* 124–9] *prose Weber* 124 SD] *Spencer* 125–9] *Q1 lines* two, / hold, / lye / not / mistaken. / 125 SD] *Spencer* stage] *Q1;* stagge *Q2* 128 God] heaven *Q4* 129 SD] *Gurr; Enter with* Megra *Q2; they come downe to the King. Q1; Enter* MEGRA *below.* | *Dyce*

Made by a painter and a pothecary,
Thou troubled sea of lust, thou wilderness
Inhabited by wild thoughts, thou swollen cloud   135
Of infection, thou ripe mine of all diseases,
Thou all sin, all hell, and last all devils! Tell me,
Had you none to pull on with your courtesies
But he that must be mine and wrong my daughter?
By all the gods, all these [*pointing at Gentlemen*], and
   all the pages   140
And all the court shall hoot thee through the court,
Fling rotten oranges, make ribald rhymes
And sear thy name with candles upon walls.
Do ye laugh, lady Venus?

MEGRA   Faith, sir, you must pardon me;
I cannot choose but laugh to see you merry.   145
If you do this, O King, nay, if you dare do it,
By all those gods you swore by and as many
More of my own, I will have fellows, and such
Fellows in it as shall make noble mirth.
The princess, your dear daughter, shall stand by me   150
On walls and sung in ballads, anything –
Urge me no more: I know her and her haunts,
Her lays, leaps and outlays, and will discover all –
Nay, will dishonour her. I know the boy
She keeps, a handsome boy, about eighteen;   155

138 **courtesies** ironic
142 **Fling rotten oranges** Cf. *MA*, 4.1.30, 'Give not this rotten orange to your friend'; the phrase suggests that such oranges were thrown in the pillory.
144 **lady Venus** an ironic reference to the goddess of love
153 **lays** lodgings, lairs (*OED n.*[7] 2a)
leaps sexual encounters
outlays 'Outlying places, out-of-the-way lairs' (*OED n.* 1a, citing this line)

133–6] *Q1 lines* lust, / thoughts, / diseases, /   133 a pothecary] Apothecaries *Q1*   137 all hell] and hell *Q1*   140–4 By . . . Venus] *Q1 lines* Court / orrenges: / candles / *Venus?* /   140 SD] *this edn* and] *om. Q1*   142 ribald] *(*ribal'd*); reball *Q1*   144 ye] you *Q1*   144–59 Faith . . . height] *Q1 lines* laugh, / King; / by, / fellows, / mirth: / me, / more, / leaps / her, / eighteene, / when; / madnesse, / height – /   149 as] that *Q1*   151 On] Vpon *Q1*   anything] or any thing *Q1*   153 lays,] fayre *Q1*   outlays] out-lying *Q1*   154 Nay] and *Q1*

Know what she does with him, where and when.
Come, sir, you put me to a woman's madness,
The glory of a fury, and if I do not
Do it to the height –
KING   What boy is this she raves at?
MEGRA

Alas, good-minded prince, you know not these things.   160
I am loath to reveal 'em. Keep this fault
As you would keep your health from the hot air
Of the corrupted people, or by heaven
I will not fall alone. What I have known
Shall be as public as a print; all tongues   165
Shall speak it as they do the language they
Are born in, as free and commonly. I'll set it
Like a prodigious star for all to gaze at,
And so high and glowing that other kingdoms far and
    foreign
Shall read it there – nay, travel with it – till they find   170
No tongue to make it more nor no more people,
And then behold the fall of your fair princess.

KING [*to Gentlemen*]

Has she a boy?

CLEREMONT

So please your grace, I have seen a boy wait
On her, a fair boy.

KING [*to Megra*]   Go, get you to your quarter.   175
For this time I'll study to forget you.

162–3 **hot . . . people** the breath of
crowds, seen as infectious. King James
was known to dislike being forced too
close to the people.

169 To improve this long line Theobald cut
And and *other*, but this is not obligatory.

170 **travel with it** use it like the pole star
for directions

156 Know] Knowes *Q1*   and] *om. Q1*   159 this] that *Q1*   164 fall] sinke *Q1*   165–72] *Q1 lines* it, /
commonly, / at, / forraigne, / tongue, / people, / Princesse. /   165 a] in *Q1*   166–7 they / Are]
they're *Q1*   170 nay] *om. Q1*   travel] (trauaile)   173 SD] *this edn*   174 SP] LEON *Q1*   175 SD] *this
edn*   175 quarter] quarters *Q1*

MEGRA

Do you study to forget me, and I'll study

To forget you. *Exeunt King, Megra [and the] Guard.*

CLEREMONT   Why, here's a male spirit fit for Hercules! If

ever there be nine worthies of women, this wench shall   180

ride astride and be their captain.

DION   Sure she has a garrison of devils in her tongue, she

uttered such balls of wild-fire. She has so nettled the

King that all the doctors in the country will scarce cure

him. That boy was a strange-found-out antidote to cure   185

her infections! That boy, that princess's boy, that brave,

chaste, virtuous lady's boy, and a fair boy, a well-spoken

boy! All these considered can make nothing else – but

there I leave you, gentlemen.   189

THRASILINE   Nay, we'll go wander with you. *Exeunt.*

3.1 *Enter* CLEREMONT, DION *[and]* THRASILINE.

CLEREMONT

Nay, doubtless 'tis true.

179 **male spirit** Megra's aggressiveness is regarded as unfeminine.
Hercules Greek hero, son of Zeus and Alcmena, famous for performing twelve difficult labours
180 **nine worthies** The nine worthies were usually three from the Bible (Joshua, David and Judas Maccabaeus), three from the classics (Hector of Troy, Alexander the Great and Julius Caesar) and three from romance (Arthur, Charlemagne and Godfrey of Bouillon). But there were frequent substitutions; in the show put on for the Princess in *LLL*, Pompey the Great and Hercules are included.
181 **ride astride** with one leg on either side of the horse rather than sidesaddle, the usual riding position for women
185 **strange-found-out** unexpectedly discovered
3.1 Location: the court
1 **'tis** a reference to the accusation of what Arethusa *does* with her boy (2.4.156)

177–8] Do so, and I'le forget your – *Q1*   178 SD *and the*] *Q1; not in Q2*   179 Why] *om. Q1*   180 worthies] worthy *Q1*   181 astride] aside *Q1*   182–9] *Q1 lines* tongue, / King, / him, / infections; / braue, / wel-spoken boy, / else, / Gentlemen. /   183 nettled] *Q1;* metled *Q2*   184 scarce] not *Q1*   186 princess's] *(Princesse)*   186–7 brave, / chaste] chast, braue *Q1*   189 you] yee *Q1*   190 SD] *Exit three Gentlemen Q1*   3.1] *(Actus 3. Scaena I.)*   0 SD] *Enter three Gentlemen. Q1*   and] *F*   1 Nay] And *Q1*   1+ SP2] LEON *Q1*

DION   Ay, and 'tis the gods
That raised this punishment to scourge the King
With his own issue. Is it not a shame
For us that should write noble in the land,
For us that should be free men, to behold   5
A man that is the bravery of his age,
Philaster, pressed down from his royal right
By this regardless king? And only look
And see the sceptre ready to be cast
Into the hands of that lascivious lady   10
That lives in lust with a smooth boy, now to be
Married to yon strange thing – who, but that people
Please to let him be a prince, is born a slave
In that which should be his most noble part,
His mind.

THRASILINE   That man that would not stir with you   15
To aid Philaster – let the gods forget
That such a creature walks upon the earth.

CLEREMONT

Philaster is too backward in't himself.
The gentry do await it, and the people,
Against their nature, are all bent for him,   20

---

the gods Throughout this act there
is little sign of censorship; *the gods*,
but not God, are repeatedly invoked
(3.1.16, 97, 129, 148, 230, 238, 268;
3.2.89, 129, 157).
3 **issue** child
4 **write** be considered
6 **bravery** a gallant or grandee (*OED* 5,
citing Jonson, *Epicoene*, 1.3, 'Hee is one
of the Braueries, though he be none o'
the Wits')
8 **regardless** heedless, indifferent
11 **smooth boy** beardless youth

12 **thing* Q1 clarifies the discrepancy
between the *thing* Pharamond is and
the *prince* he is permitted to be. Q2's
'Prince' may be an anticipation of 13 by
the scribe or compositor.
12–13 **people ... prince** a dangerous
suggestion of democratic power,
recalling the uprising described in
1.1.33–8 and prefiguring the *mutiny*
of 5.3–5.4
19–22 **people ... way** In the courtiers'
view, the mob is usually fickle and
divided.

3–15 And ... mind] *Q1 lines* shame for all vs, / freemen, / age, / right, / Scepter / Lady, / boy, /
thing, / Prince, / part, / mind. / 4 us] all vs *Q1* should] *om. Q1* 7 down] *Q1;* drowne *Q2* 12
thing] *Q1;* Prince *Q2* 15–17] *Q5; Q2 lines* minde. / you, / forget, / earth. /; *Q1 lines* mind. /
Phylaster, / Creature / earth. / 18] *om. Q1* 20–2] *prose Q1*

And like a field of standing corn that's moved
With a stiff gale, their heads bow all one way.

DION

The only cause that draws Philaster back
From this attempt is the fair princess's love,
Which he admires and we can now confute.   25

THRASILINE

Perhaps he'll not believe it.

DION

Why, gentlemen, 'tis without question so.

CLEREMONT

Ay, 'tis past speech. She lives dishonestly.
But how shall we, if he be curious, work
Upon his faith?   30

THRASILINE

We all are satisfied within ourselves.

DION

Since it is true and tends to his own good,
I'll make this new report to be my knowledge:
I'll say I know it; nay, I'll swear I saw it.

CLEREMONT

It will be best.

THRASILINE   'Twill move him.

---

25 **Which** whom
  confute prove false; usually used of an argument or opinion, the verb here seems to refer to the princess or, more precisely, the basis on which Philaster loves her.
27ff. Dion's insistent distrust of the princess and his willingness to swear to knowledge he does not have make him an ambiguous character. He claims to act for Philaster's *own good* (32),

but his behaviour undercuts Philaster's assertion that 'he that tells me this is honourable, / As far from lies as she is far from truth' (138–9) and casts doubt on the prince's own judgement.
28 **past speech** not just rumour; worse than we can say
  dishonestly unchastely
29 **be curious** ask questions
29–30 **work . . . faith** persuade him
31 **satisfied** convinced

21 of] if *Q1* *om. Q1* 23 draws] draweth *Q1* 24 princess's] *(Princesse)* 25 confute] comfort *Q1* 26 it] *om. Q1* 27 SP] CLE. *Q1* 28 SP] LEON *Q1* 30] on his beleefe *Q1* 32 tends] Lords *Q1* 34 nay] *om. Q1*

DION   Here he comes. –   35

Enter PHILASTER.

Good morrow to your honour. We have spent
Some time in seeking you.
PHILASTER   My worthy friends,
You that can keep your memories to know
Your friend in miseries and cannot frown
On men disgraced for virtue, a good day   40
Attend you all. What service may I do
Worthy your acceptation?
DION   My good lord,
We come to urge that virtue which we know
Lives in your breast. Forth, rise and make a head!
The nobles and the people are all dulled   45
With this usurping king, and not a man
That ever heard the word or known such a thing
As virtue but will second your attempts.
PHILASTER

How honourable is this love in you
To me that have deserved none! Know, my friends,   50
You that were born to shame your poor Philaster
With too much courtesy, I could afford
To melt myself to thanks, but my designs
Are not yet ripe. Suffice it that ere long
I shall employ your loves, but yet the time   55

---

38 **can . . . know** do not forget   44 **make a head** start a revolution
40 **disgraced for virtue** brought low by   53 **designs** plans
   their good qualities

35–7] *Boas; Q2 lines* best. / him. / honor, / you. / friends, /; *Q6 lines* him. / honour, / friends /;
Theobald lines him. / comes. / spent / Friends, /   35 SP3] CLE. *Q1*   SD] *Dyce; opp.* best *35 Q2; opp.*
him *35 Q6* 37–48 My . . . attempts] *prose Q1* 39 frown] frame *Q1* 40 disgraced] disgrace *Q1* 42
good] *om. Q1* 44 breast. Forth] *Q1 (*breast: forth*);* breast, forth *Q2* and] *om. Q1* 45 dulled] dull
Q1 47 or known] knowes *Q1;* or knew *Q3* 49–56] *Q1 lines* me, / friends, / *Phylaster,* / selfe /
sufficient, / loues, / would. /   50 none] more *Q1* 54 Suffice it] sufficient *Q1*

175

Is short of what I would.

DION

The time is fuller, sir, than you expect.
That which hereafter will not perhaps be reached
By violence may now be caught. As for the King,
You know the people have long hated him;   60
But now the princess, whom they loved –

PHILASTER   Why, what of her?

DION

– Is loathed as much as he.

PHILASTER   By what strange means?

DION

She's known a whore.

PHILASTER   Thou liest!

DION   My lord –

PHILASTER   Thou liest,
And thou shalt feel it!   (*Offers to draw and is held.*)
                                       I had thought thy mind
Had been of honour. Thus to rob a lady   65
Of her good name is an infectious sin
Not to be pardoned. Be it false as hell,
'Twill never be redeemed if it be sown
Amongst the people, fruitful to increase
All evil they shall hear. Let me alone   70

57 **fuller** riper, later
68 **redeemed** called back
69 **fruitful** who are fruitful, eager
70–5 **Let . . . cloud** Philaster's speech
echoes the rodomontade and
obliviousness to his audience of the
famous lines of Hotspur in *1H4*,
1.3.200–7, lines Beaumont had already
parodied in *Pestle*: 'By heaven, methinks

it were an easy leap / To pluck bright
honour from the pale-faced moon, /
Or dive into the bottom of the deep, /
Where fathom-line could never touch
the ground, / And pluck up drowned
honour by the locks, / So he that
doth redeem her thence might wear, /
Without corrival, all her dignities. / But
out upon this half-faced fellowship!'

57 sir] *om. Q1*   58 will not] *om. Q1*   60 have long] long haue *Q1*   62 SP1] Tra. *Q1*   63] *Daniel;
Q2 lines* whore. / liest. / Lord – / liest. /; *Q6 lines* lyest / lyest.   SP2] *Q1; Di. Q2*   64–75
And . . . cloud] *Q1 lines* thought, / Lady / pardon'd / redeemd, / increase, / I / on hils, / all, /
necke, / clowde. /   64 SD] *opp.* ²liest 63 *Q2; He offers to draw his sword, & is held / opp. 64–8 Q1*
65 Thus] then *Q1*   69 fruitful] faithfull *Q1*

That I may cut off falsehood whilst it springs.
Set hills on hills betwixt me and the man
That utters this, and I will scale them all
And from the utmost top fall on his neck
Like thunder from a cloud.

DION [*aside*]   This is most strange.   75
    Sure he does love her.

PHILASTER [*overhearing*]   I do love fair Truth:
    She is my mistress, and who injures her
    Draws vengeance from me. Sirs, let go my arms!

THRASILINE
    Nay, good my lord, be patient.

CLEREMONT
    Sir, remember this is your honoured friend   80
    That comes to do his service and will show you
    Why he uttered this.

PHILASTER   I ask you pardon, sir.
    My zeal to truth made me unmannerly.
    Should I have heard dishonour spoke of you
    Behind your back untruly, I had been   85
    As much distempered and enraged as now.

DION
    But this, my lord, is truth.

PHILASTER   Oh, say not so!
    Good sir, forbear to say so. 'Tis then truth

75–6 **This . . . her** These lines are a kind
of failed aside, as Philaster hears them
and responds.

77 **She** *fair Truth* (76); Arethusa
mistress beloved (*OED* 6), without
sexual implication

87 **this . . . truth** Dion's insistence

on the *truth* of what he says, and
the reiteration of the word (76, 83,
87, 88) while the audience knows
that the accusation is false despite
Dion's good motives, creates the
emotional distance typical of
tragicomedy.

71 off] out *Q1*   whilst it springs] where it growes *Q1*   72 the] that *Q1*   75–6 This . . . her] *one line*
Q1   75 SD] *this edn*   76 SD] *this edn*   76–82 I . . . this] *prose Q1*   77 injures] iniuries *Q1*   82 you]
your *Q1*   83 made] makes *Q1*   84–6] *prose Q1*   85 back] backs *Q1*   87–91] *Weber subst.; Q2 lines*
truth. / say so, / false; / impossible; / light? / at it. /   88–91 Good . . . light] *prose Q1*

That womankind is false. Urge it no more:
It is impossible. Why should you think   90
The princess light?

DION   Why, she was taken at it.

PHILASTER

'Tis false, by heaven 'tis false! It cannot be,
Can it? Speak, gentlemen, for God's love speak!
Is't possible? Can women all be damned?

DION

Why no, my lord.

PHILASTER   Why, then it cannot be.   95

DION

And she was taken with her boy.

PHILASTER   What boy?

DION

A page, a boy that serves her.

PHILASTER   Oh, good gods,
A little boy?

DION   Ay. Know you him, my lord?

PHILASTER [*aside*]

Hell and sin know him. – Sir, you are deceived.
I'll reason it a little coldly with you: 100
If she were lustful, would she take a boy

89–94 **womankind … damned** Philaster's
distrust of women emerges in the
rapidity with which he generalizes from
Arethusa to *women all*.

91 **light** sexually promiscuous
taken at it found engaged in sex

98 **A little boy** Bellario's age is somewhat
ambiguous. At 3.2.16 the King thinks
Bellario is *About eighteen*, which does
not suggest a *little boy*, and the length
of Bellario's part, the longest for a boy
(or the longest female role) in the play,

would have required an experienced
actor. Boy actors in adult companies
like the King's Men were adolescents,
'no younger than twelve and no older
than twenty-one or twenty-two, with a
median of around sixteen or seventeen'.
The youngest boys played only minor
parts, 'but boys across the entire
rest of the age range can be found
playing demanding lead female roles'
(Kathman, 220, 245). See 3.2.16n. and
pp. 61–2.

---

89 womankind is] women all are *Q1*   90 It is] 'tis *Q1*   92–4] *Q1 lines* be, / damn'd? /   93–4
for . . . possible] *om. Q1*   94–8] *Boas; Q2 lines* damn'd? / Lord. / be. / boy. / boy? / her. / boy? /
Lord? /; *Q6 lines* Lord. / boy. / her. / Lord? /   95 Why . . . lord] *om. Q1*   SP2] Tra. *Q1*   96 SP1]
Cle. *Q1*   99 SD] *Dyce*   100 coldly] milder *Q1*   101–5] *prose Q1*

That knows not yet desire? She would have one
Should meet her thoughts and know the sin he acts,
Which is the great delight of wickedness.
You are abused, and so is she, and I.   105

DION

How you, my lord?

PHILASTER   Why, all the world's abused
In an unjust report.

DION   Oh, noble sir, your virtues
Cannot look into the subtle thoughts of woman.
In short, my lord, I took them, I myself.

PHILASTER

Now all the devils thou didst! Fly from my rage.   110
Would thou hadst ta'en devils engendering plagues
When thou didst take them. Hide thee from mine eyes!
Would thou hadst ta'en thunder on thy breast
When thou didst take them or been strucken dumb
Forever, that this foul deed might have slept   115
In silence.

THRASILINE [*aside to Cleremont*]   Have you known him so
   ill-tempered?

CLEREMONT [*aside to Thrasiline*]
Never before.

PHILASTER   The winds that are let loose
From the four several corners of the earth
And spread themselves all over sea and land

---

105 Like Othello and Posthumus in *Cym*,
Philaster instinctively recognizes his
beloved's innocence even as he accuses
her.

109 **took them** found them (by
implication, *in flagrante*)
113 **ta'en . . . breast** been struck by
thunder

102 desire] desires *Q1*   103 he] she *Q1*   106 SP1] CLE. *Q1*   106–9] Boas; *Q2 lines* Lord? / abusde,
/ report. / vertues / woman. / selfe. /; *Q1 lines* Lord? / report. / looke / Lord, / selfe. /   108
woman] women *Q1*   113 ta'en thunder on] taken daggers in *Q1*   114–16 silence] *Q1 lines* them, /
fault / silence. /   114 strucken] stuacke *Q1*   115 foul deed] fault *Q1*   116 SP] CLE. *Q1*   SD] *this
edn*   117 SP1] TRA. *Q1*   SD] *this edn*   118 several] *om. Q1*   119 spread themselves] spreads them
selfe *Q1*

179

Kiss not a chaste one. What friend bears a sword   120
To run me through?

DION

Why, my lord, are you so moved at this?

PHILASTER

When any fall from virtue I am distracted;
I have an interest in't.

DION

But good my lord, recall yourself and think   125
What's best to be done.

PHILASTER   I thank you, I will do it.
Please you to leave me, I'll consider of it.
Tomorrow I will find your lodging forth
And give you answer.

DION   All the gods direct you
The readiest way.

THRASILINE [*aside to Cleremont*] He was extreme impatient.   130

CLEREMONT [*aside to Thrasiline*]

It was his virtue and his noble mind.

Exeunt Dion, Cleremont [and] Thrasiline.

PHILASTER

I had forgot to ask him where he took them;
I'll follow him. Oh, that I had a sea
Within my breast to quench the fire I feel!
More circumstances will but fan this fire.   135

120–1 **What . . . through** Philaster's
consistent reaction to crisis is to
contemplate death, by his own hand
or another's: cf. 4.5.56, 61, and 5.5.73,
79, 124.

123 **distracted** driven mad; see Neely on

the range of mental disturbance that
distraction connoted in early modern
England.

130 **extreme impatient** deeply upset

132 Philaster's failure to make enquiries is
a sign of the limitations of his character.

120 Kiss not a chaste one] Meetes not a fayre on *Q1* 122 SP] TRA. *Q1* 122–4] *Dyce lines* you /
this? / virtue, / in't /   124 an] *om. Q1* 125–6] *Weber; Q2 lines* selfe, / done. / it: /   126 do it] do't
Q1 128 I will] i'le *Q1* lodging] lodgings *Q1* forth] *om. Q1* 129 SP] OMNES. *Q1* 130 SD] *this
edn* 130–1 He . . . mind] *om. Q1* 131 SD1] *this edn* SD2] *(Exit. Di. Cle. Tra.); Exit three Gent.
Q1 and*] *F* 132 him] vm *Q1* them] her *Q1* 133–8] *Q1 lines* breast, / circumstances / now, /
simply, / honourable, /   135 will] Would *Q1* fan] flame *Q1*

It more afflicts me now to know by whom
This deed is done than simply that 'tis done.
And he that tells me this is honourable,
As far from lies as she is far from truth.
Oh, that like beasts we could not grieve ourselves   140
With that we see not! Bulls and rams will fight
To keep their females, standing in their sight,
But take 'em from them and you take at once
Their spleens away, and they will fall again
Unto their pastures, growing fresh and fat,   145
And taste the waters of the springs as sweet
As 'twas before, finding no start in sleep.
But miserable man!

Enter BELLARIO.

See, see, you gods:
He walks still, and the face you let him wear
When he was innocent is still the same,   150
Not blasted. Is this justice? Do you mean
To entrap mortality, that you allow
Treason so smooth a brow? I cannot now
Think he is guilty.
BELLARIO   Health to you, my lord.
The princess doth commend her love, her life   155

140–7 **Oh . . . sleep** Cf. *Oth*, 3.3.339–46:
'I swear 'tis better to be much abused
/ Than but to know't a little . . . /
What sense had I of her stolen hours
of lust? / I saw't not, thought it not, it
harmed not me, / I slept the next night
well, fed well, was free and merry; / I
found not Cassio's kisses on her lips; /
He that is robbed, not wanting what is
stolen, / Let him not know't, and he's
not robbed at all.'
144 **spleens** hot tempers, passions
147 **start** 'Sudden fit of passion, grief,
joy' (*OED n.*² 4d); cf. *1H4*, 3.2.124–6,
'Thou that art like enough, through
vassal fear, / Base inclination and the
start of spleen, / To fight against me'.
151 **blasted** as if by heavenly lightning
152 **entrap mortality** set a trap for
humankind

137 This] the *Q1*   'tis] it is *Q1*   143 'em] them *Q1*   146–54 And . . . guilty] *Q1 lines* before. / man,
/ weare / blush. / mortalitie, / brow: / guilty. /   148 SD] *opp. gods Q2; Enter boy. Q1*   See] *Q1;
Phi. See Q2*   151 blasted] blush *Q1*

181

And this unto you.   [*He gives him a letter.*]
PHILASTER   Oh, Bellario,
Now I perceive she loves me. She does show it
In loving thee, my boy. She has made thee brave!
BELLARIO
My lord, she has attired me past my wish,
Past my desert; more fit for her attendant,   160
Though far unfit for me who do attend.
PHILASTER
Thou art grown courtly, boy. [*aside*] Oh, let all women
That love black deeds learn to dissemble here,
Here, by this paper. She does write to me
As if her heart were mines of adamant   165
To all the world besides, but unto me
A maiden snow that melted with my looks. –
Tell me, my boy, how doth the princess use thee?
For I shall guess her love to me by that.
BELLARIO
Scarce like her servant, but as if I were   170
Something allied to her or had preserved
Her life three times by my fidelity;
As mothers fond do use their only sons;
As I'd use one that's left unto my trust,
For whom my life should pay if he met harm: 175

---

162 **grown courtly** are dressed as if for court; use convoluted language like a courtier (see 160–1)

165 **adamant** an alleged rock or mineral to which fabulous properties were ascribed, showing a confusion of ideas between the diamond and the loadstone or magnet, and consequently a poetical name for the embodiment of surpassing hardness (*OED*)

168 **how . . . thee** ostensibly a general enquiry about Bellario's treatment, and so taken by him, but with a covert suggestion of sexual *use*

171 **allied** related

156 SD] *Q1; not in Q2*   156–8 Oh . . . brave] *Q1 lines* me, / boy, / braue. /   159 My] *om. Q1*   161 Though] But *Q1*   who] that *Q1*   162–8] *Q1 lines* boy. / here, / me / Adamant / snow, / boy, / thee? /   162 boy] my boy *Q1*   SD] *Dyce, opp.* looks. – *167*   164 by] with *Q1*   165 mines] twines *Q1*   168 doth] dos *Q1*   169] *om. Q1*   171–6 Something . . . me] *Q1 lines* life / fond, / trust, / pay, / me. /   175 met] meete *Q1*

So she does use me.

PHILASTER   Why, this is wondrous well.
But what kind language does she feed thee with?

BELLARIO

Why, she does tell me she will trust my youth
With all her loving secrets, and does call me
Her pretty servant; bids me weep no more   180
For leaving you, she'll see my services
Regarded, and such words of that soft strain
That I am nearer weeping when she ends
Than ere she spake.

PHILASTER   This is much better still.

BELLARIO

Are you not ill, my lord?

PHILASTER   Ill? No, Bellario.   185

BELLARIO

Methinks your words
Fall not from off your tongue so evenly
Nor is there in your looks that quietness
That I was wont to see.

PHILASTER   Thou art deceived, boy.
And she strokes thy head?

BELLARIO   Yes.   190

PHILASTER

And she does clap thy cheeks?

BELLARIO   She does, my lord.

PHILASTER

And she does kiss thee, boy? Ha?

185–9 **Are . . . see** an example of dialogue   189 **deceived** deceivèd
   intended to direct the actors   191, 192 **And she does** does she

176 this is] tis *Q1*   178–84 Why . . . spake] *prose Q1*   179 loving secrets] maiden store *Q1*
181 services] seruice *Q1*   182 Regarded] rewarded *Q1*   184 spake] speakes *Q1*   185 ill] well
Q1   186–9 Methinks . . . see] *prose Q1; Turner lines* tongue / lookes / see. /   187 not] out
Q1   off] *om. Q1*   evenly] vneuenly *Q1*   188 quietness] quicknesse *Q1*   189–90 Thou . . . head]
one line Q1

BELLARIO   How, my lord?

PHILASTER

  She kisses thee?

BELLARIO   Never, my lord, by heaven.

PHILASTER

  That's strange: I know she does.

BELLARIO   No, by my life!

PHILASTER

  Why, then she does not love me. Come, she does: 195
  I bade her do it. I charged her by all charms
  Of love between us, by the hope of peace
  We should enjoy, to yield thee all delights
  Naked, as to her lord; I took her oath
  Thou shouldst enjoy her. Tell me, gentle boy,   200
  Is she not parallelless? Is not her breath
  Sweet as Arabian winds when fruits are ripe?
  Are not her breasts two liquid ivory balls?
  Is she not, all, a lasting mine of joy?

BELLARIO

  Ay, now I see why my disturbed thoughts   205
  Were so perplexed. When first I went to her
  My heart held augury. You are abused;

201–3 Is not . . . balls Similar elements of a female *blazon* are distributed throughout early modern poetry and prose. Close analogies or sources are the anonymous *A Larum for London* (1602), 'from her nostrils comes / A breath, as sweete as the Arabian spice' and *Luc*, where Tarquin admires 'Her breasts like ivory globes circled with blue / A pair of maiden worlds unconquered' (407–8). In his frantic jealousy Philaster metaphorically performs a similar corruption of Arethusa's unconquered maidenhood.

201 parallelless without parallel; *OED*'s only example

204 mine of joy Cf. Donne, *Elegie XIX*, 'Going to Bed': 'My Myne of precious stones, My Emperie, / How blest am I in this discovering thee!'

207–8 You . . . abused you Like Philaster, Bellario intuits the truth. Cf. Emilia, 'The Moor's abused by some most villainous knave' (*Oth*, 4.2.141), and Pisanio, 'it cannot be / But that my master is abus'd: some villain . . . hath done you both / This cursed injury' (*Cym*, 3.4.120–3).

193 Never . . . heaven.] Not so my Lord *Q4*   194 That's strange] Come come *Q4*   195–217] *Q1 lines* me, / *followed by prose*   196 bade] *(*bad*);* bid *Q1*   do it] do't *Q1*   198 delights] delight *Q1*   199 lord] *Q1;* bed *Q2*   201 parallelless] *(*parrallesse*);* paradise *Q1*   205 Ay] Yes *Q1*   disturbed] discurled *Q1*   207 augury] auguries *Q1*

Some villain has abused you. I do see
Whereto you tend. Fall rocks upon his head
That put this to you! 'Tis some subtle train   210
To bring that noble frame of yours to naught.

PHILASTER
Thou think'st I will be angry with thee. Come,
Thou shalt know all my drift: I hate her more
Than I love happiness, and placed thee there
To pry with narrow eyes into her deeds.   215
Hast thou discovered? Is she fallen to lust,
As I would wish her? Speak some comfort to me.

BELLARIO
My lord, you did mistake the boy you sent.
Had she the lust of sparrows or of goats,
Had she a sin that way, hid from the world,   220
Beyond the name of lust, I would not aid
Her base desires, but what I came to know
As servant to her I would not reveal
To make my life last ages.

PHILASTER   Oh, my heart!
This is a salve worse than the main disease.   225
Tell me thy thoughts, for I will know the least
That dwells within thee or will rip thy heart
To know it. I will see thy thoughts as plain
As I do now thy face.

BELLARIO   Why, so you do.
She is, for aught I know, by all the gods   230
As chaste as ice, but were she foul as hell
And I did know it, thus: the breath of kings,

---

228 **I . . . thoughts** Cf. Othello: 'If thou
dost love me, / Show me thy thought'
(3.3.118–19).

232–4 **the . . . me** a negative statement,
with 'neither' understood. Despite
this assertion, Bellario will be

209 Whereto] where *Q1*   211 frame] friend *Q1*   219 or] and *Q1*   220–4 Had . . . ages] *Q1 lines* lust,
/ desires, / her, / ages. /   220 way, hid] weighed *Q1*   222 came] come *Q1*   225 disease] deceit
Q1   229 now] know *F2*   229–30 Why . . . gods] *one line Q1*   229 do.] do. *Kneels*. | *Weber*   230 gods]
gods, *Kneels*. | *Daniel*

The points of swords, tortures nor bulls of brass
Should draw it from me.

PHILASTER   Then 'tis no time
To dally with thee. I will take thy life,   235
For I do hate thee. I could curse thee now.

BELLARIO

If you do hate, you could not curse me worse:
The gods have not a punishment in store
Greater for me than is your hate.

PHILASTER   Fie, fie,
So young and so dissembling! Tell me when   240
And where thou didst enjoy her, or let plagues
Fall upon me if I destroy thee not.   [*He draws his sword.*]

BELLARIO

By heaven I never did, and when I lie
To save my life may I live long and loathed.
Hew me asunder, and whilst I can think   245
I'll love those pieces you have cut away
Better than those that grow, and kiss those limbs
Because you made 'em so.

PHILASTER   Fear'st thou not death?
Can boys contemn that?

BELLARIO   Oh, what boy is he

moved by threats of torture: see
5.5.81–5.

233 **bulls of brass** mythic instruments
of torture. As recounted by Cicero,
the tyrant Phalaris of Acragas had
a brass bull made by Perilaus of
Athens. Victims were shut inside
it, a fire was kindled underneath,
and the shouts of those roasting

inside emerged through pipes and
sounded like the bellowing of the
bull.

240 **So . . . dissembling** Cf. the exchange
between Lear and Cordelia: 'So young
and so untender? So young, my lord,
and true' (*KL*, 1.1.107–8).

249 **contemn** treat as of small value;
scorn, slight

234–6] *Theobald; Q2 lines* me. / with thee; / hate thee: / now. /; *Q1 lines* me. / life, / now. /   234
draw] wrack *Q1*   237 hate] hate me *Q1*   239–42] *Theobald; Q2 lines* hate. / dissembling. / her, /
not. /; *Q1 lines* hate. / where, / me, / not. /   239 Greater for] To *Q1*   242 upon] *Q1*; on *Q2*   SD]
Q1; not in Q2; after 226 least *Weber subst.*   243–7] *Q1 lines* life, / asunder, / away / limbes /   248–9
Fear'st . . . that?] *one line Q1*   249–52 Oh . . . reason?] *Q1 lines* liue / passionate, / reason. /

Can be content to live to be a man   250
That sees the best of men thus passionate,
Thus without reason?

PHILASTER   Oh, but thou does not know
What 'tis to die.

BELLARIO   Yes, I do know, my lord:
'Tis less than to be born; a lasting sleep;
A quiet resting from all jealousy;   255
A thing we all pursue. I know besides
It is but giving over of a game
That must be lost.

PHILASTER   But there are pains, false boy,
For perjured souls. Think but on those, and then
Thy heart will melt and thou wilt utter all.   260

BELLARIO
May they fall all upon me whilst I live
If I be perjured or have ever thought
Of that you charge me with. If I be false,
Send me to suffer in those punishments
You speak of. Kill me.

PHILASTER [*aside*]   Oh, what should I do?   265
Why, who can but believe him? He does swear
So earnestly that if it were not true
The gods would not endure him. – Rise, Bellario.
Thy protestations are so deep, and thou
Dost look so truly when thou utter'st them,   270

---

251 **passionate** moved by emotion rather
   than reason
254–6 **'Tis . . . pursue** Cf. *Ham*, 3.1.59–
   63: 'to sleep – / No more, and by a sleep

to say we end / The heartache and the
thousand natural shocks / That flesh is
heir to: 'tis a consummation / Devoutly
to be wished'.

250 Can] could *Q1*   252–3 Thus . . . lord] *Dyce; Q2 lines* reason? / dye. / Lord: /   252 but] *om.*
Q1   253–7 Yes . . . game] *Q1 lines* borne, / iealousie, / againe, /   257 over of a game] ore againe
Q1   259–60] *Q1 lines* melt, / all. /   260 thou] then thou *Q1*   261–5 May . . . me] *Q1 lines* liue, / with,
/ of / me. /   265 SP] *Q1; not in Q2*   SD] *Spencer*   265–82 Oh . . . thee] *Q1 lines* beleeue him? /
followed by prose   268 him.] him. *Sheaths his sword.* | *Dyce*   Bellario.] Bellario: [Bellario *rises.* | *Dyce*

187

That though I know 'em false as were my hopes,
I cannot urge thee further. But thou wert
Too blame to injure me, for I must love
Thy honest looks and take no revenge upon
Thy tender youth. A love from me to thee   275
Is firm, whate'er thou dost. It troubles me
That I have called the blood out of thy cheeks
That did so well become thee. But, good boy,
Let me not see thee more. Something is done
That will distract me, that will make me mad,   280
If I behold thee. If thou tender'st me
Let me not see thee.

BELLARIO   I will fly as far
As there is morning ere I give distaste
To that most honoured mind. But through these tears
Shed at my hopeless parting, I can see   285
A world of treason practised upon you
And her and me. Farewell for evermore.
If you shall hear that sorrow struck me dead
And after find me loyal, let there be
A tear shed from you in my memory,   290
And I shall rest at peace.   *Exit.*

PHILASTER   Blessing be with thee,
Whatever thou deservest. Oh, where shall I
Go bathe this body? Nature too unkind
That made no medicine for a troubled mind.   *Exit.*

---

273 **Too blame** too culpable; too much
  to blame
279–81 **Something . . . thee** Cf. *Ham*,
  3.1.145–6, 'Go to, I'll no more on't. It
  hath made me mad.'
283 **distaste** offence (*OED n.* 4)

294 **no . . . mind** a commonplace; in *Wit
  of a Woman* (1604, D1ᵛ), Bario asks the
  doctor, 'I pray you tell me in rules of
  Phisicke, haue you no medicine for the
  malady of the minde?'

271 know] knew *Q1*   273 injure] iniuie *Q1*   275 tender youth] honest lookes *Q1*   277 the blood] thy
blood *Q1*   282–91 I . . . peace] *Q1 lines* farre, / *followed by prose*   284 mind] frame *Q1*   285 hope-
less] haplesse *Q1*   288 sorrow] sorrowes *Q1*   291 SD] *(Exit. Bell.); after* deservest 292 *Dyce*   291–4
Blessing . . . mind] *Q1 lines* deseruest. / vnkind, / minde. /   292 Whatever] *(*What euer*);* what ere
Q1   294 made] mad'st *Q1*   for] to *Q1*   SD] *(Ex. Phi.)*

[3.2]   *Enter* ARETHUSA.

ARETHUSA

I marvel my boy comes not back again.
But that I know my love will question him
Over and over how I slept, waked, talked,
How I remembered him when his dear name
Was last spoke, and how, when, I sighed, wept, sung   5
And ten thousand such, I should be angry
At his stay.

Enter KING.

KING   What, at your meditations?
Who attends you?
ARETHUSA   None but my single self.
I need no guard. I do no wrong, nor fear none.
KING

Tell me, have you not a boy?
ARETHUSA   Yes, sir.   10
KING

What kind of boy?
ARETHUSA   A page, a waiting boy.
KING

A handsome boy?
ARETHUSA   I think he be not ugly;
Well-qualified and dutiful I know him.

3.2 Location: Arethusa's chamber
1   **marvel** am surprised
4   **How . . . him** what I said about him
6   **such** such questions
7   **at your meditations** Like Ophelia
in *Ham*, 3.1, a nubile young woman
could 'colour' or excuse being
alone by 'devotions' visage' or the

appearance of prayer.
13 **Well-qualified** accomplished. The
accomplishments the King then
enumerates are speaking well, singing
and playing an instrument (15). Bellario
is said to play the lute (67) but is never
called upon to do so. This may indicate
a limitation of the actor available.

3.2] *Weber*   1–7 I .   stay] *Q1 lines* backe, / and oucr, / him, / spoken, / such, / stay. /   1 again]
om. Q1   3 waked, talked] make talke *Q1*   4 remembered] remember *Q1*   5 spoke] spoken *Q1*   how]
how spoke *Q1*   sighed, wept, sung] sight song *Q1*   7–9] *Turner; Q2 lines* stay / you? / guard: / none.
/   7 at] in *Q1*   12 ugly] vgly Sir *Q1*

I took him not for beauty.

KING

    He speaks and sings and plays?

ARETHUSA   Yes, sir.   15

KING

    About eighteen?

ARETHUSA   I never asked his age.

KING

    Is he full of service?

ARETHUSA   By your pardon,

    Why do you ask?

KING   Put him away.

ARETHUSA   Sir?

KING

    Put him away, I say. He's done you

    That good service shames me to speak of.

ARETHUSA   Good sir,   20

    Let me understand you.

KING   If you fear me,

    Show it in duty. Put away that boy.

ARETHUSA

    Let me have reason for it, sir, and then

    Your will is my command.

KING

    Do not you blush to ask it? Cast him off   25

---

16 **About eighteen** John Rice, who probably played Bellario in the first production, was baptized in 1591 and would have been eighteen in 1609. In 1661, when Pepys saw Edward Kynaston play Bellario, he was seventeen and eight months. See Kathman, 243–4.

17 **full of service** an ambiguous phrase with sexual overtones; 'Performance of the duties of a servant' (*OED* service *n.*[1] II 6a) shades into '*the flesh's service*, sexual intercourse' (II 6c), which is the *good service* (20) the King is worried about.

18 **Put him away** discharge him

23–4 Arethusa's demand for a reason to obey a direct order by her father and king is strikingly rebellious.

17–21] *Turner; Q2 lines* seruice? / aske? / away. / Sir. / seruice / speake of. / you. / me, /; *Daniel lines* service? / ask? / say. / speak of. / me, /   19 He's] (*has*)   20 of] off *Q1*   21–2 If . . . boy] *one line Q1*   23–4] *one line Q1*   23 sir] *om. Q1*   24 my] a *Q1*   25–9] *Boas; Q2 lines* off, / one / selfe, / selfe, / done. / Lord? /; *Q1 lines* off: / me, / gods, / selfe, / done. / done? /

Or I shall do the same to you. You're one
Shame with me and so near unto my self
That, by my life, I dare not tell myself
What you, myself, have done.

ARETHUSA   What I have done, my lord?

KING

'Tis a new language that all love to learn.   30
The common people speak it well already;
They need no grammar. Understand me well.
There be foul whispers stirring. Cast him off,
And suddenly. Do it! Farewell.   *Exit.*

ARETHUSA

Where may a maiden live securely free,   35
Keeping her honour fair? Not with the living:
They feed upon opinions, errors, dreams,
And make 'em truths. They draw a nourishment
Out of defamings, grow upon disgraces,
And when they see a virtue fortified   40
Strongly above the battery of their tongues,
Oh, how they cast to sink it! And, defeated,
Soul-sick with poison, strike the monuments
Where noble names lie sleeping till they sweat

26–7 **You're . . . me** Anything shameful you do reflects upon me.

27–9 **so near . . . done** The King's insistence on his identification with his daughter is not affectionate but political.

32 **grammar** grammar book

34 **suddenly** immediately

39 **defamings** slander
grow upon get fat with

42 **cast** scheme; cf. 'a strange Land, / Where Mothers cast to poyson their onely sonnes' (*King and No King*, 3.1.44–5).

43–5 **the . . . melt** There are many images of melting the marble-hearted but no precise precedent for Arethusa's claim here. In Richard Fanshawe's translation of Guarini's *Il Pastor Fido* (1647) Titiro is told that his daughter, 'being brought before the Priest, / Did not alone from the beholders wrest / Salt tears; but (trust me) made the marble melt, / And the hard flint the dint of pity felt' (5.2),

---

26 the same] that shame *Q1*   You're] *(Y'are); ye are Q1*   27 unto] *om. Q1*   28 my life] the gods *Q1*   I] I'd *Q1*   29 my lord] *om. Q1*   32–4] *Q1 lines* foule / it, / farewell. /   34 SD] *(Exit King.)*   35 maiden] maid *Q1*   37–43] *Q1 lines* truth / defamings, / fortified, / tongues. / foule / mountaines, /   38 truths] truth *Q1*   42 cast] mind *Q1*   43 Soul-sick] *(Soule sicke);* foule / Sicke *Q1*   monuments] mountaines *Q1*   44 lie] be *Q1*

And the cold marble melt.   45

Enter PHILASTER.

PHILASTER
Peace to your fairest thoughts, dearest mistress!
ARETHUSA
Oh, my dearest servant, I have a war within me.
PHILASTER
He must be more than man that makes these crystals
Run into rivers. Sweetest fair, the cause?
And as I am your slave, tied to your goodness,   50
Your creature, made again from what I was
And newly spirited, I'll right your honour.
ARETHUSA
Oh, my best love: that boy!
PHILASTER   What boy?
ARETHUSA
The pretty boy you gave me –
PHILASTER   What of him?
ARETHUSA
– Must be no more mine.
PHILASTER   Why?   55
ARETHUSA
They are jealous of him.
PHILASTER   Jealous! Who?
ARETHUSA
The King.
PHILASTER   Oh, my misfortune!
Then 'tis no idle jealousy. Let him go.

and in *Custom of the Country* Arnoldo   47 **dearest servant** follower, in courtly love
complains, ''Twold melt a Marble /   48–9 **crystals . . . rivers** eyes shed tears
And tame a savage man, to feele my   51 **made again** revived; recreated
fortune' (1.1.1–2).   56 **jealous** suspicious

47] *Q1 lines* seruant, / me. /   48–52] *prose Q1*   57 my misfortune] *Q1;* my mi fortune *Q2;* my my
fortune *Q3;* my fortune *Q4*

ARETHUSA

Oh, cruel!

Are you hard-hearted too? Who shall now tell you   60
How much I loved you? Who shall swear it to you,
And weep the tears I send? Who shall now bring you
Letters, rings, bracelets? Lose his health in service?
Wake tedious nights in stories of your praise?
Who shall sing your crying elegies   65
And strike a sad soul into senseless pictures
And make them mourn? Who shall take up his lute
And touch it till he crown a silent sleep
Upon my eyelids, making me dream and cry,
'Oh, my dear, dear Philaster!'

PHILASTER [*aside*]   Oh, my heart!   70
Would he had broken thee that made thee know
This lady was not loyal. – Mistress, forget
The boy. I'll get thee a far better.

ARETHUSA

Oh, never, never such a boy again
As my Bellario!

PHILASTER   'Tis but your fond affection.   75

ARETHUSA

With thee, my boy, farewell forever

---

64 **Wake** help pass; stay awake
65 **your crying elegies** technically, poems written in elegiac metre, but used more generally for love poems; cf. *AYL*, 3.2.346–9, 'There is a man haunts the forest . . . hangs . . . elegies on brambles . . . deifying the name of Rosalind.'
66 **strike . . . pictures** bring the images alive through his singing; cf. Iachimo describing the chimney piece in

Innogen's chamber, 'never saw I figures / So likely to report themselves' (*Cym*, 2.4.82–3).
67–9 **Who . . . dream** Brutus's page Lucius plays his 'instrument', almost certainly a lute, for the weary Brutus but succeeds in putting only himself to sleep (*JC*, 4.3.254–70).
72 **loyal** (sexually) faithful
75 **fond** foolish

59–70] *Theobald; Q2 lines* too? / you? / send? / bracelets? / nights / sing / soule / mourne? / till / eye-lids, / deere, / *Philaster*? / heart? /   61 loved] love *Turner*   64 Wake] make *Q1*   65 shall] shall now *Q1*   67 mourn] warme *Q1*   69 making] Make *Q1*   70–3] ²Oh . . . better] *Q1 lines* broken thee, / loyall, / better. /   70 SD] *Dyce, after* loyal 72   73 thee] you *Q1*   74–5] *Boas; Q2 lines* againe, / Bellario. / affection. / ; *Q1 lines* Bellario. / affection. /   75 SP] *Q1; Bell. Q2*

All secrecy in servants; farewell faith
And all desire to do well for itself.
Let all that shall succeed thee, for thy wrongs,
Sell and betray chaste love.   80

PHILASTER
And all this passion for a boy?

ARETHUSA
He was your boy and you put him to me,
And the loss of such must have a mourning for.

PHILASTER
O thou forgetful woman!

ARETHUSA   How, my lord?

PHILASTER
False Arethusa!   85
Hast thou a medicine to restore my wits
When I have lost 'em? If not, leave to talk,
And do thus.

ARETHUSA   Do what, sir? Would you sleep?

PHILASTER
Forever, Arethusa. O you gods,
Give me a worthy patience! Have I stood   90
Naked, alone, the shock of many fortunes?
Have I seen mischiefs numberless and mighty

---

78 **do . . . itself** instead of for reward
81–2 **all . . . your boy** See pp. 48–50
for discussion of the various ways in
which boys were understood to arouse
passion, and in whom; see also Masten;
Miller; Radel.
82 **put him** gave or sent him
88 **do thus** Exactly what Philaster does
is unclear, but apparently he indicates
death in some way. Gurr suggests that

he closes his eyes and that 'Arethusa's
bewildered misunderstanding is a
typical piece of tragicomic pathos'
(66). Alternatively, Philaster may pull
out his sword, suggesting that he seeks
the *sleep* of death.
91 **shock . . . fortunes** Cf. *Malcontent*,
4.5, 'we foure must stand full shocke
of Fortune'.

77–9] *Q1 lines* all / that / wrongs, /   77 secrecy] seruice *Q1*   78 desire] Desires *Q1*   itself] thy
sake *Q1*   82 to] vnto *Q1*   87–8] *Theobald; Q2 lines* talke, / thus. / sleepe? /; *Q1 lines* not, / thus.
/ sleepe? /   88 do] to do *Theobald*   thus] thus. *Offers to fall.* | *Turner*   89 SP] *om. Q1*   you gods]
ye gods, ye gods *Q1*   90–102 Give . . . lust] *Q1 lines* naked / mischiefe, / me: / bosome, / mirth, /
King, / Mourners, / length / cursed boy, / lust. /   90 worthy] wealthy *Q1*   91 alone] Aboue *Q1*
92 mischiefs] mischiefe *Q1*

Grow like a sea upon me? Have I taken
Danger as stern as death into my bosom
And laughed upon it, made it but a mirth,   95
And flung it by? Do I live now like him,
Under this tyrant king, that languishing
Hears his sad bell and sees his mourners? Do I
Bear all this bravely and must sink at length
Under a woman's falsehood? Oh, that boy,   100
That cursed boy! None but a villain boy
To ease your lust?

ARETHUSA   Nay, then I am betrayed.
I feel the plot cast for my overthrow.
Oh, I am wretched!

PHILASTER

Now you may take that little right I have   105
To this poor kingdom. Give it to your joy,
For I have no joy in it. Some far place,
Where never womankind durst set her foot
For bursting with her poisons, must I seek
And live to curse you.   110

---

98 **his sad bell** the bell of his own funeral;
cf. Donne, *Devotions XVII*, 'never send
to know for whom the *bell* tolls; It tolls
for *thee*' (87).
101 **cursed** cursèd
102 **betrayed** 'Placed in the power of
an enemy by treachery or disloyalty'
(*OED v.*[1]), not 'proven false' (*OED v.*[2]).
Cf. Desdemona, told by Othello that
Iago has 'ta'en order' for Cassio's death
and thus Cassio cannot testify to her
innocence: 'Alas, he is betrayed, and I
undone' (*Oth*, 5.2.72–5).
107–26 **Some . . . distinguish** This
attack on women by Philaster parallels

Posthumus's speech on being informed,
falsely, of Innogen's betrayal: 'Is there
no way for men to be, but women
/ Must be half-workers', especially
the lines beginning, 'Could I find out
/ The woman's part in me' (*Cym*,
2.4.153ff.). Like Philaster, Posthumus
accuses women of lying, flattering,
deception and mutability. Cf. also *Ham*,
3.1.141–6.
109 **For** for fear of
bursting . . . poisons It is unclear why
the *far place* would make the woman,
imagined as a serpent or scorpion full
of poison, burst.

94 stern] deepe *Q1*   96 flung] flowing *Q1*   98 Hears] heare *Q1*   99 must] *om. Q1*   105–24] *Q1 lines*
this / it: / foote, / seeke, / Caue, / are; / more hell, / Scorpyons, / wouen, / by you: / face, / haue,
/ behind you, / night, / you are, / altogether. /   109 poisons] poyson *Q1*

There dig a cave, and preach to birds and beasts
What woman is, and help to save them from you.
How heaven is in your eyes, but in your hearts
More hell than hell has. How your tongues, like scorpions,
Both heal and poison. How your thoughts are woven   115
With thousand changes in one subtle web,
And worn so by you. How that foolish man
That reads the story of a woman's face,
And dies believing it, is lost forever.
How all the good you have is but a shadow,   120
I'th' morning with you and at night behind you,
Past and forgotten. How your vows are frosts:
Fast for a night and with the next sun gone.
How you are, being taken altogether,
A mere confusion and so dead a chaos   125
That love cannot distinguish. These sad texts
Till my last hour I am bound to utter of you.
So farewell, all my woe, all my delight.   *Exit.*

ARETHUSA

Be merciful, ye gods, and strike me dead!
What way have I deserved this? Make my breast   130
Transparent as pure crystal, that the world,
Jealous of me, may see the foulest thought

114–15 **scorpions . . . poison** The flesh, or sometimes the oil, of the scorpion was supposed to be a cure for its own sting; the gendered metaphorical usage recurs in *Custom of the Country*, 'women . . . rellish much of Scorpions, / For both have stings, and both can hurt, and cure too' (5.5.202–4).

123 **Fast** fixed, apparently permanent
126 **cannot distinguish** cannot tell the difference between these opposite qualities in woman's character
130 **What . . . this?** Cf. Desdemona's response to being struck by the jealous Othello, 'I have not deserved this' (*Oth*, 4.1.240).

111 There] and there *Q1* birds and beasts] beasts and birds *Q1* 112 woman is] women are *Q1* and . . . you] om. *Q1* 115 are] *om. Q1* 117 so] *om. Q1* man] men *Q1* 118 reads] reade *Q1* 122–3 frosts: / Fast] (frosts, / Fast*); frost fast, *Q1* 128 SD] *(Exit Phi.)* 129 ye] you *Q1* 130–5] *Q1 lines* transparant, / me, / holds: / constancie? / now! / 131 as pure crystal] *om. Q1*

My heart holds. Where shall a woman turn her eyes
To find out constancy?

Enter BELLARIO.

                    Save me, how black
And guiltily, methinks, that boy looks now!   135
[*to Bellario*] O thou dissembler, that before thou
   spakest
Wert in thy cradle false! Sent to make lies
And betray innocents! Thy lord and thou
May glory in the ashes of a maid
Fooled by her passion, but the conquest is   140
Nothing so great as wicked. Fly away;
Let my command force thee to that which shame
Would do without it. If thou understood'st
The loathed office thou hast undergone,
Why, thou wouldst hide thee under heaps of hills   145
Lest men should dig and find thee.
BELLARIO   Oh, what god,
Angry with men, hath sent this strange disease
Into the noblest minds? Madam, this grief
You add unto me is no more than drops
To seas, for which they are not seen to swell.   150
My lord hath struck his anger through my heart
And let out all the hope of future joys.
You need not bid me fly, I came to part,

---

137 **Sent** both *sent* to this world, continuing the image of infancy in the preceding sentence, and *sent* by Philaster to serve her

144 the task Arethusa believes Bellario has fulfilled in lying about her
loathed loathèd

133 a woman] women *Q1*   her] their *Q1*   134 SD] *Q1; opp.* blacke *Q2*   BELLARIO] *boy Q1*   135 guiltily] vile *Q1;* guilty *Q3*   136 SD] *this edn*   spakest] spokst *Q1*   138 betray innocents] to betray innocence *Q1*   139–43] *Q1 lines* passion / wicked, / that, / vnderstoodst. /   139 May] Maist *Q1*   144 undergone] vndertooke *Q1*   146–7] *Q5; Q2 lines* thee. / god, / disease /; *Q1 lines* thee. / desease /   146 Lest] *(*Least*)*   men] we *Q1*   147 men] me *Q1*   151 hath] has *Q1*   153 You] Ye *Q1*

197

To take my latest leave. Farewell forever.
I durst not run away in honesty   155
From such a lady, like a boy that stole
Or made some grievous fault. The power of gods
Assist you in your sufferings; hasty time
Reveal the truth to your abused lord
And mine, that he may know your worth, whilst I   160
Go seek out some forgotten place to die.   *Exit.*

ARETHUSA

Peace guide thee! Thou'st overthrown me once,
Yet if I had another Troy to lose,
Thou, or another villain with thy looks,
Might talk me out of it and send me naked,   165
My hair dishevelled, through the fiery streets.

Enter a LADY.

LADY

Madam, the King would hunt and calls for you
With earnestness.

ARETHUSA   I am in tune to hunt.
Diana, if thou canst rage with a maid

---

155 **run . . . honesty** simply run away without saying farewell
158–9 **hasty . . . Reveal** may a short time uncover
159 **abused** abusèd
161 **forgotten** hidden, unknown
163–6 **I . . . streets** A recollection of 1 Player's speech describing the fall of Troy and Hecuba, the queen, who was seen to '*Run barefoot up and down, threatening the flames / With bisson rheum, a clout upon that head / Where late the diadem stood and, for a robe, / About her lank and all-o'erteemed loins, / A blanket in the alarm of fear caught up*' (*Ham*, 2.2.443–7).
167 **King . . . hunt** Hunting was a favourite activity of King James, who was often absent from court for this reason.
168 **In earnestness** urgently
   in tune to in the mood to
169–73 Arethusa wishes to become a female version of Actaeon, the *man* who while hunting came upon *Diana*, goddess of the hunt, while she was

154–61] *Q1* lines leaue, / euer. / Lady, / fault, / suffering: / mine, / seeke / die. /   157 grievous] greater *Q1*   158 sufferings] suffering *Q1*   161 SD] *(Exit Bell.)*   162 Thou'st] (tha'st); thou hast *Q1*   163 Yet] But *Q1*   Troy] time *Q1*   165 talk] take *Q1*   166 SD] *Enter. Q1*   167 SP] Wo. *Q1*   167–70 I . . . thee] *Q1 lines* hunt, / earnestnesse. / canst / thee /

As with a man, let me discover thee   170
Bathing, and turn me to a fearful hind,
That I may die pursued by cruel hounds
And have my story written in my wounds.   *Exeunt.*

4.1   *Enter* KING, PHARAMOND, ARETHUSA, GALLATEA,
              MEGRA, DION, CLEREMONT, THRASILINE
                   and Attendants.

KING

What, are the hounds before, and all the woodmen?
Our horses ready and our bows bent?
DION   All, sir.
KING [*to Pharamond*]
You're cloudy, sir. Come, we have forgotten
Your venial trespass; let not that sit heavy
Upon your spirit. Here's none dare utter it.   5
DION [*aside to Gentlemen*]   He looks like an old surfeited
stallion after his leaping, dull as a dormouse. See how

bathing. Angry at being exposed, the
goddess turned him into a stag or *hind*
and he was torn to pieces by his own
hounds.
4.1 Location: the woods. Throughout this
act the scene moves about the woods, and
the dialogue indicates which characters
are present together and which are
elsewhere. The stage direction in Q1,
'Philaster *creepes out of a bush*' (4.6.83),
may suggest that in the original staging
some representation of shrubbery was
put on the stage. See also the illustration
on the title-page of Q1, Fig. 10.
1   **before** out in advance; cf. *MND*,

5.1.375–6, 'I am sent with broom before,
/ To sweep the dust behind the door.'
3   **cloudy** gloomy, in a bad mood
4   **venial trespass** minor or pardonable
error; theologically sins are divided
between venial and mortal. The King's
jocular description of Pharamond's
behaviour   contrasts   with   his
condemnation of Megra at 2.4.132–7
and to Philaster's reaction to allegations
of Arethusa's unfaithfulness.
7   **leaping** sexual activity
      dormouse a small rodent notable for
its hibernation and hence a symbol of
dullness or sleepiness

173 SD] *Exit Princesse. Q1*   **4.1**] *(Actus 4. Scaena I.)*   0.3 *Attendants*] *two Wood-men Q1*   3 SD]
Dyce   You're] *(Y'are);* You are *Q1*   4 trespass] trespasses *Q1*   5 dare] dares *Q1*   6–9] *Q1 lines* leaping / *followed by prose*   6 SD] *Ashe subst.*

he sinks? The wench has shot him between wind and
water and, I hope, sprung a leak.

THRASILINE [*aside to Gentlemen*]   He needs no teaching;   10
he strikes sure enough! His greatest fault is he hunts
too much in the purlieus. Would he would leave off
poaching!

DION [*aside to Gentlemen*]   And for his horn, he's left it
at the lodge where he lay late. Oh, he's a precious lime-   15
hound: turn him loose upon the persue of a lady and, if
he lose her, hang him up i'th' slip. When my fox-bitch
Beauty grows proud, I'll borrow him.

KING [*to Arethusa*]
Is your boy turned away?

ARETHUSA
You did command, sir, and I obeyed you.   20

KING
'Tis well done. Hark ye further.   [*They talk apart.*]

CLEREMONT   Is't possible this fellow should repent?

---

8 **sinks** droops, suggesting erectile
disfunction

8–9 **The wench . . . leak** Using the
metaphor of a great ship that has been
brought down by a cannon *shot* during
naval warfare, Dion suggests 'the
woman has given him the pox'.

11 **strikes sure enough** ostensibly, makes
his way well, but Thrasiline ironically
implies the figurative meaning: hauls
down his flag, surrenders (*OED v.* 17c).
Cf. Jonson, *Poetaster*, 3.4, 'what, will he
saile by, and not once strike, or vaile to
a *Man of warre?*'

11–12 **hunts . . . purlieus** spends too
much time pursuing illicit love. *Purlieus*
were lands on the edge of the forest
from which the laws controlling hunting

of game had been lifted.

13 **poaching** trespassing in pursuit of
game; chasing inappropriate sexual
partners. *OED n.*[2] 1 gives this line for
the figurative meaning.

14 **horn** hunting horn; erect penis

15 **lodge** hunting lodge; his room at the
palace, where he was found with Megra

15–16 **lime-hound** canine stud; Dion's
insult is based on *OED* lime *v.*[3], 'To
impregnate a bitch'.

16 **persue** track of blood left by a
wounded deer or other quarry in a
hunt

17 **i'th' slip** in his leash
fox-bitch the female of fox-hound, a
variety of dog trained and used for fox-
hunting, rather than a female fox

---

9 leak] lake *Q1*   10–13] *Q1 lines* enough, / purlewes, / poaching. /   10 SP] CLE. *Q1*   SD] *Ashe
subst.*   14 SP] TRA. *Q1*   SD] *Ashe subst.*   he's] *(*has*)*   15 precious] pernitious *Q1*   16 loose] *om.*
Q1   persue] *(*pursue*);* pursuite *Q4*   a] any *Q1*   19 SD] *Gurr*   21 SD] *Weber*   22–31] *Q1 lines*
repent, / him, / member, / mouth, / now, / presently / Almanacke, / liuer, / dog-whip. / lookes, /
neighbours, / face, / honest. /   22 SP] LEON *Q1*

Methinks that were not noble in him, and yet he looks
like a mortified member, as if he had a sick man's salve
in's mouth. If a worse man had done this fault, now,   25
some physical justice or other would presently, without
the help of an almanac, have opened the obstructions of
his liver and let him blood with a dog whip.

DION   See, see, how modestly yon lady looks, as if she
came from churching with her neighbours. Why, what   30
a devil can a man see in her face but that she's honest?

THRASILINE   Faith, no great matter to speak of: a foolish
twinkling with the eye that spoils her coat, but he must
be a cunning herald that finds it.

DION   See how they muster one another! Oh, there's a   35

---

24 **mortified member** a member of the
church or what the Book of Common
Prayer calls a 'member of Christe', who
has brought his body and passions into
subjection by 'self-denial, abstinence,
or bodily discipline' (*OED* mortify 4a,
citing Colossians, 3.5 in Tyndale's 1526
translation: 'Mortifie therfore youre
members which are on the erth'). Also,
a detumescent penis. Fletcher repeats
the joke in *Knight of Malta*, 5.2.69–72,
where Norandine refuses to join the
Knights because 'I have too much flesh
for this spirituall Knighthood, / And
therefore do desire forbearance, sir, /
Till I am older, or more mortifide, / I
am too sound yet.'
sick man's salve *The Sick Man's
Salve*, a devotional work by Thomas
Becon (1561) 'wherein the faithful
Christians may learn both how to behave
themselves patiently and thankfully in
the time of sickness, and also virtuously
to dispose their temporal goods, and
finally to prepare themselves gladly and
godly to die'. In *Eastward Ho!* one sign
of Quicksilver's conversion is that 'He
can tell you almost all the stories of
The Book of Martyrs, and speak you all
The Sick Man's Salve without book'

(5.2). In *Epicoene*, 4.4.114–16, Trusty's
mother is said to be cured of madness
by reading it.
26–8 **physical justice . . . whip** would
have beat him till he bled. *Physical
justice* is corporal punishment; the
metaphor is from medical blood-letting,
which was recommended at regular
seasons of the year and thus with the
help of an almanac.
30 **churching** the public appearance of
a woman at church to return thanks
after childbirth; for discussion of the
practice and differences in the Anglican
and Roman Catholic ritual, see Cressy,
197–229, and Bicks, 161–88.
31 **honest** chaste
33 **spoils her coat** defaces her coat of
arms, shows her status as less than
noble; given the canine imagery
in 15–18, the phrase may suggest
'besmirches her well-groomed fur'.
34 **herald** court officer whose duty it was
to record the names and pedigrees of
those entitled to armorial bearings
35 **muster one another** The military
imagery that follows (*regiment, colours,
drum major*) suggests that the primary
meaning of *muster* is *OED v.*[1] 2b, to
collect or assemble (especially soldiers)

29 SP] TRA. *Q1*   31 a man] you *Q1*   32 SP] CLE. *Q1*   35 SP] TRA. *Q1*   one] on *Q1*

rank regiment, where the devil carries the colours and his dam is drum major. Now the world and the flesh come behind with the carriage.

CLEREMONT   Sure this lady has a good turn done her against her will. Before, she was common talk; now 40 none dare say cantharides can stir her. Her face looks like a warrant, willing and commanding all tongues, as they will answer it, to be tied up and bolted when this lady means to let herself loose. As I live, she has got her a goodly protection and a gracious, and may use 45 her body discreetly, for her health sake, once a week, excepting Lent and dog-days. Oh, if they were to be got for money, what a large sum would come out of the city for these licences! 49

to be counted, enlisted into service, or sent into battle, but also implied is *OED v.*[1] 6, 'take stock of' each other: cf. *Custom of the Country*, 5.5.66–7, 'With what a greedy hawkes eye she beholds me? / Marke how she musters all my parts.'

36 **rank** lustful, licentious (*OED a.*13); cf. *MV*, 1.3.75–6, 'The ewes being rank . . . turned to the rams.'

36–7 **devil . . . flesh** The enemies of the soul were the world, the flesh and the devil: cf. the Book of Common Prayer of 1549, 'from al the deceytes of the worlde, the fleshe, and the deuill: Good lorde deliuer us'.

36–7 ***devil . . . major** By adding *is* (see 37 t.n.) Theobald clarifies that the *drum major* is a person, not a large instrument carried by the devil's *dam*. The *colours* are the regimental flag.

39 **has** has had

41 **cantharides** an aphrodisiac. Andrew in *Elder Brother* observes his old master wooing: 'Now must I play at Bo-peepe – / A banquet – well,

Potatoes and Eringoes, / And as I take it, Cantharides. – Excellent, / A priapisme followes, and as Ile handle it, / It shall, old lecherous Goate in authority. / Now they beginne to bill; how he slavers her' (4.4.5–10).

42–3 **tongues . . . bolted** Cf. Pharamond's suggestion at 2.2.124–8 that Gallatea needs a tongue bolt to control her wit.

44 **let . . . loose** engage in sexual activity

44–7 **she . . . dog-days** She has obtained an official permission, a 'licence', to have sex (*use her body*) at regular intervals, with the exception of Lent and the hottest days of summer. For parody of the abuse of special licences to eat meat for health's sake during Lent, see *Chaste Maid*, 2.2.

47 **dog-days** the days around the time of the heliacal rising of the dog-star, varying from mid-July to mid-August; noted from ancient times as the hottest and most unwholesome period of the year

48–9 **out of the city** from the wealthy citizens

36 regiment] regient *Q1*   37 dam is] *Theobald;* Dam *Q2;* damn'd *Q1*   the world and the flesh] the flesh and the world *Q1*   39 SP] LEON *Q1*   her] *om. Q1*   41 dare] dares *Q1*   44–5 got her] got *Q1*   47 excepting] except *Q1*

KING

To horse, to horse! We lose the morning, gentlemen. *Exeunt.*

[**4.2**]   *Enter two* WOODMEN.

1 WOODMAN   What, have you lodged the deer?

2 WOODMAN   Yes, they are ready for the bow.

1 WOODMAN   Who shoots?

2 WOODMAN   The princess.

1 WOODMAN   No, she'll hunt.   5

2 WOODMAN   She'll take a stand, I say.

1 WOODMAN   Who else?

2 WOODMAN   Why, the young stranger prince.

1 WOODMAN   He shall shoot in a stone-bow for me. I
never loved his beyond-sea-ship since he forsook the   10
say for paying ten shillings. He was there at the fall of
a deer and would needs, out of his mightiness, give ten
groats for the doucets; marry, the steward would have

4.2 Location: the woods

1 **lodged** driven into their 'lodge' or lair, so they can be shot at (*OED v.* II 9)

2 **ready for the bow** prepared for the hunters

3–6 **shoots . . . hunt . . . stand** The Woodmen debate whether the princess will *hunt* the deer while riding (cf. Fig. 2) or whether she will *shoot* from within a *stand* or concealed standing-place. In *LLL*, 4.1.7–10, the Princess of France asks, 'where is the bush / That we must stand and play the murderer in?' and the Forester replies, 'Hereby, upon the edge of yonder coppice; / A stand where you may make the fairest shoot'.

9 **He . . . me** For all I care he can use a catapult; cf. *King and No King*, 5.1.59–60, 'Children will shortly take him for a wall, / And set their stone-bowes in his

forhead.'

10 **his beyond-sea-ship** a pun on 'his lordship', emphasizing Pharamond's foreignness

10–11 **forsook . . . shillings** refused the inspection of the deer's fat, conventionally awarded to the person of highest rank present, because he would have been expected to tip the woodmen ten shillings. The *say* in hunting is a 'trial of grease' (*OED n.*[2] 5, citing Chapman, *Iliad* XIX. 246, 'There, hauing brought the Bore, Atrides with his knife tooke sey'). See Fig. 6 of King James taking say.

11 **fall** bringing down

12–13 **give ten groats** The woodman expected a more generous fee.

13 **doucets** testicles of a deer
    would have wanted, asked for

---

50 SD] *Exit King and Lords, Manet Wood-men opp. 4.2.1–3 Q1*   **4.2**] *Weber; not in Q2*   0 SD] *Manet Wood-men opp. 3 Q1*   1 deer] *Deere below Q1*   8 stranger] *strange Q1*   9–18] *Q1 lines me / followed by prose*   13 the steward] *his steward Q1*

the velvet head into the bargain to turf his hat withal. I
think he should love venery. He is an old Sir Tristram,   15
for if you be remembered, he forsook the stag once to
strike a rascal milking in a meadow, and her he killed in
the eye. Who shoots else?

2 WOODMAN   The lady Gallatea.

1 WOODMAN   That's a good wench, and she would not   20
chide us for tumbling of her women in the brakes.
She's liberal and, by the gods, they say she's honest and
whether that be a fault, I have nothing to do. There's
all?

2 WOODMAN   No, one more: Megra.   25

1 WOODMAN   That's a firker, i'faith, boy! There's a wench

14 **to . . . withal** to use as a facing or
border for his hat (*OED* turf, *v.*²).
OED cites Robert Greene's *Defence of
Conny-Catching*, 'A beaver hatte turft
with velvet, so quaintly as if he had
been some Espagnolo trickt up', which
suggests that elaborate 'turfing' was
associated with Spanish extravagance
in dress.

15 **venery** The Woodman puns on the
word's two meanings, the sport of
hunting and the practice or pursuit of
sexual pleasure.

Sir Tristram an ironic comparison.
In tales of chivalry Sir Tristram was
an authority on matters to do with the
chase: cf. *FQ*, 6.2.31, where Tristram
asserts that 'my most delight hath
alwaies been / To hunt the saluage
chace amongst my peres, / Of all that
raungeth in the forrest greene; / Of
which none is to me vnknowne, that
eu'r was seene'.

16–17 **forsook . . . meadow** A *rascal* is
one of the 'young, lean, or inferior
deer of a herd, as distinguished
from the full grown antlered

bucks or stags' (*OED* 5a, citing an
example from 1607: 'What Deere
hath the Lord of this Mannor in
his Parke . . . how many of Antler,
and how many rascall'). The rascal
milking was either a female nursing
a fawn, or, Turner suggests, a young
male sucking milk from a cow,
'the usual inhabitant of a *meadow*'
(489). In either case Pharamond
is effeminized by forsaking manly
pursuit of the stag to attack a weak
animal engaged in suckling.

20 **and** if

21 **her women** The Woodman's phrase
may refer to Gallatea's own servants
or may suggest that Gallatea has
general authority over the other waiting
women. In that case she could be the
person Pharamond refers to as the
reverend mother at 2.2.3.

22 **liberal** tips well, unlike Pharamond

26 **firker** To *firk* is to press hard, move
briskly or dance, but the sexual meaning
(fuck) is present in the verb and constant
in the noun. In *Woman's Prize*, 2.6.36–7,
the rebellious women 'have got a stick of

14 turf] tuft *Theobald*   15 is an] and *Q1*   16 you] ye *Q1*   the stag] a Stagge *Q1*   17 milking] mitch-
ing *Theobald*   17–18 in the] i'the *Q1*   20 and] an *Q1*   22 she's honest] honest *Q1*   23 fault] fault or
no *Q1*   24 all?] all. *Q1*

will ride her haunches as hard after a kennel of hounds
as a hunting saddle, and when she comes home, get 'em
clapped, and all is well again. I have known her lose
herself three times in one afternoon – if the woods have   30
been answerable – and it has been work enough for one
man to find her, and he has sweat for it. She rides well
and she pays well. Hark, let's go.   *Exeunt.*

[**4.3**]   *Enter* PHILASTER.

PHILASTER

Oh, that I had been nourished in these woods
With milk of goats and acorns and not known
The right of crowns nor the dissembling trains
Of women's looks, but digged myself a cave
Where I, my fire, my cattle and my bed   5

Fiddles and they firke it / In wondrous
waies'; *OED* cites Rowley, *A Woman
never Vext*, 4.1, 'These briske factors are
notable firkers.'
26–9 There's . . . again The Woodman
suggests Megra's eagerness in hunting
and her desire to get her haunches
clapped, which here means something
like 'pressed close', with sexual
innuendo. Cf. Middleton, *Trick*,
2.1.331–2, 'Clap sure to him, widow.'
29–30 lose herself by implication so that
a man can *find her* and they can engage
in sex. This comment prepares for the
anxiety when Arethusa is missing at the
beginning of 4.4.
31 answerable suitable, meeting
requirements
32 rides well is a good horsewoman; has
good sex
4.3 Location: the woods
1–13 based on Juvenal's *Satire 6*, in
which he warns a friend against

marriage and attacks women for
sexual promiscuity and the corruption
of civilization. The first lines read, in
Braund's translation: 'I can believe
that Chastity lingered on earth during
Saturn's reign and that she was visible
for a long time during the era when
a chilly cave provided a tiny home,
enclosing fire and hearth god and
herd and its owners in communal
gloom, when a mountain wife made
her woodland bed with leaves and
straw and the skins of her neighbours,
the beasts . . . she offered her paps
for her hefty babies to drain, and she
was often more unkempt than her
acorn-belching husband.' However,
this Golden Age ended when Astraea,
the goddess of Justice, 'withdrew to
the gods above with Chastity as her
companion. The two sisters ran away
together' (*Juvenal*, 235–7).
3 trains tricks

30–1 have / been] had beene *Q1*   31 it] *om. Q1*   32 he] *om. Q1*   for it] for't *Q1*   33 let's go] else
Q1   SD] *om. Q1*   **4.3]** *Spencer (Daniel); not in Q2*   0 SD] *Enter* PHILASTER *solus. Q1*   1 these] the
Q1   4 women's looks] cruell loue *Q1*

Might have been shut together in one shed.
And then had taken me some mountain girl,
Beaten with winds, chaste as the hardened rocks
Whereon she dwells, that might have strewed my bed
With leaves and reeds and with the skins of beasts,   10
Our neighbours, and have borne at her big breasts
My large, coarse issue. This had been a life
Free from vexation.

Enter BELLARIO.

BELLARIO   Oh, wicked men!
An innocent may walk safe among beasts;
Nothing assaults me here. See, my grieved lord   15
Sits as his soul were searching out a way
To leave his body. [*to Philaster*] Pardon me that must
Break thy last commandment, for I must speak.
You that are grieved can pity. Hear, my lord!

PHILASTER
Is there a creature yet so miserable   20
That I can pity?

BELLARIO   Oh, my noble lord,
View my strange fortune and bestow on me
According to your bounty – if my service
Can merit nothing – so much as may serve

---

14 For images of nature as less dangerous
than the courts of men, see Innogen's
surprise, 'Gods, what lies I have heard! /
Our courtiers say all's savage but at court;
/ Experience, O, thou disprov'st report!'
(*Cym*, 4.2.32–4), and cf. Gonzalo's ideal
society where 'All things in common
nature should produce / Without sweat

or endeavour; treason, felony, / Sword,
pike, knife, gun, or need of any engine
/ Would I not have; but nature should
bring forth / Of its own kind all foison,
all abundance, / To feed my innocent
people' (*Tem*, 2.1.160–5).
18 **thy last commandment** i.e., 'Let me
not see thee more', 3.1.279

8 hardened rocks] rocke *Q1*   9 dwells] dwelt *Q1*   11 at] Out *Q1*   13–19 Oh . . . lord!] *Q1 lines* beasts,
/ as / body. / speake: / Lord. /   14 among] amongst *Q1*   15 See] I see *Q1*   17 SD] *Gurr; Aside
| Dyce* must] *om. Q1*   20–1 Is . . . pity?] *one line Q1*   21–6 Oh . . . hunger] *Q1 lines* fortunes, /
bounty, / keepe / hunger. /   22 fortune] fortunes *Q1*

To keep that little piece I hold of life   25
From cold and hunger.

PHILASTER   Is it thou? Be gone.
Go sell those misbeseeming clothes thou wearest
And feed thyself with them.

BELLARIO
Alas, my lord, I can get nothing for them.
The silly country people think 'tis treason   30
To touch such gay things.

PHILASTER   Now, by the gods, this is
Unkindly done, to vex me with thy sight.
Th'art fallen again to thy dissembling trade.
How shouldst thou think to cozen me again?
Remains there yet a plague untried for me?   35
Even so thou wept'st, and look'st, and spok'st, when
      first
I took thee up: curse on the time! If thy
Commanding tears can work on any other,
Use thy art; I'll not betray it. Which way
Wilt thou take, that I may shun thee?   40
For thine eyes are poison to mine, and I
Am loath to grow in rage. This way or that way?

BELLARIO
Any will serve, but I will choose to have
That path in chase that leads unto my grave.
            Exeunt Philaster [and] Bellario severally.

26–31 **Is . . . things** Q1 omits this exchange,
  possibly because of its suggestions of
  economic hostility between court and
  country. See 4.5.74 SDn. on COUNTRY
  FELLOW and pp. 39–40.
27 **misbeseeming** inappropriate
33 **dissembling trade** dishonesty,
  described as if it were Bellario's regular
  business

34 **cozen** cheat, defraud
36 **look'st** This form represents the past
  tense 'lookedst', parallel to the other
  verbs in Philaster's complaint, *wept'st*
  and *spok'st*, but elided for euphony.
38 **Commanding tears** powerfully moving tears, but perhaps also 'commanded
  tears', conjured up by Bellario's *art* (39)
43–4 **have . . . chase** pursue that route

26–31 PHILASTER . . . things] *om. Q1*   31–42 Now . . . way?] *Q1 lines* me / trade, / againe, / so / thee,
/ worke / which way / are / rage: / way?   31 the gods] my life *Q4*   33 Th'art] thou art *Q1*   36–7
first / I] I first *Q1*   37 up] *om. Q1*   42 way?] way? *Exit* PHYLASTER *Q1*   44 SD] *Exit* BOY. *Q1*   *and*] F

[4.4]   *Enter* DION *and the* WOODMEN.

DION   This is the strangest sudden chance! You,
        woodman!

1 WOODMAN   My lord Dion.

DION   Saw you a lady come this way, on a sable horse
        studded with stars of white?   5

2 WOODMAN   Was she not young and tall?

DION   Yes. Rode she to the wood or to the plain?

2 WOODMAN   Faith, my lord, we saw none.

DION   Pox of your questions, then!   *Exeunt Woodmen.*

                      Enter CLEREMONT.

        What, is she found?   10

CLEREMONT   Nor will be, I think.

DION   Let him seek his daughter himself. She cannot stray
        about a little necessary natural business but the whole
        court must be in arms. When she has done we shall
        have peace.   15

CLEREMONT   There's already a thousand fatherless tales
        amongst us: some say her horse ran away with her;
        some, a wolf pursued her; others, 'twas a plot to kill
        her, and that armed men were seen in the wood. But
        questionless, she rode away willingly.   20

                 Enter KING *and* THRASILINE.

4.4 Location: the woods
4   **sable** black (heraldic)
12–13 **stray . . . business** go privately to
      relieve herself
14 **When . . . done** when she has finished

what she is doing
16 **fatherless tales** sourceless rumours
17–19 **her   horse . . . wood**   Such
      incidents are the stuff of romance plots
      in early modern prose and drama.

4.4] *Spencer (Daniel); not in Q2* 0 SD] *Enter* LEON, CLE. *and Wood-men* Q1 1 SP] CLE. *Q1* 3
Dion] *Leon Q1* 5 studded] starre-dyed *Q1* 6 SP] 1 WOOD. *Q1* 9 your] *Q1;* you *Q2* SD1] *Dyce;
Exit Woodmen. opp.* none *8 Q2; om. Q1* SD2] *Dyce; after Exit Woodmen. 8 Q2* 12–15] *Q1 lines* stray
/ businesse: / armes, / peace. / 16–20] *Q1 lines* vs, / pursu'd her / seene / willingly. / 17 ran]
run *Q1* 20 SD] *Enter the King,* TRA. *and other Lords. Q1*

KING

    Where is she?

CLEREMONT   Sir, I cannot tell.

KING   How's that?

    Answer me so again! —

CLEREMONT   Sir, shall I lie?

KING

    Yes, lie and damn, rather than tell me that!

    I say again, where is she? Mutter not.

    [*to Dion*] Sir, speak you. Where is she?

DION   Sir, I do not know.   25

KING

    Speak that again so boldly and, by heaven,

    It is thy last. You fellows, answer me!

    Where is she? Mark me all, I am your king!

    I wish to see my daughter; show her me.

    I do command you all, as you are subjects,   30

    To show her me! What, am I not your king?

    If ay, then am I not to be obeyed?

DION

    Yes, if you command things possible and honest.

KING

    'Things possible and honest'? Hear me, thou,

---

23 **damn** be damned. For the rare passive sense *OED* cites only this line and Massinger's *New Way* (1625).

28–31 **I am . . . king?** The reversal from statement to question reflects the King's uncertainty about his status and recalls his situation as a usurper.

29 Cf. 'The King would speak with Cornwall, the dear father / Would with his daughter speak' (*KL*, 2.2.290–1).

32–3 This exchange mirrors King James's continuing conflict with the House of Commons and the common law lawyers and judges over the limits of the royal prerogative. It echoes specifically the confrontation between the king and Sir Edward Coke, the Lord Chief Justice of Common Pleas, on 13 November 1608, when Coke asserted that the law protected the king and not the king the law. See pp. 23–5.

33 Cf. Arethusa's reply to her father's order at 3.2.23–4.

21–2] *Boas; Q2 lines* she? / tell. / againe. / lie? /; *Q6 lines* tell. / lie? /   21 SP2] LEON *Q1*   22 SP] LEON *Q1*   25 SD] *this edn*   26–48] *prose Q1*   32 then] why then *Q1*   34 thou] then *Q1*

Thou traitor, that dar'st confine thy king to things   35
Possible and honest: show her me,
Or let me perish if I cover not
All Sicily with blood!

DION   Faith, I cannot,
Unless you tell me where she is.

KING

You have betrayed me: you've let me lose   40
The jewel of my life! Go, bring her me
And set her here before me. 'Tis the King
Will have it so, whose breath can still the winds,
Uncloud the sun, charm down the swelling sea
And stop the clouds of heaven. Speak, can it not?   45

DION

No.

KING   No! Cannot the breath of kings do this?

DION

No, nor smell sweet itself if once the lungs
Be but corrupted.

KING   Is it so? Take heed!

DION

Sir, take you heed how you dare the powers
That must be just.

KING   Alas, what are we kings?   50

---

35 **traitor** King James said that Coke's
'was a traitorous speech' (Gurr,
lv).

41 **jewel . . . life** Despite his high-
handedness regarding his daughter's
marriage, there is no reason to doubt
the King's affection for Arethusa.

42–5 **'Tis . . . heaven** The King's
assertions of his power are so

excessive that they invite a satirical
reading. Cf. Richard II's claims for
divinely supported royal power, *R2*,
3.2.47–61.

50–5 **Alas . . . threatenings** Cf. Henry
V's soliloquy on kingship before
Agincourt (*H5*, 4.1.227–81), especially
'What infinite heart's ease / Must kings
neglect that private men enjoy! / And

35–6 things / Possible and honest] possible and honest, things *Q1* 38–9] *Boas; Q2 lines* blood.
/ is. / 39 you] you'le *Q1* 40 you've] (y'haue); you haue *Q1* 43 so,] *Q1;* So 1 *Q2* 46 kings] a
king *Q1* 47 SP] C L E. *Q1* nor] more *Q1* 48 Is . . . heed!] Take you heed? *Q1* 49 Sir] *om. Q1*
50–3 Alas . . . thunder] *Q1 lines* gods / adord, / Thunder, /

Why do you gods place us above the rest
To be served, flattered and adored, till we
Believe we hold within our hands your thunder,
And when we come to try the power we have,
There's not a leaf shakes at our threatenings?   55
I have sinned, 'tis true, and here stand to be punished,
Yet would not thus be punished. Let me choose
My way, and lay it on.
DION [*aside*]   He articles with the gods; would somebody
would draw bonds for the performance of covenants   60
betwixt them.

Enter PHARAMOND, GALLATEA *and* MEGRA.

KING

What, is she found?
PHARAMOND   No. We have ta'en her horse;
He galloped empty by. There's some treason.
You, Gallatea, rode with her into the wood;
Why left you her?   65
GALLATEA

She did command me.

what have kings that privates have not
too, / Save ceremony, save general
ceremony? / . . . O be sick, great
greatness, / And bid thy ceremony
give thee cure! / Think'st thou the fiery
fever will go out / With titles blown
from adulation? / Will it give place to
flexure and low-bending? / Canst thou,
when thou command'st the beggar's
knee, / Command the health of it?'
56–8 The King must say these lines aloud,
or as a failed aside, as Dion hears them.
(See 3.1.75–6 for a similar moment.)

His unconcealed admission of guilt is
a sign of how disturbed he is to lose his
daughter. Cf. Leontes, who believes he
is punished for his jealousy by his son's
death: 'Apollo's angry, and the heavens
themselves / Do strike at my injustice'
(*WT*, 3.2.146–7).
59 **articles** bargains
60 **bonds . . . covenants** legal documents
to guarantee the keeping of agreements;
see p. 21 for the topical resonance.
63 **treason** Pharamond repeats the King's
charge at 35.

52 till] Still *Q1*   54 power] power we thinke *Q1*   56 stand] I stand *Q1*   57–8] *Q1 lines* way, /
on. /   57 thus] these *Q1*   59 SD] *Gurr*   60 covenants] couenant *Q1*   61 SD *and*] *om. Q1*   62–5
No . . . her] *prose Q1*   64–5] *assigned to King by Buckingham*   64 with . . . wood] into the Wood with
her *Q1*   65–6] *Daniel; Q2 lines* her? / me. / not. /; *Boas lines* me. / not. /

KING   Command! You should not –

GALLATEA

'Twould ill become my fortunes and my birth
To disobey the daughter of my king.

KING

You're all cunning to obey us for our hurts,
But I will have her.

PHARAMOND   If I have her not,   70
By this hand, there shall be no more Sicily!

DION [*aside*] What, will he carry it to Spain in's pocket?

PHARAMOND

I will not leave one man alive but the King,
A cook and a tailor.

DION [*aside*] Yes, you may do well to spare your lady   75
bedfellow, and her you may keep for a spawner.

KING [*aside*]

I see the injuries I have done must be revenged.

DION

Sir, this is not the way to find her out.

KING

Run all: disperse yourselves. The man that finds her
Or, if she be killed, the traitor, I'll make him great.   80

DION I know some would give five thousand pounds to
find her.

---

69 **for our hurts** to our detriment
73–4 **King . . . tailor** Fools in early modern drama are sometimes characterized
  by their choice of essential servants. In
  Old Law Simonides fires his father's
  Cook, Tailor, Butler and Bailiff, keeping
  only the Footman to win him wagers by
  running races and the Coachman to
  'hurry me to my whore' (2.1.260).
76 **spawner** a female to bring forth brood

81–2 It is unclear whether those who
  would *give five thousand pounds* wish
  to find Arethusa in order to be *great* in
  status – in which case the line is one
  of many slurs on King James's sale of
  knighthoods and other honours (see,
  e.g., *Eastward Ho!*) – or whether they
  wish to be alone with the princess,
  presumably for the sexual opportunity
  it would present. See 4.5.108–9.

66 SP2] PHA. *Q1*   69 You're] O y'are *Q1*   70–1 If . . . Sicily] *prose Q1*   71 hand] sword *Q1*   72 SD]
Boas   pocket] pockets *Q1*   73–4] *Q1 lines* aliue, / Taylor /   75 SD] *Boas*   spare] leaue *Q1*   76
her . . . spawner] here for a spincer *Q1*   77 SD] *Boas*   79–80] *prose Q1*   81] *aside* | *Boas*   know] *om. Q1*

212

PHARAMOND

Come, let us seek.

KING

Each man a several way; here, I myself.

DION   Come, gentlemen, we here.   85

CLEREMONT   Lady, you must go search, too.

MEGRA [*aside*]   I had rather be searched myself.

Exeunt omnes [severally].

[4.5]   *Enter* ARETHUSA.

ARETHUSA

Where am I now? Feet, find me out a way
Without the counsel of my troubled head;
I'll follow you boldly about these woods,
O'er mountains, through brambles, pits and floods.
Heaven I hope will ease me. I am sick.   [*She sits down*.]   5

Enter BELLARIO.

BELLARIO [*aside*]

Yonder's my lady. God knows I want nothing,
Because I do not wish to live. Yet I
Will try her charity.   [*Approaches Arethusa*.]
                        O hear, you that have plenty,
From that flowing store drop some on dry ground. See,

---

84 **several** separate
87 SD1 Megra seems unlikely to make this admission publicly.
87 **searched** examined inwardly or thoroughly, with sexual implication: cf. *Changeling*, 4.1.102–3, 'She will not search me, will she, / Like the

forewoman of a female jury?', lines that allude to the notorious history of Frances Howard. See p. 38.
4.5 Location: the woods
5–11 **sick . . . faints** Arethusa's weakness parallels Innogen's in *Cym*, 3.6 and 4.2.
8 **try** test, attempt

83 SP] K. *Q1*   84 SP] PHA. *Q1*   87 SP] GAL. *Q1*   87 SD1] *this edn*   searched] the search *Q1*   SD2] *Q1; Exit omnes Q2   severally*] *Boas*   4.5] *Spencer*; 4.3 *Weber; not in Q2*   0 SD] *Enter the Princesse solus. Q1*   1–18] *prose Q1*   1 me] *om. Q1*   a] the *Q1*   4 O'er] *(O're); or Q1*   5 SD1] *Q1; not in Q2*   6 SD] *Dyce after* charity   8   Yonder's my lady] Yonder my Lady is *Q1*   God] gods *Q1*   8 SD] *this edn*   9 ground] grounds *Q1*

The lively red is gone to guard her heart;   10
I fear she faints. Madam, look up! She breathes not!
Open once more those rosy twins and send
Unto my lord your latest farewell. Oh, she stirs!
How is it, madam? Speak comfort.

ARETHUSA

'Tis not gently done   15
To put me in a miserable life
And hold me there. I prithee, let me go!
I shall do best without thee. I am well.

Enter PHILASTER.

PHILASTER

I am too blame to be so much in rage.
I'll tell her coolly when and where I heard   20
This killing truth. I will be temperate
In speaking and as just in hearing.
   [*Sees Arethusa and Bellario.*]
Oh, monstrous! Tempt me not, you gods; good gods,
Tempt not a frail man! What's he that has a heart
But he must ease it here?

BELLARIO   My lord, help!   25

Help the princess!

ARETHUSA   I am well; forbear.

PHILASTER

Let me love lightning, let me be embraced

---

12 **rosy twins** lips
21 **I ... temperate** As his behaviour
in this scene and the next will
demonstrate, temperance, a cardinal

virtue, is precisely what Philaster lacks.
24–5 **heart ... ease it** playing on
heartsease, tranquillity or peace of mind
26 **forbear** keep away (from me)

12 more] *om. Q1* 14 is it] is't *Q1* 18 I am well] *om. Q1* 21–5 This . . . here] *Q1 lines* speaking,
/ not / *followed by prose* 22 SD] *Gurr subst.* 24 What's] who's *Q1* 25–6] *this edn; Q2 lines* here?
/ Princesse. / forbeare. /; *Dyce lines* here! / help, help! / princess! / forbear. / 25 here] with his
tongue *Q1* 27–40 Let . . . you] *Q1 lines* kist / Basaliskes / women: / vp, / act. / fire / teares, / beds,
/ face, / issues, / you. / 27 lightning] lightnings *Q1*

And kissed by scorpions or adore the eyes
Of basilisks, rather than trust the tongues
Of hell-bred women. Some good god look down   30
And shrink these veins up. Stick me here a stone,
Lasting to ages, in the memory
Of this damned act. Hear me, you wicked ones:
You have put hills of fire into this breast
Not to be quenched with tears, for which may guilt   35
Sit on your bosoms, at your meals and beds
Despair await you. What, before my face?
Poison of asps between your lips, diseases
Be your best issues! Nature make a curse
And throw it on you.

ARETHUSA   Dear Philaster, leave   40
To be enraged and hear me.

PHILASTER   I have done.
Forgive my passion. Not the calmed sea
When Aeolus locks up his windy brood
Is less disturbed than I. I'll make you know't.
Dear Arethusa, do but take this sword   45
And search how temperate a heart I have.

---

28 **scorpions** arachnids 'having a pair of large nippers and a general resemblance to a miniature lobster . . . The intense pain caused by the sting of the scorpion (situated at the point of the tail) is proverbial' (*OED*). In *Faithful Shepherdess*, 4.2, the wounded Alexis feels 'some poynted thing / Passe through my Bowels, sharper then the stinge / Of *Scorpion*'. See 3.2.114–15 and note.
29 **basilisks** See 1.2.71n.
31 **Stick . . . stone** set up a monument
39 **make a curse** Cf. *H8*, 3.1.123–4.
42 **calmed** calmèd
43 **Aeolus** ruler of the winds

45–61 **take . . . Kill me** Philaster repeatedly seeks death, at his own hand or at the hand of Arethusa or Bellario; besides the examples here, see 5.5.79 and 124. The insistence of his death wish exaggerates and parodies Hamlet's and suggests pathology, whether viewed in religious terms as a violation of the Everlasting's 'canon 'gainst self-slaughter' (*Ham*, 1.2.131–2) or in early modern psychoanalytic terms as dangerous melancholia, the 'troubled mind' he considers incurable at 3.1.294.
46 **search** probe, as a wound; cf. *Valentinian*, 1.3.63, 'You search

30 women] *Q1;* woman *Q2*   32 ages, in the] *om. Q1*   34 this] my *Q1*   40 throw] *Q1;* through *Q2*   41 be enraged] inrage *Q1*   42–54] *Q1 lines Eolus / I, / sword, / you, / controule. / me, / thoughts / now? / pulse, / more / die. /*   44 know't] know *Q1*   45 do but] *om. Q1*

Then you, and this your boy, may live and reign
In lust without control.
            [*Offers his sword to Arethusa, who refuses it.*]
                              Wilt thou, Bellario?
I prithee, kill me. Thou art poor and mayst
Nourish ambitious thoughts. When I am dead   50
Thy way were freer. Am I raging now?
If I were mad I should desire to live.
Sirs, feel my pulse. Whether have you known
A man in a more equal tune to die?

BELLARIO

Alas, my lord, your pulse keeps madman's time.   55
So does your tongue.

PHILASTER   You will not kill me, then?

ARETHUSA

Kill you?

BELLARIO   Not for the world.

PHILASTER   I blame not thee,
Bellario. Thou hast done but that which gods
Would have transformed themselves to do. Be gone;
Leave me without reply. This is the last   60
Of all our meeting.   *Exit Bellario.*
      [*to Arethusa*]   Kill me with this sword;
Be wise, or worse will follow. We are two
Earth cannot bear at once. Resolve to do

the soare too deep.' But the sado-
masochism and sexuality of the
relationship is underscored by the
echo of Megra's 'I had rather be
searched myself' (4.4.87).
53 **Sirs** The term could be addressed
indifferently to men and women; an
actor might also choose to address this

phrase to the audience (GM).
58–9 **done . . . do** Notably, Jupiter
transformed himself to conduct
love affairs: he became a bull to carry
away Europa, a swan to make love
to Leda, and a golden shower to
reach Danae shut in the tower. See
2.2.45n.

48 SD] *Dyce subst. after* sword *45*   51 Thy] *Q1;* This *Q2*   53 have you] you haue *Q1*   54 a more]
more *Q1*   55 SP] Prin. *Q1*   madman's] madmens *Q1*   57] *Boas; Q2 lines* you? / world. / thee, /;
Q6 lines World. / thee, /   SP1] Boy. *Q1*   SP2] Prin. *Q1*   the] a *Q4*   57–68 I . . . there] *Q1 lines*
that / do, / last / wise, / *followed by prose*   61 meeting] meetings *Q1*   SD1] *Weber; opp.* 60 last
Q2   SD2] *this edn*

216

Or suffer.

ARETHUSA

If my fortune be so good to let me fall   65
Upon thy hand, I shall have peace in death.
Yet tell me this: there will be no slanders,
No jealousy, in the other world, no ill there?

PHILASTER

No.

ARETHUSA   Show me, then, the way.

PHILASTER   Then guide
My feeble hand, you that have power to do it,   70
For I must perform a piece of justice. If your youth
Have any way offended heaven, let prayers,
Short and effectual, reconcile you to it.

ARETHUSA

I am prepared.

Enter a COUNTRY FELLOW.

65–6 **let . . . hand** allow me to be killed
by you
68 **no ill there** *no ill* may be a printer's
misreading of 'will'; in that case the
sentence would conclude with Arethusa
asking for confirmation: 'will there?'
(GM). Q1's phrasing 'no ill here', if
taken literally, would mean that there
will be no ill in *this world* once Arethusa
is dead.
69 **the way** to the *other world* (68)
71 **a piece of justice** Like Othello,
Philaster sees himself as carrying out
a just revenge; cf. 'O balmy breath, that
dost almost persuade / Justice to break
her sword!' (*Oth*, 5.2.16–17).
71–3 **If . . . it** Cf. 'Have you prayed
tonight, Desdemon? . . . If you bethink

yourself of any crime / Unreconciled
as yet to heaven and grace, / Solicit for
it straight' (*Oth*, 5.2.25–8).
73 **effectual** of prayers, earnest and
urgent (*OED* 3a); cf. the King James
Bible's translation of James, 5.16, 'The
effectual fervent prayer of a righteous
man availeth much.'
74 SD COUNTRY FELLOW Q1 calls this
character a 'Countrey Gallant', and
its title-page illustration labels him 'A
Cuntrie Gentellman'. The promotion
in status may relate to Q1's omission
of 4.3.26–31, lines which report the
reaction of the *silly country people* to
Bellario's *gay clothes*; both emendations
attempt to reduce suggestions of class
conflict. However, Q1 does not alter

65 fortune] fortunes *Q1*   66 in death] with earth *Q1*   68–71] *Turner; Q2 lines* there? / No. / way. /
guide / it, / youth /; *Q6 lines* No. / guide / it / youth / ; *Boas lines* there? / hand, / must / youth
/   68 there] here *Q1*   69 then, the way] the way to ioy *Q1*   69–73 Then . . . it] *Q1 lines* power / Iustice:
/ heauen, / to't. /   73 to it] to't *Q1*   74 SD FELLOW] *Gallant Q1*

COUNTRY FELLOW   I'll see the King if he be in the forest.   75
I have hunted him these two hours. If I should come
home and not see him, my sisters would laugh at me.
I can see nothing but people better horsed than myself
that outride me. I can hear nothing but shouting. These
kings had need of good brains: this whooping is able   80
to put a mean man out of his wits. [*Sees Philaster and
Arethusa.*] There's a courtier with his sword drawn – by
this hand, upon a woman, I think!

PHILASTER
Are you at peace?

ARETHUSA   With heaven and earth.

PHILASTER
May they divide thy soul and body.   85
   [*Philaster wounds her.*]

COUNTRY FELLOW   Hold, dastard! Strike a woman?
Th'art a craven, I warrant thee: thou wouldst be loath

---

the language of the countryman in
any notable way (see t.n. on 75–81);
in both texts he remains socially and
linguistically distinct from the courtiers
he encounters.

75 **I'll see** I must see

76 **hunted him** searched for him; the
inversion of the royal pastime of
hunting is ominous.

77 **my . . . laugh** Cf. the entrance of the
clown in *WT*: 'Let me see; what am I to
buy for our sheep-shearing feast? Three
pound of sugar, five pound of currants,
rice – what will this sister of mine do
with rice? But my father hath made her
mistress of the feast, and she lays it on'
(4.3.36–40).

78 **better horsed** As the countryman is or
was mounted, he is not a mere clown or
peasant.

80 **whooping** crying 'whoop', shouting
in excitement; cf. Drayton, Eclogue 4,
'With that the shepheard whoop'd for
ioy' (*OED*).

81 **put . . . wits** drive an ordinary
person mad; the Country Fellow's
suggestion that superior people would
be unaffected ironically occurs just as
he catches sight of the maddened but
noble Philaster.

86 **dastard** 'One who meanly or basely
shrinks from danger; a mean, base, or
despicable coward' (*OED n.* and *a.* A2)
strike a woman an unfortunately
frequent habit of Fletcher's heroes
(GM). The action is more shocking
here than in *Cupid's Revenge* and *Maid's
Tragedy*, where the women struck are in
male disguise.

87 **craven** coward

75–81] *Q1 lines* Forrest, / home, / me, / selfe, / shouting, / braines, / wits: / *followed by prose*   75 I'll]
I will *Q1*   76 these] this *Q1*   78 than] *Q1* (then); then then *Q2*   80 good] strong *Q1*   80–1 this . . . to]
The whooping would *Q1*   81 mean] *om. Q1*   81–2 SD] *this edn*   84–5] *Thorndike; Q2 lines* peace?
/ earth. / body. /; *Daniel lines* they / body! /   85 May] Nay *Q1*   SD] *Q1 opp.* peace 84; *not in Q2*
87 craven, I warrant thee:] *Q1*; crauen I warrant thee, *Q2*   thou wouldst] thoud'st *Q1*

to play half a dozen venies at wasters with a good fellow
for a broken head.

PHILASTER

Leave us, good friend.   90

ARETHUSA

What ill-bred man art thou to intrude thyself
Upon our private sports, our recreations?

COUNTRY FELLOW   God 'uds me, I understand you not,
but I know the rogue has hurt you.

PHILASTER

Pursue thy own affairs. It will be ill   95
To multiply blood upon my head, which thou
Wilt force me to.

COUNTRY FELLOW   I know not your rhetoric, but I can lay
it on if you touch the woman.

---

88 **venies** or *venues*, hits or thrusts in
a fencing match; cf. *MW*, 1.1.264–7,
'I bruised my shin th'other day with
playing at sword and dagger with a
master of fence – three venues for a
dish of stewed prunes.'
wasters 'fencing with a "waster";
single-stick, cudgel-play' (*OED* waster
*n.*² 3, citing Greene, *Selimus*, 'I thought
my selfe as proper a fellow at wasters, as
any in all our village')

91 **ill-bred . . . thyself** Arethusa's reaction
is an extreme manifestation of early
modern class prejudice, somewhat
excused by her devotion to Philaster.

92 **our private . . . recreations** Intentionally or not, Arethusa's phrases suggest
that her interaction with Philaster is sexual; that the furious passion, abjection
and violence is a form of play; and that
her wounding substitutes metaphorically
and physically for sexual penetration.

93 **God 'uds me** This expletive is a bit of
linguistic confusion on the part of the
countryman, as *'uds* was 'a form of the
name of God common in expletive oaths
in the 17th century' (*OED*); cf. *Honest
Man's Fortune*, 2.4.130, 'Udsprecious,
we have lost a brother.'

96 **multiply . . . head** make me wound or
hurt more people

98 **rhetoric** 'Elegance or eloquence
of language' but also 'language
characterized by artificial or
ostentatious expression' (*OED n.*¹ 2a,
citing Richard Brathwaite, *Strappado*
(1615), 'Heere is no substance, but a
simple peece Of gaudy Rhetoricke').
The Countryman insists that he
recognizes and will respond to
the reality of the situation despite
Philaster's linguistic flourishes.

98–9 **lay it on** deal blows vigorously; cf.
Mac, 5.8.33–4, 'lay on, Macduff, / And
damn'd be him that first cries, "Hold,
enough!"'

88 venies] *Q4;* veneis *Q1;* veines *Q2*   good fellow] man *Q1*   91–2] *prose Q1*   93–4] *Q1 lines* not, / ye.
/   93 'uds] iudge *Q1*   94 you] ye *Q1*   95–7] *Dyce; Q2 lines:* ill / head. / to. /; *prose Q1*   98 rhetoric]
(rethoricke); Rethrack *Q1*

PHILASTER

    Slave, take what thou deservest.   *They fight.*   100

ARETHUSA

    Heaven guard my lord!   [*Both men are wounded.*]

COUNTRY FELLOW   Oh, do you breathe?

PHILASTER

    I hear the tread of people. I am hurt.

    The gods take part against me. Could this boor

    Have held me thus, else? I must shift for life.   105

    Though I do loathe it, I would find a course

    To lose it rather by my will than force.   *Exit.*

COUNTRY FELLOW   I cannot follow the rogue. – I prithee,

wench, come and kiss me now.

Enter PHARAMOND, DION, CLEREMONT, THRASILINE
and WOODMEN.

PHARAMOND   What art thou?   110

---

100 SD–101 SD The placement of both
directions will depend upon an
editor's or director's interpretation
of the action, but Q1's positioning
of *They fight* after 100 seems more
logical than after 99, as in Q2. If, as
suggested here, both men are wounded
(103, 111) only after Arethusa invokes
Heaven's aid, the irony recalls the
entrance of Lear carrying the dead
Cordelia immediately after Albany
prays 'The gods defend her' (*KL*,
5.3.254).

102 **breathe** pause. Apparently Philaster
has stopped fighting.

104–8 **boor . . . rogue** The reciprocal
name-calling – the Country Fellow
refers to Philaster as a *rogue* at 94, 108
and 126, and *boor* is a term for a rustic
or peasant 'with lack of refinement
implied' (*OED* 3) – highlights the early

modern debate about whether worth
should be evaluated by social status or
by behaviour.

105 **shift for life** provide for my own
safety (as in 'shift for oneself'); remove
myself from here to save myself

109 **come . . . me** By harassing Arethusa
sexually the Country Fellow loses the
sympathy he gained by his outrage
at seeing Philaster *strike a woman*
(86). Beaumont and Fletcher recreate
this moment in *Coxcomb* when Viola
is rescued from threatened rape by
Valerio only to have him demand, 'We
are alone, shew me how thou wilt kisse
/ And hug me hard . . . 'Tis lust I wish
indeed' (3.3.74–81).

110–27 The verse breaks down as the
crowd of courtiers reacts to finding the
wounded Arethusa with the Country
Fellow.

---

100 SD] *Q1; opp.* woman *99 Q2*   101 Heaven] Gods *Q1*   SD] *this edn*   103–7] *prose Q1*   104 Could]
would *Q1*   106 loathe] lose *Q1*   107 SD] *(*Exit. Philaster.*); Exit* PHY. *opp.* rogue *108 Q1*   108–9] *Q1*
lines rogue, / now. /   109 and] *om. Q1*

220

COUNTRY FELLOW   Almost killed I am, for a foolish
    woman. A knave has hurt her.

PHARAMOND   The princess, gentlemen! Where's the
    wound, madam? Is it dangerous?

ARETHUSA   He has not hurt me.   115

COUNTRY FELLOW   By God, she lies: he's hurt her in the
    breast. Look else!

PHARAMOND   Oh, sacred spring of innocent blood!

DION   'Tis above wonder! Who should dare this?

ARETHUSA   I felt it not.   120

PHARAMOND   Speak, villain! Who has hurt the princess?

COUNTRY FELLOW   Is it the princess?

DION   Ay.

COUNTRY FELLOW   Then I have seen something yet.

PHARAMOND   But who has hurt her?   125

COUNTRY FELLOW   I told you, a rogue. I ne'er saw him
    before, I.

PHARAMOND
    Madam, who did it?

ARETHUSA   Some dishonest wretch,
    Alas, I know him not, and do forgive him.

COUNTRY FELLOW   He's hurt, too, he cannot go far. I   130
    made my father's old fox fly about his ears.

116–17 **hurt . . . breast** The wound
    is clearly visible in the title-page
    illustration of Q1 (see Fig. 10). The
    location of the wound makes it a
    political as well as a physical injury:
    the future king has wounded the future
    queen in the nurturing part of her body.
    King James called himself a 'nourish-
    father' to the nation.

124 **something yet** i.e., something to tell
    his sisters so they will not laugh at him
    (76–7)

131 **old fox** A *fox* is a type of sword
    (*OED* 6); the class implications
    of the Country Fellow having one
    are uncertain. In *Cupid's Revenge*,
    4.3.1–2, the Citizen sends his boy to
    'go fetch my Foxe from the Cutlers:
    There's money for the scowring', but
    in *Love's Cure*, 3.4.69–70, Alvarez, a
    military hero, threatens Lucio, 'On
    sir; put home: or I shall goad you
    here / With this old Fox of mine.'
    The sword held by the 'Cuntrie

111–12] *Q1 lines* woman, / her. /   113 SP] LEON *Q1*   116 he's] (has) in the] i'the *Q1*   118 sacred]
secret *Q1*   123 SP] OMNES *Q1*   125 hurt her] done it *Q1*   128–9] *Boas; Q2 lines* it? / not, / him. /;
Theobald lines it? / Wretch; / him. /   128 SP1] LEON *Q1*   131 made] let *Q1*   about his] about's *Q1*

221

PHARAMOND

How will you have me kill him?

ARETHUSA

Not at all. 'Tis some distracted fellow.

PHARAMOND   By this hand, I'll leave never a piece of him

bigger than a nut, and bring him all to you in my hat.   135

ARETHUSA

Nay, good sir,

If you do take him, bring him quick to me

And I will study for a punishment,

Great as his fault.

PHARAMOND

I will.

ARETHUSA   But swear.

PHARAMOND   By all my love, I will.   140

Woodman, conduct the princess to the King,

And bear that wounded fellow to dressing.

Come, gentlemen, we'll follow the chase close.

Exeunt [separately] Arethusa and 1 Woodman
[and] Pharamond, Dion, Cleremont and Thrasiline.

COUNTRY FELLOW   I pray, you, friend, let me see the

King.   145

2 WOODMAN   That you shall, and receive thanks.

COUNTRY FELLOW   If I get clear of this, I'll go to see no

more gay sights.   *Exeunt.*

[4.6]   *Enter* BELLARIO.

Gentellman' in the woodcut on the
title-page of Q1 is unusual in its
combination of a basket around
the knuckles with a long curved
crossguard; it suggests 'rusticity and/

or cultural conservatism' (Forgeng).
137 **quick** quickly; alive. Arethusa
does not wish her intentions to be
understood.
4.6 Location: the woods

134 hand] ayre *Q1*   of him] *om. Q1*   135 to you] *om. Q1*   136–9] *prose Q1*   139 fault] sinne *Q1*   140]
Boas; Q2 lines will. / sweare. / *followed by prose*   141–3] *Dyce; prose Q2*   141 to] vnto *Q1*   143 SD] *Exit*
Q1   separately ... and] *Dyce subst.*   146 SP] CLE. *Q1*   147 go to] *om. Q1*   148 SD] *opp.* thankes *146*
Q2; opp. Enter the BOY *4.6.0 Q1*   **4.6**] *Spencer;* 4.4 *Weber; not in Q2*   0 SD BELLARIO] *the* BOY *Q1*

BELLARIO

A heaviness near death sits on my brow
And I must sleep. Bear me, thou gentle bank,
Forever if thou wilt. You sweet ones all,
Let me, unworthy, press you. I could wish
I rather were a corpse strewed o'er with you   5
Than quick above you. Dullness shuts mine eyes
And I am giddy. Oh, that I could take
So sound a sleep that I might never wake.   [*Lies down.*]

Enter PHILASTER.

PHILASTER

I have done ill: my conscience calls me false
To strike at her that would not strike at me.   10
When I did fight, methought I heard her pray
The gods to guard me. She may be abused
And I a loathed villain. If she be,
She will conceal who hurt her. He has wounds
And cannot follow, neither knows he me.   15
Who's this? Bellario sleeping? If thou beest
Guilty, there is no justice that thy sleep
Should be so sound and mine, whom thou hast wronged,
So broken.   (*Cry within.*)
                    Hark, I am pursued. You gods,
I'll take this offered means of my escape.   20

2–6 **Bear . . . above you** Perdita assures
Florizel that she would strew him with
flowers 'like a bank, for love to lie and
play on: / Not like a corpse; or if – not
to be buried, / But quick, and in mine
arms' (*WT*, 4.4.130–2).

3 **sweet ones all** the flowers

12–13 **She . . . villain** reiterating his
suspicion at 3.1.105; cf. Bellario, 'You
are abused; / Some villain has abused
you' (3.1.207–8).

13, 41 **loathed** loathèd

14 **He** the Country Fellow

---

1 A heaviness near] Oh heauens! heauy *Q1*   3 ones] on *Q1*   6–8] *Q1 lines* giddy, / sleepe, / wake.
/   6 mine] my *Q1*   7 Oh] *om. Q1*   8 SD1] *Boas, after 3* all; *Falls asleep* | *Weber*   13–25] *Q1 lines*
conceale / follow, / sleeping, / sleepe / wrong'd, / broken. / take / escape. / blood, / mischiefe /
once. / body, / mortall, / thee. /   19 SD] *Q1; opp.* sleepe *17 Q2*

They have no mark to know me but my wounds
If she be true; if false, let mischief light
On all the world at once. Sword, print my wounds
Upon this sleeping boy. I ha' none, I think,
Are mortal, nor would I lay greater on thee.   25
    Wounds him.

BELLARIO

Oh, death I hope is come! Blessed be that hand;
It meant me well. Again, for pity's sake!

PHILASTER

I have caught myself.   *Philaster falls [down.]*
The loss of blood hath stayed my flight. Here, here
Is he that struck thee: take thy full revenge.   30
Use me, as I did mean thee, worse than death.
I'll teach thee to revenge. This luckless hand
Wounded the princess. Tell my followers
Thou didst receive these hurts in staying me,
And I will second thee. Get a reward.   35

BELLARIO

Fly, fly, my lord, and save yourself.

PHILASTER   How's this?
Wouldst thou I should be safe?

BELLARIO   Else were it vain
For me to live. These little wounds I have
Ha' not bled much. Reach me that noble hand;
I'll help to cover you.

---

21 **mark . . . me** way to identify me
23 **print** copy
26 **death . . . come** Bellario expresses a death wish much like Philaster's.

28 **caught myself** created my own danger
34 **staying me** making me stop
39 **Reach . . . hand** Philaster is still lying on the stage.

21 wounds] blood *Q1*   24 this sleeping boy] his sleeping body *Q1*   I ha'] He has *Q1*   25 SD] *opp.* mortall *Q1*   26–7] *prose Q1*   27 meant] wisht *Q1*   pity's sake] pittie *Q1*   28 SD] *opp.* Here *29 Q1; Phi. falls Q2*   29–30] *Q1 lines* flight here, / reuenge, /   33–4] *Q1 lines* thou / me. /   36 Fly, fly] Hide, hide *Q1*   36–7 How's . . . safe] *one line Q1*   36 How's] How is *Q1*   37–40 Else . . . you] *Q1 lines* liue. / much, / you. /   37 were it] it were *Q1*   38 little] *om. Q1*   39 Ha'] has *Q1*

PHILASTER   Art thou true to me?   40

BELLARIO

Or let me perish loathed. Come, my good lord,
Creep in among those bushes. Who does know
But that the gods may save your much-loved breath?

PHILASTER

Then I shall die for grief, if not for this,
That I have wounded thee. What wilt thou do?   45

BELLARIO

Shift for myself well. Peace, I hear 'em come.

[*Philaster creeps away.*]

WITHIN

Follow, follow, follow! That way they went!

BELLARIO

With my own wounds I'll bloody my own sword.
I need not counterfeit to fall: Heaven knows
That I can stand no longer.   [*Bellario falls down.*]   50

Enter PHARAMOND, DION, CLEREMONT [*and*] THRASILINE.

PHARAMOND   To this place we have tracked him by his
blood.

CLEREMONT   Yonder, my lord, creeps one away.

DION   Stay, sir, what are you?

---

40 **cover** conceal
51 **tracked** Both quartos have 'tract',
which could be modernized either as
'tracked' or as 'traced'; *OED* track,
n. explains 'It is noticeable that the
senses of the verbs *trace* and *track* are
sometimes identical; also that *track*

and *tract* were often identified in
pronunciation and use.' Nevertheless,
Theobald's interpretation seems the
most likely: cf. *OED* track *v.*[1], citing
'An Indian Souldier . . . track'd
them by the bloud about half a Mile'
(1716).

---

40 true] then true *Q1*   41 good] *om. Q1*   42 among] amongst *Q1*   those] these *Q1*   43 much-loved
breath] breeth in't, Shromd, *Q1*   46 myself well. Peace] *(*my selfe well; peace, *)*; my selfe: Well,
peace, *Q1*   SD] *Weber subst.*   47 [3]follow] *om. Q1*   50 That] *om. Q1*   SD1] *Q1 (Boy falls downe.); not
in Q2*   SD2 and] *Q1 (&)*   51 we have] I *Q1*   tracked] *(tract);* track'd *Theobald;* traced *Gurr*   53
SP] LEON *Q1*   lord, creeps] *Q1;* Lord creepes, *Q2*   54 SP] CLE. *Q1*

BELLARIO

A wretched creature wounded in these woods   55
By beasts. Relieve me if your names be men,
Or I shall perish.

DION   This is he, my lord,
Upon my soul, that hurt her; 'tis the boy,
That wicked boy that served her.

PHARAMOND

O thou, damned in thy creation!   60
What cause couldst thou shape to strike the princess?

BELLARIO

Then I am betrayed.

DION

Betrayed! No, apprehended.

BELLARIO   I confess –
Urge it no more – that big with evil thoughts
I set upon her and did make my aim   65
Her death. For charity let fall at once
The punishment you mean and do not load
This weary flesh with tortures.

PHARAMOND   I will know
Who hired thee to this deed.

BELLARIO   Mine own revenge.

PHARAMOND

Revenge! For what?

BELLARIO   It pleased her to receive   70
Me as her page, and when my fortunes ebbed,

---

62 **betrayed** found out
67–8 **do . . . tortures** Bellario's fear of
torture will be reiterated in 5.5.
68 **will know** insist upon being told

55–7 A . . . perish] *Q1 lines* beasts, / men, / perish. /   57–9 This . . . her] *Q1 lines* her. /
her. /   57 SP] TRA. *Q1*   58 'tis] It is *Q1*   59–60] *one line Q6*   60–1] *prose Q1*   62–3] *Daniel; Q2 lines*
betrayed. / apprehended. / confess: /; *Q6 lines* apprehended. / confesse; /   63–8 I . . . tortures]
Q1 lines thoughts, / death: / meane. / tortour, /   68–70] *Boas; Q2 lines* tortures. / deed, / revenge.
/ what? / receiue /; *Theobald lines* know. / Revenge. / what? / receive /   68 tortures] tortour *Q1*
69 Mine] My *Q1*   70 SP] CLE. *Q1*   70–82 It . . . revenged] *Q1 lines* Page, / carelesse. / me, /
ouer-flowde / them, / turnde / streames / contem'd / great, / liue: / reueng'd. /

That men strode o'er them careless, she did shower
Her welcome graces on me and did swell
My fortunes till they overflowed their banks,
Threatening the men that crossed 'em, when, as swift   75
As storms arise at sea, she turned her eyes
To burning suns upon me and did dry
The streams she had bestowed, leaving me worse
And more contemned than other little brooks
Because I had been great. In short, I knew   80
I could not live and therefore did desire
To die revenged.

PHARAMOND   If tortures can be found
Long as thy natural life, resolve to feel
The utmost rigour.

CLEREMONT   Help to lead him hence.

PHILASTER *creeps out of a bush.*

PHILASTER
Turn back, you ravishers of innocence!   85
Know ye the price of that you bear away
So rudely?

PHARAMOND   Who's that?

DION   'Tis the lord Philaster.

PHILASTER
'Tis not the treasure of all kings in one,
The wealth of Tagus, nor the rocks of pearl

---

75 **when** at which point
85 **you ravishers** To *ravish* in this sense
is to seize upon and carry away forcibly,
but *ravishers of innocence* suggests sexual
violation as well.
88 **in one** combined
89 **wealth of Tagus** The Tagus or

modern *Tajo*, a river in Spain, is
traditionally said to contain gold in
its sands; cf. Juvenal, *Satire* 3: 'Don't
prize all the sand of rich Tagus and
all the gold that's rolled into the sea
so much that you lose sleep' (*Juvenal*,
171).

72 strode] *(strid)*   75 'em] *(vm);* them *Q1*   77 suns] Sines *Q1*   82–4 If . . . rigour] *Q1 lines* life,
/ vigor /   84 rigour] vigor *Q1*   SD] *Q1; opp.* rigour *Q2*   85 innocence] innocents *Q1*   86 ye] you
Q1   that] what *Q1*   87] *Theobald; Q2 lines* rudely? / that? / *Philaster.* /   'Tis the] My *Q1*   88 all]
all the *Q1*

That pave the court of Neptune, can weigh down   90
That virtue. It was I that hurt the princess.
Place me, some god, upon a pyramid
Higher than hills of earth and lend a voice
Loud as your thunder to me, that from thence
I may discourse to all the underworld   95
The worth that dwells in him.

PHARAMOND

How's this?

BELLARIO   My lord, some man
Weary of life, that would be glad to die.

PHILASTER

Leave these untimely courtesies, Bellario.

BELLARIO

Alas, he's mad. Come, will you lead me on?   100

PHILASTER

By all the oaths that men ought most to keep
And gods do punish most when men do break,
He touched her not. Take heed, Bellario,
How thou dost drown the virtues thou hast shown
With perjury. By all the gods, 'twas I!   105
You know she stood betwixt me and my right.

PHARAMOND

Thy own tongue be thy judge.

CLEREMONT

It was Philaster!

DION   Is't not a brave boy?

---

92 **pyramid** *OED* uses this line to illustrate pyramid *n.* 2, 'A building or monument with a square or triangular base and sloping sides that meet in a point at the top', but it is worth noting that early modern mentions of pyramids often treat them as any structure of pyramidal form, 'as a spire, pinnacle, obelisk . . . gable' (*OED n.* 3).
95 **underworld** those who stand below the *pyramid* (92)
106 **my right** to the throne

92–6] *Q1 lines* then / you / teach / him. /   92 upon] on *Q1*   pyramid] *(Piramis);* Pyramades *Q1*   94 your] you *Q1*   95 discourse to all] teach *Q1*   96–7] *Daniel; Q2 lines* him. / this? / man, /; *Q5 lines* this? / man   97–8 My . . . die] *one line Q1*   99 these] this *Q1*   courtesies] courtesie *Q1*   100 lead me on] beare me hence *Q1*   102 do] to *Q1*   103 not] nor *Q1*   108 SP1] Leon. *Q1*

Well, sirs, I fear me we were all deceived.

PHILASTER
Have I no friend here?

DION   Yes.

PHILASTER   Then show it. Some   110
Good body lend a hand to draw us nearer.
Would you have tears shed for you when you die?
Then lay me gently on his neck, that there
I may weep floods and breathe forth my spirit.
'Tis not the wealth of Plutus, nor the gold   115
Locked in the heart of earth, can buy away
This armful from me. This had been a ransom
To have redeemed the great Augustus Caesar
Had he been taken. You hard-hearted men,
More stony than these mountains, can you see   120
Such clear, pure blood drop and not cut your flesh
To stop his life? To bind whose bitter wounds
Queens ought to tear their hair, and with their tears
Bathe 'em. – Forgive me, thou that art the wealth
Of poor Philaster!

Enter KING, ARETHUSA *and a Guard.*

KING   Is the villain ta'en?   125

111–13 **draw . . . neck**   Philaster's
command, if carried out, will create a
powerfully homosocial stage picture of
two men lying side by side, with one
body partially above the other.
115–17 **'Tis . . . me**   Cf. the similar
phrasing of De Flores in *Changeling*:
'The wealth of all Valencia shall not buy

/ My pleasure from me' (3.4.163–4).
115 **Plutus** the god of wealth
118 **Augustus Caesar** the first Roman
emperor, whose name was originally
Octavius
119 **taken** captured in battle
122 **stop his life** prevent his life's blood
from flowing out; save him

108 SP2] TRA. *Q1*   109 Well, sirs, I fear me] Well, I feare me sir, *Q1*   all] *om. Q1*   110–11] *Boas; Q2*
lines here? / . Yes. / it: / neerer /; *Theobald lines* Yes. / some / nearer. /   110 SP1] BOY. *Q1*   SP3]
BOY. *Q1*   110–25 Then . . . Philaster] *prose Q1*   115 'Tis not] Not all *Q1*   Plutus] *Pluto Q1*
121 clear] a cleere *Q1*   123 hair] haires *Q1*   124 'em] them *Q1*

229

PHARAMOND
　　Sir, here be two confess the deed, but sure
　　It was Philaster.
PHILASTER　　　　　　Question it no more.
　　It was.
KING　　　The fellow that did fight with him
　　Will tell us that.
ARETHUSA [*aside*]　　Ay me, I know he will.
KING
　　Did not you know him?
ARETHUSA　　　　　　　　Sir, if it was he,　　　　　　130
　　He was disguised.
PHILASTER　　　　　　I was so. [*aside*] Oh, my stars,
　　That I should live still!
KING　　　　　　　　　　Thou ambitious fool,
　　Thou that hast laid a train for thy own life!
　　Now I do mean to do I'll leave to talk.
　　Bear him to prison.　　　　　　　　　　　135
ARETHUSA
　　Sir, they did plot together to take hence
　　This harmless life. Should it pass unrevenged
　　I should to earth go weeping. Grant me, then,
　　By all the love a father bears his child,
　　Their custodies and that I may appoint　　　140
　　Their tortures and their deaths.
DION [*aside to Gentlemen*]　　Death? Soft, our law will not
　　reach that for this fault.

---

131 **I was so** While this is a lie told to
　　support Arethusa, in a sense Philaster
　　was disguised by temporary madness.
134 **mean to do** intend to take action

141–3 **Their . . . fault** See p. 51 for
　　the difference between English and
　　continental laws on torture.

126–32] *Dyce; Q2 lines* two, / *Philaster.* / was. / that. / will. / him? / disguised. / still. / foole;
/　126–7 Sir . . . Philaster] *one line Q1*　126 SP] LEON. *Q1*　sure] *Dyce;* say *Q2;* sute *Q1*　127 SP]
KING. *Q1*　128 SP] PHA. *Q1*　129 SD] *this edn*　he will] him well *Q1*　130 was] were *Q1*　131 SD]
this edn　132–41 Thou . . . deaths] *prose Q1*　135 him] them *Q1*　138 go] *om. Q1*　139 love] loues
Q1　140 and] *om. Q1*　142 SD] *Spencer subst.*　our] your *Q1*

KING

'Tis granted. Take 'em to you, with a guard.

Come, princely Pharamond, this business passed,   145

We may with more security go on

To your intended match.   [*Exeunt King and Pharamond.*]

CLEREMONT [*aside to Gentlemen*]   I pray that this action

lose not Philaster the hearts of the people.

DION [*aside to Gentlemen*]   Fear it not; their overwise   150

heads will think it but a trick.   *Exeunt.*

5.1   *Enter* DION, CLEREMONT *and* THRASILINE.

THRASILINE   Has the King sent for him to death?

DION   Yes, but the King must know 'tis not in his power

to war with heaven.

CLEREMONT   We linger time; the King sent for Philaster

and the headsman an hour ago.   5

THRASILINE   Are all his wounds well?

DION   All they were but scratches, but the loss of blood

made him faint.

150–1 **overwise heads** too clever brains (ironic)

5.1 Location: the court

1 **sent . . . death** called him to his execution

5 **headsman** executioner. In early modern England noblemen were beheaded, but ordinary criminals were hanged.

7 **All they** all of them, they all; in early modern English a pronoun (*they*) could be modified by a quantifier, in this case

all (JH). The phrase 'all they' meaning 'all of them' was common: it reappears at 5.4.120–1, when Pharamond says he would be willing 'To be as many creatures as a woman / And do as all they do' rather than remain captive. Cf. *Night Walker*, 2.3.47, 'Here's nothing comes, all they are mad', and *AW*, 2.3.86, 'Do all they deny her?' Nevertheless, some editors repunctuate so that *All* is an answer to Thrasiline's question and *they* starts a new clause; see t.n.

146 may] shall *Q1*   147 To your] With our *Q1*   SD] *Q1 (Exit King and* PHARAMONT*); not in Q2*   148 SP] LEON. *Q1*   SD] *Spencer subst.*   150–1] *Q1 lines* heads / trick. /   150 SP] CLE. *Q1*   SD] *Spencer subst.*   151 SD] *Q1; Finis Actus quarti. Exeunt omnes. Q2*   5.1] *(Actus Quintus. Scena prima.)*   1 SP] LEON. *Q1*   2 SP] CLE. *Q1*   4 SP] TRA. *Q1*   6 SP] LEON. *Q1*   7 SP] TRA. *Q1*   All] All; *Colman*

CLEREMONT   We dally, gentlemen.

THRASILINE   Away!   10

DION   We'll scuffle hard before he perish.   *Exeunt.*

[**5.2**]   *Enter* PHILASTER, ARETHUSA [*and*] BELLARIO
[*in prison*].

ARETHUSA

Nay, faith, Philaster, grieve not. We are well.

BELLARIO

Nay, good my lord, forbear; we're wondrous well.

PHILASTER

O Arethusa! O Bellario! Leave to be kind.

I shall be shot from heaven, as now from earth,

If you continue so. I am a man   5

False to a pair of the most trusty ones

That ever earth bore. Can it bear us all?

Forgive and leave me. But the King hath sent

To call me to my death. Oh, show it me

And then forget me! And for thee, my boy,   10

I shall deliver words will mollify

The hearts of beasts to spare thy innocence.

BELLARIO

Alas, my lord, my life is not a thing

Worthy your noble thoughts. 'Tis not a life,

5.2 Location: a prison

0.2 *in prison* Q1's addition to the direction may indicate either recollection of staging or a scribe clarifying action for a reader. Without moveable scenery at either the Globe or the Blackfriars, the prison could only have been suggested. In both *Eastward Ho!* (1605) and *Antonio and Mellida* (1599) a grate represented the barred opening through which those held in London prisons begged passersby for charity.

2 **forbear** cease, be patient

4 **shot** expelled

10 SP] LEON. *Q1*   11 SP] TRA. *Q1*   scuffle] shufle *Q1*   SD] *Exit opp.* Away *10 Q1*   **5.2**] *Weber*   0.1 *and*] *F2*   0.2 *in prison*] *Q1; not in Q2*   2 we're] *(were); we are Q1*   3–12] *Q1 lines Bellario, / heauen, / paire / bore. / leaue me; / death, / boy, / beasts, / innocence. /*   3 O Bellario] and *Bellario Q1*   4 shot] shut *Q1*   as . . . earth] *om. Q1*   6 most trusty] truest *Q1*   8 Forgive] forgiue me *Q1*   13–20] *Q1 lines* worthy / peece / you, / honour: / close / periurie, / nothing. /

'Tis but a piece of childhood thrown away.   15
Should I outlive you, I should then outlive
Virtue and honour, and when that day comes,
If ever I shall close these eyes but once,
May I live spotted for my perjury
And waste my limbs to nothing.   20

ARETHUSA

And I, the woeful'st maid that ever was,
Forced with my hands to bring my lord to death,
Do by the honour of a virgin swear
To tell no hours beyond it.

PHILASTER   Make me not hated so.

ARETHUSA

Come from this prison, all joyful to our deaths.   25

PHILASTER

People will tear me when they find you true
To such a wretch as I; I shall die loathed.
Enjoy your kingdoms peaceably whilst I
Forever sleep, forgotten with my faults.
Every just servant, every maid in love   30
Will have a piece of me if you be true.

ARETHUSA

My dear lord, say not so.

BELLARIO   A piece of you?
He was not born of woman that can cut it
And look on.

---

15 'Tis . . . childhood another comment
complicating the question of Bellario's
age. Although he is assumed to be old
enough to have sexual relations with
Arethusa, this line makes him sound
not yet adolescent. See 3.1.98n.
18 if I do not die right away

24 To . . . hours not to live
26 tear me to pieces; see 31.
28 Enjoy your kingdoms Philaster
echoes Arethusa, 'I must enjoy these
kingdoms' (1.2.54). Q1's alteration to
the singular (see t.n.) strongly suggests
censorship.

16 then] *om. Q1*   17 comes] come *Q1*   20 my limbs] *Q3;* by limbs *Q2;* by time *Q1*   21 was] liu'd
Q1   24 hours beyond] houre behind *Q1*   28–31] *Q1 lines* sleepe, / loue, / true. /   28 kingdoms]
Kingdome *Q1*   30 servant] maiden *Q1*   32 dear lord] deerest *Q1*   32–4 A . . . on] *prose Q1*   33–4]
Daniel; Q2 lines it / on. / you, /; *Theobald lines* cut / you, /   33 woman] *Q1;* women *Q2*

PHILASTER   Take me in tears betwixt you,
For my heart will break with shame and sorrow.   35

ARETHUSA
Why, 'tis well.

BELLARIO
Lament no more.

PHILASTER   What would you have done,
If you had wronged me basely and had found
Your life no price compared to mine? For love, sirs,
Deal with me truly.

BELLARIO   'Twas mistaken, sir.   40

PHILASTER
Why, if it were?

BELLARIO   Then, sir, we would have asked
Your pardon.

PHILASTER   And have hope to enjoy it?

ARETHUSA
Enjoy it? Ay.

PHILASTER   Would you, indeed? Be plain.

BELLARIO
We would, my lord.

PHILASTER   Forgive me, then.

ARETHUSA   So, so.   44

---

39 ***Your . . . mine** Philaster challenges his companions to imagine the reverse of their actual situation, that is, the action they would have taken if *they* had wronged *him* and then found themselves worthless (*no price*) in comparison with him. The emendation here, proposed by Weber and found separately in Buckingham's *Restauration*, assumes that the pronouns were accidentally reversed. It is, however, possible that Philaster asks what they would do if they had found his life *priceless* compared with their own.

42 **hope** Philaster abandons the conditional mode he has been using, requiring 'hoped', and admits his current desire for forgiveness (cf. 44).

36–7] *Theobald; Q2 lines* well. / more. / done? /; *Q6 lines* more. / done / 36 Why,] Why? *Q1* 37 What] Why? what *Q1* 39–40 Your . . . truly] *Q1 lines* loue, / truely. / 39 Your . . . mine] *Restauration; Weber (Mason);* My . . . yours *Q2* price] whit *Q1* mine? For] yours for *Q1* 40–5] *Boas; Q2 lines* truely. / Sir. / were. / pardon. / it? / I. / plaiue. [*sic*] / Lord. / then. / so. / now? / death. /; *Q6 lines* truely. / were. / pardon. / I. / Lord. / so. / Death. / 41 SP1] PRIN. *Q1* 42 Your] you *Q1* 44 SP1] PRIN. *Q1*

BELLARIO

'Tis as it should be now.

PHILASTER   Lead to my death.   *Exeunt.*

[5.3]   *Enter* KING, DION, CLEREMONT
                              [*and*] THRASILINE.

KING

Gentlemen, who saw the prince?

CLEREMONT

So please you, sir, he's gone to see the city
And the new platform, with some gentlemen
Attending on him.

KING   Is the princess ready
To bring her prisoner out?

THRASILINE   She waits your grace.   5

KING

Tell her we stay.   [*Exit Thrasiline.*]

5.3 Location: a presence room in the palace
1 **the prince** Pharamond
2 **the city** Throughout these scenes references to *the city* may suggest not merely the urban area surrounding the King's court but the City of London, frequently visited and described by foreign tourists.
3 **the new platform** Gurr argues convincingly that this is a topical reference to the 'great platform' on which Phineas Pett constructed a full-size model of Prince Henry's ship, the *Prince Royal*. Following charges of corruption and poor design, on 8 May 1609 King James himself went to Woolwich to hear evidence. Pett, the builder, records that because there were differing claims about the size of the 'ship's flat in the midships ... [which] could not be tried

upon the small plats, his Majesty referred the trial to be made on the great platform, which was purposely framed of planks to the full scale of the ship'. Pett is here using *platform* to mean primarily, 'A surface or area on which something may stand, *esp.* a raised level surface' (*OED n.* 1); he could also mean 'The area or ground occupied by a structure' (*OED n.* 4, citing Evelyn's translation of *Freart's Parallel of the Ancient Architecture with the Modern*, 'The Area or Floor, by Artists often call'd the Plan or Plat-forme'). For implications for the dating of the play, see pp. 5–6.

5 **waits your grace** is waiting for your highness's presence or permission; *wait* (*OED v.*[1] 5a), to look forward to with desire or apprehension, is now usually superseded by 'await'.

---

45 SD] *Q2c; not in Q2u* **5.3]** *Weber* 0.1 KING] *the King Q1* 0.2 *and*] *F2* THRASILINE] TRA. *and a guard. Q1* 2 SP] LEON. *Q1* city] *(City)* 3 platform] Plot-forme *Q1* 4–5 Is ... out?] *one line Q1* 5 SP] CLE. *Q1* 6 SD1] *Q1; not in Q2* SD2] *Q1 opp. lightly 8; not in Q2*

DION [*aside*]   King, you may be deceived yet:
The head you aim at cost more setting on
Than to be lost so lightly. If it must off,
Like a wild overflow that swoops before him
A golden stack and with it shakes down bridges,   10
Cracks the strong hearts of pines whose cable roots
Held out a thousand storms, a thousand thunders,
And so made mightier takes whole villages
Upon his back and in that heat of pride
Charges strong towns, towers, castles, palaces   15
And lays them desolate, so shall thy head,
Thy noble head, bury the lives of thousands
That must bleed with thee like a sacrifice
In thy red ruins.

Enter PHILASTER, ARETHUSA [*and*] BELLARIO *in a*
robe and garland [*, escorted by* THRASILINE].

KING   How now, what masque is this?

9–16 **Like . . . desolate** The image is of
a river overflowing, gaining strength
as it goes and destroying everything
in its path.
9 **swoops** sweeps away
10 **golden stack** haystack
11 **cable roots** roots as thick and strong as
cables
12 **Held out** resisted, sustained
16 **thy head** Philaster's head; the subject
of Dion's comment switches from the
King to Philaster.
19 **red ruins** the bloody (severed) head
and body
19.1–2 **in . . . garland** Bellario is dressed
as an attendant of Hymen, the god
of marriages (see 41–2 and Fig. 15).
In Jonson's *Hymenaei* of 1606, the

wedding masque for the Earl of Essex
and Frances Howard, Hymen was
followed by a '*youth*, attyred in white,
bearing another light, *of white thorne*;
vnder his arme, a little wicker *flasket*,
shut'. *TNK* begins with a wedding
procession: '*Enter Hymen with a torch*
burning; a Boy, *in a white robe, before,*
singing and strewing flowers' (1.1.0.1–2).
19.2 *escorted by* THRASILINE Thrasiline
must return, as he speaks at 133.
19 **what . . . this?** The King's question
alerts the audience to the elements of
the following scene that are adapted
from or suggest a wedding masque.
Masques were an important form of
entertainment at the court of King
James and Queen Anne, particularly

6–19 King . . . ruins] *Q1 lines* ayme at, / lightly: / him, / bridges, / rootes / thunders, / back, /
Townes, / desolate. / liues. / sacrifice, / ruines. /   8 be lost] lose it *Q1*   9 overflow] *Q2c;* ouer-throw
Q2u   swoops] *Langbaine;* soopes *Q2*   10 stack] stocke *Q1*   13 mightier] weightier *Q1*   14 that] the
Q1   16 lays] leaues *Q1*   19.1 *and*] *F2*   19.1–2 *in a robe and garland*] *with a garland of flowers on's head*
Q1   19.2 *escorted by* THRASILINE] *Dyce subst.*   19 masque] (Maske)

BELLARIO

Right royal sir, I should   20
Sing you an epithalamion of these lovers,
But having lost my best airs with my fortunes,
And wanting a celestial harp to strike
This blessed union on, thus in glad story
I give you all. These two fair cedar branches,   25
The noblest of the mountain, where they grew
Straightest and tallest, under whose still shades
The worthier beasts have made their lairs and slept

in the hands of Ben Jonson; Beaumont
would write one for the wedding of the
Princess Elizabeth in 1613. Entrance
to these performances was severely
limited; *Maid's Tragedy*, 1.2, comically
depicts people trying to push their way
in. To satisfy the substantial sections
of the theatre audience who could
never attend a court masque, plays of
the period often stage either partial
or, as in *Maid's Tragedy*, complete
masques.

21 **epithalamion** or epithalamium, a
nuptial song; Spenser's is a famous
example. In the quarto of *Hymenaei*,
after the exit of the bride and groom
to the 'nuptial bower', Jonson includes
a lengthy epithalamion and explains
that at the performance 'onely one
Staffe was sung; but because I made it
both in *Forme*, and *Matter* to aemulate
that kinde of *Poeme*, which was called
Epithalamium, and (by the Auntients)
vs'd to be song, when the *Bride* was
led into her Chamber, I have here set
it down whole'. The refrain is '*On
Hymen, Hymen call, / This Night is
Hymen's all*'.

22 **lost . . . airs** Although this loss serves
as a metaphor for all that the threesome
has suffered, an *air* or song might
have been expected in this masque-

like section. The lack may indicate the
limitations of the original boy actor. At
3.2.65–8 Arethusa describes Bellario's
'crying elegies' and lute playing, but the
actor is never called upon to sing or to
play.

23 **celestial harp** as if he were an angel
celebrating the *blessed union*

24 **blessed** blessèd
story tale; Bellario will present an
allegorical account of the action.

25 **cedar branches** Cedar, a precious
wood valued for its resistance, is a
frequent metaphor for royalty. The
soothsayer in *Cym* so interprets the
reference to the '*stately cedar*' with
'*lopp'd branches*' in the prophecy left
with Posthumus: 'The lofty cedar, royal
Cymbeline, / Personates thee: and thy
lopp'd branches point / Thy two sons
forth' (5.5.439, 454–6). In *H8* Cranmer
describes the future James I: 'He shall
flourish, / And, like a mountain cedar,
reach his branches / To all the plains
about him' (5.4.52–4).

28 **worthier . . . lairs** more valuable
animals (such as stags) have made their
resting places. *Lair* has no necessarily
negative connotation when used of
animals; cf. *OED n.*[1] 4b, citing Nicholas
Breton, *Fantasticks* (1626), 'The stately
Hart is at Layre in the high wood'.

20–66 Right . . . me] Sir, / *followed by prose Q1*   20 should] shal *Q1*   21 of these lovers] *om. Q1*   24
on] *om. Q1*   25 all.] all *Q1*   26 mountain] *Q2c*; Mountaines *Q2u*   28 lairs] *Q2c* (layars); baytes
Q2u; layers *Q1*

Free from the Sirian star and the fell thunderstroke,
Free from the clouds when they were big with humour   30
And deliver in thousand spouts their issues to the
    earth –
Oh, there was none but silent quiet there!
Till never-pleased Fortune shot up shrubs,
Base underbrambles to divorce these branches,
And for a while they did so and did reign   35
Over the mountain and choke up his beauty
With brakes, rude thorns and thistles, till the sun
Scorched them even to the roots and dried them there.
And now a gentler gale hath blown again
That made these branches meet and twine together,   40
Never to be divided. The god that sings
His holy numbers over marriage beds
Hath knit their noble hearts and here they stand,
Your children, mighty King, and I have done.

KING

    How? How?

ARETHUSA   Sir, if you love it in plain truth,   45
For now there is no masquing in't: this gentleman,

29 **Sirian star** the dog-star, the brightest in the heavens
   fell dangerous
30–1 **were . . . deliver** Q4 may be correct in making the second verb also past tense; see t.n.
33 **never-pleased** never-pleasèd
35–6 **reign . . . mountain** metaphorically, rule the kingdom. The *base underbrambles* who temporarily *divorce* or separate Arethusa and Philaster include Pharamond and Megra.
37 **brakes** clumps of bushes or brambles
37–8 **sun . . . there** Usually the *sun* is an

image of the King: cf. *R2*, 3.2.36–53, where Richard compares himself to the 'searching eye of Heaven' and imagines 'rising in our throne the east'. However, if *them* refers to the *shrubs* (33) and *thorns and thistles* (37), so far the King has stopped only Megra. If *them* refers to the *cedar branches*, the scorching *sun* may refer to the King's hostility to Philaster and Arethusa.
40 **made** has made
46 **no . . . in't** no playing or pretence. Arethusa is anxious to cut through the metaphor.

29 from] from the firuer of *Q1* 31 deliver] deliverd *Q4* their] *Q2c;* there *Q2u;* that *Q1* 34 underbrambles] vnder branches *Q1* divorce] deuour *Q1* 36 choke] did choake *Q1* 38 even] *om. Q1* roots] roote *Q1* them] vm *Q1* 39 gentler] gentle *Q1* hath] has *Q1* 41 divided] vnarmde *Q1* sings] *Q2c;* slings *Q2u* 42 holy] *om. Q1* numbers] *Q4;* number *Q2* over] ore *Q1* 43 Hath] has *Q1* 44 mighty] worthy *Q1*

The prisoner that you gave me, is become
My keeper, and through all the bitter throes
Your jealousies and his ill fate have wrought him,
Thus nobly hath he struggled and at length   50
Arrived here my dear husband.

KING   Your dear husband! –

Call in the captain of the citadel. –
There you shall keep your wedding. I'll provide
A masque shall make your Hymen
Turn his saffron into a sullen coat   55
And sing sad requiems to your departing souls!
Blood shall put out your torches, and instead
Of gaudy flowers about your wanton necks
An axe shall hang like a prodigious meteor,
Ready to crop your loves' sweets. Hear, you gods: 60
From this time do I shake all title off
Of father to this woman, this base woman,
And what there is of vengeance in a lion
Chased among dogs or robbed of his dear young,

---

48 **My keeper** In the 'Solemnization of Matrimony' as set down in the Anglican Book of Common Prayer (1559), the groom is asked if he promises to 'honour and keepe her, in sickennesse, and in health? And forsakynge all other, keepe thee onely to her'. The bride makes the same promise.

53–60 **I'll . . . sweets** Adopting the metaphor, the King adds Hymen's *saffron . . . coat*, *torches* and *flowers* to the marriage masque elements enumerated in Bellario's speech and then reverses their usual meaning.

56 **requiems** dirges or chants for the repose of the dead, replacing the

epithalamion of 21

57 **your torches** Masquers were regularly accompanied by torchbearers; cf. *RJ*, 1.4.11–12, 'Give me a torch, I am not for this ambling. / Being but heavy I will bear the light.'

59 **prodigious** appalling, portentous, like an evil omen

60 **crop . . . sweets** an image suggesting the loss of the hymen

63–4 **lion . . . young** The comparison suggests that the King is not only offended because his royal authority has been challenged by inferiors (*dogs*) but also suffering psychologically as a father *robbed* of his daughter by another man, her new husband.

---

48 throes] threats *Q1*   51–6] *this edn; Q2 lines* husband. / in / keepe / make / coat, / soules; / ; *Dyce lines* husband. / husband! – / Citadel. – / provide / saffron / requiems / souls; / ; *Boas lines* husband! – / Citadel. – / provide / saffron / requiems / souls; /   51 here my] here: / My *Q1*   53 There] where *Q1*   63 vengeance in] venge- / in *Q1*   64 Chased] (Chast); chaft *Q1*   among] amongst *Q1*

The same enforced more terrible, more mighty,   65
Expect from me.

ARETHUSA   Sir,
By that little life I have left to swear by,
There's nothing that can stir me from myself.
What I have done, I have done without repentance,
For death can be no bugbear unto me   70
So long as Pharamond is not my headsman.

DION [*aside*]

Sweet peace upon thy soul, thou worthy maid,
Whene'er thou diest. For this time I'll excuse thee
Or be thy prologue.

PHILASTER   Sir, let me speak next,
And let my dying words be better with you   75
Than my dull living actions. If you aim
At the dear life of this sweet innocent,
You're a tyrant and a savage monster
That feeds upon the blood you gave a life to.
Your memory shall be as foul behind you   80
As you are, living. All your better deeds

---

70 **bugbear** hobgoblin, image of dread
71 **my headsman** the executioner who cuts off my head; the man who takes my maidenhead. Cf. *RJ*, 1.1.20–5, 'SAMPSON . . . I will show myself a tyrant: when I have fought with the men I will be civil with the maids, I will cut off their heads. GREGORY The heads of the maids? SAMPSON Ay, the heads of the maids, or their maidenheads; take it in what sense thou wilt.'
74 **be thy prologue** die first, fighting for you
75 **be . . . you** find more acceptance from you

78 **You're a tyrant** a very powerful charge. In the early modern period a tyrant was either one who seized sovereign power without legal right, that is, a usurper like the King in *Philaster*, or an anointed king who behaved in a manner so oppressive, unjust or cruel as to justify his deposition. Macduff threatens to have Macbeth's head 'Painted upon a pole, and underwrit, "Here may you see the tyrant"', and then presents Malcolm with 'Th'usurper's cursed head' (5.8.26–7, 5.9.21).
81–2 **All . . . writ** 'To write in water' is proverbial (Dent, W114); cf. *H8*,

66 Expect] looke *Q1*   67 life] life that *Q1*   68 that] *om. Q1*   70 can . . . me] to me can be no bugbare *Q1*   71] *Q1 lines* Pharamont, / heads-man. / So] as *Q1*   72 SD] *Dyce, opp.* prologue *74*   73–4 Whene'er . . . prologue] *prose Q1*   74 Or be] ore by *Q1*   76–103] *Q1 lines* life / monster, / to, / liuing: / writ; / you, / men: / Pelion, / brasse, / Pyramides; / gods, / faults, / issues, / wisedomes, / off: / selfe, / king, / sinne / soule. / long / you, / die, / in't. /   77 dear] *om. Q1*   78 You're] *(Y'are)*; you are *Q1*   79] *Q1; not in Q2*

Shall be in water writ, but this in marble.
No chronicle shall speak you, though your own,
But for the shame of men. No monument,
Though high and big as Pelion, shall be able   85
To cover this base murder. Make it rich
With brass, with purest gold and shining jasper
Like the pyramids, lay on epitaphs
Such as make great men gods – my little marble,
That only clothes my ashes, not my faults,   90
Shall far outshine it. And for after-issues:
Think not so madly of the heavenly wisdoms
That they will give you more for your mad rage
To cut off, unless it be some snake, or something
Like yourself, that in his birth shall strangle you.   95
Remember my father, King! There was a fault –
But I forgive it. Let that sin persuade you
To love this lady. If you have a soul,
Think, save her, and be saved. For myself,
I have so long expected this glad hour,   100
So languished under you and daily withered,
That, by the gods, it is a joy to die;

4.2.45–6, 'Men's evil manners live in brass, their virtues / We write in water.'

82 **marble** symbolic of hardness and durability; cf. *Son* 55, 'Not marble, nor the gilded monuments / Of princes, shall outlive this powerful rhyme.'

83–4 **No . . . men** No history book, not even one about you or written for you, will say you are anything but a disgrace to mankind.

84–9 **No . . . gods** Some of the tombs of kings were as elaborate as the *monument* described here; see 82n. and Llewellyn.

85 **Pelion** a mountain in Thessaly, high and difficult to access. Proverbially, 'to pile Pelion upon Ossa' was to add difficulty to difficulty.

86–7 **rich / With brass** Cf. *Son* 107, 'And thou in this shalt find thy monument, / When tyrants' crests and tombs of brass are spent.'

87 **jasper** a precious stone; any bright-coloured chalcedony except carnelian, the most esteemed being green

89 **little marble** simple tombstone

91 **after-issues** further children

94–5 **snake . . . you** a reversal of the myth of Hercules, who while still in his cradle strangled two snakes sent by Hera to kill him

102–3 **it is . . . in't** Philaster again reveals his depression and self-destructiveness. His comment that dying is a *recreation* recalls the

84 the] a *Q1*   87 with purest] *om. Q1*

I find a recreation in't.

Enter a MESSENGER.

MESSENGER
Where's the King?
KING   Here.
MESSENGER   Get you to your strength
And rescue the Prince Pharamond from danger.   105
He's taken prisoner by the citizens,
Fearing the Lord Philaster.
DION [*aside*]   Oh, brave followers!
Mutiny, my fine dear countrymen, mutiny!
Now, my brave valiant foremen, show your weapons
In honour of your mistresses!

Enter another MESSENGER.

2 MESSENGER   Arm, arm, arm, arm!   110
KING
A thousand devils take 'em!
DION [*aside*]   A thousand blessings on 'em!
2 MESSENGER
Arm, O King, the city is in mutiny,
Led by an old grey ruffian who comes on

---

wounded Arethusa's objecting to the Country Fellow's intrusion on 'our private sports, our recreations' (4.5.91–2).

104 **strength** military power (*OED* 1e, citing Kyd, *Spanish Tragedy*, 1.4, 'Their fight was long . . . Their strength alike, their strokes both dangerous.')

109 **foremen** Although he appreciates

the action of his countrymen, Dion cannot think of them without insisting on their social status. Presumably he considers the mutineers *foremen*, principal workmen, because they support Philaster. See 165–6n.

109–10 **show . . . mistresses** In this phrase the *weapons* are suggestively phallic.

---

103 SD MESSENGER] Gentleman *Dyce* 104 SP1, SP3] *1. Messenger | Turner* you] *om. Q1* 107 Fearing] For *Q1* 107–10 Oh . . . mistresses] *prose Q1* 107 SD] *Dyce, opp.* mistresses *110* follow-ers] fellowes *Q1* 110 SD] *om. Q1; Enter a* Second Gentleman *Dyce* SP] *Q1; Mes. Q2; Sec. Gent. | Dyce* ⁴arm] *om. Q1* 111] *this edn; Q2 lines* take vm. / on vm. / take 'em] take these Citizens *Q1* SD] *Dyce* on 'em] on them *Q1* 112 SP] *Daniel; Mes. Q2; Sec. Gent. | Dyce*

In rescue of the Lord Philaster.

KING

Away to the citadel. I'll see them safe   115
And then cope with these burghers.

Exeunt [Messengers] with Arethusa, Philaster [and] Bellario.

Let the guard
And all the gentlemen give strong attendance.   *Exit.*

CLEREMONT

The city up! This was above our wishes.

DION

Ay, and the marriage, too! By my life,
This noble lady has deceived us all.   120
A plague upon myself, a thousand plagues,
For having such unworthy thoughts of her dear honour!
Oh, I could beat myself, or do you beat me
And I'll beat you, for we had all one thought.

CLEREMONT

No, no; 'twill but lose time.   125

DION   You say true. Are your swords sharp? Well, my dear
countrymen what-ye-lacks, if you continue and fall not

---

115 **citadel** fortress commanding the city
see them safe make certain that
Arethusa, Philaster and Bellario are
confined. In an ironic contradiction,
s*afe* also suggests 'out of danger'.

116 **burghers** citizens; more specifically,
inhabitants of a burgh or borough. *City*
derives from the Latin *civitas*, while the
Old English form *burh* became *borough*.
Cf. *MV*, 1.1.9–10, 'your argosies
with portly sail / Like signiors and
rich burghers on the flood'. Despite
different attitudes towards the mutiny,
the King and Dion share a sense of
class superiority.

118 **up** in rebellion

119–24 It is uncertain whether these lines
are intended as verse, prose or a mixture
(see t.n.). Q2 switches to prose at 120,
yet that line is a perfect pentameter.
The immediate confusion may be that
of the scribe or compositor, but the
basic difficulty derives from the iambic
rhythm of much of Beaumont and
Fletcher's prose.

127 **what-ye-lacks** shopkeepers, identified by their usual invitation to customers. Cf. the apprentice's cry in
Eastward Ho!, 1.1, 'What do ye lack,
sir? What is't you'll buy, sir?' and the

---

116 SD] *this edn; Exit with Ara. Phi. Bellario. opp.* Philaster *114 Q2; after* citadel *115* |
Daniel   Messengers] *Gurr; Messenger* | *Thorndike; some of the Guard* | *Turner*   117 SD] *(Exit King. /
Munent Dion, Clermond, Trasiline.)*   119–24] *Colman; Q2 lines* life, / *followed by prose; prose Q1*   119
my life] al the gods *Q1*   126–32] *Q1 lines* deere / not / Chronicled, / prais'd, / ballads, / seculorum,
/ Countrimen. /   127 what-ye-lacks] what you lackes *Q1;* what ye lacke *Q3*

back upon the first broken shin, I'll have ye chronicled
and chronicled, and cut and chronicled, and all-to-
be-praised, and sung in sonnets, and bathed in new   130
brave ballads, that all tongues shall troll you *in saecula*
saeculorum, my kind can-carriers.

THRASILINE   What if a toy take 'em i'th' heels now
and they run all away and cry 'The devil take the
hindmost!'   135

DION   Then the same devil take the foremost, too, and
souse him for his breakfast! If they all prove cowards,
my curses fly among them and be speeding. May they
have murrains reign, to keep the gentlemen at home
unbound in easy frieze. May the moths branch their   140

almost identical phrases of Mistress
Openwork, a citizen's wife, in *Roaring*
Girl, 2.1.1–2.
continue keep up the rebellion
127–8 **fall . . . shin** do not run away at the
first minor injury
128 **chronicled** recorded in history books
131 **troll** sing; cf. *Tem*, 3.2.117–18, 'Will
you troll the catch / You taught me but
whilere?'
131–2 *in saecula saeculorum* for ever and
ever (Latin)
132 **can-carriers** like Cob, the water
carrier in Jonson's *Every Man Out*
(1599)
133 **a toy** 'A foolish or idle fancy; a whim'
(*OED* 4a)
134–5 **they . . . hindmost**   Fletcher
stages such a scene in *Bonduca*, 4.2.70–
2, as soldiers flee a battle: '*1. Souldier.*
Flee, flee, he kills us. *2. Souldier.* He
comes, he comes. *Judas.* The devil take
the hindmost. *Hengist.* Run, run, ye
Rogues, ye precious Rogues, ye rank
Rogues.'
137 **souse** pickle

138–50 **May . . . debts** Dion's *curses* are
directed at the economic interests of
the citizens as shopkeepers. He assumes
they deal particularly in varieties of
cloth, a primary English manufacture
and export.
138–40 **May . . . frieze** May infectious
diseases (*murrains*) be epidemic (*reign*)
so that wealthy potential purchasers
(*gentlemen*) remain in their own houses
where they can dress informally (be
unbound) in coarse woollen cloth
(*frieze*). Jacobean male attire of the
upper classes was elaborate and made
of fine materials, including silks
and velvets. Colman's reading, may
'murrains rain', although mocked by
Dyce, is also possible.
140–1 **moths . . . velvets** playing ironically on *OED* branch *v.* 6, 'To adorn
or embroider with gold or needlework
representing flowers or foliage'. The
citizens' Captain is similarly ironic in
urging his troops to *ravel* Pharamond,
'Branch me his skin in flowers like a
satin' (5.4.43–5).

128 shin] skin *Q1*   have] see *Q1*   ye] you *Q1*   130–1 new brave] braue new *Q1*   132 can-carriers]
Countrimen *Q1*   137 souse] *(*sowce*)*; sawce *Q1*   138 fly] flush *Q1*   among] amongst *Q1*   them]
vm *Q1*   be] ill *Q1*   139 murrains reign] *(*Murriens raigne*)*; iniurious raine *Q1*; murrains rain
Colman   140 unbound in easy] in rasine *Q1*   moths] moth *Q1*

velvets and their silks only be worn before sore eyes.
May their false lights undo 'em and discover presses,
holes, stains and oldness in their stuffs, and make them
shop-rid. May they keep whores and horses, and break
and live mewed up with necks of beef and turnips. May   145
they have many children, and none like the father. May
they know no language but that gibberish they prattle
to their parcels, unless it be the goatish Latin they write
in their bonds, and may they write that false and lose
their debts!   150

Enter the KING.

KING   Now the vengeance of all the gods confound them!
How they swarm together! What a hum they raise!
Devils choke your wild throats! If a man had need to

---

141 **silks . . . eyes** valuable materials not
be seen and appreciated; 'only enough
silk [be] bought as may be worn for
eye-bandages' (Gurr)

142 **false . . . discover** A common charge
was that merchants kept the light in
their shops low so that defects in their
cloth would not be noticed or *discovered*;
cf. Dekker and Webster, *Westward Ho*,
Act I, where men suspected of being
cuckolds are said to 'weare their hats
ore their eye-browes, like pollitick
penthouses, which commonly make
the shop of a Mercer, or a Linnen
Draper, as dark as a roome in Bedlam',
and Middleton, *Michaelmas*, where
Quomodo the woollen draper, whose
assistant is aptly named Falselight,
assures his wife that 'my shop is not
altogether so dark as some of my
neighbours', where a man may be
made cuckold at one end, while he's
measuring with his yard at t'other'
(2.3.36–9).

presses creases

143 **stuffs** materials

144 **shop-rid** worn out from lying in the
shop

break go bankrupt

145 **mewed up** shut away, confined; cf.
Humorous Lieutenant, 4.5.17, 'They
keep me mew'd up here, as they mew
mad folkes.'

146 **none . . . father** suggesting that they
are the product of the wife's extra-
marital affairs

148 **goatish Latin** To show contempt for
the inadequate Latin of the citizens,
Dion calls it *goatish* rather than *gothic*,
which itself means barbarous or
uncouth.

149–50 **lose . . . debts** be unable to press
their claims on those who have signed
agreements (*bonds*) and owe money to
them

152 **swarm . . . hum** The King describes
the citizens as noisy bees swarming out
of a hive.

146–7 May they] and *Q1*   151–66] *Q1 lines* them, / raise. / neede / for't, / sheepe: / heate, / me, /
Lord / Prince, / him, / wits. / pin / me, / bakon, / fat / liking. /   153 wild] wide *Q1*

use their valours, he must pay a brokage for it, and
then bring 'em on, and they will fight like sheep. 'Tis   155
Philaster, none but Philaster, must allay this heat. They
will not hear me speak, but fling dirt at me and call me
tyrant. [*to Cleremont*] Oh, run, dear friend, and bring
the lord Philaster. Speak him fair, call him 'Prince', do
him all the courtesy you can, commend me to him. Oh,   160
my wits, my wits!   *Exit Cleremont.*

DION [*aside*]   Oh, my brave countrymen! As I live, I will
not buy a pin out of your walls for this; nay, you shall
cozen me, and I'll thank you and send you brawn
and bacon and soil you every long vacation a brace   165
of foremen that at Michaelmas shall come up fat and
kicking!

KING   What they will do with this poor prince, the gods
know – and I fear.

DION [*aside*]   Why, sir, they'll flay him and make church-   170

---

154 **use their valours** employ them in an
action requiring courage
a brokage a broker or middleman's fee;
the *OED* comments that while often
'the exact sense cannot be fixed . . . In
most cases the word has an ill favour'
and cites, among others, this line and
Florio's *Montaigne*, 'By the brokage or
panderizing of the lawes'.
157–8 **call me tyrant** See 78n.
163 **buy . . . walls** purchase the slightest
thing except in your shops
164–5 **brawn and bacon** typical gifts from
country gentlemen to those who lived in
the city; *brawn* is the flesh of a boar.
165 **soil you** fatten for you; *OED* soil
$v.^4$ gives this as the first citation, and
cf. soiled, *ppl.a.²*, 'fed with fresh-cut
green fodder', as in *KL*, 4.6.120–1,
'The fitchew, nor the soiled horse, goes

to 't with a more riotous appetite.'
165-6 **a brace of foremen** One would
normally fatten a *brace* or pair of geese.
See 109, and cf. *Love's Pilgrimage*,
1.1.145–9: 'I could at his years Gossips
/ (As temperate as you see me now)
have eaten / My brace of ducks, with
my half goose, my cony, / And drink
my whole twelve Marvedis in wine /
As easie as I now get down three olyffs.'
170 **flay him** strip him of his skin.
Fletcher repeats the idea of employing
flayed human skin in *Woman's Prize*,
2.4.44–5, 'She flead her husband in her
youth, and made / Raynes of his hide
to ride the Parish.' Q2's *flea* is merely a
spelling variant.
170–1 **church-buckets** buckets kept in
the parish church for use in case of fire,
OED's earliest example

---

154 their] your *Q1*   he] we *Q1*   for it] for't *Q1*   155 'em] *om. Q1*   they] you *Q1*   158 SD] *this
edn*   159 fair] well *Q1*   160 courtesy] courtesies *Q1*   161 SD] *om. Q1*   162 countrymen] Citizens
Q1 SD] *Dyce*   165 and soil you] *om. Q1*   every] *Q1;* euer *Q2*   vacation] vocation *Q1*   165–6
a . . . Michaelmas] and soule *Q1*   167 kicking] in braue liking *Q1*   168 this] that *Q1*   169 and] *om.
Q1*   170 SD] *Daniel*   sir] *om. Q1*   flay] *(*flea*)*

buckets o'his skin to quench rebellion, then clap a rivet
in's sconce and hang him up for a sign.

Enter CLEREMONT *with* PHILASTER.

KING

Oh, worthy sir, forgive me; do not make
Your miseries and my faults meet together
To bring a greater danger. Be yourself,   175
Still sound amongst diseases. I have wronged you,
And though I find it last and beaten to it,
Let first your goodness know it. Calm the people
And be what you were born to. Take your love
And with her my repentance, all my wishes   180
And all my prayers. By the gods, my heart speaks this,
And if the least fall from me not performed,
May I be struck with thunder.

PHILASTER   Mighty sir,
I will not do your greatness so much wrong
As not to make your word truth. Free the princess   185
And the poor boy, and let me stand the shock
Of this mad sea-breach, which I'll either turn
Or perish with it.

KING   Let your own word free them.

171–2 **clap . . . sign** put a nail through his
head (*sconce*) and use it as a shop sign.
Elizabethan and Jacobean shops and
taverns were identified by images rather
than numbers; quartos of *Philaster* were
to be sold 'at the signe of the Eagle and
Childe'. The plot of *The Merry Devil
of Edmonton* (acted and published 1608)
turns on the transference of the pub

sign of The George from one side of
the street to the other.
175–9 **Be . . . born to** Under pressure the
King acknowledges Philaster's right to
the kingship.
177 **beaten** have been beaten
182 **least** slightest promise
187 **mad sea-breach** Cf. Dion's image
at 9–16.

171 o'his] (on's)   172 a] *Q1; not in Q2*   SD] *Enter* PHYLASTER. *Q1*   173–83 Oh . . . thunder] *Q1*
lines miseries / danger, / you, / to't, / be / repentance, / gods, / me, / thunder. /   177 to it] to't
Q1   178 first] me *Q1*   it] *om. Q1*   181 this] all this *Q1*   183–8 Mighty . . . it] *Q1 lines* wrong, / boy,
/ sea-breach, / it. /   184 your] *Q1;* you *Q2*   186 poor] *om. Q1*   188 them] her *Q1*

PHILASTER
Then thus I take my leave, kissing your hand,
And hanging on your royal word. Be kingly   190
And be not moved. Sir, I shall bring you peace
Or never bring myself back.
KING   All the gods go with thee.   *Exeunt.*

[5.4]   *Enter an old* CAPTAIN *and* CITIZENS *with*
                    PHARAMOND.

CAPTAIN   Come, my brave Myrmidons, let's fall on. Let
your caps swarm, my boys, and your nimble tongues
forget your mother gibberish of 'what-do-you-lack',
and set your mouths ope, children, till your palates fall
frighted half a fathom, past the cure of bay salt and   5
gross pepper.

5.4 Location: the city
1–19 The Captain begins and ends the scene speaking prose to the citizens, but throughout the remainder of the scene most of his lines can be read either as prose or as exuberant verse. The insistent iambic rhythm suggests the latter, especially when the Captain addresses the two princes.
1 **Myrmidons** 'Members of a warlike people . . . whom Achilles led to the siege of Troy' (*OED* 1); by extension, members of a retinue, faithful followers (*OED* 2). In *Woman's Prize* Livia creeps past the quarters 'fierce *Petrucio* / Keepes with his Myrmidons' (2.2.8–9 and cf. 2.2.34). The Captain's line may recall Shakespeare's Achilles, 'Come here about me, you my Myrmidons' (*TC*, 5.7.1).
3 **mother gibberish** a jocular variant of 'mother tongue'
what-do-you-lack the cry of the

merchant sitting in his shop to a potential customer; cf. 5.3.127n.
5–6 **past . . . pepper** The Captain's joke seems to be based on two meanings of *cure*, *OED n.*[1] 6a, successful medical treatment (citing Shakespeare, *LLL*, 5.2.28, 'past care is still past cure'), and *OED n.*[1] 9, 'the curing or preserving of fish, pork, etc.' *OED*'s earliest example of the latter meaning dates from 1743, but meat was prepared for keeping by salting (*OED* cure *v.*[1] 7) much earlier than that. Pepper, along with other spices, was used in preserving: cf. Cerimon's shock on finding the apparently dead body of Thaisa 'Balmed and entreasured with full bags of spices!' (*Per*, 3.2.64).
5 **bay salt** salt obtained in large crystals by slow evaporation; originally, salt from sea-water dried by the sun's heat
6 **gross pepper** pepper coarsely ground, in large particles

190 royal] noble *Q1* 191 you] *Q1;* your *Q2* 192 All] Now all *Q1* SD] *(Exeunt omnes); om. Q1* Note: For scenes 5.4 and 5.5 changes in lineation and emendations in other editions are collated, but *Q1* is only noted when variants in its text are adopted into this edition. 5.4] *Weber* 1–8] *this edn; prose Q1; Q2 lines* caps / mother / mouthes / halfe a / Pepper, / *Philaster,* / ding dongs, /; *Weber lines* on! / tongues / lack, / Palates / cure / cry / *Philaster* / ding-dongs, / 2 your caps] *Q1;* our caps *Q2* 4 ope] *Q1 (*ope'*);* Vp *Q2*

And then cry 'Philaster, brave Philaster!'
Let Philaster be deeper in request, my dingdongs,
My pairs of dear indentures, kings of clubs,
Than your cold water chamlets or your paintings 10
Spitted with copper. Let not your hasty silks
Or your branched cloth of bodkin or your tissues,

8 **dingdongs** a variant on dingding, a term of endearment, but also an onomatopoeic suggestion of the noisy crowd; *OED* 1 cites Cotgrave, *A Dictionary of the French and English Tongues* (1611), '*Dindan*, the ding-dong, or ringing out of bells'.

9 **pairs . . . indentures** An indenture is a deed between two or more parties and, particularly, 'the contract by which an apprentice is bound to the master who undertakes to teach him a trade . . . Originally both copies were written on one piece of parchment or paper, and then cut asunder in a serrated or sinuous line, so that when brought together again at any time, the two edges exactly tallied and showed that they were parts of one and the same original document: hence the expression "pair of indentures"' (*OED* 1, 2). Gurr asserts that 'the mob is largely composed of indentured apprentices', presumably because the Captain refers to his followers as *children* (4) and *boys* (21). However, to the Captain, an *old grey ruffian* (5.3.113), the crowd seems youthful. More importantly, he instructs the citizens to *bring your wives* (148). Apprentices were not permitted to marry, so the crowd must include the apprentices' masters.
kings of clubs 'Prentices and clubs' was the rallying cry of the London apprentices (*OED* club *n.* 1c). Cf. Dekker and Middleton, *Honest Whore 1*, 4.3.91–2, 'Sfoot clubs, clubs, prentices, downe with em, ah you roagues, strike a Cittizen in's shop'.

10–17 The Captain addresses the citizens as dealers in various kinds of cloth. The names of materials, some of which no longer exist in their seventeenth-century forms, serve as the basis for a series of puns in which the names are more important than the precise sense.

10 **cold water chamlets** Chamlet or camlet was originally a soft, fine fabric made of the hair of the chamois. By the fifteenth century the name was applied to a fine material made either of silk or of the hair of the Angora goat. 'By 1525, chamlets were made to show a "watered" or moiré appearance, and thereafter they were designated "unwatered" or "watered", the latter called "cold water chamblets" in *Philaster*' (Linthicum, 74). According to Holland's *Pliny*, 1601, watered chamlet, with its wavy surface, 'was from the beginning esteemed the richest and brauest wearing' (*OED*). Clearing the way for the christening in *H8*, the Porter addresses, 'You i'th' chamblet' (5.3.86).

10–11 **paintings . . . copper** painted cloth embroidered with copper thread

11 **hasty silks** 'silks stiffened with gum, a cheap way of giving a temporary shine to a fabric' (Gurr, 106)

12 **branched** See 5.3.140–1n.
cloth of bodkin 'raised work' on cloth of gold or tissue, 'characterized by raised designs of animals, plants, branches and geometric figures, and made in many colours' (Linthicum, 115). The term was used generally for rich embroidered stuff and brocade. Bodkin or baudekin originated in Baghdad (to which the name is etymologically related). After the fourteenth century it was not made exclusively in the east but continued to be regarded as a valuable import: cf. the materials expected when the 'Ships come home' in *City Madam*: 'Silk . . . / Cloth of Bodkin, / Tissue,

Dearly beloved of spiced cake and custards,
You Robin Hoods, Scarlets and Johns, tie your affections
In darkness to your shops. No, dainty duckers,   15
Up with your three-piled spirits, your wrought valours,
And let your uncut cholers make the King feel
The measure of your mightiness. Philaster!
Cry, my rose nobles, cry!

ALL   Philaster, Philaster!

CAPTAIN
How do you like this, my lord prince?   20

Gold, Silver, Velvets, Sattins, Taffaties' (2.1.70–2). The word is not related to 'bodkin', a short pointed dagger or small pointed instrument for piercing holes in cloth.

tissues rich materials, 'of precious metals, or of these metals and silk . . . distinguished from the plain weave of cloth of gold, for both warp and woof of tissue were composed of twisted threads' (Linthicum, 117–18). Cf. 'she did lie / In her pavilion, cloth-of-gold of tissue' (*AC*, 2.2.198–9).

14 *You Robin Hoods, Scarlets and Johns** To explain his emendation (see t.n.) Theobald writes, 'All, who know anything of the Story of *Robin-hood*, must know that *Scarlet* and *John* were two of his Favourite Dependants.' Nevertheless, Q2's 'Your Robin-hoods scarlets' may suggest a pun, as scarlet was 'in early use, some rich cloth, often of a bright red colour'. See 2.2.23n.

15 **duckers** duck hunters; ducks (a term of affection); 'servile head-bobbing tradesmen' (Gurr). *OED* gives only this line for 'a cringer' and notes that the meaning is uncertain.

16 **three-piled** Three-pile was 'velvet in which the loops of the pile-warp (which constitutes the nap) are formed by three threads, producing a pile of treble thickness' (*OED*); it was frequently

used metaphorically. Cf. *Scornful Lady*, 3.1.91–5, 'And for you, tender Sir, whose gentle bloud / Runnes in your nose, and makes you snuffe at all / But three pil'd people, I doe let you know, / He that begot your worships sattin sute, / Can make no men Sir.'

wrought valours a pun on 'wrought velvets', that is, cloth 'decorated or ornamented, as with needlework; elaborated, embellished, embroidered' (*OED* wrought, *ppl.a.* 3b)

17 **uncut cholers** The Captain puns on *choler* (anger) and *collar*. The citizens' *cholers* are *uncut* or, in Q1's reading, 'acute', because they have not been assuaged and because their *uncut collars* afford them no cooling ventilation. 'Cut' or ornamentally slashed clothes were fashionable; cf. Middleton, *Hengist*, 2.4.86–9, 'this is like the vanity of your Roman gallants that cannot wear good suits but they must have 'em cut and slashed into gigots that the very crimson taffeta sits blushing at their follies'.

18 **measure** strength; mercer's measuring rod

19 **rose nobles** 'A gold coin current in the fifteenth and sixteenth centuries . . . with the figure of a rose stamped upon it' (*OED* 1); 'commercial nobles, as distinct from the great nobles' (Gurr)

---

13 custards] Custard *Q4* 14 You] *Theobald;* Your *Q2* 17 cholers] *Dyce;* Collers *Q2;* Coller *Q5;* choler *Colman* 20–4] *Weber; Q2 lines* boyes, / top-sailes / Argosie / Cockels. /

These are mad boys, I tell you; these are things
That will not strike their topsails to a foist
And let a man of war, an argosy,
Hull and cry cockles.

PHARAMOND

Why, you rude slave, do you know what you do?   25

CAPTAIN

My pretty prince of puppets, we do know
And give your greatness warning that you talk
No more such bug's-words, or that soldered crown
Shall be scratched with a musket. Dear Prince Pippen,
Down with your noble blood, or as I live   30
I'll have you coddled. – Let 'im loose, my spirits.
Make us a round ring with your bills, my Hectors,
And let me see what this trim man dares do. –

22–4 **strike . . . cockles** Metaphorically, the citizens will not yield (*strike . . . sails*) to the insignificant Pharamond while Philaster is disregarded and made to undertake activities (like crying or hawking fish) unworthy of his greatness. A *foist* was a light galley, propelled by sails and oars, or a small boat used on the river, insignificant vessels compared with an *argosy*, a warship or merchant-vessel of the largest size. Cf. Petrucio denigrating his wife's power: 'This Pinck, this painted Foyst, this Cockle-boat' (*Woman's Prize*, 2.6.17). To *hull*, according to Smith's *Sea Grammar*, was to 'bear no sail', especially 'before a storm, when they strike their sails'.

28 **bug's-words** swaggering or threatening language; cf. Sophocles' indignation when Maria announces she will come down to her new husband only when he agrees to her demands: 'By'r Lady these are Bugs-words' (*Woman's Prize*, 1.3.119).

28–9 **soldered . . . musket** Pharamond is uninjured, but the Captain speaks as if

both his head and his royal diadem were stuck together with metallic solder.

29–31 **Pippen . . . coddled** 'Pippens' or apples were frequently stewed (*coddled*).

32 **bills** weapons with a long wooden handle culminating in a blade, axe or spearhead; halberds. Such weapons were carried by constables and were frequently associated with pikes: *OED* cites Drayton, *Barons' Wars*, 1603, 'Wer't with the speare, or Browne Bill, or the Pike' (Canto 2, 37). Cf. 42 and *Custom of the Country*, 'He was still in quarrels, scorn'd us Peace-makers, / And all our bill-authority' (2.3.131–2).
Hectors Hector was Troy's greatest military hero. The Captain has forgotten that he called the Citizens *Myrmidons* (1), and that at Achilles' direction the Myrmidons killed Hector.

33 **trim** ironically, 'fine, nice, pretty' (*OED adj.* 3); cf. Calianax's anger at Melantius, 'And theres / Another of 'em, a trim cheating souldier' (*Maid's Tragedy*, 2.2.97–8).

33 me] vs *Q3*

Now, sir, have at you. Here I lie,

And with this washing blow – do you see, sweet prince? –   35

I could hulk your grace and hang you up cross-legged

Like a hare at a poulter's, and do this with this wiper.

PHARAMOND

You will not see me murdered, wicked villains?

1 CITIZEN   Yes, indeed, will we, sir. We have not seen one

so a great while.   40

CAPTAIN

He would have weapons, would he?

Give him a broadside, my brave boys, with your pikes.

Branch me his skin in flowers like a satin,

And between every flower a mortal cut.

Your royalty shall ravel. Jag him, gentlemen: 45

I'll have him cut to the kell, then down the seams.

Oh, for a whip to make him galloon laces:

I'll have a coach whip.

PHARAMOND   Oh, spare me, gentlemen!

CAPTAIN

Hold, hold, the man begins to fear and know himself.

He shall for this time only be seeled up   50

---

35 **washing** swashing (*OED ppl.a.* 2), either
literal ('Gregory, remember thy washing
blow', *RJ*, 1.1.59–60) or figurative (''Tis
a lustie wench: now I could spend my
forty-pence . . . to have but one fling at
her; / To give her but a washing blow',
Wild Goose Chase, 5.4.36–8)
36 **hulk** disembowel (*OED v.* 2, citing this
line)
37 **poulter's** poultry dealer's shop
wiper slang for a weapon (*OED* 3,
citing this line)
40 ***so** treated so; Q2's 'foe' is probably a
misreading of a long *s*.
42 Slap him with the flat sides of your
blades.

45 **ravel** unwind, disintegrate: cf. 'do's my
Lord rauell out, do's he fret?' (Marston,
Fawn, 2.1, STC 17483, 1606).
Jag stab, pierce with a sharp instrument
46 **kell** membrane covering the intestines
47 **make him** make him into
galloon laces gold or silver braid,
frequently used for trimming servants'
liveries and hence particularly
offensive to Pharamond. Cf. 'Thou
Galloone gallant, and Mamon you /
That build on golden mountaines'
(*Sea Voyage*, 1.4.81–2).
50–2 **seeled . . . going** To *seel* was to
sew up a bird's eyelids as part of the

---

35 washing] swashing *Q3*   40 so] *F2* (soe); foe *Q2;* for *Weber*   41–7] *Weber; Q2 prose to 46* then /
followed by Laces, / Coach-whip. /   42 boys, with your pikes.] *Theobald;* boyes with your Pikes, *Q2*
49] Hold, hold; / himself; | *Weber*

With a feather through his nose, that he may only see
Heaven and think whither he's going. —
Nay, my beyond-sea sir, we will proclaim you.
You would be king!
Thou tender heir apparent to a church-ale,   55
Thou slight prince of single sarcenet,
Thou royal ringtail, fit to fly at nothing
But poor men's poultry and have every boy
Beat thee from that, too, with his bread and butter!

PHARAMOND

Gods keep me from these hellhounds!   60

1 CITIZEN   Shall's geld him, Captain?

CAPTAIN

No, you shall spare his doucets, my dear donsels.
As you respect the ladies, let them flourish.
The curses of a longing woman kills
As speedy as a plague, boys.   65

1 CITIZEN   I'll have a leg, that's certain.

2 CITIZEN   I'll have an arm.

taming process; *OED* cites Sidney's *Arcadia*, 'Now she brought them to see a seeled Doue, who the blinder she was, the higher shee straue.' The Captain proposes to seel the eyes of Pharamond so that, unlike the birds, he can see only up (to *Heaven*) rather than down, for prey.

55 **church-ale** festive gathering at church. These had a reputation for sexual licentiousness: Stubbes complains of them in *The Anatomy of Abuses* (1583), and in Jonson's *Masque of Queens* (1609) a witch has 'Kill'd an infant, to haue his fat. / A Piper it got, at a Church-ale' (176–7).

56 **single sarcenet** fine, soft silk material. Double sarcenet was heavy but single sarcenet was very thin, and stage references use the term metaphorically

'to suggest contemptuous slightness' (Linthicum, 121). Hotspur objects to weak oaths as 'sarcenet surety' (*1H4*, 3.1.247).

57–8 **ringtail . . . poultry** The ringtail is the juvenile or female of the hen harrier and thus a weak bird of prey, *fit to fly* only at domestic *poultry*; *OED* 1 cites *The Thracian Wonder*, 5.1 (?Rowley and Heywood), 'no Faulcon but dares venter upon a *Ring-tale*'.

62–4 **spare . . . kills** 'at the fall of the deer' Pharamond 'would needs . . . give ten groats for the doucets' or testicles (4.2.11–13); the Citizens seem aware of Pharamond's philandering, though they may not identify Megra as the *longing woman* who would suffer from his castration.

62 **donsels** young gentlemen

56 sarcenet] *(scarcenet)*

3 CITIZEN   I'll have his nose, and at mine own charge
   build a college and clap't upon the gate.

4 CITIZEN   I'll have his little gut to string a kit with, for   70
   certainly a royal gut will sound like silver.

PHARAMOND   Would they were in thy belly and I past my
   pain once.

5 CITIZEN   Good Captain, let me have his liver to feed
   ferrets.   75

CAPTAIN   Who will have parcels else? Speak.

PHARAMOND   Good gods, consider me. I shall be
   tortured.

1 CITIZEN   Captain, I'll give you the trimming of your
   two-hand sword, and let me have his skin to make false   80
   scabbards.

2 CITIZEN   He has no horns, sir, has he?

CAPTAIN   No, sir, he's a pollard. What wouldst thou do
   with horns?

2 CITIZEN   Oh, if he had had, I would have made rare   85
   hafts and whistles of 'em, but his shinbones, if they be
   sound, shall serve me.

Enter PHILASTER.

69 **build . . . gate** punning on the name of Brasenose College, Oxford

70 **kit** a small fiddle (*OED n.* 2); cf. Jonson, *Sad Shepherd*, 1.4.45–6, 'And each did dance, some to the Kit, or Crowd, / Some to the Bag-pipe.'

75 **ferrets** or polecats, kept for hunting rats

79–81 1 Citizen offers the Captain a decoration for his sword if he will let him use Pharamond's skin; *false scabbards* may be early modern condoms, human skin being better than the usual leather (GM). There is certainly some sexual suggestion: in *Family of Love*, 5.1, G4^r, 1608, *scabbard* means vagina: 'Since he has strooke with the sword, strike you with the Scabbard: in plaine termes Cuckold him,' and in *Chances* wild Don John asks his lascivious landlady, 'Worshipfull Lady, / How does thy Velvet scabbard?' (3.1.74–5).

83 **pollard** 'a male deer that has cast its antlers' (*OED n.* 2). The Captain impugns Pharamond's potency now that he has been captured.

86 **hafts** handles

82 has . . . has] *Colman;* had . . . had *Q2*

ALL

Long live Philaster, the brave Prince Philaster!

PHILASTER

I thank you, gentlemen. But why are these
Rude weapons brought abroad to teach your hands   90
Uncivil trades?

CAPTAIN   My royal Rosicleer,
We are thy Myrmidons, thy guard, thy roarers,
And when thy noble body is in durance,
Thus do we clap our musty morions on
And trace the streets in terror. Is it peace,   95
Thou Mars of men? Is the King sociable
And bids thee live? Art thou above thy foemen
And free as Phoebus? Speak. If not, this stand
Of royal blood shall be a-broach, a-tilt, and run

90 **Rude weapons** the citizens' coarse or rough *clubs* (9) and *bills* (32), as opposed to more refined weapons such as swords

91 **Uncivil** barbarous, not fit for citizens. Etymologically *civil* derives from Latin *civis*, of or pertaining to citizens.
Rosicleer a hero of the Spanish chivalric romance by Diego Ortúñez de Calahorra, known as *The Mirror of Knighthood*. The title-page of the earliest English translation (1578), by M[argaret] [Tyler], epitomizes the style: '*The mirrour of princely deedes and knighthood wherein is shewed the worthinesse of the Knight of the Sunne, and his brother Rosicleer, sonnes to the great Emperour Trebetio: with the strange loue of the beautifull and excellent princesse Briana, and the valiant actes of other noble princes and knightes.*' Rafe, the 'Knight of the Burning Pestle', complains of the deterioration of knighthood: 'one that *Rosicler* would have cal'd right beauteous Damsell, they will call dam'd bitch' (1.1.237–8).

92 **roarers** or roaring boys, noisy bullies much noted in London in the Jacobean period. In Middleton and Rowley's

Quarrel (1617) Chough, a Cornish simpleton, attends a 'roaring school' in London, and in *Bartholomew Fair*, 2.3, Knockem is 'Captaine o'the Roarers'.

93 **in durance** imprisoned

94 **morions** brimless helmets worn by foot soldiers; those belonging to the citizens are *musty* from disuse.

95 **trace . . . terror** walk through the streets frightening people. To trace is to 'pass along or over, tread', as in J. Reynolds, *God's Revenge against Murder* (1621), 'Tracing the street in a neate perfumed boote with iangling spurres' (cited *OED v.*[1] 3).

96 **Mars of men** Cf. 'the Black Prince, that young Mars of men' (*R2*, 2.3.101).
sociable disposed to be friendly

98 **Phoebus** the sun god; Gurr sees confusion with donsel dol Phoebo or the Knight of the Sun, Rosicleer's brother in *The Mirror of Knighthood* (see 91n).

98–100 **stand . . . lees** The Captain threatens to *broach* or pierce Pharamond, the *stand* (or position, *OED n.*[1] II 11b) *of royal blood*, and let his blood flow out as if he were a cask of wine.

99 a-broach, a-tilt] *(a broach, a tilt)*

Even to the lees of honour. 100

PHILASTER

Hold and be satisfied. I am myself
Free as my thoughts are. By the gods, I am.

CAPTAIN

Art thou the dainty darling of the King?
Art thou the Hylas to our Hercules?
Do the lords bow and the regarded scarlets 105
Kiss their gummed golls and cry 'We are your
  servants!'?
Is the court navigable and the presence stuck
With flags of friendship? If not, we are thy castle,
And this man sleeps.

PHILASTER

I am what I do desire to be, your friend. 110
I am what I was born to be, your prince.

PHARAMOND

Sir, there is some humanity in you;
You have a noble soul. Forget my name
And know my misery. Set me safe aboard

---

104 **Hylas . . . Hercules** Hylas was a beautiful young man loved by the Greek hero Hercules; see 2.4.17n. By the time of *Philaster* King James's penchant for young men was well known at court, but there is no suggestion of such a relation between the King and Philaster.

105–6 **regarded . . . golls** respected courtiers kiss their hands to you, but the choice of words indicates contempt. In Sidney's *Arcadia* rustic Mopsa 'put to her golden gols among them' (cited *OED*). See also 148n. *Gummed* can mean sweet-smelling ('perfum'd / With gummes of *paradise*', Jonson, *Alchemist*, 2.2.93–4), but also false and sticky, e.g. *Woman Hater*, 4.2.183–4, where Oriana is described as 'smooth, and soft, as new Satten; shee was never gumb'd yet boy,

nor fretted'. The Captain may imply that the lords take bribes.

105 **scarlets** a scarlet is 'one who wears a scarlet uniform or insignia; e.g. a judge' (*OED* scarlet *n.* and *a.* 4a, citing this line). Cf. 2.2.23n and 14n.

107–8 The Captain's metaphor uses a formal meeting at sea to describe one at court. The *presence* or presence chamber is a place of ceremonial attendance ('the two great Cardinals / Wait in the presence', *H8*, 3.1.16–17), but it is *stuck* (adorned) with flags like an admiral's ship expecting a visit. Similarly, the *castle* is both a stronghold and a large warship (*OED* 4 and 5).

109 **sleeps** dies

114 **aboard** on or into a ship; cf. 'her fortunes brought the maid aboard

107 stuck] struck *Q6*

From these wild cannibals and, as I live,   115
I'll quit this land forever. There is nothing –
Perpetual prisonment, cold, hunger, sickness
Of all sorts, of all dangers, and altogether
The worst company of the worst men, madness, age,
To be as many creatures as a woman   120
And do as all they do, nay, to despair –
But I would rather make it a new nature
And live with all these than endure one hour
Amongst these wild dogs.

PHILASTER

I do pity you. Friends, discharge your fears;   125
Deliver me the prince. I'll warrant you
I shall be old enough to find my safety.

3 CITIZEN   Good sir, take heed he does not hurt you; he's
a fierce man, I can tell you, sir.

CAPTAIN

Prince, by your leave, I'll have a surcingle   130
And make you like a hawk.   *Pharamond strives.*

PHILASTER

Away, away! There is no danger in him.
Alas, he had rather sleep to shake his fit off.
Look you, friends, how gently he leads. Upon my word
He's tame enough; he needs no further watching.   135

us' (*Per*, 5.3.11). The word may be a
misreading for 'abroad' (GM); either
way, Pharamond wishes to leave Sicily.
117 **prisonment** obsolete form of
imprisonment
120–1 **To . . . they do** Pharamond's
comment reflects his association with
changeable and unfaithful women
such as Megra (see 1.1.53–61), but his
defection from Arethusa demonstrates
his own, male fickleness.
125 **discharge your fears** Do not worry
about me.

130 **surcingle** a girth for a horse or
other animal, here apparently to bind
Pharamond so that he will obey his
'keeper', like a tamed bird
131 SD *Q7's correction, *strives* (see t.n.),
clarifies that Pharamond is still being
restrained by the group of Citizens.
134 **leads** is led, can be led
135 **tame . . . watching** falconry terms:
to 'watch' is to keep the bird awake until
it is tamed. Cf. *TS*, 4.1.175–83, and
Woman's Prize, 1.2.149–57.

117 sickness] *F2;* sicknesse, *Q2*   128–9] *Turner; Q2 lines* you, / Sir. /   131 SD] *Q7 (He strives); He strives Q2; He stirres Q3*   135 needs] *Q9;* neede *Q2*

Good my friends, go to your houses,
And by me have your pardons and my love,
And know there shall be nothing in my power
You may deserve but you shall have your wishes:
To give you more thanks were to flatter you.   140
Continue still your love, and for an earnest
Drink this.   [*Gives 'em his purse.*]

ALL   Long mayst thou live, brave prince, brave prince,
brave prince!   *Exeunt Philaster and Pharamond.*

CAPTAIN   Go thy ways, thou art the king of courtesy. Fall   145
off again, my sweet youths; come, and every man trace
to his house again and hang his pewter up. Then to the
tavern, and bring your wives in muffs. We will have
music, and the red grape shall make us dance and rise,   149
boys.   *Exeunt.*

[5.5]   *Enter* KING, ARETHUSA, GALLATEA, MEGRA,
            CLEREMONT, DION, THRASILINE, BELLARIO
                    and Attendants.

KING
Is it appeased?

137 **pardons** By rising in the streets the
citizens incur the risk of punishment
for rioting, which could be death.
140 **flatter you** Philaster's distrust of
those who 'could well be flattered' is in
evidence from his first meeting with his
supporters (1.1.312).
141 **earnest** pledge of something (often
money) afterwards to be received in
greater abundance (*OED n.*[2] 1); cf. 'It
is an earnest of a further good' (*Cym*,
1.5.65).
147 **pewter** weapon or armour made of

pewter (*OED* 3b, citing only this line)
or pewter coloured (*OED* B2); cf.
'These pewter coates canne neuer sit so
wel as Satten doublets' (*Campaspe*, 5.3).
148 **in muffs** Cf. *Woman Hater*, 5.4.170–
1, where a woman baiting Gondarino
makes him hold out his hands and says,
'Alas how cold they are poore golls, why
do'st thou not get thee a muffe?'
149 **rise** sexually
5.5 Location: the palace
1 **it** the riot or *mad sea-breach* (5.3.187) of
the Citizens

136–7] *Colman; prose Q2*   142 SD] *Q1; not in Q2*   144 prince] *(Prine)*   SD *Exeunt*] *(Exit)*
145–50] *Gurr; Q2 lines* Curtesie, / man / then to / haue / Boyes. /; *Theobald lines* Courtesy; /
followed by prose   5.5] *Weber*   0.3 Attendants] *Q4; attendance Q2*

DION

Sir, all is quiet as this dead of night,
As peaceable as sleep. My lord Philaster
Brings on the prince himself.

KING   Kind gentleman!

I will not break the least word I have given   5
In promise to him. I have heaped a world
Of grief upon his head, which yet I hope
To wash away.

Enter PHILASTER *and* PHARAMOND.

CLEREMONT   My lord is come.

KING [*Embraces Philaster.*]   My son,

Blest be the time that I have leave to call
Such virtue mine. Now thou art in mine arms   10
Methinks I have a salve unto my breast
For all the stings that dwell there. Streams of grief
That I have wronged thee, and as much of joy
That I repent it, issue from mine eyes;
Let them appease thee. Take thy right; take her –   15
She is thy right, too – and forget to urge
My vexed soul with that I did before.

PHILASTER

Sir, it is blotted from my memory,

2 **this** Theobald, following Seward,
emends to *the* on the grounds that it is
not actually midnight.

4 ***gentleman** Although a number of
courtiers or *gentlemen* (see t.n.) are
present to whom the King could be
speaking, his praise indicates that he
refers to Philaster, who has rescued
Pharamond from the riot *himself.*

5 **word . . . given** the promises at
5.3.178–83, reiterated at 15–17, that
Philaster may be what he was *born to*

and take Arethusa as well.

13 ***wronged** Q2's 'wrought' may
result from a two-stage compositorial
error, first inverting the *n* and then
completing the apparent word. The
error was not caught before Theobald.
Ashe suggests 'wrought' may be 'meant
in the obsolete sense of "agitated"',
but OED *ppl.adj.* 5 gives that sense
only for the sea.

16–17 **urge . . . with** remind me about

17 **vexed** vexèd

4 gentleman] *Theobald (Seward);* Gentlemen *Q2*   8] *Boas; Q2 lines* away. / come. / sonne, / ; *Q6 lines*
away. / sonne! /   SD2] *Gurr*   13 wronged] *Theobald;* wrought *Q2*

Past and forgotten. – For you, prince of Spain,
Whom I have thus redeemed, you have full leave   20
To make an honourable voyage home.
And if you would go furnished to your realm
With fair provision, I do see a lady
Methinks would gladly bear you company.
How like you this piece?

MEGRA   Sir, he likes it well,   25
For he hath tried it and hath found it worth
His princely liking. We were ta'en abed;
I know your meaning. I am not the first
That nature taught to seek a fellow forth.
Can shame remain perpetually in me   30
And not in others? Or have princes salves
To cure ill names that meaner people want?

PHILASTER
What mean you?

MEGRA   You must get another ship
To bear the princess and her boy together.

DION
How now?   35

MEGRA

Others took me, and I took her and him
At that all women may be ta'en sometime.
Ship us all four, my lord: we can endure
Weather and wind alike.

26 **tried** tested sexually
28–37 **I am . . . sometime** Megra articulates a spirited, feminist defence of women's sexual needs and practices as natural and common, but it is weakened by her lies about Arethusa and by her suggestion that women of higher status are not held to the same standard of chastity. The reactions of the King and Philaster to the accusations against Arethusa refute the latter charge.
31–2 **Or . . . want** Cf. the conversation between Dion and the King in 4.4 on the limitations of royal power.

34 her] the *Q3*

KING [*to Arethusa*]

   Clear thou thyself or know not me for father.   40

ARETHUSA

   This earth,

   How false it is! What means is left for me

   To clear myself? It lies in your belief.

   My lords, believe me, and let all things else

   Struggle together to dishonour me.   45

BELLARIO

   Oh, stop your ears, great King, that I may speak

   As freedom would. Then I will call this lady

   As base as are her actions. Hear me, sir:

   Believe your heated blood when it rebels

   Against your reason sooner than this lady.   50

MEGRA

   By this good light, he bears it handsomely.

PHILASTER

   This lady! I will sooner trust the wind

   With feathers or the troubled sea with pearl

   Than her with anything. Believe her not!

   Why, think you if I did believe her words   55

   I would outlive 'em? Honour cannot take

   Revenge on you. Then what were to be known

   But death?

KING   Forget her, sir, since all is knit

   Between us. But I must request of you

   One favour, and will sadly be denied.   60

42–3 **What . . . myself** Unlike Megra, Arethusa does not attempt a defence.

47 **As freedom would** freely

55–6 **think . . . 'em** the first of Philaster's threats of suicide in this scene; see

79 SD, 124 SD.

56–7 **Honour . . . you** Philaster cannot honourably challenge Arethusa's accuser because of her gender.

60 **sadly** unwillingly

40 SD] *this edn*   48 are] *om. Q3*

PHILASTER

    Command whate'er it be.

KING   Swear to be true

    To what you promise.

PHILASTER   By the powers above,

    Let it not be the death of her or him,

    And it is granted.

KING   Bear away that boy

    To torture. I will have her cleared or buried.   65

PHILASTER

    Oh, let me call my word back, worthy sir!

    Ask something else. Bury my life and right

    In one poor grave, but do not take away

    My life and fame at once.

KING   Away with him!

    It stands irrevocable.   70

PHILASTER

    Turn all your eyes on me. Here stands a man,

    The falsest and the basest of this world.

    Set swords against this breast, some honest man,

    For I have lived till I am pitied.

    My former deeds were hateful, but this last   75

    Is pitiful, for I unwillingly

    Have given the dear preserver of my life

    Unto his torture. Is it in the power

    Of flesh and blood to carry this and live?

       Offers to kill himself.

61–4 **Swear . . . granted** another of the promises and counterpromises between the King and Philaster

65 **torture** The threat to torture Bellario here, along with the imagined stripping of his *tender flesh* (81) – an even more titillating possibility if the audience has suspicions about Bellario's gender – is eliminated in Q1. Instead the mob threatens to torture Pharamont.
    buried burièd

66 **word** promise

70 **It** the order to torture Bellario

74 **pitied** pitièd

76 **pitiful** worthy of your sympathy

61–2] *Dyce; Q2 lines* be. / promise. / aboue, / once. / irreuocable. /   79 SD] *Q9; opp. 78–9 Q2*   66 word] words *Q4*   69–70] *this edn; Q2 lines*

ARETHUSA

    Dear sir, be patient yet. Oh, stay that hand!   80

KING

    Sirs, strip that boy.

DION   Come, sir, your tender flesh

    Will try your constancy.

BELLARIO   Oh, kill me, gentlemen!

DION

    No help, sirs.

BELLARIO   Will you torture me?

KING   Haste there!

    Why stay you?

BELLARIO   Then I shall not break my vow,

    You know, just gods, though I discover all.   85

KING

    How's that? Will he confess?

DION   Sir, so he says.

KING

    Speak, then.

BELLARIO   Great King, if you command

    This lord to talk with me alone, my tongue,

    Urged by my heart, shall utter all the thoughts

    My youth hath known, and stranger things than these   90

81–2 ***your . . . constancy** The tenderness of your flesh will test or challenge your ability to remain constant under torture. Gurr, who retains 'tire' (see 82 t.n.), sees a quibble on 'be sufficient clothing for' and 'make weary', that is, Bellario's constancy is dressed in tender flesh.

83 ***No help, sirs** Q2's punctuation, 'No, help sirs', suggests that Dion asks for assistance in overcoming the struggles of the slight 'boy' Bellario. More probably he warns the other courtiers

away as they move to protect the page.

84–5 **Then . . . all** Bellario's decision to reveal his identity is more credible because he has already shown a fear of torture at 4.6.66–83, when Pharamond threatened tortures 'long as thy natural life'.

90 ***things** The plural is required by the agreement with *these*; the compositor may have had difficulty with the type for *g*, as the letter is inverted in the catchword *King* only two lines below on I1v.

81–7] *Boas; Q2 lines* boy. / constancy. / Gentlemen. / sirs. / me? / you? / vow, / all. / confesse? / sayes. / then. / command /*; Q6 lines* boy / constancy. / sirs. / you? / vow, / all. / sayes / command /   82 try] *Q3 (*trie*);* tire *Q2*   83 No help, sirs] *Q9;* No, helpe sirs *Q2*   90 things] *Q3;* thing *Q2*

You hear not often.

KING   Walk aside with him.

    [Dion and Bellario walk apart.]

DION

   Why speak'st thou not?

BELLARIO   Know you this face, my lord?

DION

   No.

BELLARIO   Have you not seen it, nor the like?

DION

   Yes, I have seen the like, but readily
   I know not where.

BELLARIO   I have been often told   95
   In court of one Euphrasia, a lady
   And daughter to you, betwixt whom and me
   They that would flatter my bad face would swear
   There was such strange resemblance that we two
   Could not be known asunder, dressed alike.   100

DION

   By heaven, and so there is.

BELLARIO   For her fair sake,
   Who now doth spend the springtime of her life
   In holy pilgrimage, move to the King
   That I may scape this torture.

DION   But thou speak'st
   As like Euphrasia as thou dost look.   105
   How came it to thy knowledge that she lives

---

91 **Walk ... him** The conversation between Dion and Bellario must be heard by the audience but not by the other courtiers, as Dion will announce its result at 126.

92–112 **Know ... Euphrasia** For discussion of the parallels between this conversation and the interview between Pericles and the unknown Marina, see pp. 12–13.

96 **Euphrasia** the first mention of the name, which means 'mind-gladdening' (Gurr); at 1.1.333 she is referred to merely as 'a virtuous gentlewoman'. The name does not appear in Q1.

103 **move to** beg

91 SD] *Dyce*   92 speak'st] *Q3;* speak't *Q2*

In pilgrimage?

BELLARIO   I know it not, my lord,
But I have heard it – [*aside*] and do scarce believe it.

DION

Oh, my shame! Is't possible? Draw near
That I may gaze upon thee. Art thou she,   110
Or else her murderer? Where wert thou born?

BELLARIO

In Siracusa.

DION   What's thy name?

BELLARIO   Euphrasia.

DION

Oh, 'tis just, 'tis she!
Now I do know thee. Oh, that thou hadst died,
And I had never seen thee nor my shame!   115
How shall I own thee? Shall this tongue of mine
E'er call thee daughter more?

BELLARIO

Would I had died indeed; I wish it too,

---

108 and SD *aside . . . it* The last phrase
makes little sense unless Bellario
indicates his true knowledge by
speaking it aside, just before revealing
the truth. Alternatively, *scarce* could be
an error for a word such as 'firm'.
112 **Siracusa** on the east coast of Sicily,
near the mythological Arethusa's
well; the similarity of Arethusa and
Euphrasia is insisted upon.
Euphrasia At this point in Q1
Euphrasia '*Kneels to* Dion, *and
discovers her hair*', which may recall
early performance practice. However,
as Ashe points out, in Q1 the display
of Euphrasia's hair is appropriate
because the conversation between
father and daughter is private, but

in Q2 it is not feasible 'because
other characters on stage await
Dion's announcement of Bellario's
identity'. Furthermore, the action in
Q1 replaces much of 92–122 in Q2;
see facing pages in Appendix and
pp. 90–1.
113 **just** just so, the truth; Gurr sees an
echo of 'the secret justice of the gods'.
114–15 **that . . . my shame** Cf. the
egotistic reaction of Antonio to
Claudio's accusations against his
daughter Hero, *MA*, 4.1.120–54.
116 **own** recognize; acknowledge
118 **Would . . . died** Like Philaster,
Bellario/Euphrasia is depressive,
crying 'death I hope is come' when
Philaster wounds her (4.6.26).

106–7] *Theobald; Q2 lines* liues / Pilgrimage? / Lord, / ; *Q6 lines* Pilgrimage? / Lord, /   108 SD] *this
edn*   112] *Boas; Q2 lines* Siracusa. / name? / *Euphrasia.* / ; *F2 lines* name? / *Euphrasia.* /   Euphrasia.]
Behold me sir. *Kneeles to* LEON, *and discovers her haire. Q1*

And so must have done by vow ere published
What I have told, but that there was no means   120
To hide it longer. Yet I joy in this:
The princess is all clear.

KING [*to Dion*]   What have you done?

DION

All's discovered.

PHILASTER   Why, then, hold you me?
All is discovered! Pray you, let me go.

He offers to stab himself.

KING

Stay him.

ARETHUSA   What is discovered?

DION   Why, my shame.   125
It is a woman; let her speak the rest.

PHILASTER

How? That again.

DION   It is a woman.

PHILASTER

Blest be you powers that favour innocence!

KING [*Points to Megra.*]

Lay hold upon that lady.

PHILASTER

It is a woman, sir! Hark, gentlemen,   130
It is a woman! Arethusa, take
My soul into thy breast, that would be gone
With joy. It is a woman! Thou art fair

---

119 **published** publishèd

122 **What . . . done** Without punctuation, as in Q2, the entire phrase may refer to the conversation of Dion and Euphrasia or to some action of hers, such as kneeling. Alternatively, with a comma after *What* (see t.n.), *have you*

done means 'have you finished?'

126–33 **It is a woman** Five iterations of this phrase, especially with a boy actor representing Euphrasia, risk arousing laughter. The tone of Beaumont and Fletcher's tragicomedies is often puzzling.

---

119 so] so I *Q4*   122 SD] this edn   What] What, *Dyce*   125] *Boas; Q2 lines* discouered? / shame / 129 SD] *this edn;* Megra *is seized.* | *Weber*

And virtuous still to ages, in despite of malice.

KING [*to Bellario, pointing at Dion*]
    Speak you. Where lies his shame?

BELLARIO   I am his daughter.   135

PHILASTER
    The gods are just.

DION [*Kneels to Philaster and Arethusa.*]
    I dare accuse none, but before you two,
    The virtue of our age, I bend my knee
    For mercy.

PHILASTER [*Raises him.*]   Take it freely, for I know
    Though what thou didst were undiscreetly done,   140
    'Twas meant well.

ARETHUSA   And for me,
    I have a power to pardon sins as oft
    As any man has power to wrong me.

CLEREMONT
    Noble and worthy!

PHILASTER   But, Bellario –
    For I must call thee still so – tell me why   145
    Thou didst conceal thy sex. It was a fault,
    A fault, Bellario, though thy other deeds
    Of truth outweighed it. All these jealousies
    Had flown to nothing if thou hadst discovered
    What now we know.

BELLARIO   My father oft would speak   150

---

134 **virtuous** virt'ous
   despite Theobald's emendation,
   'spight, would regularize the metre.
140 **what thou didst** a reference
   to Dion's assertion that he saw the
   Princess and the boy together and that
   she is *known a whore* (3.1.63)
   undiscreetly indiscreetly, unwisely

149 **discovered** revealed
150–83 The speech recalls Othello's account
   of wooing Desdemona, which begins,
   'Her father loved me, oft invited me', and
   its account of how Desdemona, when
   she could 'with haste dispatch' the house
   affairs, would 'come again, and with a
   greedy ear / Devour up my discourse'

---

134 despite] 'spight *Theobold*   135–7] *Boas; Q2 lines* shame? / Daughter. / iust. / two, /; *Q6 lines*
Daughter. / two /; *F2 lines* shame? / just. / two. /   135 SD] *this edn*   137 SD] *Dyce subst.*   139
SD] *Dyce subst.*

Your worth and virtue, and as I did grow
More and more apprehensive, I did thirst
To see the man so raised. But yet all this
Was but a maiden longing, to be lost
As soon as found, till sitting in my window,   155
Printing my thoughts in lawn, I saw a god,
I thought – but it was you – enter our gates.
My blood flew out and back again as fast
As I had puffed it forth and sucked it in
Like breath. Then was I called away in haste   160
To entertain you. Never was a man
Heaved from a sheepcote to a sceptre, raised
So high in thoughts as I. You left a kiss
Upon these lips then which I mean to keep
From you forever. I did hear you talk   165
Far above singing. After you were gone,
I grew acquainted with my heart and searched
What stirred it so. Alas, I found it love –
Yet far from lust, for could I but have lived
In presence of you, I had had my end.   170
For this I did delude my noble father
With a feigned pilgrimage and dressed myself

(*Oth*, 1.3.129–70). Desdemona and Euphrasia each subsequently flee a father to follow a beloved.

152 **apprehensive** understanding

153 **raised** admired, standing above other men. Settle apparently considered this an error for *praised* (see t.n.), and the reiteration of *raised* at 162 may indicate compositorial anticipation here.

156 **Printing . . . lawn** embroidering on fine linen cloth

161–3 ***Never . . . So high** Q2's punctuation (see t.n.) makes the person *raised* the man *heaved* up from a sheepcote, but the referent is Euphrasia,

whose thoughts are elevated by her contact with Philaster.

169 ***could I** As Q3 recognized, this is hypothetical rather than declarative.

170 **my end** that which I desired; death from love

172 **feigned pilgrimage** a romance convention; cf. Helena in *AW*, 4.3.46–7, 'Her pretence is a pilgrimage to Saint Jaques' and Cariola's objection to the Duchess of Malfi's plan, 'I do not like this jesting with religion, / This feigned Pilgrimage' (*Malfi*, 3.2.317–18).

172–3 **dressed . . . boy** The trope of the cross-dressed girl following her beloved

153 raised] praised *Settle*   162 sheepcote . . . sceptre, raised] *Langbaine;* sheepe-coate, . . . Scepter rais'd, *Q2*   169 could I] *Q3;* I could *Q2*

In habit of a boy. And for I knew
My birth no match for you, I was past hope
Of having you. And understanding well   175
That when I made discovery of my sex
I could not stay with you, I made a vow,
By all the most religious things a maid
Could call together, never to be known,
Whilst there was hope to hide me from men's eyes,   180
For other than I seemed, that I might ever
Abide with you. Then sat I by the fount
Where first you took me up.

KING   Search out a match
Within our kingdom, where and when thou wilt,
And I will pay thy dowry, and thyself   185
Wilt well deserve him.

BELLARIO   Never, sir, will I

---

recurs throughout Jacobean drama, for
example in the Beaumont and Fletcher
canon in *Maid's Tragedy*, *Mad Lover*
and *Cupid's Revenge* or in Middleton's
Valour (1622) and *Dissemblers* (1619).
Euphrasia most closely resembles Julia
of *TGV*, who calls herself a 'true-
devoted pilgrim' (2.7.9) as she pursues
Proteus. He, like Philaster and like
Orsino in *TN*, uses her as a messenger
to his (new) beloved.

174 **My . . . you** Euphrasia's conviction
that her social status will keep her from
Philaster echoes Laertes' statement that
Hamlet's 'greatness weighed, his will
is not his own. / For he himself is
subject to his birth' (1.3.17–18 in F)
and Polonius's warning to Ophelia that
'Lord Hamlet is a prince out of thy
star' (2.2.138). Philaster's inaccessibility
is, however, never contradicted, while
Gertrude claims she hoped Ophelia
'shouldst have been my Hamlet's wife'
(5.2.233).

183–5 **Search . . . dowry** *AW* concludes
as the King for the second time offers

a maiden, 'Choose thou thy husband
and I'll pay thy dower' (5.3.322). Diana,
who has earlier announced that 'Marry
that will, I live and die a maid' (4.2.74),
makes no reply.

186–7 **Never . . . vow** Euphrasia's refusal
to accede to a heteronormative marriage
violates the usual comic conclusion,
which requires the neat pairing-off of
all unmarried females, even widows
such as Paulina in *WT*. Q1 reimposes
the standard ending, keeping Euphrasia
silent while her father agrees to
'surrender of all the right a father has'
and gives her to the courtier indicated
by Philaster. See Appendix 1.

186–7 **Never . . . Marry** The phrasing
is ambiguous. As punctuated by
Q2, *Marry* completes Euphrasia's
affirmation. But she may reply to the
King's offer more comprehensively,
asserting that she will do nothing
that he suggests, neither search out
a match, accept a dowry nor deserve
a husband. In that case *Marry* is
merely an intensifier, as at 4.2.13.

Marry. It is a thing within my vow.
But if I may have leave to serve the princess,
To see the virtues of her lord and her,
I shall have hope to live.

ARETHUSA   I, Philaster,   190
Cannot be jealous, though you had a lady
Dressed like a page to serve you, nor will I
Suspect her living here. – Come live with me,
Live free as I do. She that loves my lord,
Cursed be the wife that hates her.   195

PHILASTER

I grieve such virtue should be laid in earth
Without an heir. Hear me, my royal father:
Wrong not the freedom of our souls so much
To think to take revenge of that base woman;
Her malice cannot hurt us. Set her free   200
As she was born, saving from shame and sin.

KING

Set her at liberty, but [*to Megra*] leave the court.
This is no place for such. – You, Pharamond,
Shall have free passage and a conduct home
Worthy so great a prince. When you come there,   205
Remember 'twas your faults that lost you her
And not my purposed will.

The syntactic parallel between
Arethusa's 'nor will I suspect'
(192–3) and Euphrasia's 'never will
I marry' makes Q2's punctuation
more likely.
191 **Cannot be jealous** In contrast
to the triangles at the ends of *TN*
and *MV*, where the participants are
two men and a woman, Arethusa
announces her willingness to live
with another woman who is openly
in love with her husband. Such

situations were not unknown but
had not been seen at the English
court since Henry VIII. Arethusa's
feminine rejection of jealousy
contrasts with the behaviour of
many dramatic heroes, e.g. Othello,
Posthumus and Philaster.
195 a short line, whether or not *cursed* =
cursèd
196–7 **I . . . heir** In Q1 Philaster's
statement is translated into active
matchmaking.

194 free] free, *Q6*   202 SD] *this edn*

PHARAMOND   I do confess,
Renowned sir.

KING

Last, join your hands in one. Enjoy, Philaster,
This kingdom, which is yours, and after me   210
Whatever I call mine. My blessing on you.
All happy hours be at your marriage joys,
That you may grow yourselves over all lands
And live to see your plenteous branches spring
Wherever there is sun. Let princes learn   215
By this to rule the passions of their blood,
For what heaven wills can never be withstood.   *Exeunt.*

FINIS

208 **Renowned** renownèd
214–15 **your . . . sun** Cf. the image of the 'two fair cedar branches, / The noblest of the mountain' in Bellario's epithalamion, which announces the marriage of Philaster and Arethusa once 'a gentler gale hath blown again / That made these

branches meet and twine together, / Never to be divided' (5.3.25–41).
215–16 **Let . . . blood** The concluding lines return to the themes of tyranny and temperance, the latter conspicuously absent from both the King and Philaster.

214] live *Q6;* like *Q2*   217 SD] *(Exeunt omnes); om. Q1*

APPENDIX 1

PARALLEL PAGES FROM Q1 (*PHYLASTER*) AND Q2 (*PHILASTER*)

PHILASTER (Q2)

1.1   *Enter* DION, CLEREMONT *and* THRASILINE.

CLEREMONT   Here's nor lords nor ladies.

DION   Credit me, gentlemen, I wonder at it. They received strict charge from the King to attend here. Besides, it was boldly published that no officer should forbid any gentlemen that desired to attend and hear.   5

CLEREMONT   Can you guess the cause?

DION   Sir, it is plain about the Spanish prince that's come to marry our kingdom's heir and be our sovereign.

PHYLASTER (Q1)

1.1   *Enter at several doors* Lord LEON; TRASILINE *follows him;* CLERIMON *meets them.*

TRASILINE   Well o'erta'en, my lord.

LEON   Noble friend, welcome – and see who encounters us: honourable good Clerimon!

CLERIMON   My good Lord Leon, most happily met!
Worthy Trasiline! Come, gallants, what's the news?   5
The season affords us variety. The novelists of our time
runs on heaps to glut their itching ears with airy sounds
trotting to th' Burse, and in the Temple walk with

Where the texts of Q1 and Q2 are identical, notes are not repeated. Q2 is quoted in the modernized text.

0.1 *at several doors* Leon, followed by Trasiline, comes from one of the two doors which stood to the left and right of the central 'discovery space' in the tiring-house wall; Clerimon enters from the other door.

1   **Well o'erta'en** The greetings between the gentlemen set the scene at court less clearly than in Q2, where the men come together at a 'strict charge from the King to attend here' (1.1.3).

5   **what's the news?** The phrase was proverbial among the gallants who frequented Paul's Walk, and usually had a political meaning. Walkley, publisher of both Q1 and Q2, 'was ideally positioned to offer news of Westminster politics to this audience of "Paul's walkers", courtiers, and Parliament men' (Lesser, 159).

6   **novelists** 'Newsmongers or carriers of news' (*OED* 4), although the earliest *OED* entry for this meaning is from

1706. The usual seventeenth-century meaning is innovators, persons who favour novelty (*OED* 1, citing Andrew Willet, *Hexapla in Exodum* (1608), 'Augustine doth directly oppose himselfe to all such Dogmatistes and Nouelistes'). The word is not found elsewhere in seventeenth-century drama, but cf. Brathwaite on the 'base *Monopolist*, Church-peace-disturbing-factious *Novelist*' (*Honest Ghost*, 14).

8   **th' Burse** Britain's Burse, or the New Exchange, built by Sir Robert Cecil as a commercial centre to capture the fashionable trade moving westward towards the court at Westminster. It was the location of Thomas Walkley's publishing business. See Dillon, 109–23.

   the Temple one of the Inns of Court, home to lawyers and law students; the name permits Clerimon to pun on the difference between those who frequent a religious institution, a pious *temple* or church, and those who seek only news and novelties.

1.1.0 SD LEON] *(LYON)*   2 SP, 15 SP] *(LYON)*   5–10 Come . . . cherubims] *Ashe; Q1 lines* newes, / variety, / heapes, / sounds, / walke / lye, / Cherubins / *but does not capitalize lines*   6 novelists] *(*nouilsts*)*

THRASILINE   Many that will seem to know much say she
looks not on him like a maid in love.   10

DION   Faith, sir, the multitude, that seldom know anything
but their own opinions, speak that they would have. But
the prince, before his own approach, received so many
confident messages from the state that I think she's
resolved to be ruled.   15

CLEREMONT   Sir, it is thought with her he shall enjoy
both these kingdoms of Sicily and Calabria.

DION   Sir, it is, without controversy, so meant. But 'twill
be a troublesome labour for him to enjoy both these
kingdoms with safety, the right heir to one of them   20
living, and living so virtuously – especially the people
admiring the bravery of his mind and lamenting his
injuries.

CLEREMONT   Who, Philaster?

DION   Yes, whose father, we all know, was by our late King   25
of Calabria unrighteously deposed from his fruitful

greater zeal to hear a novel lie than a pious anthem,
though chanted by cherubims.   10

TRASILINE   True, sir, and holds set counsels to vent their
brainsick opinions, with presagements what all states
shall design.

CLERIMON   That's as their intelligence serves.

LEON   And that shall serve as long as invention lasts. Their   15
dreams they relate as spoke from oracles or if the gods
should hold a synod and make them their secretaries.
They will divine and prophesy, too. But come and
speak your thoughts of the intended marriage with
the Spanish prince. He is come, you see, and bravely   20
entertained.

TRASILINE   He is so, but not married yet.

CLERIMON   But like to be, and shall have in dowry with
the princess this kingdom of Sicily.

LEON   Soft and fair. There is more will forbid the banns   25
than say 'amen' to the marriage. Though the King

---

10 **cherubims** *cherubins* was the usual
Jacobean form; the modernized
cherubims follows the Hebrew plural.

12 **presagements** predictions

14 **intelligence** information

17 **synod** assembly or council
secretaries persons 'entrusted with
private or secret matters' (*OED n.*[1] 1a)

18 **divine** have or claim magical insight
into; predict

19–22 **intended . . . yet** These phrases
are less explicit than in Q2, where
the prince is described as coming 'to
marry our kingdom's heir and be our
sovereign' and the princess 'looks not
on him like a maid in love' (1.1.8, 10).

24 **kingdom of Sicily** Cf. Q2, 'both
these kingdoms of Sicily and Calabria'
(1.1.17). The change probably results
from censorship.

25 **Soft and fair** 'not so fast'; *OED* cites
Cotgrave's dictionary, 1611, which
translates the French phrase *tout beau*
as 'take your leisure, soft and faire, not
too fast'.
forbid the banns make a formal
objection to the marriage

26–8 **the King . . . Phylaster** The
political history here differs from
that in Q2, where the 'late King of
Calabria' deposed Philaster's father
'from his fruitful Sicily' (1.1.25–7);
that is, the usurpation took place
in the previous generation. In Q1
neither man's father is mentioned,
and it instead seems that during
the *nonage* of Phylaster the current
king, perhaps holding the position of
regent, usurped the kingdom from
Phylaster himself.

---

10 cherubims] *(*Cherubins*)*   11–13] *Ashe; Q1 lines* Sir: / opinions / designe / *but does not capitalize*
lines   15–16 And . . . oracles] *Ashe; Q1 lines* lastes, / Oracles, / *but does not capitalize lines*   20–1
He . . . entertained] *one line Q1*   24 Sicily] *(Cycele)*

275

Sicily. Myself drew some blood in those wars which I
would give my hand to be washed from.

CLEREMONT   Sir, my ignorance in state policy will not
let me know why, Philaster being heir to one of these   30
kingdoms, the King should suffer him to walk abroad
with such free liberty.

DION   Sir, it seems your nature is more constant than to
inquire after state news. But the King, of late, made a
hazard of both the kingdoms – of Sicily and his own   35
– with offering but to imprison Philaster. At which
the city was in arms, not to be charmed down by any
state order or proclamation till they saw Philaster
ride through the streets pleased and without a guard.
At which they threw their hats and their arms from   40
them, some to make bonfires, some to drink, all for his

usurped the kingdom during the nonage of the prince
Phylaster, he must not think to bereave him of it quite.
He is now come to years to claim the crown.

TRASILINE   And lose his head i'the asking.   30

LEON   A diadem worn by a headless king would be
wondrous. Phylaster is too weak in power.

CLERIMON   He hath many friends.

LEON   And few helpers.

TRASILINE   The people love him.   35

LEON

I grant it. That the King knows too well
And makes this contract to make his faction strong.
What's a giddy-headed multitude
That's not disciplined nor trained up in arms
To be trusted unto? No, he that will   40
Bandy for a monarchy must provide

---

27 **nonage** legal minority. In the common law, by the seventeenth century this lasted until twenty-one. However, the sovereign attained majority at eighteen: see James, 22.

28 **quite** wholly

29 **He . . . years** he has reached the age. If Leon is describing the legal situation Phylaster has turned eighteen (see 27n.), but he may mean more generally that Phylaster is adult enough to register his claim.

32 **weak in power** without support of arms

33–4 **many . . . helpers** This phrase sounds proverbial but the closest analogy is Dent F694, 'A friend is never known till a man have need'.

36–40 **That . . . unto** Q2 emphasizes the political power of the people rather than their weakness and lack of discipline, and consequently the King 'labours to bring in the power of a foreign nation to awe his own with'. See Q2, 1.1.43-4.

39 **trained** trainèd

40–51 **No . . . them** These lines, which

do not appear in Q2, are probably a later interpolation. They parallel the situation of Frederick, the Elector Palatine, who in August 1619 claimed the monarchy of Bohemia. In July 1620 Frederick was ejected from his new realm by Spanish Habsburg forces; in November he lost the Battle of the White Mountain, and soon thereafter, threatened with *Famine*, fled to The Hague with his wife Elizabeth, the daughter of King James. James's failure to go to the assistance of his daughter and son-in-law, or to *supply them*, infuriated many of his Protestant subjects. Assuming the lines were an insertion, they support the theory that Q1 was prepared for performance in 1619–20, when urging Frederick's troops to grow 'more valiant the more danger threats' and *hold their courage* would have pleased sections of the audience. The verse is notably more regular than the surrounding lines.

41 **Bandy** contend, fight (*OED v.* 8); give blows for (*OED v.* 6)

27 nonage] (non-age)

deliverance. Which, wise men say, is the cause the King labours to bring in the power of a foreign nation to awe his own with.

[*Enter* GALLATEA, *a* LADY *and* MEGRA.]

THRASILINE   See, the ladies. What's the first?   45

DION   A wise and modest gentlewoman that attends the princess.

CLEREMONT   The second?

DION   She is one that may stand still discreetly enough and ill-favouredly dance her measure, simper when she   50
is courted by her friend, and slight her husband.

CLEREMONT   The last?

DION   Faith, I think she is one whom the state keeps for the agents of our confederate princes. She'll cog and lie with a whole army before the league shall break. Her   55
name is common through the kingdom and the trophies of her dishonour advanced beyond Hercules' pillars. She loves to try the several constitutions of men's bodies and indeed has destroyed the worth of her own

Brave martial troops with resolution armed
To stand the shock of bloody, doubtful war,
Not daunted though disastrous Fate doth frown
And spit all spiteful fury in their face,   45
Defying horror in her ugliest form,
And grows more valiant the more danger threats.
Or let lean Famine her affliction send,
Whose pining plagues a second hell doth bring;
They'll hold their courage in her height of spleen   50
Till valour win plenty to supply them.
What think ye: would your feast-hunting citizens
endure this?

TRASILINE   No, sir. A fair march a mile out of town, that
their wives may bring them their dinners, is the hottest   55
service that they are trained up to.

CLERIMON

I could wish their experience answered their loves.
Then should the much-too-much-wronged Phylaster
Possess his right in spite of don and the devil.

TRASILINE

My heart is with your wishes.

---

50 **spleen** violent ill nature
54 **fair . . . town** The city militia trained
at the eastern edge of London at Mile
End. It is frequently mentioned in the
Beaumont and Fletcher canon (e.g.
Monsieur Thomas, 3.3.46, *Wit Without
Money*, 3.2.96 and *Wife for a Month*,
epilogue) and repeatedly invoked in
Pestle. Mistress Merrythought assures
Michael that 'Mile-end is a goodly
matter, there has bene a pitch-field my
child betweene the naughty *Spaniels*
and the *English-men*' (2.2.70–3) and the
Wife asks Rafe to 'call all the youthes
together in battle-ray, with drums, and
guns, and flags, and march to Mile-

end in pompous fashion' (5.5.57–9).
In his death speech Rafe explains he
was 'chosen Citty Captaine at *Mile-
end*, / With hat and feather and with
leading staffe, / And train'd my men
and brought them all off cleere, / Save
one man that berai'd him with the
noise' (5.5.300–3).

55–6 **hottest service** warmest meal; most
dangerous military undertaking; most
intense sexual activity

58, 63 **wronged** wrongèd

59 **don . . . devil** The alliteration
emphasizes the gentlemen's general
attitude towards the Spanish, not only
don or prince Pharamont.

52–3] *prose this edn; Q1 lines* Citizens / this? /   54–6] *this edn; Q1 lines* may / they / to. / *but does
not capitalize lines; Ashe lines* town / dinners, / to. /

279

body by making experiment upon it for the good of the 60
commonwealth.

CLEREMONT   She's a profitable member!

MEGRA [*to Gallatea and Lady*]   Peace, if you love me.
You shall see these gentlemen stand their ground and
not court us. 65

GALLATEA   What if they should?

LADY   'What if they should'!

MEGRA [*to Lady*]   Nay, let her alone. [*to Gallatea*] What if
they should? Why, if they should, I say, they were never
abroad; what foreigner would do so? It writes them 70
directly untravelled.

GALLATEA   Why, what if they be?

LADY   'What if they be'!

MEGRA [*to Lady*]   Good madam, let her go on. [*to
Gallatea*] What if they be? Why, if they be, I will 75
justify they cannot maintain discourse with a judicious
lady, nor make a leg, nor say 'excuse me'.

GALLATEA   Ha, ha, ha!

MEGRA   Do you laugh, madam?

DION   Your desires upon you, ladies. 80

MEGRA   Then you must sit beside us.

DION   I shall sit near you, then, lady.

MEGRA   Near me, perhaps. [*Indicates Gallatea.*] But there's
a lady endures no stranger, and to me you appear a very
strange fellow. 85

LADY   Methinks he's not so strange; he would quickly be
acquainted.

THRASILINE   Peace, the King!

LEON   And so is mine,   60
    And so should all that loves their true-born prince.
    Then let us join our forces with our minds
    In what's our power to right this wronged lord,
    And watch advantage as best may fit the time
    To stir the murmuring people up,   65
    Who is already possessed with his wrongs
    And easily would in rebellion rise,
    Which full well the King doth both know and fear.
    But first our service we'll proffer to the prince
    And set our projects as he accepts of us.   70
    But hush't, the King is coming.   *Sound music within.*

61–6 **all . . . loves; people . . . is** These phrases appear to make plural subjects agree with singular verbs, but these are third person plural forms ending in /s. The Northern personal pronoun rule permitted a variety of plural endings in early modern English. The /s ending for plural verbs is frequent in relative clauses, as here. See Hope, 161–2.

66 **possessed** possessèd

60] *Ashe; Q1 lines* wishes. / mine, /

Enter KING, PHARAMOND, ARETHUSA *and train.*

KING

    To give a stronger testimony of love

    Than sickly promises, which commonly   90

    In princes find both birth and burial

    In one breath, we have drawn you, worthy sir,

    To make your fair endearments to our daughter

    And worthy services known to our subjects

    Now loved and wondered at. Next, our intent   95

    To plant you deeply, our immediate heir,

    Both to our blood and kingdoms. For this lady,

    The best part of your life, as you confirm me

    And I believe: though her few years and sex

    Yet teach her nothing but her fears and blushes,   100

    Desires without desire, discourse and knowledge

    Only of what herself is to herself

    Make her feel moderate health, and when she sleeps,

    In making no ill day, knows no ill dreams.

    Think not, dear sir, these undivided parts   105

    That must mould up a virgin are put on

    To show her so, as borrowed ornaments,

    To talk of her perfect love to you or add

    An artificial shadow to her nature.

    No, sir, I boldly dare proclaim her yet   110

    No woman. But woo her still, and think her modesty

    A sweeter mistress than the offered language

    Of any dame

Enter the KING, PHARAMONT, *the* PRINCESS, *the*
Lady GALLATEA, *the* Lady MEGRA, *a* GENTLEWOMAN,
with Lords attending. The King takes his seat.

KING

Fair prince,
Since heaven's great guider furthers our intents
And brought you with safety here to arrive
Within our kingdom and court of Sicily,   75
We bid you most welcome, princely Pharamont,
And that our kingly bounty shall confirm.
Even whilst the heavens hold so propitious aspect
We'll crown your wished desires with our own.
Lend me your hand, sweet prince. Hereby enjoy   80
A full fruition of your best contents.
The interest I hold I do possess you with –
Only a father's care and prayers retain
That heaven may heap on blessings. Take her, prince;
A sweeter mistress than the offered language of any
    dame,   85

71 SD2 The mass entrance of the court here absorbs lines 45–88 of the first scene in Q2, during which the ladies enter, are described by Dion and have a conversation in which Megra asserts her attraction to foreigners or 'strangers'. As in the final scene of Q1, the length of the women's parts played by boys is severely reduced.

72–85 The speeches of the King in Q1 and Q2 come together at line 85, which is the same in both, but the opening section is almost twice as long in Q2. Notably omitted from Q1 are the King's sexualized description of Arethusa, which emphasizes the princess's 'dreams', 'desires without desire', 'undivided parts' and virginity. Also reduced is the political import: where in Q2 Pharamond is to be declared 'immediate heir' (1.1.96), in

Q1 the emphasis is on his *desires* and the *interest* the King holds in his daughter rather than in his state.

75 **kingdom . . . Sicily** In the equivalent speech in Q2 the King intends to name Pharamond heir to 'our . . . kingdoms' (1.1.97). See 24n.

82 **interest I hold** The King asserts patriarchal rights over his daughter as his possession, which he can thus pass on to Pharamont.

85 The confusing comparison between the *sweeter mistress* and the *offered language* is clarified by Q2, where the King instructs Pharamond to think Arethusa's 'modesty / A sweeter mistress than the offered language / Of any dame' (1.1.111–13), that is, to be more attracted by the princess's chaste reticence than by the forwardness of other women.

71 SD2] Enter *King, Pharamond, Arathusa,* and traine *after 88 Q2; Enter* Gallatea, Megra, *and a Lady opp. 44–5 Q2*   85] *the final line on B2ʳ*

[5.4]   *Enter an old* CAPTAIN *and* CITIZENS *with*
                         PHARAMOND.

CAPTAIN   Come, my brave Myrmidons, let's fall on. Let
     your caps swarm, my boys, and your nimble tongues
     forget your mother gibberish of 'what-do-you-lack',
     and set your mouths ope, children, till your palates fall
     frighted half a fathom, past the cure of bay salt and   5
     gross pepper.
     And then cry 'Philaster, brave Philaster!'
     Let Philaster be deeper in request, my dingdongs,
     My pairs of dear indentures, kings of clubs,

[5.4]   *Enter an old* CAPTAIN *with a crew of* CITIZENS
leading PHARAMONT *prisoner.*

CAPTAIN   Come, my brave Myrmidons, fall on! Let your
caps swarm and your nimble tongues forget your
gibberish of 'what do you lack?' and set your mouths
ope, children, till your palates fall frighted half a
fathom past the cure of bay salt and gross pepper,   5
and then cry 'Phylaster, brave Phylaster!' Let Phylaster
be deep in request, my ding-a-dings, my pair of dear
indentures, kings of clubs, than your cut water camlets
and your painting. Let not your hasty silks, dearly

5.4 Location: the city

1–99 Throughout the scene the prosodic
irregularity is too great to allow the
authors' or reviser's precise prose/
verse intentions to be discerned. In
particular, the Captain usually speaks
in an exuberant prose that has an
insistent iambic rhythm, thus blurring
the distinction from verse, into which
he apparently slips in lines 18–22. This
edition follows the lineation of Q1
except when noted.

7   **deep in request** (more) sought after;
see t.n.
ding-a-dings variant on dingding, a
term of endearment; an onomatopeic
suggestion of the noisy crowd

7–8 **pair . . . indentures** Gurr asserts
the 'the mob is largely composed of
indentured apprentices'; in Q2 the
Citizens must include the apprentices'
masters because they have wives, but
wives are not mentioned in Q1.

8   ***kings of clubs** Q1's 'King' is an error,

as the Captain speaks to the plural mob
throughout.

cut water camlets Cut clothes had
their edges or other parts ornamentally
slashed or indented (*OED ppl.a.*1b);
cf. 'Your Roman gallants that cannot
wear good suits but they must have 'em
cut and slashed into gigots' (*Hengist*,
2.4.87–8). Camlet or chamlet was
a soft, fine fabric, originally of silk
and camel's hair; later the name was
applied to a fine material made of silk
and the hair of the chamois or Angora
goat.

9   **painting** The Captain's reference is
unclear. If there are women in the crowd
he may refer to the use of cosmetics (cf.
Ham, 3.1.141, 'I have heard of your
paintings well enough'), or he may refer
to painted cloth.

9–10 **dearly belovers** Echoing the
priest at the marriage service, the
Captain carnivalizes religious language
throughout his speech.

5.4.3 do] *Q2; not in Q1*   4 ope] *(ope')*   7 deep] deeper *Q2*   8 kings] *Q2;* King *Q1*   than] *(thē)*
cut] cold *Q2*

Than your cold water chamlets or your paintings   10
Spitted with copper. Let not your hasty silks
Or your branched cloth of bodkin or your tissues,
Dearly beloved of spiced cake and custards,
You Robin Hoods, Scarlets and Johns, tie your
    affections
In darkness to your shops. No, dainty duckers,   15
Up with your three-piled spirits, your wrought valours,
And let your uncut cholers make the King feel
The measure of your mightiness. Philaster!
Cry, my rose nobles, cry!

ALL   Philaster, Philaster!

CAPTAIN

How do you like this, my lord prince?   20
These are mad boys, I tell you; these are things
That will not strike their topsails to a foist
And let a man of war, an argosy,
Hull and cry cockles.

belovers of custards and cheesecakes, or your branch   10
cloth of bodkins or your tiffanies, your robin-hood
scarlet and Johns, tie your affections in durance to your
shops, my dainty duckers. Up with your three-piled
spirits, that right valorous, and let your acute colours
make the King to feel the measure of your mightiness.   15
'Phylaster!' Cry, my rose nobles, cry!

ALL   Phylaster, Phylaster!

CAPTAIN

How do you like this, my lord prisoner?
These are mad boys, I can tell you.
These be things that will not strike topsail to a foist   20
And let a man of war, an argosy,
Stoop to carry coals.

PHARAMONT

Why, you damned slaves, do you know who I am?

CAPTAIN   Yes, my pretty prince of puppets, we do

10–11 **branch . . . bodkins** The cloth
is *branch* or branched, adorned or
embroidered with gold or needlework
representing flowers or foliage (*OED*
branch *v.* II. 2.6). Bodkin or baudekin
was 'raised work' on cloth of gold or
tissue. The plural here may indicate
confusion with 'bodkins', small
pointed instruments for piercing holes
in cloth.

11 **tiffanies** Tiffany is 'a thin gauze-like
fabric of soft silk and linen' (Linthicum,
100); cf. *Noble Gentleman*, 1.1.86, 'Let her
haue Velvets, Tiffinies, Jewels, Pearls'.

11–12 **your robin-hood scarlet and
Johns** Robin-hood scarlet is the
bright red cloth worn by the folk hero.
However, Q2's (edited) text, 'You Robin
Hoods, Scarlets and Johns', suggests
that these are three names from the
legend of Robin Hood.

14 **right valorous** with 'are' understood;

in Q2 this is 'wrought valours', a pun
on 'wrought velvets'.

acute colours The Captain puns on
colours and *cholers* (angers). In Q2 the
pun is on 'choler' and 'collar'.

20–2 **strike . . . coals** The Captain's
lines have the same metaphorical
meaning, that the Citizens will not
yield to the insignificant Pharamont
while Phylaster is disregarded and
humiliated, as in Q2, 5.4.21–4, but
conclude with a different image of
abjection. Where in Q2 the mad boys
will not let an argosy, a warship or
merchant-vessel of the largest size,
'hull and cry cockles', in Q1 they
refuse to let it *carry coals* or 'do
dirty or degrading work, to submit
to humiliation or insult' (*OED* coal,
12). Cf. 'on my word we'll not carry
coals' (*RJ*, 1.1.1) and *Island Princess*,
5.1.16.

11 tiffanies] Tishues *Q2*   12 scarlet] scarlets *Q2*   14 acute colours] vncut Collers *Q2*   17+ SP ALL]
(OMNES)   21 argosy] (Argosea)   22] Hull, and cry Cockels *Q2*

PHARAMOND

    Why, you rude slave, do you know what you do?   25

CAPTAIN

    My pretty prince of puppets, we do know

    And give your greatness warning that you talk

    No more such bug's-words, or that soldered crown

    Shall be scratched with a musket. Dear Prince
        Pippen,

    Down with your noble blood, or as I live   30

    I'll have you coddled. – Let 'im loose, my spirits.

    Make us a round ring with your bills, my Hectors,

    And let me see what this trim man dares do. –

    Now, sir, have at you. Here I lie,

    And with this washing blow – do you see, sweet   35
        prince? –

    I could hulk your grace and hang you up cross-legged

    Like a hare at a poulter's, and do this with this wiper.

PHARAMOND

    You will not see me murdered, wicked villains?

1 CITIZEN   Yes, indeed, will we, sir. We have not seen one

so a great while.   40

know, and give you gentle warning you talk no more   25
such bug's-words, lest that sodden crown should be
scratched with a musket. Dear prince pippin, I'll have
you coddled. Let him loose, my spirits, and make a
ring with your bills, my hearts. Now let me see what
this brave man dares do. Note, sir, have at you with this   30
washing blow. Here I lie. Do you huff, sweet prince? I
could hock your grace and hang you cross-legged like a
hare at a poulter's stall, and do thus.

PHARAMONT

Gentlemen, honest gentlemen –

1 SOLDIER   'A speaks treason, Captain; shall's knock him   35
down?

CAPTAIN   Hold, I say!

2 SOLDIER   Good Captain, let me have one maul at's
mazard. I feel my stomach strangely provoked to be at
his Spanish pot-noll. Shall's kill him?   40

---

26 **sodden crown** The Captain treats both
Pharamont's head and his royal diadem
as wet through. However, *sodden* may be
a mishearing of Q2's 'soldered'.

30 **dares do** A Fletcherian turn of phrase
(GM); cf. *Custom of the Country*,
'Hee's swolne so high, out of his owne
assurance, / Of what he dares do'
(2.1.56–7) and *Maid's Tragedy*, 5.1.7,
'Tis all I dare doe Madam'.

31 **huff** 'To puff or swell with pride
or arrogance; to speak arrogantly or
insolently; to storm, bluster' (*OED v.* 4)

32 **hock** apparently *OED v.* 2b, 'To bind
or otherwise beset (persons) in the way
practised at Hocktide', but possibly
OED v. 1, 'To disable by cutting the
tendons of the ham or hock, in man or
beast; to hough, hamstring'.

33 **poulter's** poultry dealer's

35 **SP** The change from Q2's *Citizens*
to Q1's *Soldiers* emphasizes the mob's
aggression. The reviser may have been

misled by the title *Captain*, but as
citizens served as the militia in London
the distinction was blurred. In *Island
Princess* (1621) the stage direction '*Enter
Captaine and Citizens*' is followed by the
Captain's first words, 'Up souldiers, up,
and deale like men' (2.3.58–9).

38 **maul** a heavy blow (*OED n.*[1] 4)

39 **mazard** humorously, the head; cf.
Ham, 5.1.84–5, 'knocked about the
mazard with a sexton's spade'.

40 **pot-noll** A *noll* is a head; Ashe
suggests that the *pot* refers to 'a
small steel helmet of a type worn
by cavalrymen' (*OED n.*[1] 9, citing
Verney, 1639, 'If I had a pott for
the hedd that were pistoll proofe,
it may be I would use it'). But *noll*
was often used 'With depreciative
adjective', frequently 'drunken' (*OED*
1b), so the *pot* may refer to *OED* 1c, 'a
vessel used for drinking an alcoholic
beverage (esp. beer)'.

35+SP 1 SOLDIER] *Cit. Q2*

CAPTAIN
He would have weapons, would he?
Give him a broadside, my brave boys, with your pikes.
Branch me his skin in flowers like a satin,
And between every flower a mortal cut.
Your royalty shall ravel. Jag him, gentlemen: 45
I'll have him cut to the kell, then down the seams.
Oh, for a whip to make him galloon laces:
I'll have a coach whip.

PHARAMOND   Oh, spare me, gentlemen!

CAPTAIN
Hold, hold, the man begins to fear and know himself.
He shall for this time only be seeled up   50
With a feather through his nose, that he may only see
Heaven and think whither he's going. —
Nay, my beyond-sea sir, we will proclaim you.
You would be king!
Thou tender heir apparent to a church-ale,   55
Thou slight prince of single sarcenet,
Thou royal ringtail, fit to fly at nothing
But poor men's poultry and have every boy

ALL   Ay, kill him, kill him!

CAPTAIN   Again, I say, hold!

3 SOLDIER   Oh, how rank he looks! Sweet Captain, let's geld him and send his doucets for a dish to the bordello.   45

4 SOLDIER   No, let's rather sell them to some woman chemist that useth extractions. She might draw an excellent provocative oil from them that might be very useful.

CAPTAIN   You see, my scurvy don, how precious you   50
are in esteem amongst us. Had you not been better kept at home? I think you had. Must you needs come amongst us to have your saffron hide tawed as we intend it? My don, Phylaster must suffer death to satisfy your melancholy spleen – he must, my don, he   55
must – but we your physicians hold it fit that you bleed for it. Come, my robustics, my brave regiment of rattle makers, let's call a common cornuted council and, like

---

45 **bordello** brothel

46–7 **woman chemist** Women, while not trained formally, practised a variety of kinds of medicine and pharmacy; cf. the 'herb woman' mentioned in *Per*, 4.5.90, and the title character in Heywood's *Wise Woman of Hoxton*.

47 ***useth extractions** As Daniel noted, *useth* is misplaced (see t.n.); extraction is not a verb but a noun, the 'action or process of obtaining (the constituent elements, juices, etc.) from any substance by heat, pressure' (*OED* 3, citing from 1627 'their artificiall extractions, seperations, and preparations of their medicines').

48 **provocative** The Captain assumes the *woman chemist* is sought out by clients seeking to improve their sexual performance; cf. 'Cantharides is a baudy flie, of wch the apothecarys make a provocative medicine, that stirrs vp lust beyond all performance' (*Two Noble Ladies*, 2.2.657–9).

53 **saffron hide** yellow-coloured skin, apparently an insult; cf. 'Did this companion with the saffron face / Revel and feast it at my house to–day' (*CE*, 4.4.63–4).

tawed softened by beating, like leather (*OED v.*^1 1)

57 **robustics** *OED* recognizes 'robustic' only as an adjective meaning robust or robustious, with the earliest example from 1683: 'Such People are . . . fit for all robustick, dirty, killing Imployments.'

57–8 **rattle makers** a coinage of the Captain's referring to the citizens' noise

58–9 **cornuted . . . branched crests** A 'cornuto' is a cuckold, traditionally said to have horns or, in the Captain's words, a 'branched crest'. The Captain's satire is directed not at his *regiment* but at more usual authorities, *senators* and the common council.

---

47 useth] *this edn (Daniel); after* from *48 Q1; not in Q2*

Beat thee from that, too, with his bread and butter!

PHARAMOND

Gods keep me from these hellhounds! 60

1 CITIZEN   Shall's geld him, Captain?

CAPTAIN

No, you shall spare his doucets, my dear donsels.

As you respect the ladies, let them flourish.

The curses of a longing woman kills

As speedy as a plague, boys. 65

1 CITIZEN   I'll have a leg, that's certain.

2 CITIZEN   I'll have an arm.

3 CITIZEN   I'll have his nose, and at mine own charge build a college and clap't upon the gate.

4 CITIZEN   I'll have his little gut to string a kit with, for 70 certainly a royal gut will sound like silver.

PHARAMOND   Would they were in thy belly and I past my pain once.

5 CITIZEN   Good Captain, let me have his liver to feed ferrets. 75

CAPTAIN   Who will have parcels else? Speak.

PHARAMOND   Good gods, consider me. I shall be tortured.

1 CITIZEN   Captain, I'll give you the trimming of your two-hand sword, and let me have his skin to make false 80 scabbards.

2 CITIZEN   He has no horns, sir, has he?

CAPTAIN   No, sir, he's a pollard. What wouldst thou do with horns?

2 CITIZEN   Oh, if he had had, I would have made rare 85 hafts and whistles of 'em, but his shinbones, if they be sound, shall serve me.

grave senators, bear up our branched crests in sitting
upon the several tortures we shall put him to and, with   60
as little sense as may be, put your wills in execution.
SOME *(Cry.)*   Burn him, burn him!
OTHERS   Hang him, hang him!

---

60 **several tortures** In Q2 it is Bellario
who is threatened with torture in 5.5.

The threat, eliminated in Q1, may leave
its trace here.

62 SOME *(Cry.)*] *(*SOME CRIES*)*

Enter PHILASTER.

ALL

    Long live Philaster, the brave Prince Philaster!

PHILASTER

    I thank you, gentlemen. But why are these

    Rude weapons brought abroad to teach your hands   90

    Uncivil trades?

CAPTAIN   My royal Rosicleer,

    We are thy Myrmidons, thy guard, thy roarers,

    And when thy noble body is in durance,

    Thus do we clap our musty morions on

    And trace the streets in terror. Is it peace,   95

    Thou Mars of men? Is the King sociable

    And bids thee live? Art thou above thy foemen

    And free as Phoebus? Speak. If not, this stand

    Of royal blood shall be a-broach, a-tilt, and run

    Even to the lees of honour.   100

PHILASTER

    Hold and be satisfied. I am myself

    Free as my thoughts are. By the gods, I am.

CAPTAIN

    Art thou the dainty darling of the King?

    Art thou the Hylas to our Hercules?

    Do the lords bow and the regarded scarlets   105

    Kiss their gummed golls and cry 'We are your
        servants!'?

    Is the court navigable and the presence stuck

    With flags of friendship? If not, we are thy castle,

    And this man sleeps.

PHILASTER

    I am what I do desire to be, your friend.   110

    I am what I was born to be, your prince.

PHARAMOND

    Sir, there is some humanity in you;

294

Enter PHYLASTER.

CAPTAIN   No, rather let's carbonado his codshead and cut
    him to collops. Shall I begin?   65

PHYLASTER
    Stay your furies, my loving countrymen.

ALL   Phylaster is come! Phylaster, Phylaster!

CAPTAIN   My porcupines of spite, make room, I say, that
    I may salute my brave prince. And is Prince Phylaster
    at liberty?   70

PHYLASTER
    I am, most loving countrymen.

CAPTAIN   Then give me thy princely goll, which thus
    I kiss, to whom I crouch and bow. But see, my royal
    spark: this headstrong swarm that follow me humming
    like a master bee have I led forth their hives and, being   75
    on wing and in our heady flight, have seized him shall
    suffer for thy wrongs.

ALL   Ay, ay, let's kill him! Kill him!

PHYLASTER
    But hear me, countrymen –

CAPTAIN   Hear the prince, I say, hear Phylaster!   80

ALL   Ay, ay, hear the prince! Hear the prince!

PHYLASTER   My coming is to give you thanks, my dear
    countrymen, whose powerful sway hath curbed the
    prosecuting fury of my foes.

ALL   We will curb 'em, we will curb 'em!   85

---

64 **carbonado** grill; cf. *WT*, 4.4.265–6,
'how she longed to eat adders' heads
and toads carbonadoed'.

65 **collops** slices of meat; pieces of flesh

66, 71 **loving countrymen** The repetition may be either a printing error
or a deliberate repetition showing
Phylaster's respect for the people.

68 **porcupines** referring to the points
on the ring of bills (29) surrounding
Pharamont.

72 **goll** hand

74–76 **headstrong ... flight** In Q2 the
image of the bees is used by the King
at 5.3.152: 'How they swarm together!
What a hum they raise!'

64 carbonado] *(carbinade)*

You have a noble soul. Forget my name
And know my misery. Set me safe aboard
From these wild cannibals and, as I live,   115
I'll quit this land forever. There is nothing –
Perpetual prisonment, cold, hunger, sickness
Of all sorts, of all dangers, and altogether
The worst company of the worst men, madness, age,
To be as many creatures as a woman   120
And do as all they do, nay, to despair –
But I would rather make it a new nature
And live with all these than endure one hour
Amongst these wild dogs.

PHILASTER

I do pity you. Friends, discharge your fears;   125
Deliver me the prince. I'll warrant you
I shall be old enough to find my safety.

3 CITIZEN   Good sir, take heed he does not hurt you; he's
a fierce man, I can tell you, sir.

CAPTAIN

Prince, by your leave, I'll have a surcingle   130
And make you like a hawk.   *Pharamond strives.*

PHILASTER

Away, away! There is no danger in him.
Alas, he had rather sleep to shake his fit off.
Look you, friends, how gently he leads. Upon my word
He's tame enough; he needs no further watching.   135
Good my friends, go to your houses,
And by me have your pardons and my love,
And know there shall be nothing in my power
You may deserve but you shall have your wishes:
To give you more thanks were to flatter you.   140
Continue still your love, and for an earnest
Drink this.   [*Gives 'em his purse.*]

ALL   Long mayst thou live, brave prince, brave prince,
brave prince!   *Exeunt Philaster and Pharamond.*

PHYLASTER

I find you will.
But if my interest in your loves be such
As the world takes notice of, let me crave
You would deliver Pharamont to my hand
And from me accept this testimony of my love,   90
   (*Gives 'em his purse.*)
Which is but a pittance of those ample thanks
Which shall redound with showered courtesies.

CAPTAIN   Take him to thee, brave prince, and we thy
bounty thankfully accept and will drink thy health,
thy perpetual health, my prince, whilst memory lasts   95
amongst us. We are thy Myrmidons, my Achilles, we
are those will follow thee and in thy service will scour
our rusty morions and our bilbo–blades, most noble
Phylaster, we will. Come, my routists, let's retire till
occasion calls us to attend the noble Phylaster.   100

ALL   Phylaster, Phylaster, Phylaster!

Exeunt Captain and Citizens.

PHARAMONT

Worthy sir, I owe you a life,
For but yourself there's nought could have prevailed.

PHYLASTER

'Tis the least of service that I owe the King,   104
Who was careful to preserve ye.   *Exeunt.*

---

90 In Q1 the line is divided (see t.n.) to
allow room for the stage direction in the
right margin.
92 **redound** be plentiful; bring honour
98 **rusty morions** disused brimless
helmets worn by foot soldiers; in Q2
they are 'musty' rather than *rusty*.
   bilbo–blades swords noted for the
temper and elasticity of the blade; the

best blades were said to come from
Bilbao, in Spain, long called Bilboa in
England (*OED*).
99 *****routists** The Captain creates the word
from *OED* rout *n.*[1] 8, 'riot, disturbance';
cf. *Othello* demanding, 'Give me to
know / How this foul rout began'
(2.3.205–6). Cf. 5.5.24, *mutineers*.

90] *this edn; Q1 lines* this / loue. / SD] *opp.* this *Q1*   92 redound] *(redowne)*   98 morions]
(murins)   bilbo-blades] *(bill-bow-blades)*   99 routists] *(rowtists)*   101 SD *Exeunt] (Exit)*   105
SD] *(Exit.)*

297

CAPTAIN   Go thy ways, thou art the king of courtesy. Fall   145
off again, my sweet youths; come, and every man trace
to his house again and hang his pewter up. Then to the
tavern, and bring your wives in muffs. We will have
music, and the red grape shall make us dance and rise,   149
boys.   *Exeunt.*

[5.5]

Enter KING, ARETHUSA, GALLATEA, MEGRA,
CLEREMONT, DION, THRASILINE, BELLARIO
and Attendants.

KING

Is it appeased?

DION

Sir, all is quiet as this dead of night,
As peaceable as sleep. My lord Philaster

[5.5]   *Enter* LEON, TRASILINE *and* CLERIMON.

TRASILINE   I ever thought the boy was honest.

LEON   Well, 'tis a brave boy, gentlemen.

CLERIMON   Yet you'd not believe this.

LEON   A plague on my forwardness! What a villain was
I to wrong 'em so. A mischief on my muddy brains!   5
Was I mad?

TRASILINE   A little frantic in your rash attempt, but that
was your love to Phylaster, sir.

LEON   A pox on such love! Have you any hope my
countenance will e'er serve me to look on them?   10

CLERIMON   Oh, very well, sir.

LEON   Very ill, sir. 'Uds death, I could beat out my brains
or hang myself in revenge.

CLERIMON   There would be little gotten by it. E'en keep
you as ye are.   15

LEON   An excellent boy, gentlemen, believe it. Hark, the
King is coming.   *Cornets sounds.*

Enter the KING, PRINCESS, GALLATEA, MEGRA,
BELLARIO, *a* GENTLEWOMAN *and other Attendants.*

5.5 Location: the palace

5 'em Arethusa and Bellario, wronged by
his accusations in his *rash attempt* (7) to
persuade Phylaster to rebel. It is possible,
however, that Q1's *vm* = *'im* and refers
only to Bellario, the *brave boy* (2).
muddy muddled, confused; *OED* cites

Ford, *Perkin Warbeck*, 'Muddie-braynd
peasants?' and *WT*, 1.2.325–6, 'Dost
think I am so muddy, so unsettled, /
To appoint myself in this vexation?'

12 'Uds death a strong oath, derived from
'God's death'

14 gotten obtained

5.5.5 'em] *(*vm*)*

Brings on the prince himself.

KING   Kind gentleman!

    I will not break the least word I have given   5

    In promise to him. I have heaped a world

    Of grief upon his head, which yet I hope

    To wash away.

Enter PHILASTER *and* PHARAMOND.

CLEREMONT   My lord is come.

KING [*Embraces Philaster.*]   My son,

    Blest be the time that I have leave to call

    Such virtue mine. Now thou art in mine arms   10

    Methinks I have a salve unto my breast

    For all the stings that dwell there. Streams of grief

    That I have wronged thee, and as much of joy

    That I repent it, issue from mine eyes;

    Let them appease thee. Take thy right; take her –   15

    She is thy right, too – and forget to urge

    My vexed soul with that I did before.

PHILASTER

    Sir, it is blotted from my memory,

    Past and forgotten. – For you, prince of Spain,

    Whom I have thus redeemed, you have full leave   20

    To make an honourable voyage home.

    And if you would go furnished to your realm

    With fair provision, I do see a lady

    Methinks would gladly bear you company.

    How like you this piece?

MEGRA   Sir, he likes it well,   25

    For he hath tried it and hath found it worth

    His princely liking. We were ta'en abed;

    I know your meaning. I am not the first

    That nature taught to seek a fellow forth.

    Can shame remain perpetually in me   30

KING

No news of his return?
Will not this rabble multitude be appeased?
I fear their outrage, lest it should extend   20
With dangering of Pharamont's life.

Enter PHYLASTER *with* PHARAMONT.

LEON

See, sir, Phylaster is returned.

PHYLASTER

Royal sir,
Receive into your bosom your desired peace.
Those discontented mutineers be appeased,   25
And this foreign prince in safety.

KING

How happy am I in thee, Phylaster,
Whose excellent virtues begets a world of love.
I am indebted to thee for a kingdom.
I here surrender up all sovereignty: 30
Reign peacefully with thy espoused bride.
Assume, my son, to take what is thy due.
     Delivers his crown to him.

PHARAMONT

How, sir, your son? What am I, then?
Your daughter you gave to me.

---

21 **dangering . . . life** Not mentioned at
this point in Q2; in 5.3 in both quartos
the Messenger urges the King to rescue
the prince *from danger*.

32 **Assume . . . to take** These verbal forms
seem redundant; Philaster will either
assume the throne or *take* his due.

32 SD, 61 SD These explicit stage direc-

tions may reflect a production, either
the original or a Jacobean revival.

33–4, 42–4, 82–6 Although Q1 offers a
much shorter version of the scene than
Q2, Pharamont's part is expanded. In
Q2 he has only one two-line speech
but remains onstage throughout.

21 SD] *after 21 Q1*   26 foreign] *(*fortaigne*)*   32 Assume] *(*Ashume*)*   SD] *opp. 31–2 Q1*   33–4]
this edn; prose Q1   33 your] *(*yer*)*

And not in others? Or have princes salves
To cure ill names that meaner people want?

PHILASTER

What mean you?

MEGRA   You must get another ship
To bear the princess and her boy together.

DION

How now?   35

MEGRA

Others took me, and I took her and him
At that all women may be ta'en sometime.
Ship us all four, my lord: we can endure
Weather and wind alike.

KING [*to Arethusa*]

Clear thou thyself or know not me for father.   40

ARETHUSA

This earth,
How false it is! What means is left for me
To clear myself? It lies in your belief.
My lords, believe me, and let all things else
Struggle together to dishonour me.   45

BELLARIO

Oh, stop your ears, great King, that I may speak
As freedom would. Then I will call this lady
As base as are her actions. Hear me, sir:
Believe your heated blood when it rebels
Against your reason sooner than this lady.   50

MEGRA

By this good light, he bears it handsomely.

PHILASTER

This lady! I will sooner trust the wind
With feathers or the troubled sea with pearl
Than her with anything. Believe her not!
Why, think you if I did believe her words   55
I would outlive 'em? Honour cannot take

KING

But heaven hath made assignment unto him   35
And brought your contract to a nullity.
Sir, your entertainment hath been most fair,
Had not your hell-bred lust dried up the spring
From whence flowed forth those favours that you
    found.
I am glad to see you safe. Let this suffice: 40
Yourself hath crossed yourself.

LEON [*to Pharamont*]   They are married, sir.

PHARAMONT

How, married!
I hope your highness will not use me so.
I came not to be disgraced and return alone.

KING

I cannot help it, sir.   45

LEON

To return alone? You need not, sir.
Here is one will bear you company.
You know this lady's proof, if you
Failed not in the say taking.

---

36 **nullity** 'With reference to marriage: the fact or condition of being void or voidable' (*OED* 1b); cf. *Epicoene*, 5.3.79–81, 'as wee say in the Canon-law, *not take away the bond, but cause a nullitie therein*'.

37 **entertainment** reception, treatment

41 **They are married** As the King has already been told, Philaster has become Arethusa's 'dear husband' (5.3.51).

48 **proof** 'The condition of having successfully stood a test, or the capability of doing so' (*OED* 9a); cf. *Wild Goose Chase*, 3.1.459, 'We must be patient; I am vext to the proof too.'

49 *****say taking** Pharamond is accused of having *taken* a *say* or assay of Megra,

that is, of having tested the merchandise. Ironically, this recalls the Woodmen's complaint in 4.2 that Pharamont 'forsook the say' – the 'trial of grease' (*OED* n.² 5) or inspection of the deer's fat, conventionally awarded to the person of highest rank present – because he would have been expected to tip ten shillings. The phrase is also used of the testing of metals to ascertain their standard of purity (*OED* say n.² 4 = assay, *n.* 6) and may have particular resonance for a Spanish prince; *OED* cites Lord Sandwich's translation of *Barba's Metals* (1669): 'All the Mines . . . in that Province have been found out, and first taken say of, by the Spaniards.'

---

41 SD] *this edn*   42–3] *this edn; one line Q1*   49 say taking] *Ashe;* say-taging *Q1*

Revenge on you. Then what were to be known
But death?

KING   Forget her, sir, since all is knit
Between us. But I must request of you
One favour, and will sadly be denied.   60

PHILASTER
Command whate'er it be.

KING   Swear to be true
To what you promise.

PHILASTER   By the powers above,
Let it not be the death of her or him,
And it is granted.

KING   Bear away that boy
To torture. I will have her cleared or buried.   65

PHILASTER
Oh, let me call my word back, worthy sir!
Ask something else. Bury my life and right
In one poor grave, but do not take away
My life and fame at once.

KING   Away with him!
It stands irrevocable.   70

PHILASTER
Turn all your eyes on me. Here stands a man,
The falsest and the basest of this world.
Set swords against this breast, some honest man,
For I have lived till I am pitied.
My former deeds were hateful, but this last   75
Is pitiful, for I unwillingly
Have given the dear preserver of my life
Unto his torture. Is it in the power
Of flesh and blood to carry this and live?
   Offers to kill himself.

ARETHUSA
Dear sir, be patient yet. Oh, stay that hand!   80

MEGRA

I hold your scoffs in vilest base contempt.   50
Or is there said or done aught I repent
But can retort even to your grinning teeths
Your worst of spites. Though princesses' lofty steps
May not be traced, yet may they tread awry.
That boy there –

51 **Or . . . aught** there is nothing either
  said or done
53 **princesses' lofty steps** In Q2
  Megra makes her point by comparing
  meaner people to 'princes' generally

(31), with vaguer gender implications.
Nevertheless in Q2 Megra's defence
is that she has done that at which 'all
women may be ta'en sometime'; the
speech is less feminist in Q1.

50 vilest] *(*vildest*)*   53 princesses'] *(*Princesse*)*

KING

    Sirs, strip that boy.

DION   Come, sir, your tender flesh

    Will try your constancy.

BELLARIO   Oh, kill me, gentlemen!

DION

    No help, sirs.

BELLARIO   Will you torture me?

KING   Haste there!

    Why stay you?

BELLARIO   Then I shall not break my vow,

    You know, just gods, though I discover all.   85

KING

    How's that? Will he confess?

DION   Sir, so he says.

KING

    Speak, then.

BELLARIO   Great King, if you command

    This lord to talk with me alone, my tongue,

    Urged by my heart, shall utter all the thoughts

    My youth hath known, and stranger things than these   90

    You hear not often.

KING   Walk aside with him.

    [*Dion and Bellario walk apart.*]

DION

    Why speak'st thou not?

BELLARIO   Know you this face, my lord?

DION

    No.

BELLARIO   Have you not seen it, nor the like?

DION

    Yes, I have seen the like, but readily

    I know not where.

BELLARIO   I have been often told   95

    In court of one Euphrasia, a lady

    And daughter to you, betwixt whom and me

They that would flatter my bad face would swear
There was such strange resemblance that we two
Could not be known asunder, dressed alike.   100

DION

By heaven, and so there is.

BELLARIO   For her fair sake,
Who now doth spend the springtime of her life
In holy pilgrimage, move to the King
That I may scape this torture.

DION   But thou speak'st
As like Euphrasia as thou dost look.   105
How came it to thy knowledge that she lives
In pilgrimage?

BELLARIO   I know it not, my lord,
But I have heard it – [*aside*] and do scarce believe it.

DION

Oh, my shame! Is't possible? Draw near
That I may gaze upon thee. Art thou she,   110
Or else her murderer? Where wert thou born?

BELLARIO

In Siracusa.

DION   What's thy name?

BELLARIO   Euphrasia.

DION

Oh, 'tis just, 'tis she!
Now I do know thee. Oh, that thou hadst died,
And I had never seen thee nor my shame!   115
How shall I own thee? Shall this tongue of mine
E'er call thee daughter more?

BELLARIO

Would I had died indeed; I wish it too,
And so must have done by vow ere published
What I have told, but that there was no means   120
To hide it longer. Yet I joy in this:
The princess is all clear.

BELLARIO   If to me ye speak, lady,   55
          I must tell you you have lost yourself
          In your too much forwardness and hath forgot
          Both modesty and truth. With what impudence
          You have thrown most damnable aspersions
          On that noble princess and myself,   60
          Witness the world. Behold me, sir.
               Kneels to Leon and discovers her hair.

LEON

          I should know this face. My daughter!

BELLARIO   The same, sir.

PRINCESS

          How? Our sometime page, Bellario, turned woman?

55–61 SD This passage condenses lines
   40–135 of Q2, which include the
   King's order that Bellario, who
   denies Megra's accusations, be
   tested by torture; Philaster's horror
   at discovering that he has agreed
   to endanger his preserver and his

consequent attempt to kill himself;
Bellario's promise that if he may talk
to Dion (= Q1 Leon) he will reveal
all; and a conversation between the
two concluding with the identification
of Bellario as 'Euphrasia', a name that
never appears in Q1.

60–1] *this edn; Q1 lines* world; / sir. /

KING [*to Dion*]　　　　　　　What have you done?

DION

　　All's discovered.

PHILASTER　　　　　Why, then, hold you me?

　　All is discovered! Pray you, let me go.

　　　　He offers to stab himself.

KING

　　Stay him.

ARETHUSA　　　What is discovered?

DION　　　　　　　　　　　　Why, my shame.　　125

　　It is a woman; let her speak the rest.

PHILASTER

　　How? That again.

DION　　　　　　　It is a woman.

PHILASTER

　　Blest be you powers that favour innocence!

KING [*Points to Megra.*]

　　Lay hold upon that lady.

PHILASTER

　　It is a woman, sir! Hark, gentlemen,　　　130

　　It is a woman! Arethusa, take

　　My soul into thy breast, that would be gone

　　With joy. It is a woman! Thou art fair

　　And virtuous still to ages, in despite of malice.

KING [*to Bellario, pointing at Dion*]

　　Speak you. Where lies his shame?

BELLARIO　　　　　　　　I am his daughter.　　135

PHILASTER

　　The gods are just.

DION [*Kneels to Philaster and Arethusa.*]

　　I dare accuse none, but before you two,

　　The virtue of our age, I bend my knee

　　For mercy.

PHILASTER [*Raises him.*]　　Take it freely, for I know

　　Though what thou didst were undiscreetly done,　　140

'Twas meant well.

ARETHUSA   And for me,
I have a power to pardon sins as oft
As any man has power to wrong me.

CLEREMONT
Noble and worthy!

PHILASTER   But, Bellario –
For I must call thee still so – tell me why   145
Thou didst conceal thy sex. It was a fault,
A fault, Bellario, though thy other deeds
Of truth outweighed it. All these jealousies
Had flown to nothing if thou hadst discovered
What now we know.

BELLARIO   My father oft would speak   150
Your worth and virtue, and as I did grow
More and more apprehensive, I did thirst
To see the man so raised. But yet all this
Was but a maiden longing, to be lost
As soon as found, till sitting in my window,   155
Printing my thoughts in lawn, I saw a god,
I thought – but it was you – enter our gates.
My blood flew out and back again as fast
As I had puffed it forth and sucked it in
Like breath. Then was I called away in haste   160
To entertain you. Never was a man
Heaved from a sheepcote to a sceptre, raised
So high in thoughts as I. You left a kiss
Upon these lips then which I mean to keep
From you forever. I did hear you talk   165
Far above singing. After you were gone,
I grew acquainted with my heart and searched
What stirred it so. Alas, I found it love –
Yet far from lust, for could I but have lived
In presence of you, I had had my end.   170
For this I did delude my noble father

BELLARIO

Madam, the cause induced me to transform myself
Proceeded from a respective modest   65
Affection I bear to my lord,
The prince Phylaster, to do him service,
As far from any lascivious thought
As that lady is far from goodness.
And if my true intents may be believed   70
And from your highness, madam, pardon find,
You have the truth.

PRINCESS

I do believe thee. Bellario I shall call thee still.

PHYLASTER

The faithfulest servant that ever gave attendance.

LEON [*to Megra*]

Now, Lady Lust, what say you to th' boy now?   75
Do you hang the head, do ye? Shame would steal

64–72 This passage condenses Bellario's
lengthy speech, 150–83 of Q2, reducing
the narrative of her history and
eliminating elaborate metaphors and
Shakespearean echoes.

75–8 In Q2 Philaster orders Megra set at
liberty with her shame, and the King
orders her out of the court.

66 my] *Gurr;* my my *Q1*   75 SD] *this edn*

With a feigned pilgrimage and dressed myself
In habit of a boy. And for I knew
My birth no match for you, I was past hope
Of having you. And understanding well   175
That when I made discovery of my sex
I could not stay with you, I made a vow,
By all the most religious things a maid
Could call together, never to be known,
Whilst there was hope to hide me from men's eyes,   180
For other than I seemed, that I might ever
Abide with you. Then sat I by the fount
Where first you took me up.

KING   Search out a match
Within our kingdom, where and when thou wilt,
And I will pay thy dowry, and thyself   185
Wilt well deserve him.

BELLARIO   Never, sir, will I
Marry. It is a thing within my vow.
But if I may have leave to serve the princess,
To see the virtues of her lord and her,
I shall have hope to live.

ARETHUSA   I, Philaster,   190
Cannot be jealous, though you had a lady
Dressed like a page to serve you, nor will I
Suspect her living here. – Come live with me,
Live free as I do. She that loves my lord,
Cursed be the wife that hates her.   195

PHILASTER
I grieve such virtue should be laid in earth
Without an heir. Hear me, my royal father:
Wrong not the freedom of our souls so much
To think to take revenge of that base woman;
Her malice cannot hurt us. Set her free   200
As she was born, saving from shame and sin.

314

Into your face, if ye had grace to entertain it.

Do ye slink away?   *Exit Megra hiding her face.*

KING

Give present order she be banished the court

And straitly confined till our further   80

Pleasure is known.

PHARAMONT [*aside*]   Here's such an age of transformation

that I do not know how to trust myself. I'll get me gone,

too. [*to the King*] Sir, the disparagement you have

done must be called in question. I have power to right   85

myself, and will.

KING

We fear ye not, sir.   *Exit Pharamont.*

PHYLASTER

Let a strong convoy guard him through the kingdom.

With him, let's part with all our cares and fear

And crown with joy our happy love's success.   90

KING

Which to make more full, Lady Gallatea,

Let honoured Clerimon acceptance find

In your chaste thoughts.

PHYLASTER   'Tis my suit too.

---

80 **straitly** strictly, narrowly
84–6 **Sir . . . will** Pharamont makes no
 similar threats in Q2.
84 **disparagement** generally, dishonour
 (*OED* 2), but particularly 'Marriage
 to one of inferior rank; the disgrace
 or dishonour involved in such a
 misalliance' (*OED* 1), a reference to
 the suggestion that Megra bear him
 company
88 **strong convoy** armed escort
91–107 In its most radical variance
 from Q2, Q1 imposes a standard
 comic ending, tying up all loose ends

in a series of unexpected marriages.
In Q2 Gallatea remains without a
partner, and Bellario asserts, 'Never,
sir, will I / Marry. It is a thing within
my vow.' Her request to serve the
princess and Arethusa's invitation
to 'Come live with me, / Live free
as I do' create a permanent *ménage à
trois* not present in Q1. Patriarchy is
further enforced in Q1 by Bellario's
silence while Leon transfers his
rights in her to Trasiline, whose
relationship to Bellario has not
previously been mentioned.

82 SD] *this edn*   84 SD] *this edn*   87 SD] *after 86 Q1*   92 Clerimon] *(Clerimont)*

KING

    Set her at liberty, but [*to Megra*] leave the court.
    This is no place for such. – You, Pharamond,
    Shall have free passage and a conduct home
    Worthy so great a prince. When you come there,   205
    Remember 'twas your faults that lost you her
    And not my purposed will.

PHARAMOND   I do confess,
    Renowned sir.

KING

    Last, join your hands in one. Enjoy, Philaster,
    This kingdom, which is yours, and after me   210
    Whatever I call mine. My blessing on you.
    All happy hours be at your marriage joys,
    That you may grow yourselves over all lands
    And live to see your plenteous branches spring
    Wherever there is sun. Let princes learn   215
    By this to rule the passions of their blood,
    For what heaven wills can never be withstood.   *Exeunt.*

FINIS

PRINCESS

Such royal spokesmen must not be denied.

GALLATEA

Nor shall not, madam.

KING   Then thus I join your hands.   95

GALLATEA

Our hearts were knit before.   *They kiss.*

PHYLASTER [*to Bellario*]

But 'tis you, lady, must make all complete

And give a full period to content.

Let your love's cordial again revive

The drooping spirits of noble Trasiline.   100

What says Lord Leon to it?

LEON

Marry, my lord, I say, I know she once loved him –

At least made show she did.

But since 'tis my lord Phylaster's desire,

I'll make a surrender of all the right   105

A father has in her. [*to Trasiline*] Here, take her, sir,

With all my heart, and heaven give you joy.

KING

Then let us in, these nuptial feasts to hold.

Heaven hath decreed, and fate stands uncontrolled.

[Exeunt.]

---

108 In Q2 the King announces not only submission to 'heaven' but a political moral, that princes must learn 'to rule the passions of their blood'.

97 SD] *Ashe*   98 give] *(giues)*   period] *(perod)*   106 SD] *this edn*   109 SD] *this edn*

APPENDIX 2

CASTING *PHILASTER*

The chart below shows *Philaster* cast with six boys; six adult male actors playing major roles without doubling; one adult male actor doubling two roles; and five actors playing all other minor adult male parts, for a total of six boys and twelve men. Boys are marked with a +, silent parts are marked with a *. This is a minimum casting; if the company had more actors available they could have swollen the King's 'train' (1.1.88 SD) and increased the number of Guards in 2.4 and of Attendants in the court scenes. Other adjustments are possible; for example, one of the boys playing the Lady or the Gentlewoman could play one of the Citizens. The total of eighteen here is, with the possible exception of the number of boys, within the norms for the King's Men in the early seventeenth century.

Boys did not usually double, and six boys may have been more than Jacobean companies could always produce: Q1's list of *The Actors Names* includes only five (Arethusa, Gallatea, Megra, A Waiting Gentlewoman and the disguised Bellario). It appears that an attempt was made to combine Arethusa's Gentlewoman and Q2's nameless court 'Lady', though the bad Q1 text may not report the changes entirely accurately. In the first scene of Q1 there is no description of the three ladies. The '*Gentlewoman*' who enters with '*the Lady* GALLATEA' and '*the Lady* MEGRA' could be the same Gentlewoman who calls Philaster to Arethusa at the end of the scene, as the 'Ladies' exit together about twenty-five lines before the Gentlewoman (re)enters. In Q1's 3.2 the Lady's lincs are assigned to 'Wo'. However, in Q1's equivalent of 2.4, the stage direction calls for the entrance of '*the three Gentlewomen, Megra, Gallatea, and another Lady*', and immediately thereafter Pharamont enters with '*the Princesse boy, and a woman*'. Arethusa is also on stage (see 2.4.8 SDn.), which would make a total of six boys.

The minor parts are usually distributed with enough time allowed to permit easy doubling. For example, the Messengers who have brief parts in 5.3 exit at line 116, and the scene continues for 75 more lines before they need to re-enter as Citizens. However, if the Citizens who appear in 5.4 reappear as the King's Attendants in 5.5 there is no time allowed for their change. Nevertheless, since the Guards and Attendants are mute, any simple piece of costuming rapidly donned, for example a helmet, might be sufficient to suggest new identities.

Actor	1.1	1.2	2.1	2.2	2.3	2.4	3.1	3.2	4.1
1	King					King		King	King
2+	Arethusa	Arethusa			Arethusa	Arethusa		Arethusa	Arethusa
3	Philaster	Philaster	Philaster				Philaster	Philaster	
4	Pharamond	Pharamond		Pharamond		Pharamond			Pharamond
5	Dion					Dion	Dion		Dion
6	Claremont					Claremont	Claremont		Claremont
7	Thrasiline					Thrasiline	Thrasiline		Thrasiline
8+			Bellario		Bellario	Bellario	Bellario	Bellario	
9+	Gallatea			Gallatea	Gallatea	Gallatea			Gallatea
10+	Megra			Megra		Megra			Megra
11+	Lady							Lady	
12+	Gentlewoman	Gentlewoman			Gentle-woman				
13									
14	1 Attendant*					1 Guard*			1 Attendant*
15	2 Attendant*					2 Guard*			2 Attendant*
16									
17									
18									

Actor	4.2	4.3	4.4	4.5	4.6	5.1	5.2	5.3	5.4	5.5
1			King		King			King		King
2+				Arethusa	Arethusa		Arethusa	Arethusa		Arethusa
3		Philaster		Philaster	Philaster		Philaster	Philaster	Philaster	Philaster
4			Pharamond	Pharamond	Pharamond				Phara-mond	Pharamond
5			Dion	Dion	Dion	Dion		Dion		Dion
6			Claremont	Claremont	Claremont	Claremont		Claremont		Claremont
7			Thrasiline	Thrasiline	Thrasiline	Thrasiline		Thrasiline		Thrasiline
8+		Bellario		Bellario	Bellario		Bellario	Bellario		Bellario
9+			Gallatea							Gallatea
10+			Megra							Megra
11+										
12+										
13				Country Fellow					Captain	
14					1 Guard*			1 Messenger	5 Citizen	1 Attendant*
15								2 Messenger	4 Citizen	2 Attendant*
16	1 Woodman	1 Woodman		1 Woodman					1 Citizen	
17	2 Woodman	2 Woodman		2 Woodman					2 Citizen	
18									3 Citizen	

ABBREVIATIONS AND REFERENCES

Quotations and references relating to *Philaster* are keyed to this edition. Works of Shakespeare are cited from the most recent Arden editions. *OED* references are to *OED²*, accessed before January 2009. Biblical citations are from the Bishops' Bible (1573) STC 2108, unless otherwise noted. Place of publication is London unless otherwise noted.

ABBREVIATIONS

ABBREVIATIONS USED IN NOTES

*	precedes commentary notes involving readings altered from the base text
c.w.	catchword
n.	commentary note
n.s.	new series
om.	omitted
SD	stage directions
SP	speech prefix
subst.	substantially
this edn	a reading adopted or proposed for the first time in this edition
t.n.	textual note

WORKS BY AND PARTLY BY SHAKESPEARE

AC	*Antony and Cleopatra*
AW	*All's Well that Ends Well*
AYL	*As You Like It*
CE	*The Comedy of Errors*
Cor	*Coriolanus*
Cym	*Cymbeline*
Ham	*Hamlet*
1H4	*King Henry IV, Part I*
2H4	*King Henry IV, Part II*
H5	*King Henry V*

2H6	*King Henry VI, Part II*
H8	*King Henry VIII*
JC	*Julius Caesar*
KL	*King Lear*
LLL	*Love's Labour's Lost*
Luc	*The Rape of Lucrece*
MA	*Much Ado About Nothing*
Mac	*Macbeth*
MND	*A Midsummer Night's Dream*
MV	*The Merchant of Venice*
MW	*The Merry Wives of Windsor*
Oth	*Othello*
Per	*Pericles*
R2	*King Richard II*
R3	*King Richard III*
RJ	*Romeo and Juliet*
Son	*Sonnets*
TC	*Troilus and Cressida*
Tem	*The Tempest*
TGV	*The Two Gentlemen of Verona*
TN	*Twelfth Night*
TNK	*The Two Noble Kinsmen*
TS	*The Taming of the Shrew*
VA	*Venus and Adonis*
WT	*The Winter's Tale*

REFERENCES

EDITIONS OF *PHILASTER* COLLATED

Q1	*Phylaster*, The First Quarto (1620)
Q2	*Philaster*, The Second Quarto (1622)
Q3	*Philaster*, The Third Quarto (1628)
Q4	*Philaster*, The Fourth Quarto (1634)
Q5	*Philaster*, The Fifth Quarto (1639) – identified as Q4
Q6	*Philaster*, The Sixth Quarto (1652) – identified as Q5
Q7	*Philaster*, The Seventh Quarto (*c.* 1661, dated 1652 and identified as Q5)
Q8	*Philaster*, The Eighth Quarto (undated, but *c.* 1661 – identified as Q6)
F	*Philaster*, in *Fifty Comedies and Tragedies* (1679)
Q9	*Philaster*, the Ninth Quarto (1687)

Ashe	Dora Jean Ashe, ed., *Philaster* (Lincoln, NE, 1974)
Boas	F. S. Boas, ed., *Philaster* (1898)
Colman	G. Colman, ed., *Dramatic Works of Beaumont and Fletcher*, 10 vols (1778)
Daniel	P. A. Daniel, ed., *Philaster*, in *The Works of Francis Beaumont and John Fletcher*, ed. A. H. Bullen, 4 vols, the Variorum Edition (1904–12)
Dyce	Alexander Dyce, ed., *The Works of Beaumont and Fletcher*, 11 vols (1843–6)
Gurr	Andrew Gurr, ed., *Philaster* (1969)
Langbaine	*The Works of Beaumont and Fletcher*, 7 vols (1711)
Spencer	Hazelton Spencer, ed., *Elizabethan Plays* (Boston, MA, 1933)
Strachey	J. St Loe Strachey, ed., *The Works of Beaumont and Fletcher*, 2 vols (1887)
Theobald	L. Theobald, T. Seward and J. Sympson, eds, *The Works of Beaumont and Fletcher*, 10 vols (1750)
Thorndike	Ashley H. Thorndike, ed., *Philaster and The Maid's Tragedy* (Boston, MA, 1912)
Turner	Robert K. Turner, Jr, ed., *Philaster*, in Beaumont and Fletcher
Weber	Henry Weber, ed., *The Works of Beaumont and Fletcher*, 14 vols (Edinburgh, 1812)

OTHER WORKS CITED

Antonio and Mellida	John Marston, *Antonio and Mellida*, STC 17473, in Marston
Astrophil and Stella	*Astrophil and Stella*, in *The Poems of Sir Philip Sidney*, ed. W. A. Ringler, Jr (Oxford, 1962)
Adkins	Mary Grace Muse Adkins, 'The Citizens in *Philaster*: Their Function and Significance', *Studies in Philology* (1946), 203–12
Aubrey	John Aubrey, *Aubrey's Brief Lives*, ed. Oliver Lawson Dick (1949)
Baldwin	Thomas Whitfield Baldwin, *The Organization and Personnel of the Shakespearean Company* (Princeton, NJ, 1927)
Bawcutt	N. W. Bawcutt, ed., *The Control and Censorship of Caroline Drama: The Records of Sir Henry Herbert Master of the Revels 1623–73* (Oxford, 1996)
Beaumont and Fletcher	*The Dramatic Works in the Beaumont and Fletcher Canon*, gen. ed. Fredson Bowers, 10 vols (Cambridge, 1966–96)

Bednarz	James P. Bednarz, 'Between Collaboration and Rivalry: Dekker and Marston's Coactive Drama', *Ben Jonson Journal*, 10 (2003), 209–34
Bentley	Gerald Eades Bentley, *The Jacobean and Caroline Stage*, 7 vols (Oxford, 1941–68)
Berek	Peter Berek, 'Cross-Dressing, Gender, and Absolutism in the Beaumont and Fletcher Plays', *Studies in English Literature*, 44 (2004), 359–77.
Bicks	Caroline Bicks, *Midwiving Subjects in Shakespeare's England* (Aldershot, 2003)
Blayney	Peter Blayney, *The First Folio of Shakespeare* (Washington, DC, 1991)
Bliss, *Beaumont*	Lee Bliss, *Francis Beaumont* (Boston, MA, 1987)
Bliss, 'Three Plays'	Lee Bliss, 'Three Plays in One', *Renaissance Drama*, 2 (1985), 153–70
Bliss, 'Tragicomic'	Lee Bliss, 'Tragicomic Romance for the King's Men, 1609–1611: Shakespeare, Beaumont, and Fletcher', in A. R. Braunmuller and J. C. Bulman (eds), *Comedy from Shakespeare to Sheridan: Change and Continuity in the English Dramatic Tradition* (Newark, NJ, 1986), 148–64
Bonduca	[John Fletcher,] *Bonduca*, Wing B1581, ed. Cyrus Hoy, in Beaumont and Fletcher
Bradley	David Bradley, *From Text to Performance in the Elizabethan Theatre* (Cambridge, 1992)
Brathwaite	Richard Brathwaite, *The Honest Ghost, or, A Voice from the Vault* (1658)
Bright	Timothy Bright, *A Treatise of Melancholy* (1586)
Brown	F. C. Brown, *Elkanah Settle His Life and Works* (Chicago, IL, 1910)
Buckingham	*Plays, Poems, and Miscellaneous Writings associated with George Villiers, Second Duke of Buckingham*, ed. Robert D. Hume and Harold Love, 2 vols (Oxford, 2007)
Butler	Martin Butler (ed.), *Cymbeline* (Cambridge, 2005)
Caelica	*Caelica*, in Fulke Greville, *Works* (1633)
Cameron	Kenneth Walter Cameron, '*Othello*, Quarto 1, Reconsidered', *PMLA*, 47 (1932), 671–83
Campaspe	John Lyly, *Campaspe*, STC 17047.5, in *Campaspe, Sappho and Phao*, ed. David Bevington (1991)
Captain	*The Captain*, Wing B1581, ed. L. A. Beaurline, in Beaumont and Fletcher

Cathcart	Charles Cathcart, 'John Fletcher in 1600–1601: Two Early Poems, and Involvement in the "Poets' War", and a Network of Literary Connections', *Philological Quarterly*, 81 (2002), 33–51
Chambers	E. K. Chambers, *The Elizabethan Stage*, 4 vols (Oxford, 1923)
Chances	[John Fletcher,] *The Chances*, Wing B1581, ed. George Walton Williams, in Beaumont and Fletcher
Changeling	[William Rowley and Thomas Middleton,] *The Changeling*, Wing M1980, ed. Douglas Bruster, in Middleton
Chaste Maid	*A Chaste Maid in Cheapside*, STC 17877, ed. Linda Woodbridge, in Middleton
Clare	Janet Clare, *'Art made tongue-tied by authority': Elizabethan and Jacobean Dramatic Censorship*, 2nd edn (Manchester, 1999)
Clark	Sandra Clark, *The Plays of Beaumont and Fletcher: Sexual Themes and Dramatic Representation* (1994)
Coleridge	Roberta Florence Brinkley (ed.), *Coleridge on the Seventeenth Century* (Durham, NC, 1955)
Collier	Susanne Collier, 'Cutting to the Heart of the Matter: Stabbing the Woman in *Philaster* and *Cymbeline*', in Gillian Murray Kendall (ed.), *Shakespearean Power and Punishment* (Madison, NJ, 1998), 39–58
Colman, 'Adaptation'	G. Colman, *Philaster, A Tragedy . . . with Alterations* (1763)
Covent Garden	A.B., *Covent Garden Drollery* (1672)
Coxcomb	*The Coxcomb*, Wing B1581, ed. Irby B. Cauthen, Jr, in Beaumont and Fletcher
Cressy	David Cressy, *Birth, Marriage and Death: Ritual, Religion, and the Life-Cycle in Tudor and Stuart England* (Oxford, 1997)
Cupid's Revenge	*Cupid's Revenge*, STC 1667, ed. Fredson Bowers, in Beaumont and Fletcher
Custom of the Country	[John Fletcher and Philip Massinger,] *The Custom of the Country*, Wing B1581, ed. Cyrus Hoy, in Beaumont and Fletcher
Danby	John F. Danby, *Poets on Fortune's Hill: Studies in Sidney, Shakespeare, Beaumont and Fletcher* (1952)
Davison	Peter Davison, 'The Serious Concerns of *Philaster*', *English Literary History*, 30 (1963), 1–15
Dekker	*The Works of Thomas Dekker*, ed. Fredson Bowers, 4 vols (Cambridge, 1958–64)
Dent	R. W. Dent, *Proverbial Language in English Drama Exclusive of Shakespeare, 1495–1616* (1984)

Dillon	Janette Dillon, *Theatre, Court and City, 1595–1610: Drama and Social Space in London* (Cambridge, 2000)
Dissemblers	*More Dissemblers Besides Women*, Wing M1989, ed. John Jowett, in Middleton
Donne, *Devotions*	John Donne, *Devotions upon Emergent Occasions*, ed. Anthony Raspa (Oxford, 1987)
Donne	*The Poems of John Donne*, ed. Herbert Grierson (Oxford, 1960)
Dryden	John Dryden, *Of Dramatic Poesy and Other Critical Essays*, ed. George Watson, 2 vols (1962)
Dutton	Richard Dutton, *Mastering the Revels: The Regulation and Censorship of Renaissance Drama* (Iowa City, 1991)
Eastward Ho!	George Chapman, Ben Jonson and John Marston, *Eastward Ho!*, ed. Suzanne Gossett and W. David Kay, in *The Cambridge Edition of the Works of Ben Jonson* (forthcoming)
Edward II	STC 17437, in Marlowe
Elder Brother	[John Fletcher and Philip Massinger,] *The Elder Brother*, STC 11066, ed. Fredson Bowers, in Beaumont and Fletcher
Eliot	T. S. Eliot, *The Sacred Wood: Essays on Poetry and Criticism* (1922)
Elyot	Thomas Elyot, *The Castle of Health* (1539; 1595)
Epicoene	*Epicoene, or The Silent Woman*, STC 14763, in Jonson
Erne	Lukas Erne, *Shakespeare as Literary Dramatist* (Cambridge, 2003)
Faithful Shepherdess	[John Fletcher,] *The Faithful Shepherdess*, STC 11068, ed. Cyrus Hoy, in Beaumont and Fletcher
Family of Love	[Lording Barry, previously attributed to Thomas Middleton], *The Family of Love* (1608), STC 17879
Fawn	John Marston, *Parasitaster, or the Fawn* (1606), STC 17483
Finkelpearl	Philip Finkelpearl, *Court and Country Politics in the Works of Beaumont and Fletcher* (Princeton, NJ, 1990)
Foakes	R. A. Foakes (ed.), *King Lear* (Walton-on-Thames, 1997)
Forgeng	Jeffrey L. Forgeng, private communication
Four Plays in One	[Nathan Field and John Fletcher,] *Four Plays or Moral Representations in One*, Wing B1581, ed. Cyrus Hoy, in Beaumont and Fletcher
FQ	Edmund Spenser, *The Fairie Queene*, ed. J. C. Smith, 2 vols (Oxford, 1909)
Gayley	Charles Mills Gayley, *Beaumont, The Dramatist* (New York, 1914)
GM	Gordon McMullan, private communication
Golden Age	Thomas Heywood, *The Golden Age* (1611), STC 13325

327

Gossett	Suzanne Gossett, 'Taking *Pericles* seriously', in Raphael Lyne and Subha Mukherji (eds), *Early Modern Tragicomedy* (Woodbridge, 2007), 101–14
Greg	W. W. Greg, *A Bibliography of the English Printed Drama to the Restoration*, 4 vols (1951)
Gripus and Hegio	Robert Baron, *Gripus and Hegio, or, The Passionate Lovers*, in *The Cyprian Academy* (1647)
Gristwood	Sarah Gristwood, *Arbella: England's Lost Queen* (New York, 2003)
Gurr, *Companies*	Andrew Gurr, *The Shakespearian Playing Companies* (Oxford, 1996)
Gurr, *Stage*	Andrew Gurr, *The Shakespearean Stage*, 3rd edn (Cambridge, 1992)
Hanson	Elizabeth Hanson, 'Torture and Truth in Renaissance England', *Representations*, 34 (1991), 53–84
Healy	Margaret Healy, '*Pericles* and the Pox', in Jennifer Richards and James Knowles (eds), *Shakespeare's Late Plays: New Readings* (Edinburgh, 1999), 92–107
Hengist	*Hengist, King of Kent; or, The Mayor of Queenborough*, Wing M1984, ed. Grace Ioppolo, in Middleton
Heywood	Thomas Heywood, *A Woman Killed With Kindness*, STC 13371, ed. Brian Scobie (1985)
Honest Man's Fortune	[Nathan Field, John Fletcher, Philip Massinger,] *The Honest Man's Fortune*, Wing B1581, ed. Cyrus Hoy, in Beaumont and Fletcher
Honest Whore 1	*The First Part of the Honest Whore*, STC 6501, in Dekker
Honigmann	Ernst Honigmann, *The Texts of Othello and Shakespearian Revision* (1996)
Hope	Jonathan Hope, *Shakespeare's Grammar* (2003)
Hoy	Cyrus Hoy, 'The Shares of Fletcher and his Collaborators in the Beaumont and Fletcher Canon I–VII', *Studies in Bibliography*, 8 (1956), 129–46; 9 (1957), 143–62; 11 (1958), 85–106; 12 (1959), 91–116; 13 (1960), 77–108; 14 (1961), 45–67; 15 (1962), 71–90
Humorous Lieutenant	[John Fletcher,] *The Humorous Lieutenant*, Wing B1581, ed. Cyrus Hoy, in Beaumont and Fletcher
Hunter	George K. Hunter, ed., *The Malcontent* (1975)
Island Princess	[John Fletcher,] *The Island Princess*, Wing B1581, ed. George Walton Williams, in Beaumont and Fletcher
James	T. E. James, 'The Age of Majority', *The American Journal of Legal History*, 4 (1960), 22–33
JH	Jonathan Hope, private communication
JJ	John Jowett, private communication

Jonson	*Ben Jonson*, ed. C. H. Herford and Percy and Evelyn Simpson, 11 vols (Oxford, 1925–52)
Juvenal	*Juvenal and Persius*, ed. and trans. Susanna Morton Braund (Cambridge, MA, 2004)
Kathman	David Kathman, 'How Old Were Shakespeare's Boy Actors?', *Shakespeare Survey*, 58 (2005), 220–46
King	Ros King, *Cymbeline: Constructions of Britain* (Aldershot, 2005)
King and No King	*A King and No King*, STC 1670, ed. George Walton Williams, in Beaumont and Fletcher
Knight of Malta	[Nathan Field and John Fletcher,] *The Knight of Malta*, Wing B1581, ed. George Walton Williams, in Beaumont and Fletcher
Larum for London	Anonymous, *A Larum for London, or The Siege of Antwerp* (1602)
Leech	Clifford Leech, *The John Fletcher Plays* (1962)
Lesser	Zachary Lesser, *Renaissance Drama and the Politics of Publication: Readings in the English Book Trade* (Cambridge, 2004)
Linthicum	M. Channing Linthicum, *Costume in the Drama of Shakespeare and his Contemporaries* (Oxford, 1936)
LION	*Literature Online*
Llewellyn	Nigel Llewellyn, *Funeral Monuments in post-Reformation England* (Cambridge, 2000)
London Stage	*The London Stage 1660–1800: A Calendar of Plays, Entertainments, and Afterpieces*, ed. William Van Lennep *et al.*, 5 parts in 11 vols (Carbondale, IL, 1960–8)
Loughlin	Marie H. Loughlin, 'Cross-Dressing and the Politics of Dismemberment in Francis Beaumont and John Fletcher's *Philaster*', *Renaissance and Reformation*, 21 (1997), 23–44
Love's Cure	[?Francis Beaumont, John Fletcher, Philip Massinger,] *Love's Cure, or the Martial Maid*, Wing B1581, ed. George Walton Williams, in Beaumont and Fletcher
Love's Pilgrimage	Wing B1581, ed. L. A. Beaurline, in Beaumont and Fletcher
McKenzie	D. F. McKenzie, 'Printers of the Mind: Some Notes on Bibliographical Theories and Printing-House Practices', *Studies in Bibliography*, 22 (1969), 1–75
McMillin	Scott McMillin, *The First Quarto of Othello* (Cambridge, 2005)
McMullan, *Fletcher*	Gordon McMullan, *The Politics of Unease in the Plays of John Fletcher* (Amherst, MA, 1994)
McMullan, *H8*	Gordon McMullan, (ed.), *King Henry VIII* (2000)

McMullan and Hope   Gordon McMullan and Jonathan Hope (eds), *The Politics of Tragicomedy: Shakespeare and After* (1992)

Mad Lover   [John Fletcher,] *The Mad Lover*, Wing B1581, ed. Robert Kean Turner, in Beaumont and Fletcher

Maguire   Laurie E. Maguire, *Shakespearean Suspect Texts; The 'bad' quartos and their contexts* (Cambridge, 1996)

Maid in the Mill   [John Fletcher and William Rowley,]*The Maid in the Mill*, Wing B1581, ed. Fredson Bowers, in Beaumont and Fletcher

Maid's Tragedy   *The Maid's Tragedy*, STC 1676, ed. Robert K. Turner, in Beaumont and Fletcher

Malcontent   *The Malcontent*, STC 17479, in Marston

Malfi   *The Duchess of Malfi*, STC 25176, ed. David Gunby and David Carnegie, in Webster

Marlowe   *Dr Faustus and Other Plays*, ed. David Bevington and Eric Rasmussen (Manchester, 1998)

Marston   *The Selected Plays of John Marston*, ed. MacDonald P. Jackson and Michael Neill (Cambridge, 1986)

Massinger   *The Plays and Poems of Philip Massinger*, ed. Philip Edwards and Colin Gibson, 5 vols (Cambridge, 1986)

Masten   Jeffrey Masten, 'Editing Boys: the Performance of Genders in Print', in Peter Holland and Stephen Orgel (eds), *From Performance to Print in Shakespeare's England* (Basingstoke, 2006), 113–34

Michaelmas   *Michaelmas Term*, STC 17890, ed. Theodore B. Leinwand, in Middleton

Middleton   *Thomas Middleton: The Collected Works*, gen. eds Gary Taylor and John Lavignino (Oxford, 2007)

Miller   Jo E. Miller, '"And All This Passion for a Boy?": Cross-dressing and the Sexual Economy of Beaumont and Fletcher's *Philaster*', *English Literary Renaissance*, 27 (1997), 129–50

Monsieur Thomas   [John Fletcher,] STC 11071, ed. Hans Walter Gabler, in Beaumont and Fletcher

Munro   Lucy Munro, *Children of the Queen's Revels: A Jacobean Theatre Repertory* (Cambridge, 2005)

Neely   Carol Thomas Neely, *Distracted Subjects: Madness and Gender in Shakespeare and Early Modern Culture* (Ithaca, NY, 2004)

New Way   *A New Way to Pay Old Debts*, STC 17638, in Massinger

Night Walker   [John Fletcher, rev. Shirley,] *The Night Walker*, STC 11072, ed. Cyrus Hoy, in Beaumont and Fletcher

Noble Gentleman	[John Fletcher,] *The Noble Gentleman*, Wing B1581, ed. L. A. Beaurline, in Beaumont and Fletcher
Norrington	Ruth Norrington, *In the Shadow of the Throne: The Lady Arbella Stuart* (2002)
Old Law	[Thomas Middleton, William Rowley, Thomas Heywood,] *The Old Law*, Wing M1048, ed. Jeffrey Masten, in Middleton
Orgel	Stephen Orgel, *Impersonations: The Performance of Gender in Shakespeare's England* (Cambridge, 1996)
Paster, *Body Embarrassed*	Gail Kern Paster, *The Body Embarrassed: Drama and the Disciplines of Shame in Early Modern England* (Ithaca, NY, 1993)
Paster, *Humoring*	Gail Kern Paster, *Humoring the Body: Emotions and the Shakespearean Stage* (Chicago, IL, 2004)
Il Pastor Fido	Giovanni Battista Guarini, *Il Pastor Fido*, trans. Richard Fanshawe (1647)
Pepys	*The Diary of Samuel Pepys*, ed. Robert Latham and William Matthews, 11 vols (Berkeley, CA, 1970–83)
Pestle	[Francis Beaumont,] *The Knight of the Burning Pestle*, STC 1674, ed. Cyrus Hoy, in Beaumont and Fletcher
Potter	Lois Potter (ed.), *The Two Noble Kinsmen* (Walton-on-Thames, 1997)
Quarrel	[Thomas Middleton and William Rowley,] *A Fair Quarrel*, STC 17911, 17911a, ed. Suzanne Gossett, in Middleton
Radel	Nicholas F. Radel, 'Fletcherian Tragicomedy, Cross-dressing, and the Constriction of Homoerotic Desire in Early Modern England', *Renaissance Drama*, n.s. 26 (1995), 53–82
Redworth	Glyn Redworth, *The Prince and the Infanta: The Cultural Politics of the Spanish Match* (New Haven, CT, 2003)
Renegado	*The Renegado*, STC 17641, in Massinger
Roaring Girl	[Thomas Middleton and Thomas Dekker,] *The Roaring Girl; or, Moll Cutpurse*, STC 17908, ed. Coppélia Kahn, in Middleton
Rouverol	Jean Rouverol, *Refugees from Hollywood: A Journal of the Blacklist Years* (Albuquerque, NM, 2000)
RP	Richard Proudfoot, Private Communication
Rulfs	Donald J. Rulfs, 'Beaumont and Fletcher on the Stage 1776–1833', *PMLA*, 63 (1948), 1245–64
Sad Shepherd	*The Sad Shepherd*, STC 14753, in Jonson
Savage	J. E. Savage, 'The "Gaping Wounds" in the text of *Philaster*', *Philological Quarterly*, 28 (1949), 443–57

Scornful Lady	*The Scornful Lady*, STC 1686, ed. Cyrus Hoy, in Beaumont and Fletcher
Sea Voyage	[John Fletcher and Philip Massinger,] *The Sea Voyage*, Wing B1581, ed. Fredson Bowers, in Beaumont and Fletcher
Settle	See Brown
Smith	J. Smith, *A Sea Grammar* (1627)
Spanish Tragedy	Thomas Kyd, *The Spanish Tragedy*, STC 15086, 15089, ed. Philip Edwards (1959)
Sprague	Arthur Colby Sprague, *Beaumont and Fletcher on the Restoration Stage* (Cambridge, MA, 1926)
STC	*A Short-Title Catalogue of Books Printed in England, Scotland, & Ireland, and of English Books Printed Abroad, 1475–1640*, 2nd edn, begun by W. A. Jackson and F. S. Ferguson, completed by Katherine F. Panzer, 3 vols (1976)
Steen	Sara Jayne Steen (ed.), *The Letters of Lady Arabella Stuart* (New York, 1994)
Stone	Lawrence Stone, *The Family, Sex and Marriage* (abridged edn) (New York, 1983)
Stubbes	John Stubbes, *Donne: The Reforming Soul* (2007)
Taylor and Jowett	Gary Taylor and John Jowett, *Shakespeare Reshaped 1606–1623* (Oxford, 1993)
Thorndike, *Influence*	Ashley Thorndike, *The Influence of Beaumont and Fletcher on Shakspere* [*sic*] (1901)
Tomalin	Claire Tomalin, *Samuel Pepys, The Unequalled Self* (New York, 2002)
Trick	*A Trick to Catch the Old One*, STC 17896, ed. Valerie Wayne, in Middleton
Turner, 'Printing'	Robert K. Turner, 'The Printing of Philaster Q1 and Q2', *The Library*, 5th series, 15 (1960), 21–32
Two Noble Ladies	*The Two Noble Ladies and the Converted Conjurer* (BL MS Egerton 1994), ed. Rebecca G. Rhoads (Oxford, 1930)
TxC	Stanley Wells and Gary Taylor, with John Jowett and William Montgomery, *William Shakespeare: A Textual Companion* (Oxford, 1987)
Valentinian	[John Fletcher,] Wing B1581, ed. Robert K. Turner, Jr, in Beaumont and Fletcher
Valour	*The Nice Valour; or, The Passionate Madman*, Wing B1581, ed. Gary Taylor, in Middleton
Vaughan	William Vaughan, *Naturall and Artificial Directions for Health* (1600)
Waith	Eugene M. Waith, *The Pattern of Tragicomedy in Beaumont and Fletcher* (New Haven, CT, 1952)

Wallis	Lawrence B. Wallis, *Fletcher, Beaumont & Company: Entertainers to the Jacobean Gentry* (New York, 1947)
Webster	*The Works of John Webster*, ed. David Carnegie, David Gunby, Antony Hammond and MacDonald P. Jackson, 3 vols (Cambridge, 1995–2007)
Werstine, 'Division'	Paul Werstine, 'Line Division in Shakespeare's Dramatic Verse: An Editorial Problem', *Analytic and Enumerative Bibliography*, 8 (1984), 73–125
Werstine, 'Othello'	Paul Werstine, 'Review of *The Texts of Othello and Shakespearian Revision*', *Shakespeare Quarterly*, 51 (2000), 240–4
Westward Ho	[Thomas Dekker and John Webster,] STC 6540, in Dekker
Wife for a Month	[John Fletcher,] *A Wife for a Month*, Wing B1581, ed. Robert Kean Turner, in Beaumont and Fletcher
Wild Goose Chase	[John Fletcher,] *The Wild Goose Chase*, Wing B1616, ed. Fredson Bowers, in Beaumont and Fletcher
Williams, *Glossary*	Gordon Williams, *A Glossary of Shakespeare's Sexual Language* (1997)
Williams, *King*	George Walton Williams (ed.), *A King and No King*, in Beaumont and Fletcher
Wilson	Harold Wilson, '*Philaster* and *Cymbeline*', *English Institute Essays 1951* (New York, 1952)
Wing	*A Short-Title Catalogue of Books Printed in England, Scotland, Ireland, Wales and British America, and of English Books Printed in Other Countries, 1641–1700*, 2nd edn, rev. and enl., compiled by Donald Wing, 4 vols (New York, 1972–98)
Wit of a Woman	Anonymous, *The Wit of a Woman* (1604), STC 25868, reprinted Malone Society (Oxford, 1913)
Wit Without Money	[John Fletcher and ?James Shirley,] STC 1691, ed. Hans Walter Gabler, in Beaumont and Fletcher
Woman Hater	*The Woman Hater*, STC 1692, ed. George Walton Williams, in Beaumont and Fletcher
Woman Killed	see Heywood
Woman's Prize	[John Fletcher,] *The Woman's Prize, or The Tamer Tamed*, Wing B1581, ed. Fredson Bowers, in Beaumont and Fletcher
Wright	George T. Wright, *Shakespeare's Metrical Art* (Berkeley, CA, 1988)

INDEX

The index covers the Introduction, the commentary notes (including those in Appendix 1) and Appendix 2. Page numbers in italics refer to figures.

334